"THE KILLING
GAME"

"THE KILLING GAME"

SELECTED WRITINGS
BY THE AUTHOR OF *DARK ALLIANCE*

GARY WEBB

EDITED WITH A PREFACE BY **ERIC WEBB**
PUBLISHER'S NOTE BY **DAN SIMON**
FOREWORD BY **TOM LOFTUS**
AFTERWORD BY **ROBERT PARRY**

7

Seven Stories Press

NEW YORK

Seven Stories Press
140 Watts Street
New York, NY 10013
www.sevenstories.com

College professors may order examination copies of Seven Stories Press titles for a free six-month trial period. To order, visit http://www.sevenstories.com/textbook or send a fax on school letterhead to (212) 226-1411.

From Kristina Borjesson, *Into the Buzzsaw: Leading Journalists Expose the Myth of a Free Press*, revised edition (Amherst, NY: Prometheus Books, 2004); www.prometheusbooks.com. Copyright © 2004 by Kristina Borjesson. All rights reserved. Used with permission of the publisher.

Book design by Jon Gilbert
Frontis photo © *The Kentucky Post*

Library of Congress Cataloging-in-Publication Data

Webb, Gary.
The killing game : selected writings by the author of Dark alliance / Gary Webb ; edited with a preface by Eric Webb ; foreword by Tom Loftus ; afterword by Robert Parry. -- Seven Stories Press 1st ed.
    p. cm.
ISBN 978-1-58322-932-3 (pbk.)
I. Webb, Eric, 1988- II. Title.
PN4874.W35A25 2011
070.4--dc22

                                    2010048503

Printed in the United States

9 8 7 6 5 4 3 2 1

To my mother, for always being there.
—EW

Contents

Preface

When my father's editor and publisher at Seven Stories first approached my mother and me with the idea of putting together a second book to collect my father's other writings, I was a second-year journalism student at junior college in Sacramento, California. I had a good knowledge of story structure, the AP stylebook, and copy-editing skills, and had experience editing my college newspaper for a couple semesters. I had seen and studied investigative stories in my lower-division journalism and English classes. I also believed that I had a fair knowledge of my father's work, at least his more recent articles. None of that prepared me fully for the task of editing this book. Doing so has been an arduous journey for me, a difficult emotional assignment, one that in the end has given me a new perspective on my father's work and on journalism as a whole.

I'd been too young to really appreciate what my father did for a living while he was still alive. He died when I was sixteen, and at that age my father was much more of a fellow videogame fanatic and punk rocker rather than a journalist, although those realms did overlap every now and then. Since his death I had considered journalism as my own career choice, but it has only been through this process, reading then transcribing tens of thousands of his words, that I've grown close to him professionally. This closeness grew out of my profound respect for the courage he had to have to do the type of reporting he did, and the effort it took to do the research behind the writing, and how those two elements came together to produce journalism of the highest caliber.

But in my father's eyes, courage and effort had little to do with his work. The way he saw it, investigative reporting was what he was born to do, and he was damn good at it. He loved researching, he loved writing, and he got high off of nailing the "bad guys" in his stories. I remember from a young age how my father boasted, not about his own exploits but about the media's responsibility to keep everyone in check and to print the truth regardless of who it pissed off.

Like my father says himself in this book, he was a poster child for investigative reporters—basking in the awards and in the freedom he had to choose the stories he covered. If there was ever a believer in the power of the press, it was my father.

But I also saw that poster torn down, and I saw a man crushed, when the very principles and institutions and people he believed in turned their backs on him. He didn't just lose his job, or his career . . . he lost his dream.

He was never quite the same after his own newspaper and the newspapers of record vilified him for the "Dark Alliance" story, even though he did a lot of great writing later in his life. He felt betrayed by his profession and couldn't see any hope for it if such a firm believer and so highly respected a practitioner as himself could be so easily scorned.

The majority of the articles in *The Killing Game* were written long before I was born, at a time when journalism itself was somewhat more respected, and perhaps more exciting and risqué—at least for print reporters—than it is today. The code of ethics for newspapers has become more restricted, more corporate, perhaps less antagonistic to the powers that be. It goes without saying that many of my father's earlier articles might not have been published today.

If you know where to find it, this kind of hardcore investigative journalism still does exist. It probably won't be on your front page, though. It is my hope for my generation of journalists that we don't forget where we came from. We must remember that it is our responsibility to be thorough and responsible, and to always print the truth.

—Eric Webb
September 2010

Publisher's Note*

Almost a year after his 1996 "Dark Alliance" series in the *San Jose Mercury News* hit the stands and created a furor on the internet, Gary Webb set to work with me on the book-length version of his controversial story. Webb was one of America's top investigative reporters. His awards included a Pulitzer in 1990 as part of a team, and at least four other major prizes for his solo work. But the "Dark Alliance" story had been attacked so prominently in the mainstream press that by that summer of 1997 when we signed on to be his publisher, he'd already completed his spectacular fall from grace and was living in its aftermath: no longer a star reporter, but still a working journalist and a recently minted hero of the Left. (*Esquire* referred to us as "publisher of last resort" when we took him on, and we liked the designation so much that we featured it in our next catalogue.) I hadn't met Gary before. I found him funny, generous, warm, and charismatic.

What would turn out to be the biggest story of his life ran as a three-day series beginning on August 18, 1996. Here's how it started:

> For the better part of a decade, a Bay Area drug ring sold tons of cocaine to the Crips and Bloods street gangs of Los Angeles and funneled millions in drug profits to a Latin American guerrilla army run by the US Central Intelligence Agency, a *Mercury News* investigation has found.

The series documented a network of collusion in the 1980s that joined together the crack cocaine explosion, the Contras, and the CIA. But it might have vanished without a trace had the paper not chosen this story to create a splash for its website, complete with graphics and links to a treasure trove of original source documents. It became the first big internet news story, with as many as 1.3 million hits in a single day. Talk radio picked it up off the internet, and citizens' groups and media watchdogs soon followed. The CIA launched its own internal investigation. For around two months, Gary's star had never shone more brightly.

That all changed suddenly in October 1996, when *The New York Times*, the *Washington Post*, and the *Los Angeles Times* all began their coverage as page-one news. Instead of picking up the story from the *Mercury News* or conducting their own investigations—as to whether the CIA had played a part in the siphoning of drugs to America's cities and the profits to Ronald Reagan's "freedom fighters" in Nicaragua—they attacked the messenger, Gary himself. The papers charged ahead with the unprecedented personal vilification of a distinguished journalist that would turn out to be completely unfounded. As Webb's editor at the *Mercury News*, Jerry Ceppos, commented at the time, these newspapers did this although they "could not find a single significant factual error." But after that the series was described frequently as "discredited," and soon even Ceppos changed sides: he wrote an editorial that was read as an apology, in effect distancing the paper from the series and hanging Webb out to dry. Webb left the paper, more or less disgraced, even though the evidence supporting the "Dark Alliance" story had never been stronger, and was growing steadily.

Two years later, the CIA's internal investigation would validate the assertions in the "Dark Alliance" story, showing that if anything the story was bigger and more widespread than Gary had claimed. Another internal investigation at the Justice Department also shored up the allegations and assertions made in the "Dark Alliance" series. As we worked on updating the book for the forthcoming paperback edition, Gary took solace in being vindicated by these findings, even as he remained mystified as to how the mainstream press could fail to reassess its earlier, erroneous findings.

I remember Gary talking to me about how he had not gone looking for the "Dark Alliance" story, and even when it did find him, he hadn't wanted it at first and had pushed quite hard against taking it on. Gary, who described his family to me, especially on his mother's side, as "Nixonian Republicans," certainly wasn't looking for a story that would tie together key members of our federal government with drug dealers and the crack epidemic that was plaguing our inner cities. What I understood Gary to be saying was that, from the get-go, this was a scary story, even to this reporter who had spent his career going after scary stories.

Gary seemed to relish turning the "Dark Alliance" series into a book. He enjoyed writing long format and was good at it—it tickled him that there were no length restrictions. When the book finally appeared, two of the three papers that originally dismissed the story reviewed it positively, and one major newspaper that had attacked the story originally, the *Baltimore Sun*, publicly acknowledged its earlier error. But neither the *Times*, the *Post*, nor the *Los Angeles Times* would ever do so—at least they haven't yet.

Meanwhile the alternative media, to their credit, lionized Gary. In 1996 he won the James Aronson Award for Social Justice Journalism from Hunter College, at City University in New York. Also in 1996, he won the Freedom Fighter Award from the California NAACP, and the Journalist of the Year Award from the Bay Area Society of Professional Journalists. In 1997 he won the Media Hero Award at the 2nd Annual Media & Democracy Congress. In 1998 when the book *Dark Alliance* came out, it won a Firecracker Alternative Book (FAB) Award in the Politics category, was nominated as the Best Nonfiction Book by the Bay Area Book Reviewers Association, and Gary himself was a finalist for the PEN/Newman's Own First Amendment Award. Finally, in 1999, he won the Oakland PEN First Amendment Award for *Dark Alliance*.

But the community of Gary's peers in journalism never again embraced him. And as brave as he was, he never did recover from the sense of betrayal he felt. As an investigative reporter Gary had been looking for that one big story for his entire career. He found it with "Dark Alliance." It was the story of the betrayal by our government of the people it is supposed to protect.

Now six years have passed since Gary's death. When we first thought to follow *Dark Alliance* with a volume selecting Gary's other journalistic writings, we approached Sue Bell, Gary's ex-wife and the mother of his sons. Sue sent us copies of the articles that Gary had kept, presumably because they represented the writings he thought best represented his career as a journalist. Reading them for the first time two years ago, I was blown away by how good and how consistent Gary's investigative reporting was. "Dark Alliance" wasn't some kind of anomaly after all. Every one of these writings displays the same homing instinct for finding the story's deepest cave, and Gary's incredible gift for taking the story all the way to that inner sanctum, to the place where the corruption and criminality and power brokers all get cozy together—whether it was in the Kentucky coal industry, the Ohio state medical board, or the army's video gaming initiative. Gary's younger son Eric, a journalism student, signed on as editor of this collection of his father's writings. Eric did a tremendous job putting the book together. Later, we reached out to Gary's co-writers, editors, and colleagues at many of the newspapers and magazines he wrote for, asking if they would like to help us. In every case the journalists we approached not only agreed, but did more than we asked of them. Some volunteered hours of proofreading, others helped us obtain permissions. In the cases of Bob Parry, Tom Loftus, Kristina Borjesson, Annie Nocenti, and Tom Scheffey, they did even more. And all had stories to tell about Gary. This was clearly someone they couldn't and wouldn't forget—someone whose influence has continued to grow long after we lost the pleasure of his company.

Dan Simon
February 7, 2011
New York City

*Sections of this Publisher's Note were included in "The Tragedy of Gary Webb," which appeared in the February 2005 issue of the *Progressive*.

Foreword

Reporter Gary Webb was both an editor's dream and an editor's nightmare. From the outset of his career, Webb went after big stories. Stories that grabbed attention. Stories that often won awards. Stories that sometimes got his newspaper sued.

Editors love awards. They loathe lawsuits. Webb considered lawsuits part of the job of a serious investigative reporter. An avid ice hockey fan, Webb knew the best players were aggressive players who spent their share of time in the penalty box.

My bet is that most of his editors—at least among those who worked with him prior to his days at the *San Jose Mercury News*—consider the stories they did with Webb among the most significant of their careers. Unlike many who call themselves investigative reporters, Webb delivered.

Webb was an example of the meritocracy of the journalism business. He didn't hold a degree from a prestigious J-school, or any J-school for that matter. He never held a coveted fellowship. Still, Webb succeeded. He was recruited by the *Mercury News* when that newspaper may have been the hottest place in the country for a young reporter to work. He got the job offer because his clips showed he could deliver.

I knew Webb when his clipbook was thin and mostly featured rock 'n' roll reviews. He was still a student at Northern Kentucky University when he walked into the newsroom of the *Kentucky Post* looking for work.

The *Post*'s editor later described Webb as "green as grass but eager as hell." He put him to work right away at the minimum Newspaper Guild wage. Webb started as a deadline legman covering fires, shootings, and car wrecks. He spent time driving across a twelve-county circulation area picking up News of Record items (crime reports, lawsuits, etc.). On Friday nights in the fall, he was assigned along with other young city desk reporters to cover high school football games.

While making his bones with grunt work, Webb was already on the trail of a big story.

An unsolved slaying of the owner of a Newport adult bookstore captured his attention. Editors lost interest in the case, but enticing details caused Webb and a fellow reporter to dig for more on their own time. They found the victim's long and violent criminal record, involvement with shady deals in Kentucky's coal industry, high-level business and political associations, and even a photograph of the victim with Ronald Reagan. Eventually they wrote an award-winning series of stories about organized crime in the coal business.

I was lucky to eventually work with Webb on stories that accused the powerful Kentucky energy secretary of a conflict of interest in an odd coal export agreement the state had struck with Italy.

Gary was smart. Even in his early twenties he had highly advanced skills as a researcher. He knew what could be found at the courthouse, public libraries, and government record repositories. He refined his record-gathering skills by endlessly filing requests under the Freedom of Information Act and state Open Records Acts. When denied a record, he relentlessly appealed until he got the goods.

He knew how to read audits and corporate balance sheets. I know—for years I vetted my most complicated stories with him.

Webb was not intimidated, no matter how complex the story, no matter how powerful his target. He was unshakable once he concluded the public good was being trampled by the greed and dishonesty of government institutions or big business.

I would like to have worked more with Webb, but his work at the *Post* soon earned him a job at the *Plain Dealer* in Cleveland where he established a reputation as a hard-hitting investigative reporter. He continued to build an impressive body of work at the *Mercury News*.

The best of his work is contained in this volume, with the exception of the "Dark Alliance" series, which Gary expanded into the book he wrote— his only book—under the same title.

Busy with my own work far away, I did not read most of these stories when they were first published. But I remained in contact with Webb. And I was not surprised when the "Dark Alliance" series appeared with its international implications and devastating personal repercussions. (For an understanding of the "Dark Alliance" story, I recommend numerous articles written by journalist Robert Parry.)

I can't pretend to be unbiased about Gary. He was a close friend. On occasion—rare occasion, I suggest—he was aggressive and self-confident to a fault. He did not suffer fools easily, particularly if they were editing his copy.

The point to remember as you read this collection is that it is the work of a skilled reporter who—in the course of exposing the selfishness and stupidity of the powerful—never pulled his punches for fear of offending a source or in the hope of landing a lucrative press secretary's job.

During the "open microphone" memorial service that followed Gary's death in 2004, a diverse group of family, colleagues, and friends spoke. Predictably, the most fitting description of Gary's career—indeed, his life— came not from a journalist but a teammate in the local ice hockey league.

"Gary had the enthusiasm, and he was fast," his teammate said of Gary on the ice. "His problem was he didn't know how to stop. The guy just had no brakes."

—Tom Loftus

The Coal Connection

Gary Webb and Thomas Scheffey

Kentucky Post (May 31–June 17, 1980)

INTRODUCTION BY THOMAS SCHEFFEY

Any smart editor would have tried to discourage Gary Webb and me from pursuing the story that eventually became the seventeen-part series, "The Coal Connection," for the *Kentucky Post*.

Vance H. Trimble, our editor at the time, was more than just smart. He was a Pulitzer Prize–winning investigative reporter in his own right, who knew how nearly impossible it would be to nail down a story like this. It started as a police beat murder story, but was seeping outward into a tale of exotic international financial swindling. The lowest criminals were mixed up with top state and national political figures—something neither liked to talk about. And the dramatic themes that made the story exciting also would make it maddeningly tough and time-consuming to document. "Your trench coat is flapping in the wind," Trimble told Gary. Undaunted, he pursued the story on his own time, and I offered what encouragement and assistance I could during the three years I was in law school (I worked at the *Post* on weekends and summers). With Freedom of Information Act requests, scores of telephone and in-person interviews, and even cold-calling peoples' phone records, we sifted through the pieces of the puzzle. There were individual stories of coal swindles around the country and abroad. Sometimes the value of the coal itself fueled the scams. Sometimes the money was in the easy-to-fence earth-moving equipment used for strip mines. Then there were aggressive coal tax–shelter scams, as advertised to Wall Street. They succeeded richly—so long as no coal was actually mined!

In spite of all the hurdles—or maybe because of them—Gary got the story. He amassed five bankers boxes of files, hours of taped interviews, and a stunning photo of Ronald Reagan in front of his first private campaign jet that was supplied by a hardened ex-con who had made the FBI's Ten Most Wanted list.

It wasn't easy for two twenty-something reporters to penetrate international commodities finance swindles, or securities tax fraud. For a law school special

1

project, I worked with the state securities department researching coal scams. While organizing the series, we were inspired by Jonathan Kwitny's book, *The Fountain Pen Conspiracy*. It chronicled complex securities swindles of a decade earlier, and featured some of the same unsavory characters, who were moving from stock swindles to coal frauds.

Gary's research and organization paid off. Most interview subjects can sense if a questioner is ill-informed or just fishing, and clam up. Just as important, Gary had an engaging approach with people that was wonderful to witness. He could charm the most hard-boiled detective into sharing rich details. Even accomplished swindlers, encouraged by Gary's wry humor, regaled us with explanations of how they pulled off their boldest schemes and called back when they had new escapades to brag about, partly because Gary was irreverent, lively, and spontaneous—a pleasure to talk with. The best of listeners, he made people feel understood, and would lend a serious and attentive ear to the people who had lost their life savings through these schemes.

Writing up the series was comparatively a breeze, with us literally finishing each other's sentences. When the series finally saw print, prosecutors took notice and racked up successful prosecutions. "The Coal Connection" won the Investigative Reporters and Editors Award for newspapers of our size in 1980, as well as the Society of Professional Journalists Investigative Reporting Award for 1980, for the Queen City (Greater Cincinnati) Chapter. Marvin Stone, the Canadian financier who outlined how to become a millionaire in coal in two weeks, caught the attention of the US prosecutor in Pikeville, Kentucky. Our stories helped him win a three-year sentence for Stone, who served eighteen months and was later sent back to Canada. Gary had launched his meteoric and historic investigative reporting career.

While writing this, I had the good fortune to speak with Vance Trimble again, who's about to enter his ninety-ninth year. In 1960, he had won the Pulitzer for a six-month series of stories exposing flagrant nepotism and payroll abuse in Congress, which he researched and wrote on his own time, while working as night news–editor for the Scripps Howard bureau in Washington, serving the twenty-seven-paper chain.

Trimble was a formidable editor. When he told Webb that his trench coat was flapping in the breeze, a lesser reporter might have become discouraged. Instead, Webb was galvanized, inspired to press forward.

When we spoke today, Trimble observed that some of the very finest journalism comes from reporters who take their direction from the excitement of the story, not the dictates of an editor. "Your individual stuff, on your own hook—you've got more heart in it. You've got more heart in something you think is a great story yourself." And with that, he put his finger on what inspired the resourceful, unsinkable journalism of Gary Webb.

□   □   □

PART 1: THE COAL CONNECTION
MAY 31, 1980

It was a fine night for a killing.

A muffling fog had settled over downtown Newport. The garish neon blaze of Monmouth Street's strip was smeared and softened in the haze. The bars and strip joints had just closed, and the Friday night celebrants were feeling their way home. Soon, the streets were deserted.

The temperature was two degrees above freezing that night, Jan. 7, 1978. Shortly before 3 a.m., two men emerged from the gloom into the light cast by the only open shop.

One was a swarthy man wearing dark clothing. The other was tall, about six feet, with a sandy moustache hiding a harelip. He looked to be middle-aged, and he spoke with a pronounced lisp. The big man pushed open the black wooden door of Lewallen's Variety Store at 721 Monmouth St. and walked inside the seedy adult bookstore. The other man stayed slightly behind.

A portly, 45-year-old man named Lester Lee looked up from behind the counter when the tall man entered. He seemed to know the man. But this wasn't a friendly visit.

"Hit the floor!" the tall man shouted, pulling a revolver from within the folds of his beige overcoat. There were few customers around to hear his command.

One was Eddie Chambers, a friend of Lee's and a bouncer in a couple of Newport clubs. The gunman swung the pistol towards Chambers, and Chambers dropped to the floor.

Lee rounded the corner of the upraised counter/display case. The man pointed the pistol at Lee and pulled the trigger. The gun only clicked.

Lee reached for the gun he carried in his waistband, behind his back. The gun clattered to the floor and fell down the one step separating the counter area from the main floor.

As Lee reached for it, Chambers fled down a corridor housing peep show booths and hid in the dark bowels of the bookstore. The man pulled the trigger again and the gun fired. A bullet smashed into the left side of Lee's head, spinning him around. Lee crumpled to the gritty linoleum floor.

The killers dashed from the bookstore and vanished into the fog. They were not seen again. Minutes later, Newport police Sgt. Jerry Early—having heard the call when he opened the door of his unmarked cruiser at the corner of Eighth and Monmouth—sidled up to the door of the bookstore. He pulled his service revolver and poked his head inside the door.

"Lee was laying on the floor, his eyes were half open and he was making this sound, like a death rattle," recalled Early, now Dayton police chief. "I could tell then he was zonked."

By then, police cruisers and ambulances were screaming up to the scene, bathing the dim street in brilliant blues and reds.

Lee was scooped onto a stretcher and heaved into the back of the ambulance. Early climbed in with him, on the off chance Lee would regain consciousness and make a statement. He didn't.

While doctors at St. Luke Hospital in Ft. Thomas worked frantically on the comatose Lee, Jerry Early sat in the lobby of the emergency room and flipped through Lee's wallet, looking for identification.

It wasn't a wallet that belonged to a lowly bookstore clerk. Inside, Early found $835 in cash and a $2,083 check from a Hy-Test Coal Company.

Had Early looked further, he would have seen something even more curious than the check: 43 business cards, most of them from coal company presidents, stock brokers, real estate agents and investment bankers. One of the business cards would have startled even a seen-it-all-cop like Early.

Embossed on the card was the seal of the Ohio State Senate. Underneath, in large capital letters, the name "Donald E. Lukens" and below that, the words "Minority Whip".

On the back, there were three handwritten phone numbers: one for Lukens' home in Middletown, Ohio, one for his Washington, D.C., apartment and another for his apartment in Columbus, Ohio.

But Early didn't get to see those. Before he got that far, a nurse came from the emergency room and told him Lee was dead, a bullet lodged in his brain.

Since that winter night more than two years ago, a lid of silence has been clamped on the case. Newport police officials have steadfastly refused to discuss any aspect of the murder of Lester Clifford Lee.

"I can't give out any details. It's still under active investigation," said Lt. Col. Albert Garnick. The *Kentucky Post* investigated the murder of Lester Lee for 20 months, interviewing more than 125 people and filing 32 Freedom of Information Act requests with the FBI, the Bureau of Prisons, the US Parole Board, the Air Force and the Securities and Exchange Commission.

The investigation spanned 20 states and three foreign countries and produced more than 3,800 documents, 950 relating solely to Lester Lee.

It was determined:

- Lee was a convicted rapist with a long criminal record. At one time Lee had been on the FBI's 10 Most Wanted Fugitives list and was believed to have been a professional killer, responsible for dozens of contract murders.

- Lee was president of an international coal company which made apparently illicit contributions to the 1976 presidential campaign of Ronal Reagan and had under contract the services of Ohio State Sen. Donald (Buz) Lukens, a close Reagan political ally and now Midwest coordinator of the Reagan campaign.

- Lee was a close business associate of convicted gun runner Dominick E. Bartone, reputed to be a top Cleveland organized crime figure. Lee and Bartone shared a $55 million coal contract with the country of Turkey.

But more than that, it appears Lee was a piece in the sprawling jigsaw puzzle of organized crime in the American coal industry, a picture investigators are putting together piece by piece today.

It is a picture of massive fraud, bribery, narcotics trafficking, corruption and murder.

This investigative series begins with the remarkable history of Lester Lee, detailing his role in the coal racket. It also will explain, swindle by swindle, the operations of mobsters and Mafia-linked con men who have been preying on the US coal industry since the coal boom hit in the mid-1970s.

Lester Lee is finished, but men of his ilk are not. They have shown that coal is a particularly attractive industry for economic fraud.

Coal properties are easy to come by in any of 10 states, but they're off the beaten track. Law enforcement is spread paper thin, and few local lawmen really understand the complex interstate and international swindles.

Coal attracts money. With energy in short supply, customers grow desperate for a source, and investors scramble to buy into a boom. It stacks up to a mixture of confusion, greed, high stakes and lax law enforcement—a happy swindling ground.

The coal racket flourishes when energy needs are highest, and recent energy policy is shifting America to coal.

Threats of conflict in the Middle East and rapid OPEC price hikes place US oil supplies in constant jeopardy. Nuclear reactors have not proven the safe, cheap power source they once promised to be, and the era of solar energy is just dawning.

President Carter has proposed to spend billions to develop synthetic fuels and speed conversion of oil-burning electric generators to coal. Meanwhile, only $1 million has been allocated to combat the coal racket, a highly-sophisticated operation with a self-generating money supply.

The stage is set for booming years in the coal business—and booming years for the coal racket.

PART 2: FUGITIVE LEE BECOMES MODEL PRISONER
JUNE 2, 1980

Lester Clifford Lee spent Christmas Eve, 1955, in a bar in Niceville, Fla., a sleepy little fishing village about 55 miles east of Pensacola.

Niceville is a flyspeck of a town, population 2,000, on the edge of the swampy Choctawatchee Bay. The locals say Niceville is a nice place to live. But for Lee, it was a nice place to hide. Lee had spent the last 21 months running from the FBI. He'd beaten and robbed a Knoxville, Tenn., merchant of $500 in March, 1954.

The FBI wanted Lee because he'd been on parole at the time and skipped town.

Lee wasn't an easy man to find. He'd spent his boyhood traveling with carnivals, and he slipped from town to town as easily as a roving sideshow. The FBI suspected, correctly, that he'd returned to the carnival circuit.

Agents followed his trail through Tennessee, Alabama, Georgia, Mississippi and Kentucky. In Hazard, they learned Lee had been traveling with the Interstate Shows carnival.

They learned Lee and a convicted bank robber named Bob Smith had pistol-whipped a deputy sheriff and fled. Interstate Show's gate receipts had vanished too.

But Lee was always two steps ahead of the manhunt, and when his trail grew as cold as the weather, the Knoxville FBI nominated Lee for the Ten Most Wanted Fugitives Program.

On Dec. 1, 1955, Lee's picture went on display in police stations and post offices throughout the country. While Lee dallied in Niceville's Shady Oaks Café, a rookie policeman named Joe Wright shuffled papers at the police station. Wright came across Lee's wanted poster and recognized the sullen face.

The dark-haired man with the curious blue dot on his left cheek looked remarkably like a man Wright had arrested for brawling a month before.

Niceville wasn't a big town, and it didn't take long for Wright to find Lee. One look inside the Shady Oaks confirmed Wright's hunch.

Wright left to summon the police chief from nearby Valparaiso. They each deputized a bystander, and the four returned to the Shady Oaks to get their man.

It wasn't an oversized posse for the job. The FBI poster bore the warning:

"Lee may be armed and should be considered extremely dangerous. He reportedly carries a knife and wears large rings on his fingers to aid him in hand-to-hand combat."

As Lee was being led to a waiting police cruiser, he bolted. Police said they called for Lee to stop and fired a warning shot over his head. Wright then opened fire, hitting Lee in the lower back and the right thigh.

It still took a flying tackle to bring him down.

On Christmas Day, FBI Director J. Edgar Hoover sent a telegram to all Bureau offices in the country.

"Subject arrested Niceville, Florida, December twenty four, fifty five. Discontinue investigation to locate." Hoover.

It wasn't the last time the FBI would come looking for Lester Clifford Lee. And it wasn't the first time he'd been at odds with the law.

He was born Jan. 14, 1932, in Rayville, La., the only child of two carnival game operators. His father was constantly away from the Knoxville family home, on the road with his gambling game. Lester's parents divorced while he was in grade school.

Lester grew to be a wiry little tough. He was ruddy-faced, blue-eyed and lean—more than his stepmother Alice Myers Lee could handle. A staunch Catholic, she enrolled the boy in parochial school for four years. But Lester was getting another kind of education on the side.

When he was 12, he was arrested by Knoxville police for larceny and housebreaking. At 13, he stole a car. The young boy was sent to the state reform school in Nashville for three years.

He was out in a year, having convinced school officials to free him to join the Army. Instead, he joined his father on the carnival circuit and became the bingo foreman. He was 14 and earning $45 a week.

When the carnival ended in the summer of 1946, Lee joined the Army, telling the recruiting officer he was 18. He was shipped to Champaign, Ill., to train as a sheet metal worker.

While celebrating his 15th birthday in an Urbana, Ill., motel room, Lee was arrested for statutory rape, a charge later reduced to contributing to the delinquency of a minor. After serving 20 days in county jail, Lee transferred to the Air Force and was sent to Kadina Air Base in Okinawa.

Then Lester Lee began his career as a felon. On the morning of Jan. 31, 1949, Lee, drunk on rice wine, raped and sodomized a 65-year old Okinawan peasant woman. A military court sentenced him to eight years at hard labor. He was dishonorably discharged and sent to Terre Haute, Ind., federal prison to serve his sentence.

In prison, Lee acted the model prisoner. He sang tenor in the glee club, attended Mass regularly, wrote frequently to his parents and gave blood during the Red Cross drives, apparently not telling anyone he had contracted malaria, gonorrhea and syphilis while in Okinawa. But the Air Force turned down his repeated requests for clemency.

In early 1952, though, he began getting some outside help.

Howard Baker, then a Tennessee Congressman, now Senate Minority Leader, wrote to the Adjutant General of the Army, William Bergin, that Lee's "mother has written me about the possibility of leniency and I should like to have a report on the case for this purpose."

But parole was again denied, and Lee's perfect prison record went down the drain. One morning during Mass, Lee and a black inmate named Henry Curry were seen "apparently holding hands. After Mass, at breakfast, they were sitting together taking bites out of each other's food," a prison report stated.

Prison officials promptly transferred Lee to the federal prison in Lewisburg, Pa., in September, 1952.

Four months later, Rep. Baker wrote Bergin again, "Mrs. Alice Lee . . . who is the mother of the above-named prisoner, advise (sic) me that his case will be presented to the parole board again soon. She is badly in need of him at home and I will appreciate your consideration."

Gen. Bergin forwarded Baker's letter to the US Parole Board which, without explanation, reopened the case and granted Lee parole.

It was a peculiar decision, in light of the fact that just 10 days earlier, the military clemency board had unanimously rejected the idea of even reducing Lee's sentence, citing his "poor adjustment" in prison and a "prior unstable civil history."

At the end of July, 1953, Lee was free, having served just over four years of an eight-year sentence.

But his parole ended on the streets of Niceville, Fla., when he was shot down by Joe Wright, the rookie cop.

Lee was sent to the federal prison in Atlanta, Ga., to serve out a three-and-a-half year sentence as a parole violator.

Lee again became a model prisoner, enrolling in an array of educational and self-help programs. But his role as a cooperative inmate turned him into a guinea pig for secret and bizarre medical experiments.

His annual clemency report for his January, 1958, stated Lee was a "participant in the Asian Flu project and has been active in the LSD Project."

In more than 950 pages of Air Force, FBI and prison records obtained by *The Kentucky Post*, only one more passing reference is made to the Asian Flu project. Lee's participation in the LSD Project is never mentioned again, and no further explanation was made of the extent and nature of either project.

The US Bureau of Prisons states that all of Lee's records from his prison stay in Atlanta—the time when the experiments were carried out—are inexplicably missing.

The clemency review board, in light of Lee's participation in "medical research projects" concluded its report by saying Lee "has earned some further clemency." The Army ignored the board's recommendations.

His sentence ran out eight months later, however, and he was conditionally released on Aug. 25, 1958. But he quickly returned.

It wasn't Lee's vagrancy and loitering arrest in Nashville that bothered the parole people. It was the fact that he was arrested in Knoxville 10 days later for shoplifting and trying to work a swindle on a Sears Roebuck store. He served another 11 months before he was freed.

Lee's record stayed relatively clean for several years. In 1963, he and a host of other ex-con carnival workers were arrested in Fargo, N.D. Lee was charged with interstate transportation of a firearm by a convicted felon, but he was acquitted.

Lee returned to Knoxville after that and told FBI agents he was a grocer. But his biggest impact in the grocery business came in Newport, Tenn., a wild little town on the edge of the Smoky Mountains.

At 8:30, the morning of Oct. 7, 1966, a grocer named Sam Overton was robbed of $19,862 as he walked from the Famers and Planters bank to the Newport Super Dollar store where he worked.

His two assailants then shot Overton, the father of four young sons, three times. Overton died on his way to the hospital.

The gunmen were convicted of first degree murder, and Lester Lee was convicted of hiring them to rob Overton. Court records do not reflect his sentence.

The Overton murder showed up in a 1966 racketeering investigation conducted by the Cincinnati FBI.

In that report, Lee was described as a "notorious East Tennessee hoodlum who at one time or another has been associated with most all criminals in the area." The report termed Lee "emotionally unstable."

Exactly why the FBI was interested in Lee at this point is not discernible from the heavily-censored documents. The Cincinnati FBI reported the majority of its files on Lee were routinely destroyed in 1977 and 1978, while Lee was still operating in Newport and Covington.

From what files remain, though, it is clear Lee began showing up in the northern Kentucky area in the late 1960s. FBI agents in 1967 learned Lee was "operating a con game or engaged in flimflam activities in the Cincinnati-Covington area."

As time went on, Lee left Tennessee behind, visiting northern Kentucky to ostensibly tend his nightclub business.

Lee later told FBI agents he was a partner with twice-convicted burglar Vance Raleigh in the Brass Ass nightclub on Monmouth St. in Newport. Raleigh was shot to death Sept. 7, 1973, in a gun battle outside the Gladiator Club in Newport.

Lee's actual interest in Raleigh's nightclub is not known. In the early 1970s, Lee worked for The Body Shoppe, another Newport club, and his wife Anne—his third of four—reported she worked there also. Lee also reported owing money to Wilfred (Butter) Rodgers, the owner of The Spotted Calf nightclub.

Lee's relationship with Raleigh may have been nothing more than a close friendship.

"Vance and J.R. (for 'Junior,' Lee's family nickname) were real good friends. They used to babysit each other's kids when J.R. was living down there," Raleigh's mother, Bess, said.

Lee's nightclubbing was a sideline, however. His real income appears to have come from a much more gruesome business.

On June 2, 1968, Carl J. Baker got a call from an informant in Columbus, Ohio.

The man told Baker, then head of the Treasury Department's Alcohol, Tobacco and Firearms (ATF) Cincinnati office, that Lee and a man named Tommy Stilson would be passing through Cincinnati in the next few days.

"At the time the informant contacted me . . . he stated Lester Clifford Lee was a convicted felon, he was a suspect in a murder in Dayton, Ohio, he would be en route to North Carolina by way of Knoxville, Tenn., and that he had a contract to kill a man in North Carolina," Baker would later testify.

Baker, now retired and living in Lancaster, Ky., said Lee's contract was for $5,000. "My information was he had a contract on an ex-state representation," Baker said in a recent interview.

The morning of June 12, 1968, Baker got another call from his informant, who told him Lee and Stilson had just left Columbus and would be stopping in Dayton, Ohio, to pick up "four objects" from a man named Philpott.

Three hours later, ATF agents forced Lee's brown Buick off the road near the Ft. Mitchell exit on I-75. Agents found a loaded .38-cal. revolver in the trunk. Under a floormat in the front, they found four neatly-folded $100 bills, all bearing the same serial number.

Lee's gun was traced to a Westerville, Ohio, sporting goods shop where it had been stolen several months before.

Lee was charged with interstate transportation of firearms by a convicted felon and possession of counterfeit money.

At the trial in March, 1969 Stilson told the jury that he and Lee were going to Knoxville to pick up some carnival equipment from Lee's father.

But according to Baker, who followed Lee's activities for many years, Lee hadn't been in the carnival business for quite some time. At the time of his arrest, Baker said, Lee was practicing his new vocation, that of a hired killer.

"Lester Clifford Lee was a prime suspect in seven or eight homicides in and around the Columbus, Ohio, area," Baker told reporters.

According to one Dayton, Ohio, police detective, Lee was suspected of killing a local used car dealer just before his Kentucky arrest.

"We questioned him about it. It was a hit, and we knew he did it. We just couldn't prove it," he said.

Those killings were just a few of many Lee is suspected of, according to Jerry Schwartz, a former Columbus, Ohio, detective.

When asked if seven or eight murders sounded about right, Schwartz snorted. "Try 39," he said. "We had 39 separate files on him."

Lee was never charged in those cases.

But he was convicted on the counterfeiting and transportation of firearms charges and sentenced for five years in prison. His lawyers appealed to the US Supreme Court.

While his case was on appeal, Lee moved from Columbus to Burlington, Ky., where he bought a house at 2740 Petersburg Rd. from Stanley and Mary Kasper.

"We put our house up for sale and they came over to look at it," Mrs. Kasper said. "They came on real strong. Drove a big Cadillac. His wife was real pretty, and he was so nice."

She recalled Lee saying that "he was either the owner or part owner of The Pink Pussycat (nightclub) in Newport. His wife was working down there, too," Mrs. Kasper said.

(The Pink Pussycat exploded into flames and was destroyed on Christmas Eve morning, 1975. Arson investigators said the fire was deliberately set. No arrests have been made.)

After buying the house, Lee rented a two-story duplex from the Kaspers at 110 Washington St. in Burlington.

Lee "used part of it for an office," Mrs. Kasper said. The business conducted in the "office" was anything but normal.

"There were big black Cadillacs rolling up at all hours, and they'd stay all night and leave early in the morning. They kept it all locked up with a bunch of big padlocks, and they wouldn't let me upstairs," Mrs. Kasper said.

When Lee's rent was late, the Kaspers sued and appeared at the duplex with a deputy sheriff.

"They were all gone," Mrs. Kasper recalled. "They left all the phones. They had that back room wired up like nobody's business."

Three months later the Supreme Court refused to hear Lee's last appeal, and he surrendered to federal marshals to begin his five-year sentence.

On Feb. 22, 1972, the Terre Haute federal prison gates clanged shut behind him. He was back—after 22 years.

PART 3: LEE DISCOVERS NEW RACKET: COAL
JUNE 3, 1980

Lester Lee excelled at being a prisoner because he wanted to be something more.

He served his time carefully at Terre Haute, Ind., federal prison, earning glowing reports from prison social workers. Meanwhile his connections with the outside world were alive, but not well.

Lee's third wife, Anne, divorced him and was given custody of their three children. His house in Burlington, Ky., was sold at auction to pay $33,000 in personal debts.

But Lee wasn't exactly homeless. Or forgotten. By July 1973, he had a promise of a job from his long-time tax accountant, Mitchell Turner of Lexington.

"The job duties are primarily picking up and delivering books and records for our clients. The pay will be $150 a week," Turner wrote on the stationery of his Lexington accounting firm, Dealers Tax Service.

With the backing of Turner and Lexington attorney D. Cameron Hays, Lee was paroled to Dealers Tax Service and Nov. 16, 1973, serving only 19 months of a five-year sentence for possession of a fire firearm and possession of counterfeit money.

If Lee was Turner's errand boy, he didn't look the part. "He appears to be very prosperous," Lee's parole officer wrote.

But Lee later told attorneys in a deposition he made no money at Dealers Tax. And when he became president of Gamilee Management, Inc.—a Lexington commodities brokerage run by Lee, Turner and Turner's brother Gareth, who was then general manager of Dutchess Furniture Co. in Florence—Lee claimed that, too, was a non-paying job.

Lee told the incredulous attorneys he lived off "personal money I had accumulated."

But the FBI suspected that "personal money" may have been stolen.

On July 23, 1974, an 85-year old man in Malden, Mass., was swindled of $27,500 by two men posing as bank examiners.

The FBI tracked down one of the swindlers who told them Lee had acted as the middleman in the con, putting the swindlers together and finding someone in Chicago who could cash the old man's check.

The Chicago US Attorney declined prosecution because the con men were already in jail on similar charges. The case was closed.

But while the Chicago FBI was closing its file on Lee, the Louisville FBI was opening one of its own.

Lee was travelling along the East Coast at the time. Lee had lured his parole officer into extending his parole travel limits with the fanciful tale that Gamilee—housed in a squat, rundown Lexington office building that served as home for Dealers Tax and D. Cameron Hays' law office—managed "meat companies in various parts of the eastern United States."

Lee told his parole officer "he must travel to various meat companies checking their books and working undercover checking on their operations for Gamilee," the FBI report noted.

Lee was working undercover—but meat had nothing to do with it.

On Jan. 21, 1974, the Louisville FBI wrote, "(Lee) has been convicted of passing counterfeit money and is believed to be a hired gun. It is requested that a 91-New (file) be opened . . . to determine if he could be a suspect in any unsolved bank robberies."

Lee's parole officer told inquiring FBI agents Lee "had the potential to commit any type of crime, especially one of violence."

They found that the Lexington police department also had its eye on Lee. "They followed his activities for quite some time and found him to associate with many known gamblers in Lexington and northern Kentucky area," the FBI report said.

But by then, Lee had latched onto a racket more lucrative than bank robbery: coal.

When coal prices began to take off in 1974, Lee was in the process of getting on board. Among his first contacts were Sidney S. Shrine and Dominick Edward Bartone.

Their connections with coal, like Lee's, were new. But their connections with organized crime were well established.

When Sid Shine lived in Dayton, Ohio, in 1960, he owned a large portion of the now-defunct Dayton Speedway. That year, he got a $100,000 loan to operate the speedway from Cleveland multi-millionaire Sam W. Klein.

Klein was involved in business deals with New Jersey syndicate boss Gerardo (Jerry) Catena. When that relationship was made public, Klein was forced to resign from the board of Bally Pinball Co. and sell his majority stock ownership to Bally.

Documents filed recently in Campbell Circuit Court revealed Klein took over a part ownership in the Beverly Hills Supper Club in Southgate in 1967 from reputed Cleveland syndicate members Morris Kleinman, M.B. (Moe) Dalitz and Sam Tucker.

According to a confidential Florida police intelligence report obtained by *The Kentucky Post*, Shine, 62, of Atlanta, numbers among his business associates two convicted swindlers, Byron Prugh and Harold Audsley, both of Ft. Lauderdale, Fla., and Charles Verive and Lou (The Tailor) Rosanova, both identified by law enforcement agencies as Chicago crime family members. The same report states Shine reportedly fronts for Miami/Tampa Mob boss Santo Trafficante in dealings with the La Scene nightclub in Cocoa Beach, Fla.

In 1976, Shine and seven other Georgia businessmen were indicted on charges of defrauding a Chattanooga, Tenn., insurance company of $3.3 million in phony policies and bad loans underwritten by Shine's company.

Shine was acquitted of the fraud charges, but two of his partners in Vanguard Security Funding Corp. were convicted. Shine's business card, found in Lee's wallet the night Lee was killed in a seedy Newport adult bookstore, lists Shine's employer as Vanguard Security Funding. Shine was reached at the number on that business card.

Shine said he met Lee while Lee was working for Jermilee, Inc., a company Lee, Mitchell Turner and a Lexington timber broker named Jerome Jernigan set up when the Gamilee operations were abandoned in late 1974.

"Lester called me trying to sell some railroad equipment and . . . said he'd decided to come up with some coal leases. We came over to their offices and tried to work out some deal with them but . . . they could never come up with anything." Shine said.

Not for lack of trying. Jermilee's phone records show Lee called Shine dozens of times in late 1974 and early 1975.

Shine said he still owns coal land in Breathitt County through a firm called Olympic Developments, which uses the same phone number as

Vanugard Security Funding Corp. He remembered Lee as "a jolly fellow. I kind of liked him." Shine said he didn't know how Lee found him.

But Lee's other coal associate, Dominick Bartone, was more than just associating with the underworld. The rough-talking, 66-year old Bartone is reputed to be one of Cleveland's top organized crime figures.

Before Lee and Bartone got together, Bartone didn't know much about coal. His business experience was in gun running and tax fraud.

In 1959, Bartone was convicted of conspiracy to illegally export implements of war. The weapons, hidden in huge military transport planes, were destined for the Dominican Republic and Fulgencio Batista. Batista had been ousted from Cuba by Fidel Castro and was plotting a coup against Castro. The coup never came off.

For his part in the scheme Bartone was put on probation.

Three years later, his probation was revoked when he sold machine guns to Honduras. He served a year in jail.

Bartone's line of work apparently cause problems when it came to filling out his income tax returns. Some years, he didn't bother filing at all. Between 1966 and 1969, he was convicted three times of tax fraud.

Bartone got out of jail in 1971. By late 1974, he and Lee were planning to move mountains in the coal industry. Lee introduced Bartone to Island Creek Coal Co. of Lexington, the nation's fourth-largest coal company.

On March 14, 1975, Island Creek signed a letter of intent to sell the Guyan mines in southeastern Kentucky to Bartone's American Concrete Builders of Youngstown, Ohio.

The asking price was $50 million.

Copies of the agreement went to Jermilee and a Springfield, Ohio, firm called Sterling Group and Associates, run by Bartone front man Harold R. Fetter.

Fetter, who's been arrested seven times for check fraud and larceny by trick but never convicted, told *The Kentucky Post* Sterling Group was acting as "mortgage brokers" for Bartone's company.

"We were strictly a hired hand," Fetter said. Fetter soon would become one of Lee's closest associates.

Bartone was later convicted of bank fraud after the now-defunct Northern Ohio Bank loaned $250,000 to American Concrete Builders. That bank financed many Mob-controlled ventures, according to US attorneys with the Organized Crime Strike Force in Cleveland.

The bank collapsed in 1975, leaving the federal government liable for more than $30 million owed to federally insured depositors.

Bartone is in jail as a result of that conviction and since then has been convicted again of gun running, bribery and bank fraud. Fetter said he didn't know Bartone had ever been in jail.

Neither did Stonewall Jackson Barker, Jr., president of Island Creek. Barker said he didn't know anything about Bartone or his company but said Bartone seemed serious about buying the mines. Bartone and Island Creek negotiated for months.

In a deposition Lee gave in August 1975, the deal then was "at a stalemate." But Lee had not given up on his friend Bartone.

"There is a separate agreement between American Concrete and Jermilee stating that if American Concrete buys the property, they will give Jermilee a commission, I think it's for $1 million," Lee said.

Stonie Barker said he didn't "know why the deal didn't go through." Island Creek still owns the mines.

But the $50 million Guyan deal was nothing compared to what Lee and Bartone were hatching at that time.

By early 1975, Lee was putting the finishing touches on a multi-million dollar coal contract with the country of Turkey, and Bartone was planning to supply some of that coal.

It was destined to be Lester Lee's biggest score. Lee the rapist, the hired killer, the con man, was fast becoming Lee the coal baron.

PART 4: COAL BARON LEE LEARNS HOW TO PULL POLITICAL STRINGS
JUNE 4, 1980

The Russians were almost finished.

The $640 million steel plant they were building for the Turkish government in the Mediterranean port of Iskenderun was nearly complete. Soon, the Turks would need coal—loads of it—to fuel the massive furnaces.

In mid-1974, high grade metallurgical coal was selling for $50 a ton, almost triple its price the year before.

A coal boom was cresting, and whoever landed a coal contract with the Iskenderun Iron and Steel Works would be rich.

Ries Hengstmengle wanted to cash in. Hengstmengle, a bespectacled, multilingual Dutchman, knew his way around Turkish governmental circles. He'd lived in Turkey when he was employed as an executive for Royal Dutch Shell oil company. But Hengstmengle didn't know much about coal.

So he went to see his friend Robert E. Todd in Miami, Okla. Todd was developing a machine which he thought would revolutionize the coal industry; a machine capable of digging out difficult, thin seams of high quality coal, the kind the Turks would need.

It was a hand alliance. Hengstmengle had the money to quickly develop the machine—$200,000, which he promised Todd if the two managed to land a contract with the Turks. Todd had a knowledge of coal and a machine to get it out. The arrangement was convenient in other aspects, too.

Todd's uncle had an old Arkansas shell corporation, a company called Hy-Test Coal Co., which was inactive at the time. Todd said his uncle loaned him the shell—a corporation already licensed to do business but having no assets—so Todd could develop his thin seam miner.

And they could go into the contract negotiations with the Turks as representatives of a 50-year-old coal company.

About this time, Lester Clifford Lee entered the picture.

Lee was operating Jermilee Management, Inc. in Lexington, brokering coal and other commodities.

Fresh from federal prison, Lee had done well, landing several coal contracts and dealing coal properties to third parties. But Jermilee was seeing little money, and one of Lee's business partners, Lexington timber broker Jerome Jernigan, was getting suspicious.

So when Hengstmengle introduced Lee to the Turkish contract, it was fortuitous. Lee wanted out of Jermilee anyway.

How Lee and Hengstmengle found each other isn't clear. The Dutchman told *The Kentucky Post* that Todd located Lee, a man Hengstmengle now refers to as "a gangster." Todd claimed it was the other way around. Either way, Lee was in.

Todd and Hengstmengle flew to Turkey to begin the negotiations. Lee began laying the groundwork for Hy-Test Coal Co. of Kentucky.

He approached Ray Cumberledge of Lexington, then assistant registrar at the University of Kentucky. Cumberledge moonlighted in coal brokering and was well-acquainted with Lee.

"I told him I was having problems (at Jermilee) and was going to leave and was he interested in leaving the University of Kentucky and going into business?" Lee said in a deposition.

Cumberledge quickly agreed. So did Lee's parole sponsor, Lexington attorney D. Cameron Hays. They were joined by Lee's longtime friend Gareth Turner, then general manager of Dutchess Furniture Co. in Florence, Ky.

On Feb. 17, 1975, Todd sent Lee a telegram from Turkey: "We are pleased to inform you that we have been advised the Turkish coal (contract) has been awarded to our company."

Lee moved quickly, dumping the inquisitive Jernigan, whose demands for accountability were becoming more frequent. Jernigan later sued his former partners for $10 million, claiming he was cheated of the Turkish contract. That suit is pending in Fayette Circuit Court.

Six days after Todd's telegram arrived at Jermilee's offices, Cameron Hays incorporated High Test Appalachian Coal Co. with Lee, Cumberledge, Turner and himself as officers.

But the fledgling coal company had no assets or capital, no way of securing loans to develop coal property. Lee turned to his friend, Dominick Bartone, a convicted gun runner and reputed organized crime figure from Cleveland.

In March 1975 a contract was drawn up. Bartone would give Lee's coal company $400,000 in advance for coal mined in Arkansas using Todd's miracle machine. The remaining $1 million would come when the coal was shipped to Bartone. Now Lee had both capital and an asset—an impressive coal contract to show bankers.

But the Turks discovered they had ordered the wrong type of coal, so they rejected the original contract and ordered it rebid. The contract with Bartone was never completed.

This time, the Turks decided to come to the United States and inspect the mines and the coal companies firsthand.

Just before the Turks arrived in April 1975, Cameron Hays put together Hy-Test Coal Co. of Kentucky Inc., with Lee, Cumberledge, Turner and himself owning 50 percent of it. The remainder was owned by Todd, Hengstmengle and several other Dutchmen. Hy-Test went from a one-room operation to a multi-national corporation with stationery boasting worldwide offices.

A welcoming party for the Turks was whipped up.

It included an energetic young Louisville businessman named Rodney Glenn, president of American Carbon Energy; a smooth Nashville wheeler-dealer named Floyd Kephart, who was a White House aide during the Kennedy administration, a political analyst for WSM-TV in Nashville and president of Kepco, Inc., a brokerage firm; Tom Chambers, an import-export specialist from Louisville; Ray Cumberledge; Robert Todd; Ries Hengstmengle; Lee, and Dutch contractor named Ton Van Hoorn.

Chambers said Rodney Glenn, with Lee's money, chartered a DC-3 and flew the entire entourage to New York City to meet the Turkish trading emissaries.

For two days, the group wined and dined in New York's poshest clubs. Cumberledge hired a New York public relations and protocol specialist to make sure everything went smoothly. The Turks were impressed.

The two-week old Hy-Test Coal Co. of Kentucky was awarded the contract at a well-publicized event in New York. The Turks, Todd, Hengstmengle and Van Hoorn were made Kentucky Colonels by Gov. Julian Carroll's New York representative.

"Julian was quite impressed with the fact that this coal machine would ultimately come to Kentucky and that we had this $55 million contract with the Turks," Todd said.

It was a sizable contract: 930,000 tons of coal at $55.75 a ton. But it wasn't quite as large as Lee was telling people.

Lee told the Louisville *Courier-Journal* that the contract was for two million tons and would be "renegotiated for another two million tons in the following two years. He sad the contract might then be extended so it would cover more than 15 million tons."

Rodney Glenn, according to a story in the Louisville *Times*, estimated the contract was worth from "$250 million to $750 million."

The Turks, along with a couple of Spanish United Nations officials, came to Kentucky to celebrate the signing. It was Derby weekend, and the flamboyant Glenn put on quite a show.

According to Chambers, who later went to work with Glenn in American Carbon Energy, Glenn spent lavishly on a Kentucky Derby party for the visiting dignitaries.

"I've heard it expressed at $40,000, some have said $70,000. I've got to credit Rodney Glenn with knowing how to throw a super party," Chambers said.

Glenn bought enclosed boxes on the Sky Terrace at Churchill Downs, hired the Corsair Shrine Marching Band to entertain the Turks, arranged guided tours of Louisville and got invitations for the entire party to attend the Governor's Breakfast. The party went on for two days.

But the Derby bash was Rodney Glenn's downfall. Chambers said Glenn bet heavily on American Carbon's part of Hy-Test's Turkish contract and squandered money he actually owed to Skyuka Mining Co. of Manchester, Ky.

When Lee, who controlled the Turkish contract, cut Glenn out of the deal, the roof fell in. Skyuka couldn't be paid. Glenn fled Louisville and his creditors and was arrested on a fugitive warrant by the FBI in New York City.

Skyuka Mining wasn't a company to be trifled with. Its owner was the notorious swindler Alexander Guterma, convicted of a string of securities frauds in the early 1960s. (Among his victims was Bon Ami, the cleansing powder company. At one point, Guterma backed an armored truck up to Bon Ami's offices and made off with $3 million in cash and securities.)

This time, however, Guterma was on the receiving end.

Glenn was charged with fraud. Destitute, he spent 11 months in Jefferson County jail before he was acquitted. Glenn has since left Kentucky and could not be found.

Glenn wasn't the only key business partner Lee lost at this time. Hy-Test's founder, Robert Todd, abruptly quit the company in June 1975. Todd said the trouble started after he dug too deeply into Lee's background.

Todd didn't find out about Lee's rape conviction or his prior hit man activities, but what he found was disturbing enough.

"I didn't want any part of the Mafia," Todd said from his home in Houston, Texas.

He said he'd learned that "Lee used to be the bodyguard for (Teamsters Union boss) Jimmy Hoffa. I was horrified to find out I was involved with people of that type."

Todd said he confronted Lee with his findings, and Lee didn't deny them. In fact, he elaborated.

Lee told Todd "they had attempted to kill (Lee) before. That when he was serving as a bodyguard for Hoffa, somebody planted an explosive in the car but (Lee) survived the explosion."

Chambers, too, said Lee spoke often of Hoffa, who disappeared in July 1975.

"When I was introduced to Lee, I was told he had been an organizer for the Teamsters. I knew he knew Hoffa, and he had a very high admiration for Hoffa," Chambers said.

US Labor Department organized crime investigators said they could find nothing to support Lee's story of Teamsters Union connections.

Todd said he told the Hy-Test officers: "I'll just take my little patents and my coal machine, and I'll go home. And you can have your coal contract." Todd resigned June 27, 1975.

But Lee had more pressing problems than Todd's resignation. Floyd Kephart had been busy gathering miners to produce the Turkish coal, but when Hy-Test attempted to acquire dock space for the Turkish freighters in the port of Mobile, Ala., they were rebuffed.

Kephart said there were "big-time problems." Hy-Test was refused space on the crowded Alabama State Docks.

To solve that problem, Kephart went to see a college chum named James Free, who was then clerk and chief executive officer of the Tennessee House of Representatives.

"He knew all the politicos," Kephart said.

Free, Kephart and Lee boarded a private plane in Nashville and went to Alabama.

"I went to see the governor (then George C. Wallace), and he told me to contact this lawyer," Kephart said.

"This lawyer" was Mobile attorney Pierre Pelham, who had been president pro tempore of the Alabama Senate when the state docks were under construction and was a close political associate of Wallace.

Pelham said "the word was out" that the Drummond Coal Co. of Walker County, Ala.—the state's largest coal producer—"had a lock" on the state docks.

"The problem posed to me was that the Drummonds controlled this thing down here and wouldn't let anybody else come through. That was the problem I addressed myself to," Pelham said.

Pelham said he couldn't recall how he solved Hy-Test's problem. When asked why Hy-Test had sought his aid, Pelham said, "I'm a Phi Beta Kappa and an honor graduate of Harvard Law School, so I guess I'm a pretty smart fellow."

Pelham said he "checked around to make sure there wasn't any foolishness going on. I can't tell you any more than that. I got it straightened out."

Pelham wasn't the only one looking for Drummond "foolishness."

Last October, Drummond Coal Co., its president, vice-president and treasurer were indicted along with two Alabama state senators and a state representative on 19 counts of racketeering, bribery, fraud and extortion.

One of the counts alleges the Drummonds provided prostitutes to certain Alabama politicians for favorable treatment on state coal contracts. The Drummond trial is now in its fifth week and is expected to go another two or three months.

Whatever Pelham did about the Drummonds, it worked. Hy-Test got its dock space. Pelham said he got a "modest fee" for his work. Jim Free, who introduced Lee and Kephart to Pelham said he was given $1,000.

It was a lesson in politics Lee was not soon to forget.

PART 5: EMPIRE-BUILDER LEE HIRES STATE SEN. BUZ LUKENS
JUNE 5, 1980

Lester Lee had good reason to respect political pull.

In 1953, when Lee was in federal prison for rape and sodomy, letters to the parole board from US Rep. Howard Baker Jr., father of present Senate Minority leader Howard Baker Jr., immediately preceded Lee's release.

In early 1975, Lee was negotiating a multi-million dollar contract with Turkey, and he sent the Turkish Minister of Finance a new Buick sedan. The contract went to Lee's Hy-Test Coal Co.

In June, when Hy-Test was denied dock space in the port of Mobile, Ala., Lee went to see the clerk of the Tennessee House (now a Carter/Mondale campaign director) who introduced him to an influential ex-senator in Alabama. Both were paid for their help, and the dock space materialized.

Two months later, Hy-Test got the chance to hire the minority whip of the Ohio State Senate, a man who had served in the US Congress. Lee promptly signed a contract for the politician's services.

Hy-Test was in high gear.

With a $55 million Turkish coal contract in hand, the company moved from its rundown offices on Pinoak Street in Lexington to a fashionable concrete and smoked-glass headquarters on Waller Avenue.

Hy-Test financial statement dated July 31, 1975, showed the four-month-old coal company with slightly more than $1 million in sales with assets of more than half a million dollars.

The financial statement, which was unsigned and uncertified, showed expected profits from the Turkish contract to be $3.5 million. Millions of dollars worth of credit were being posted in Hy-Test's name by the Turks in international banks in Europe and Dayton, Ohio.

"Everybody was waiting for Lee to make them rich," said Fred J. Eilers Jr., then Hy-Test office manager.

Eilers, 39, Park Hills, left a job as office manager of Dutchess Furniture Co., Florence, to work for Hy-Test.

One person with a big stake in Lee was Dominick E. Bartone, a tall, corpulent man reputed to be one of the top organized crime figures in Cleveland, Ohio. Bartone, a thrice-convicted gun runner, helped Lester Lee when Hy-Test was brand new. Now Lee returned the favor.

On June 5, 1975, Hy-Test agreed to buy from Bartone's American Concrete Builders Inc., anywhere from one-quarter to one-half of the coal to supply the 930,000-ton Turkish contract. Bartone was looking to take in $19.5 million on the deal.

The contract was witnessed by Harold R. Fetter, a Springfield, Ohio, man who's been arrested seven times on charges of check fraud and larceny by trick, but never convicted. Fetter said he was hired by Bartone to "do some contract stuff, be sort of a transaction agent."

Harold Fetter, for his work, was to get as much as $420,000. Lee instructed Winters National Bank in Dayton, Ohio, to pay Bartone and Fetter directly from the Turkish letters of credit posted there.

But the Turkish coal deal turned sour on Bartone, Fetter said. Bartone bought a coal mine in Pound, Va. to supply Lee's contract, but the mine was a failure. "They had three cave-ins, got their equipment buried three or four times. You could have put in an envelope the coal they mined there," Fetter said.

Fetter said Bartone nearly went broke on that mine. "You'd never believe it about a person like Mr. Bartone, but I think he's extremely naïve. He left his bleached bones down there when they got done with him," Fetter explained.

Bartone may have been naïve about coal, but he was wise in the ways of swindlers.

In 1977, Bartone was convicted of defrauding the now-defunct Northern Ohio Bank of $249,000 in loans. Bartone claimed that money was to finance his coal ventures. In December, 1977, he and a Lyndhurst, Ohio, man named Morton Franklin were convicted of obstruction of justice in Miami for attempting to smuggle machine guns to Cuban premier Fidel Castro.

Bartone was not one to let politics stand in the way of profit. In 1959, he had been convicted of attempting to smuggle guns to ousted Cuban dictator, Fulgencio Batista, who was plotting a coup against Castro.

Bartone's relationship with Castro intrigued the House Select Subcommittee looking into the assassination of President John F. Kennedy. In March, 1978, Bartone was subpoenaed before the Subcommittee, which was exploring a possible link between Castro and the Kennedy assassination.

The same month, he and his gun running partner Morton Franklin were accused of coal-related fraud by the Securities and Exchange Commission. The SEC charged Bartone had stolen most of a $600,000 investment he had raised to mine land in West Virginia and lied to investors by telling them there was coal on the land.

Bartone signed a consent decree that permanently enjoined him from public money-raising schemes.

A month earlier, Bartone had pleaded guilty to bribing a Newark, N.J., bank officer. He also pleaded guilty to conspiring to defraud that same bank, The Trust Co. of New Jersey, of $685,000 in loans.

He is now in the federal prison in Lewisburg, Pa., serving a seven year sentence for bank fraud, bribery and obstruction of justice.

Despite the fact that Harold Fetter witnessed every contract signed between Lester Lee and Dominick Bartone, Fetter claimed there was no real connection between Bartone and Fetter's Springfield, Ohio, mortgage brokerage, Sterling Group and Associates.

"We were just a hired hand," Fetter said.

But Ohio tax records show the original incorporator of Sterling Group was a man named Bruce R. Condon, and Condon's signature appears as secretary of Bartone's American Concrete Builders, Inc. on two Hy-Test contracts.

The illegal loans from the Northern Ohio Bank were made in the name of American Concrete Builders.

Fetter's association with Hy-Test appears to have been steady. Hy-Test's phone records show Lee was in regular contact with Fetter and his company throughout 1975 and into 1976.

Bartone and Fetter's $19.5 million slice of the Turkish contract was made final Aug. 5, 1975. That same day, Lester Lee signed a one-year, $60,000 contract with a trio who called themselves The Shelley Company.

The three Shelley partners were an ex-Congressman, an ex-convict and a businessman who calls himself a "generalist."

The contract is quite clear about the services The Shelley Co. was to provide Hy-Test: "Public Relations . . . in connection with various parts of the general public, industrial public, governmental public, as well as provide advice-related to public offerings (and) increasing (Hy-Test's) profits."

What isn't clear is exactly what The Shelley Co. did to live up to its contract, and the three men found that hard to explain. The thousands of dollars they were paid is an even bigger mystery.

The ex-Congressman was Donald E. (Buzz) Lukens, a powerful conservative Republican who represents Ohio's Fourth District in the state senate. The ex-convict was Charles V. Wheeler, a New Albany Ohio commodities broker with a long criminal record. The "generalist" was Mike Meister of Columbus, Ohio, a man who claims years of experience in finance.

Lukens, 49, is a handsome political dynamo, "a fighter" he says. He served two terms in the US House of Representatives in the mid-60s and has been national chairman of the Young Republicans, executive member of the Republican National Committee, minority whip of the Ohio Senate and is presently Midwest coordinator for the Ronald Reagan campaign. Lukens is a longtime friend and political supporter of the ex–California governor.

But Lukens' political career is not spotless. In 1973, during his second bid for governor, he was barred from running for filing his 1972 state senate campaign expsenses late.

During the Senate "Koreagate" hearings, Korean rice merchant Tongsun Park testified he made two bribe payments totaling $1000 to Lukens. Lukens denies the charge.

Last summer, Lukens was under investigation by postal authorities for a nationwide direct-mail campaign soliciting money for an anti-abortion "war chest" to defeat liberal US Senators Birch Bayh (D-Ind.) and George McGovern (D-S.D.)

Bayh and McGovern complained to the US Postal Service that the mailings were "misleading"

Lukens said Lester Lee was brought to him by Charles Wheeler. According to Lukens, Lee and Wheeler were "old boyhood friends."

Wheeler is 58 and making his living as "a hustler," according to his sometime attorney Richard Vimont of Lexington. Vimont said he has defended Wheeler on charges of armed robbery and possession of counterfeit money, with mixed success.

Wheeler was convicted in 1966 of conspiracy to sell $25,000 worth of bogus $10 and $20 bills in Manchester, Ky.

Vimont recalled, "They had a roadblock set up for him. Charley did a U-turn and drove off at 100 miles an hour, throwing the funny money out of the window. Those farmers were finding money in the weeds for weeks."

Wheeler's criminal record shows 12 arrests on a variety of charges, including attempted burglary, attempted robbery, assault and battery, fraud, possession of forgeries and shooting with intent to kill. Wheeler, a Paintsville, Ky., native, served both federal and state prison sentences.

Wheeler operated a firm called International Sales and Associated Enterprises, Ltd., which used the same New Albany, Ohio, address as did The Shelley Co. Wheeler's partner in International Sales was his brother Paul Harrison Wheeler, 52.

Paul Wheeler's criminal record is even more sordid that his older brother's. According to his rap sheet, he has been sentenced to life imprisonment twice, once in 1960 for breaking and entering and armed burglary and again in 1961 for armed burglary and shooting with intent to kill. His sentence was commuted to nine years, and he was paroled in 1964.

Other arrests include theft of government property, receiving stolen property and armed assault.

The third part of the Shelley trio was Mike Meister, 60, who told *The Kentucky Post* he didn't remember how he became associated with either Wheeler or The Shelley Co.

Meister was alternately vague and argumentative when asked about his role in Shelley.

"Sometimes it's hard for me to remember what I had for breakfast," he declared.

Meister, Wheeler and Lukens' memories conflicted about what they were doing for Lester Lee and Hy-Test Coal Co.

According to Sen. Lukens, Shelley "was formed to do advertising and PR service work for Hy-Test."

Meister said, "Our primary thrust was an attempt to get a favorable financing arrangement for the country of Turkey."

Charles Wheeler said, "We didn't do anything at all."

However, all three men were in complete agreement on the amount of money Lester Lee paid them for their services, whatever they were.

Meister: "Never got paid a dime." Lukens: "I never picked up a penny from it." Wheeler: "We never did any business."

But Hy-Test office manager Fred J. Eilers Jr. didn't remember it that way. "We were just feeding them money," Eilers said of the Shelley group.

The Kentucky Post obtained copies of Hy-Test's cancelled checks and check stubs, which included five payments to Shelley totalling $28,804.

When shown copies of the checks, Lukens appeared surprised. "Jiminy Christmas," he muttered. "I never got it, I never saw anything of it. My goodness gracious."

Wheeler said he couldn't remember what the checks were for. "Maybe office furniture," he suggested.

Wheeler's name and what appears to be his handwriting appears alternately on four more checks for $24,700, made payable to "Hy-Test Field Office of Ohio." Wheeler could not explain what those checks were for or what the "field office" did.

Another Hy-Test check for $2,500 marked "PR expenses" was made payable to Wheeler personally. That check was marked for deposit to the bank account of Wheeler's International Sales and Associated Enterprises, Ltd.

Meister, who told Kentucky officials last December he was executive vice-president of International Sales, said he didn't know what any of the checks were for.

In fact, all three Shelley partners maintained that, despite the contract and the checks, they performed no public relations work for Hy-Test.

Whether or not that was the case, Hy-Test did make on public splash, and Hy-Test officers recalled The Shelley Co. arranged it.

The event was memorialized in Hy-Test's expense ledger, entries marked simply: "plane rental for Reagan trip."

PART 6: LEE FLIES REAGAN ON FOUR-STATE JAUNT
JUNE 6, 1980

When Lester Lee used to talk about Ronald Reagan, Hy-Test Coal Co. office manager Fred J. Eilers Jr. would listen skeptically.

"Lee was such a braggart. He said he'd been flying around with Ronald Reagan. I couldn't figure it. Why would Reagan fool with such a dinky outfit? I mean, we were brand new. We had nothing to offer anyone," Eilers remarked.

Eilers, 39, a tall, scholarly-looking Park Hills man, remained doubtful of Lee's talk until Hy-Test fired its bookkeeper, Lee's brother-in-law David Fleissner. Eilers inherited the green binder Fleissner used as the company ledger.

Written several times in ink on the ledger sheets were the words: "plane rental for Reagan trip."

"It was kind of a shocker," Eilers admitted. But Lester Lee surprised a lot of people.

After spending most of his life behind bars for a variety of felonies, Lee quickly became president of a multi-national coal corporation headquartered in Lexington, Hy-Test Coal Co. of Kentucky Inc.

By late summer of 1975, Hy-Test had a lot of money. Its coal contract with the country of Turkey was worth $55 million, and the company projected a $3.5 million profit by December, 1976. Lee was spending some of that money to build up Hy-Test's image. In August, 1975, he hired Ohio State Sen. Donald E. (Buzz) Lukens as a public relations consultant.

Lukens and two other men formed The Shelley Co. in New Albany, Ohio, to tend to Hy-Test's needs.

Lukens was also doing work that summer for his longtime political friend Ronald Reagan, drumming up Midwestern support for Reagan's candidacy in the 1976 presidential election.

Lukens said he invited the ex–California governor to speak at a fundraiser in Dayton, Ohio, on Sept. 25, 1975, while Reagan was on a nationwide campaign tour. But there was one problem.

Lukens said he got a call from the Reagan entourage a few days before Reagan was to appear in Dayton.

"They said: 'Man, we can't get a plane. We'd like to make your Dayton appearance.' I told them, 'Look, if you get him to Dayton I'll get you a plane.' I didn't have a plane, but I told them I'd get one,' Lukens recalled.

Lukens said he first tried to get the loan of a corporate plane from Armco Steel of Middletown, Ohio, and Champion Paper Co. of Hamilton, both of which are in Lukens' Fourth Senate District. He was not successful.

"I was getting a little desperate," he said.

So Lukens called his partner in The Shelley Co., Charles Wheeler, 59, a convicted burglar with a long criminal record, and spoke to Wheeler about the Reagan appearance.

Wheeler, Lukens said, wanted to donate money to the campaign. "I said, 'Well, great. We can use all the money we can get, but what I'd really like to do is get an airplane. Do you know anyone?"

According to Lukens, Wheeler suggested Lester Lee and Hy-Test Coal Co., Shelley's sole client. "I said, 'Jeepers do you think he'd let us use it?"

Lukens called to find out.

Lee "said he had a plane—any corporation would. I thought I was in the big time," Lukens said.

But Lee didn't have a plane either. Instead, Lee turned to Sprite Flite Jets Inc. of Lexington and rented a red and white Lear Jet for Ronald Reagan.

"They believed in doing things in style," Eilers said of Hy-Test.

Two days before Reagan's Dayton appearance, two calls were made from Hy-Test to Reagan's Los Angeles public relations firm, Deaver and Hannaford, Lukens said: "They (Hy-Test) were probably confirming the airplane."

Lukens explained that Michael Deaver, who was Reagan's chief of staff at the time, was in charge of Reagan's itinerary. Peter Hannaford is one of Reagan's closest political advisors.

The same day, Lee called Hy-Test Vice President Ton Van Hoorn at Hy-Test's Caribbean offices in the Netherlands Antilles Islands.

"I was in Curaçao, and Lee told me to come up," the young Dutch contractor said. "Lee said he had a Lear jet there and said we were going on a trip with Ronald Reagan," he added. Intrigued, Van Hoorn flew up to join the Hy-Test/Reagan trip along the way.

The reason Hy-Test agreed to provide the plane for Reagan is something best known to Lee, who was murdered while working in a Newport, Ky., adult bookstore Jan. 7, 1978.

Other Hy-Test officers said they didn't know precisely what Lee had in mind. But they knew generally.

Ries Hengstmengle, president of Hy-Test of Kentucky's Dutch arm, Hy-Test International, said: "Lee supported the campaign. As far as I can see, they bet heavily Reagan would be the next president of the United States and, you know, favors would be returned."

Ray Cumberledge, vice-president of Hy-Test of Kentucky and now director of planning for the state Justice Department, said Lee "never ever did say point blank what the purpose of the trip was, but you know far better than I do that you just don't spend money for something like that and not expect something in return."

Nor was Sen. Lukens mystified by Lee's motive. "I've never met a human being who wasn't interested in having a piece of a president," Lukens said.

"Lee pretended he was unimpressed—'Mr. Reagan, how are you? Happy to help you out'—but I'm telling you now he had the bug just like everyone else. It just didn't show as much," Lukens said.

The morning of Sept. 25, 1975, Lee flew to Memphis, Tenn., where the night before, Reagan had address a crowd of more than 900 at the Hilton Inn at Memphis International Airport, his second stop in Tennessee that day.

According to *The Commercial Appeal* in Memphis, the stops were part of a "warmup tour for the presidential campaign."

Reagan and his chief of staff Deaver boarded the jet and flew to Bluegrass Field in Lexington, where Lukens and former Kentucky Gov. Louie B. Nunn joined the entourage.

Nunn said he'd been invited by Lukens, who called him several days before the trip and told him "some of them were going down, that they were trying to a get a fundraising thing set up in Kentucky, and they wanted to talk to me about that. I guess it was for Reagan."

Nunn was certainly the right person to call about Reagan fundraisers. At that time, Nunn was one of five founding members of Citizens For Reagan, Reagan's only authorized campaign committee. By the end of September 1975, Citizens For Reagan had raised $396,462 on behalf of the former movie star.

The jet flew to Dress Regional Airport in Evansville, Ind., where it was met by Hy-Test officers Cumberledge and Van Hoorn; Lukens' partners in The Shelley Co., Charles Wheeler and Mike Meister, and a handful of local GOP leaders.

In the crowd was *The Evansville Press*' political reporter, Robert Flynn. Flynn had been tipped to Reagan's surprise visit by an unusual source.

"About two days before Reagan arrived in Evansville, a local gambler C. W. Lee Jr. called me at home and told me Reagan was coming to town. I called the county GOP chairman, and he didn't know anything about it. He seemed a little annoyed that no one had told him," Flynn said.

C.W. Lee probably learned of Reagan's trip from Lester Lee. Shortly before Flynn got his call, C.W.'s father got a $10,000 check from Hy-Test Coal Company. C.W.'s father wrote back to Lester Lee that C.W. Lee Oil Co. would use the money for an oil and gas venture. Hy-Test records show the payment of the check was stopped.

Lukens said the Evansville stop was arranged through "one of Charlie (Wheeler)'s friends there. I don't remember who that was now, someone in the party there."

Reagan landed in Evansville with little advance notice. Wrote Flynn, in the next day's *Press*:

"The Evansville non-event appeared to have been a spur of the moment decision. With (Reagan) on the plane were several representatives of Hy-Test International, Inc. The firm owned the plane and also appeared to be the host for the visit, which seemed to puzzle the local Republicans."

Reagan told Flynn: "I just wanted to have lunch with my friends in Evansville."

The group dined at the Evansville Ramada Inn, and Hy-Test Coal Co. of Kentucky picked up the $115 tab.

But the Evansville stop was for more than lunch, Lukens told *The Kentucky Post* in a recent interview on the floor of the Ohio Senate.

"It got us a lot of votes. You know, I was building a little favor for the future because we knew Reagan was going to run. We did extremely well there when the votes were cast because we'd come to that county and stopped in that town," Lukens said.

Lukens said the trip was in no way connected with his work for Hy-Test at The Shelley Co., despite the fact that all three Shelley partners were in Evansville to meet Reagan that day.

Mike Meister, 60, one of the three partners, said he couldn't remember "if we were responsible (for the Reagan trip) or not. I don't know."

Meister claimed he didn't even know why he was in Evansville. "I probably went around and put nameplates in front of luncheon dishes or something like that," he said.

Wheeler told reporters the Reagan trip never occurred.

Whatever The Shelley Co. was doing for Hy-Test in the latter part of September 1975, Hy-Test paid handsomely for Shelley's services.

On Sept. 29 and 30, Hy-Test sent The Shelley Co. three checks totaling $19,086. Neither Lukens nor Meister nor Wheeler could explain what that money was for.

After the Evansville luncheon, Louie Nunn was flown back to Lexington on another plane. Nunn said it was his understanding Hy-Test Coal Co. paid for that plane.

Hy-Test Vice President Cumberledge returned by car, and Reagan flew on to Dayton in the Hy-Test jet with Lee, Wheeler, Van Hoorn, Lukens and Meister.

That afternoon, Reagan held a press conference in the old Dayton Courthouse. Later Reagan was guest of honor at a fundraiser at the Associates Club in the University of Dayton arena. It was and odd assortment of partygoers.

Mingling with the local GOP higher-ups was Lester Lee, a convicted rapist and suspected hit man, Charles Wheeler, a convicted burglar and armed robber and Paul Wheeler, Charles Wheeler's brother and business partner, also a convicted burglar and armed robber twice sentenced to life in prison.

The cheapest tickets to the cocktail party cost $25 a couple. The most expensive $100 a couple. Lee and the Wheelers "bought the big tickets. They were all hot on Ronald Reagan," Lukens said.

After the party, Reagan spoke to a crowd of more than 500 at the arena, denying repeatedly he was a presidential candidate.

From Dayton, the Hy-Test/Reagan entourage flew to Chicago, where Reagan and Lukens got off.

Reagan may have told the Dayton crowd he wasn't a candidate, but when he addressed the Executive Club of Chicago the next morning, he certainly sounded like one.

At that gathering, Reagan delivered his most significant speech of the 1976 campaign, his famous $90 billion gaffe.

"What I propose is nothing less than a systematic transfer of authority and resources to the states, a program of creative federalism for America's third century," Reagan said.

He presented a detailed plan that was to be the economic foundation of his campaign—and he spent the rest of the campaign defending his arithmetic.

Lukens went, on Reagan's behalf, to address a national convention of office outfitters that same morning.

The trip cost Hy-Test Coal Co. of Kentucky Inc. $3,324.88 for jet plane rentals, which it paid from its account at First Security National Bank in Lexington. The $115.80 Evansville luncheon also was billed to Hy-Test, but it was never paid. It is listed in Hy-Test's bankruptcy files.

Neither expense appears as a campaign contribution, obligation or debt in the 1975–1976 records of Citizens For Reagan.

The contributions were never reported, Joe Holmes told *The Kentucky*

Post in a recent interview. Holmes was Reagan's press secretary at the time. He since has been named communications director.

"Our position is that Gov. Reagan was not a candidate in September of 1975," Holmse said. "Until you formally announce, you're not a candidate." Reagan formally announced Nov. 20, 1975.

Further, Holmes asserted, there was no need for Reagan to report the contributions because the entire Hy-Test trip was for Buz Lukens' state senate re-election campaign

Holmes' first statement is wrong, according to the Federal Election Commission. And Lukens denied the second one.

According to FEC records, Ronald Reagan legally became a candidate on July 24, 1975, the day Citizens For Reagan filed its organizational statement with the FEC and began reporting contributions to the Reagan campaign.

"A formal announcement doesn't mean a thing in terms of the federal election campaign laws," said FEC Public Affairs Director Fred Eiland.

The Federal Election Campaign Act of 1971 states that a person becomes a candidate and is legally required to report campaign contributions and expenditures when he has "received contributions or made expenditures, or has given his consent for any other person to receive or make contributions."

Eiland said Reagan could have remained a non-candidate by simply disavowing the Citizens For Reagan committee when it filed its organizational statement with the FEC in July, 1975.

Eiland cited the recent Edward Kennedy draft movement as an example. "We had some 70 committees register for Kennedy. Each time one of them registered, Kennedy wrote us and told us he was disavowing that committee," Eiland explained.

That was not the case with Ronald Reagan in 1975. Far from disavowing Citizens For Reagan, Reagan wrote the committee chairman on July 14, 1975—more than two months before the Hy-Test trip—and said he recognized "the committee must file with the Federal Elections Commission as working on my behalf. I trust this letter will suffice as my consent for purposes of allowing you to do so."

In fact, Lukens and Lee discussed contributing to Reagan's campaign while they were flying with Reagan on the Hy-Test jet.

"They were going to give big contributions. They had all these friends, these coal miners, who were going to give $1,000 each," Lukens said.

Lukens said Lee and Wheeler made "big talk. They said, 'Oh, don't worry. We'll get you $10,000 or $15,000 or $20,000.' I said, 'Look, if you want to make an impression on Reagan, the thing to do is give a *legal* contribution. Hit your friends up,'" Lukens said.

Federal election laws prohibit personal political campaign contributions in excess of $1,000.

Lukens said "nothing ever came of it. I checked." Lukens told *The Kentucky Post* he asked Reagan a few weeks after the trip, "What have you got from Kentucky or West Virginia or Ohio? Any $1,000 goodies? Nothing."

Regan's very presence on Hy-Test's jet appears to be a violation of federal election laws which prohibit corporations from giving "anything of value" to a federal office-seeker.

"Corporate contributions have been illegal since 1907," the FEC's Eiland said.

Accepting illegal contributions or failing to report contributions carries stiff civil and criminal penalties. A candidate who willfully violates the federal election laws can be fined $25,000 and imprisoned for a year.

But Reagan spokesman Holmes said the contributions weren't illegal because the entire Hy-Test trip "was not a Reagan activity. The Governor went to do a series of fundraisers for Sen. Lukens. Sen. Lukens asked Gov. Reagan to appear at fundraisers for the Senator's campaign."

Holmes was asked why a state senator from Middletown, Ohio, would be campaigning for re-election in Memphis, Tenn., Lexington, Ky., Evansville, Ind., Dayton, Ohio, and Chicago, Ill.

"I would suggest you pose that question to Sen. Lukens," Holmes replied.

Lukens flatly denied any portion of the trip was for his campaign.

"First of all, Dayton isn't even in my district, and Evansville isn't even in my state. And the Chicago stop was (Reagan's) baby," Lukens, now Reagan's Midwest campaign coordinator, said.

"I received no money from these stops. And I received no money from Lester Lee or Hy-Test, either personally or politically. Besides, how would Joe Holmes know? He wasn't even on board then," Lukens said sharply.

Citizens For Reagan co-founder Louie Nunn had no trouble deciding which candidate the Hy-Test trip benefited. "I felt it was for Reagan. I don't know why Reagan would have been down there making an appearance for Lukens in Evansville."

Holmes refused to allow *The Kentucky Post* to speak to Reagan about the campaign trips, or any other contributions Lester Lee or Hy-Test may have made to Reagan during the last election.

Lukens, when asked if Lee gave Reagan any cash contributions during the plane trip, said: "I cannot say he didn't, but I don't know that he did."

For weeks, Holmes said he would not even broach the subject with Reagan. "He can't be bothered with things like this," Holmes declared. But more recently, Holmes said, "I've talked to the Governor about anything from a Lester Lee, and he said he doesn't remember any Lester Lee."

But Lee remembered Reagan. While working at the adult bookstore on Monmouth Street, Lee would boast that he and Reagan were close friends.

Reagan's direct association with Hy-Test appears to have ended with the plane trip. But Lukens' certainly did not.

PART 7: LEE TAKES HY-TEST FOR A RIDE—ALL THE WAY DOWN
JUNE 7, 1980

Lester Lee piloted Hy-Test Coal Co. of Kentucky Inc. into the ground, but they went first class all the way down.

Lee, by the summer of 1975, was a fat, bulldog-faced man. Prison denims and handcuffs had given way to garish leisure suits and gold chains.

A year and a half earlier, Lee had been earning $10 a month as a clerk in the Terre Haute, Ind., federal prison farm office. Now, he was driving a purple Lincoln Continental Mark IV and making $70,000 a year as Hy-Test's president.

Ray Cumberledge, assistant registrar at the University of Kentucky before he met Lee, had become Hy-Test's vice-president at a salary of $50,000.

Hy-Test leased a sleek $1,800-a-month suite of offices on Lexington's Waller Avenue and outfitted it with $12,000 worth of furniture. Across the street, the company had a $200-a-month apartment complete with a color TV and a king-sized-bed.

Lee hired a staff of six secretaries, a receptionist and a switchboard operator. Lee had his own private secretary. Hy-Test leased a brand new fleet of cars and trucks.

Then Lester Lee wanted to buy himself an airplane.

"We had absolutely no money coming in, no prospect of any immediate money, and Lee wanted an airplane," Hy-Test's office manager at the time, Fred J. Eilers Jr., remembered with a sigh.

And whatever Lee wanted, he got.

"He was president, and you didn't question him. By God, you just didn't question the man," Eilers said.

So Hy-Test bought an airplane. "It was a good-sized plane, seated six, eight maybe. We bought it used and had to have it completely remodeled. I think we paid $300,000 or $400,000 for it," Eilers recalled.

But by early fall, 1975, Lee's partners were beginning to have their doubts about Lee's leadership.

"Even Cumberledge complained about the airplane, and he usually didn't complain about anything," Eilers said.

Cumberledge was also upset about another Lee extravaganza: Hy-Test's financing of a campaign trip for ex-California Gov. Ronald Reagan in September 1975.

"You bet your life I was angry about that. We were spending this money for who knows what? I couldn't see any direct benefit from it," Cumberledge said.

Lee was running his coal company like he ran his life. Amidst the flamboyance, there was an aura of furtiveness.

"He would never let me see the coal contracts so I could confirm invoices. It was all very secretive. I had no idea what I was paying for and Lee kept spending all this money," said Eilers, 39, 801 Arlington Rd., Park Hills.

Before August 1975, Hy-Test didn't have a cent to spend on anything. Banks in Dayton, Ohio, and Lexington, were lending the coal company money on the strength of $55 million coal contract Hy-Test had with Turkey.

For Hy-Test to get the Turkish coal money, it needed to ship coal to Turkey, take the shipping documents and coal analysis reports to the Winters National Bank in Dayton and present them to the bank's International Department, where the Turks had posted million-dollar letters of credit.

The banker would compare the testing reports to the coal specifications listed in the Turkish contract. If the coal measured up, Hy-Test could immediately receive 90 percent of the letter of credit.

The remaining 10 percent would be paid once the Turks inspected the coal themselves and verified it met their specifications.

The first letter of credit—for $1,338,000—was posted in the Winters Bank on Aug. 6, 1975. The first Turkish freighter, the *S.S. Erdemir*, sailed from Norfolk, Va. on Sept. 1, 1975, carrying 21,574 tons of coal. Hy-Test withdrew $1,083,000 from the Winters Bank.

A second letter of credit for $1.5 million was posted, and the second ship sailed from Norfolk on Sept. 18. Hy-Test withdrew another $1.25 million.

But according to Cumberledge, those figures were a well-guarded secret. "I was unable to get access to the books to see what was going on. Lee just wouldn't let me look at them. He said everything was fine and that I didn't need to see them," Cumberledge said.

As Hy-Test's second boatload of coal was pulling away from the Norfolk docks, Lee was taking steps to get a passport. But just why a man on parole, whose travel was restricted to eastern Kentucky until 1977, wanted a passport is not exactly clear.

According to Hy-Test officers Ries Hengstmengle and Cumberledge and Hy-Test attorney Richard Vimont, Lee paid Lexington attorney Julius Rather $5,000 to get him a passport.

Rather strongly denied he had anything to do with Lee acquiring a passport.

"That's just utterly ridiculous. It's ludicrous. It makes me sound like I used that money to pay somebody off," Rather scoffed. He confirmed, however, that Lee paid him $5,000 on Sept. 18, 1975.

The next day, Lee and his fourth wife, Roberta Fleissner Lee, had passport pictures taken at Lafayette Studios in Lexington.

Rather said he couldn't recall what he did to earn the $5,000.

The Kentucky Post filed a Freedom of Information Act request with the US Parole Commission in December 1979, to determine how Lee was able to travel overseas while on parole, but the Commission has refused to release Lee's records.

Lee eventually acquired a passport and used it to fly to Turkey and Romania in mid-October, 1975. His intentions are unclear.

"He had things set up in Curaçao (in the Netherlands Antilles). It was going to be a getaway, in my opinion, a place for him to disappear to with all the money, untouched by federal hands," said Eilers, who later became Hy-Test's bookkeeper.

The company's banking records lend support to Eilers' theory.

Lee began siphoning cash in mid-September, 1975, from Hy-Test's bank account at the Winters Bank in Dayton into the Dutch Antilles bank account of Hy-Test Holding Co. N.V., which had just been formed by a Curaçao lawyer named Franciscus A. A. Duynstee. (Duynstee would later incorporate a Caribbean company, which the Securities and Exchange Commission is prosecuting on charges of a tax fraud of more than $20 million.)

Lee sent repeated letters to the Winters Bank ordering cash transfers and soon, the three-week-old holding company showed a bank account worth $200,000. Between Sept. 13 and Sept. 23, Lee also wrote checks to himself for $15,000.

The first two coal boats had left for Turkey by Sept. 18. Lee, simply by presenting the shipping documents to the Dayton bank, was suddenly in a position to get his hands on $2.3 million. For Lee, the shipping documents were like so many cashiers checks on the Turkish millions in the Winters Bank.

Lee still hadn't gotten his passport by the time the *Erdemir* arrived in Turkey, and when lab tests revealed the quality of Hy-Test's product, the Turks were not pleased. The second boatload, they said, was even worse. The coal was unusable.

By the time Lee got his passport in mid-October, relations with the Turkish coal buyers were in jeopardy. Lee picked up his passport in Washington, D.C., and flew to Turkey in an attempt to iron out the problems.

After several days in Turkey, Lee wired Lexington for more money. "He'd run out of blown it or something, and he wanted us to send more. We'd had it with him by then," Eilers said.

Eilers said the Hy-Test bookkeeper, Lee's brother-in-law David Fleissner, was ordered not to send the money. "Then we found out Dave had wired the money after all. A couple thousand dollars," Eilers said.

Cumberledge and Gareth Turner, a Hy-Test board member and then general manager of Dutchess Furniture Co. in Florence, "told Fleissner to get out and never come back."

Eilers took over the books and was alarmed at what he saw. The books, he said, were "miserable, totally indistinguishable. I called Turner and told him what I'd found."

Turner, a friend of Lee's for 10 years, was shocked, Eilers said. "His initial reaction was panic, total panic. He tried personally contacting Lee in Turkey and couldn't get a hold of him."

Turner ordered Eilers to Norfolk to pick up the shipping documents from the third freighter, the *S.S. Erzurum*. In the meantime, Lee called from Bucharest, Romania, where he was hunting down another coal contract, and Cumberledge said Lee's secretary, Linda Webb, told Lee "something was going on, and he'd better get back here."

Lee phoned his private pilot, a Cuban named Jesus Cuevas, and told him to meet him in New York with the company plane. The race to Norfolk was on.

Eilers said the worried Turner thought Lee would try to get the shipping documents first and cash in on the $1.5 million letter of credit. He was right.

Eilers got to Norfolk on Oct. 22, 1975, and scooped up the valuable shipping documents. And not a moment too soon.

"Lee was in Norfolk the same time I was, looking for the documents. I firmly believe his sole purpose in being there was to get them and take off with the loot," Eilers said.

The letter of credit was cashed and placed in a bank in Lexington. Lee and Fleissner's signatures were removed from the account, and Cumberledge hired attorney Richard Vimont to get rid of Lester Lee.

Lee was called into the Hy-Test board room the morning of Oct. 27, handed a $10,000 check for his company stock and a letter of resignation, which he signed.

D. Cameron Hays, the Lexington attorney who was Lee's parole sponsor and the corporate attorney for Hy-Test, was shown the door also.

"Lee was very calm. He told them if they thought they could find someone who could run the company better, let them try," Hays recalled.

The next day, Hy-Test International, Inc. was incorporated in New Albany, Ohio, with Lee as chairman of the board, Charles Wheeler as president and David Fleissner as secretary-treasurer.

Wheeler, a convicted burglar and armed robber, was already working for Lee through a public relations firm called The Shelley Co. That firm was housed in the Hatch Bldg, 39 E. Main St., New Albany.

At that same address was another Wheeler firm called International Sales and Associated Enterprises, which he operated with his brother Paul, another ex-convict twice sentenced to life in prison for burglary and safecracking.

Lee's Hy-Test International set up shop in that same office.

In Lexington, Ray Cumberledge, who replaced Lee as president of Hy-Test of Kentucky, struggled to go on.

"I was nearly scared out of my wits because my wife and I had been threatened by Lester Lee," Cumberledge, now director of planning for the state Justice Department, said.

He said Lee called him and "threatened to make a parking lot out of my house." Cumberledge said he had FBI agents check the Waller Avenue offices for hidden dynamite, and he changed the locks on the office doors.

Hy-Test vice-president Ton Van Hoorn also got violent phone calls from Lee.

"He said things like my house would change to a parking lot if I didn't leave," the young Dutch contractor said. "Then I heard from the FBI that they found a bomb in my car. They said it was better to move out of the country, which I did. I never went back," he said from his home in Rotterdam, Holland.

After setting up the Ohio Hy-Test, Lee flew back to Turkey, apparently to pick up where he'd left off.

On his first trip to Ankara, Lee had signed a letter of commitment guaranteeing the Turks would get a $55 million loan to pay for Hy-Test's coal.

Turkey was in the midst of a currency crisis and if the Hy-Test contract was to continue, the Turks would need a massive dose of American dollars.

Ries Hengstmengle, president of the *real* Hy-Test International in Curaçao, said he and Lee were asked by "the Turkish government if we could arrange a loan, and Lester signed a letter which was, to my mind, *impossible!* He just signed it without a wink of an eye and said to the Turks: 'Okay, we'll arrange it.' I couldn't believe it."

While Lee was on his second excursion to Turkey, Charles Wheeler was scrambling to locate the $55 million Lee had so freely promised the Turks. He posed the problem to Ohio State Sen. Donald E. (Buz) Lukenz, who was a partner with Wheeler in The Shelley Co.

Lukens said he assumed he was still working for Hy-Test Coal Co. of Kentucky and said he didn't know Wheeler and Lee had set up Hy-Test International. But Lukens did know its incorporating attorney, Fred J. Milligan Jr.

"When I ran statewide, I met him a couple of times. He's a big Republican," Lukens said.

Lukens said the third Shelley partner, Columbus, Ohio, businessman Mike Meister asked him to go to the Export-Import Bank of the United States in Washington, D.C., (Eximbank), to see about getting the $55 million loan.

Lukens said the Eximbank turned him down. He said that was his last association with Lee and Hy-Test.

But Wheeler said the loan was all set up. The Turks were to get $55 million over five years—$5 million every six months.

Wheeler said the Eximbank was ready to approve the loan. All that was needed was approval from the Foreign Credit Insurance Association, a Eximbank subsidiary.

"We needed to have $500,000 in the bank as collateral, and Mr. Meister said we were just short of that, but that it would be okay," Wheeler said.

That money was in the Winters Bank and actually belonged to Hy-Test Coal Co. of Kentucky, however.

Wheeler said: "The people in Lexington pulled the money out when they found out we'd been asking about it." The loan fell through when the money was transferred out.

"Lester was never the same after that," Wheeler said. "He felt he'd been done in by the people in Lexington."

When the loan fell through the Turks, already angry over the low-grade coal Lee had shipped them, cancelled the contract. Hy-Test of Kentucky, which had been teetering on the brink of a financial disaster, collapsed.

"There was no way to salvage the company. Lee had us locked in on a bunch of 12-month contracts for coal we couldn't sell. It was all substandard coal, and there was no market for it," Eilers said.

In January 1976, the miners tired of waiting for their money and filed suits against Hy-Test for $309,000. Cumberledge and Turner got together on Feb. 12, 1976, and put Hy-Test Coal Co. of Kentucky into bankruptcy.

All told, the company owed $10,706,754 to 47 separate creditors. "None of them probably will ever be paid," said court-appointed trustee Jerry Truitt of Lexington.

Lester Lee's dream of a trans-global coal empire was over. Wheeler said Lee stayed in New Albany, Ohio, until May 1976, and then retreated to Newport, Ky., leaving behind a stack of unpaid bills.

Ries Hengstmengle said he forfeited the $235,000 he'd put up as a performance bond on the contract. His home in The Hague was repossessed. Van Hoorn estimated his losses at $800,000.

Nasvhille, Tenn., TV personality Floyd Kephart, who helped Lee supply coal on the contract, said he was left with $300,000 in bills. He said he's still paying on the Hy-Test fiasco.

Two of the coal suppliers for Hy-Test, NM&N Coal Co. and Pawnee Mining Co. in Alabama, went into bankruptcy themselves after Hy-Test folded. On the surface, it appears everyone involved with Hy-Test Coal Co. of Kentucky lost money. But there is still a fortune unaccounted for.

According to Turkish trading documents acquired by *The Kentucky Post*, Hy-Test withdrew $4.5 million from the Turkish letters of credit. Bookkeeper Eilers was flabbergasted when shown the accountings.

"We couldn't have gotten that much!" he said. "If we'd have gotten that money, the company would have survived. The only money we ever took in was the $1.5 million I put in the bank myself," he said.

Where the remaining $3 million went is unknown. But Lester Lee, when he arrived in Newport, "was loaded," one acquaintance said.

In August 1977, Lester Lee bought a house at 823 E. Alexandria Pike, Cold Spring, for $43,000 cash. In July 1977 he bought a half interest in a proposed adult bookstore at 708 Monmouth St., Newport, from convicted burglar and safecracker Albert (Sammy) Wright.

Shortly before that, Lee had offered $2,500 to three Newport commission candidates if they would take a hands-off approach to Lee's new bookstore. They refused the "contribution," and the bookstore never opened.

There is some evidence to indicate Lee was still involved in coal through another adult bookstore at 721 Monmouth St. That, too, was owned by Sammy Wright, who was once convicted for hiding a member of Detroit's feared Purple Gang from federal authorities.

Charles Wheeler said he received a phone call from a Belgian named Nico Steylen a few weeks before Lee was killed. Steylen is listed in Hy-Test documents as the sales manager of Hy-Test Europe. Wheeler said Steylen had come to the United States during Hy-Test's glory days and discussed buying ships with Lee.

"Steylen called me and said he and Lee were going back into the coal business. Steylen said he'd spoken to Lee at the bookstore. It was my understanding Lester was running a coal company out of the bookstore," Wheeler said.

Another associate of Lee's said Lee was receiving calls from Turkey at the bookstore. "Ronnie Smith would be able to tell you about those," the man said.

Smith, a former Green Beret, is a Sammy Wright sidekick who's been convicted of possession of dangerous drugs and assault. He is awaiting trial on another assault charge.

Smith, 29, was behind the counter of the bookstore at 721 Monmouth St. when *Kentucky Post* reporters approached him for an interview. "I don't have no comment," Smith said warily.

If Lee was going back into the coal business in late 1977, he never got the chance. He was shot to death Jan. 7, 1978, while working in Sammy Wright's bookstore.

PART 8: COAL FEVER: "EVERYONE WAS GOING TO MAKE MILLIONS"
JUNE 9, 1980

The Arab oil embargo of 1973 brought the energy crisis home to Americans. It also signaled the beginning of a coal boom.

As fuel prices rocketed and shortages sent waves of panic across the land, the nation turned to coal to ease the crunch.

The United States had more coal than any other country, and Kentucky had more coal than any other state. The dirty black mineral began to take on an allure of power and value which it had been losing steadily for two decades.

When coal prices went up, owners of struggling coal companies became instant millionaires. Strip miners were scooping it up off the ground for $10 a ton; panicky power companies and other giant buyers were eager to pay more than $40 a ton. Investors looking for a solid, embargo-proof energy investment wanted a piece of the coal rush.

The opportunity was vast—and complex. In eastern Kentucky Holiday Inns, self-proclaimed coal experts and out-of-town "financiers" huddled late into the night, putting together deals for millions of tons and millions of dollars. Other speculators plugged in by phone or wire.

One California investor, who was funneling the profits of his antique business into coal dreams, described the frenzy.

"Everybody was so afraid everybody else was going to get in on the deal, everything was code named. It was like gold fever. Everybody was going to make a million dollars in one day. I was ending up with a telephone bill each month of $1000," he said.

The supply of coal properties was virtually unlimited. Deep mines abandoned years earlier as unprofitable or unsafe were suddenly resurrected. Farmland and fields atop questionable seams of coal were touted as sure money makers.

The names of coal deposits were romantic enough to hang dreams on: Widow Taggart, Sewanee, Elkhorn and Pocahontas seams.

Investors put up millions on the strength of geological reports which were sometimes little more than wishful thinking translated into figures. Other times, they were outright lies.

The new coal companies often were kitchen tabletop operations. Their founders came from past ventures in "sure-fire" investments. Many were road contractors or homebuilders with earthmoving equipment.

"They figured that if they knew earthmoving, they knew how to mine coal," said one London, Ky., coal operator. "It just ain't the same thing, but you couldn't tell these guys that."

Reliable information was hard to get. Mining experts with the most knowledge were not always as appealing or available as the polished confidence men in their rented Lear jets and Rolls Royces who knew the lingo and little more.

They called metallurgical coal "met," and knew the finest grade was Pocahontas, or "Poky," which they always seemed to have in abundant supplies. They spoke glibly of free swelling indexes, Audibert-Arnu Contraction tests, and "hivol" of "lovol" coal.

"Of all the people I met who were brokering coal, maybe five percent knew what they were talking about," said geological engineer Lew Adams, Oklahoma City. "The remaining 95 percent had developed a line of patter."

Aggravating this lack of knowledge was a lock of communication between the experienced contract miner and his rich, out-of-state employer.

John Bond, a Hollywood, Fla., attorney and a candidate for the state legislature, oversaw a mining operation in eastern Kentucky for his father, New York attorney John L. A. Bond, during the coal boom.

"There was a resentment of outsiders coming in. The people down there thought, 'Who do these Floridians or New Yorkers coming in think they are? They think they know more than we do,'" Bond said.

"The resentment was such that it discouraged the cooperation necessary between the investors and the local labor force and property owners," he said.

Said one London-area coal operator: "They came down here and made a mistake with eastern Kentucky people. They came down here with these flashy ways, and it caught up with them. They didn't know how to deal with us, and they came up on the short end."

It was a perfect breeding ground for swindles. Greed had outstripped caution, and even if a neophyte tried to be careful, it was difficult to know whom to trust.

"I'm not a gullible person, but you'd have thought I believed the moon was made of ice cream," said the California antique dealer. "I thought everyone was telling the truth and acted accordingly."

The Kentucky coal business has been fraught with crime for years, but it was the kind of crime local police could understand: random bombings and shootings associated with labor strife.

When coal prices skyrocketed, a new type of criminal emerged, on of infinite subtlety and craft.

Men who, for years, had practiced and perfected intricate and nearly incomprehensible securities frauds moved into the coal industry and found the pickings good. And easy.

Local lawmen were not prepared to detect, let alone battle, bewildering criminal schemes that snaked through several states and involved dozens of shell corporations, dummy directors and foreign banks.

A confederacy of stock swindlers and bank fraud artists existed years before coal became a glamorous word.

In his book *The Fountain Pen Conspiracy*, investigative reporter Jonathan Kwitney wrote: "One can only guess from their activity how well they are organized. That any one man could control them, or contrive all their operations is unlikely. But that they communicate and rely on each other regularly seems beyond doubt."

The same network Kwitney explored has operated virtually unmolested in Kentucky and neighboring coal-producing states for the past seven years, *The Kentucky Post* has found.

Losses to private investors, insurance companies and lending institutions total in the billions of dollars. Half a dozen murders have resulted. To date, not one of them has been solved.

"We are seeing the same people doing the same thing in 10 different jurisdictions," said Alabama Securities Commissioner Tom Krebs, one of the first men to investigate the problem.

"We started work in December of 1976 on an informant's tip, and then we got with Kentucky and put our notes together, and the thing began to snowball. Everybody was coming up with the same stuff," Krebs said.

Said James C. Strode, director of the Kentucky Division of Securities in

Frankfort: "We're of the impression that this is a concerted, coordinated plan to defraud."

Another securities commissioner, Stephen Coons of Indiana, said: "What we have now is a lot of overlap. Associates of one associate with another. It's more than coincidence."

Fears of an energy shortage affected government policies. To spur investment in fuel production, tax and securities laws were modified to make a risky business more attractive.

It was. Well-to-do people in high tax brackets were eager to take advantage of the favorable write-offs available for coal investors. In some instances, a $50,000 investment could be written off as a $250,000 tax deduction.

What particularly concerned Krebs and the other investigators were the people who masterminded the various coal ventures.

In a confidential memo to the Justice Department in Washington, D.C., in 1977, Krebs outlined the reason for his concern:

1. Organized crime figures are in the process of acquiring substantial interests in the American coal industry.

2. Organized crime figures are defrauding foreign coal buyers and bankrupting domestic coal producers through the use of foreign coal purchase contracts.

3. Organized crime figures are defrauding domestic investors and facilitating tax frauds through the sale of limited partnership interests in coal mining ventures.

4. Organized crime figures are heavily involved in the theft and interstate transportation of stolen mining equipment.

Krebs told *The Kentucky Post*: "What we are seeing is a bunch of *extremely* questionable people taking a position of prominence in the coal industry. What's Lester Lee doing with a multi-million dollar company? What's Sandy Guterma doing? How does Dominick Bartone all of a sudden get to be a coal magnate? You see these people operating openly in the coal industry, and you've got to wonder what the hell is going on."

Krebs said the players fell into two categories. "When we speak of organized crime, we speak of it in two senses. One is the restricted sense, La Cosa Nostra or whatever. The other is the broad sense, a group of swindlers," he said. Krebs said both groups are heavily involved in coal.

And the monetary loss to the coal industry is nearly inestimable, he said.

"You look. How many finance companies have been burned on fraudulent equipment deals? There's a letter from one finance company that they lost $25 million in two years and that they were *not* going to finance any more coal. What's the cost of that, either directly or indirectly?" Krebs asked.

Coons estimated the loss to Indiana investors from tax shelter frauds alone was between $20 million and $30 million. "That's just scratching the surface," he said.

The complete picture is one of murder, bribery, kickbacks, fraud and political corruption. The players range from the top securities swindlers in the country to inept entrepreneurs driven by greed to financial ruin. Personal horror stories abound.

Florida real estate developer Christie Vitolo, once head of the third largest bowling alley construction firm in the country, said he was "skinned" in the eastern Kentucky coal fields. He estimated his personal losses at a half million dollars.

"After a while, I got to hate Kentucky. If I never see Kentucky again, it'll be too soon," he groused.

PART 9: YOU WERE DEALING WITH CROOKS AND CHARLATANS
JUNE 10, 1980

Gordon Wade doesn't like to think about his short-lived venture in Kentucky coal. It brings back too many bad memories, he said.

But then, Gordon Wade is accustomed to success. In his 41 years, he hasn't struck out very many times.

Graduating as valedictorian from Covington Holmes High School, Wade won the Kentucky Harvard College Scholarship. He graduated with honors from Harvard in 1960 with a degree in political science.

From there, Wade went on to become brand name manager for Procter and Gamble's *Bold* detergent line. He served as public relations director for the Republican National Committee during the Nixon years, head of the Kentucky GOP Central Committee, head of the Kenton County GOP Executive Committee.

Along the way, Wade became a wealthy man. He lives in a starkly modernistic home in Park Hills, from which he operates a private consulting firm.

Wade, an excitable, blue-eyed man with salt and pepper hair, said he became interested in the coal business in late 1974, when "coal fever" was running high.

Wade held a real estate license—a hobby, he said—with Crittenden real estate agent William Lillard. Wade said Lillard approached him with a proposition.

As Wade explained it, Lillard wanted to set up a company that would manage coal-producing properties for rich, absentee investors with little knowledge of coal. Lillard would use his knowledge of real estate and construction. Wade, a charismatic, well-spoken businessman, would find the investors.

"It was a good idea. It verged on being brilliant," Wade said.

It may have been a good idea, but the business was a dismal failure. The investors fell prey to a host of top-level swindlers operating in the coal industry.

1. Alexander Gaus Jr., a Chicago-area loan broker with documented Mafia connections who served 23 months in federal prison for mail and wire fraud.

2. Gaus' accountant, Archibald Barnhill, a Dallas, Tex., CPA convicted of fraud and stripped of his license.

3. Alexander Guterma, a notorious swindler convicted of a string of securities frauds in the early 1960s.

4. Saul N. Davidson, a Denver, Colo., financier convicted of fraud in connection with a nationwide Mob-linked scheme.

But none of that was apparent on Nov. 27, 1974, when Lee Lanter, then Grant County Attorney, incorporated Mineral Investment Counselors Inc., or MICI. Its directors were Lanter, Lillard, his son Ronnie, Wade and Lew Adams, a Louisville businessman with oil, gas and coal experience.

The MICI group also incorporated another company, Fedco Inc.

"The Lillard Building," a one-story shake and brick structure about two miles from I-75 on Hwy. 1548 in Crittenden was the corporate headquarters for both companies. The building also served as the office of Lillard Realtors.

MICI/Fedco's first contract was with an outfit from Carrollton, Tex., called Bilto, Inc., which had a million-ton coal contract with the government of Turkey. Wade's group was hired to manage the contract and the coal mines.

The Turkish deal fizzled, Wade and Adams said, because Bilto could not come up with a $1 million performance bond the Turks required.

But they may not have known the whole story.

Bilto's negotiators in the Turkish deal were none other than the convicted swindlers Gaus and Barnhill, who were to provide the performance bond.

Gaus told *The Kentucky Post*: "The Turkish contract was brought to me by Archie Barnhill through Bilto. Our negotiations via Bilto reached a point of final contract construction, but the Turks required a payoff. I was not prepared to accommodate them."

MICI/Fedco did no better on its next big deal.

Adams, MICI's portly, silver-haired engineer, had learned that the owners of the Skyuka Mining Co., in Manchester, Ky., were interested in selling. Adams said he prepared a 70-page summary of Skyuka's operation for a group of buyers in Florida.

The buyers were headed by Alexander Guterma, represented in the transaction by Lousiville shopping magnate John W. Waits.

"I went to Louisville and met Waits at his home four or five times," Adams said. "The next thing I knew, Waits had gone around me and was dealing directly with the owners of Skyuka."

Guterma eventually bought Skyuka Mining, and Adams said MICI was cut out of a $50,000 finders fee.

Waits could not be reached for comment.

Wade said the soured deals caused him to quit MICI and the coal business altogether.

"The coal fields were full of characters, many of them uneducated, stupid and venal. You were dealing with crooks, charlatans and mountebanks. I didn't want any more of it," he said.

Adams also began to get impatient after the Skyuka deal fell through. He'd moved from Louisville to Covington, leased a house in the Riverside district and said he hadn't made any money since joining MICI.

"It was costing me $3,000 a month just to hang around. It was eating me alive financially," he said.

By the time Adams said he left MICI in mid-1975, the company had landed just one coal contract—with Hy-Test Coal Co.

Hy-Test's president, Lester Lee of Newport, Ky., was a convicted felon, suspected hit man and a coal field con artist.

"I think that was the only contract we ever made money on," Adams said wryly.

When MICI/Fedco was finally abandoned—its officers are unsure of the date—Bill Lillard said he was left with $7,000 in phone bills. Adams said his net worth when he came to Kentucky was $400,000. By the time he left MICI/Fedco, that amount had dwindled to $40,000, he said.

To make money, Adams said he began freelancing coal properties for sale to potential buyers, hoping to make a middleman's profit. "I know how to put a package together," Adams said.

One man who liked what Adams brought him was Saul Davidson.

Despite Adams' claim that he disassociated himself from MICI in mid-1975, both his name and MICI's turned up a year later in Davidson's personal files, portions of which were acquired by *The Kentucky Post*.

In a memo dated April 27, 1976, Davidson wrote: "Last night I met in Pheonix with Lewis J. Adams, Mici, Inc., 322 E. 3rd St., Covington; Arnold Cook, Danny O'Keefe and David Sweeney. The meeting with the above individuals was to discuss various opportunities available in the coal field."

The Kentucky Post obtained a confidential Phoenix police department intelligence report which stated: "O'Keefe is closely associated with Joseph Bonanno, Frank Mossuto and William Rocco D'Ambrosio."

All three men are reputed members of the Tucson, Ariz., organized crime family, FBI sources said.

Further, the report said: "O'Keefe has been active in supplying money from organized crime sources to start new businesses in the Phoenix area."

Adams said he met with O'Keefe and Davison several times and offered to sell them coal mines. Davidson, in his memo, wrote that he bought a Pennsylvania mine from Adams for $300,000, but Adams said he never received any money from Davidson.

Davidson's files show he was planning to purchase a West Virginia mine from Adams but needed collateral for bank loans.

On July 19, 1976, Davidson wrote to Louis Pihakis, Pensacola, Fla., who had been convicted in 1971 of a multi-million dollar insurance swindle in Alabama.

Davidson described the glowing opportunities awaiting them in the coal fields. He said he needed collateral for a loan to buy a mine Adams had for sale and suggested using $1 million in stock from one of Pihakis' companies.

Pihakis' response is not known. But within six months, Davidson was in jail, charged with bilking three Denver banks of more than $500,000 by using worthless stock as collateral on loans. He was convicted and sentenced to two years in jail.

In March 1977, Davidson was indicted with nine other people for running a nationwide advance fee racket, which bilked businessmen of millions. *The New York Times* called the scheme "Mafia-directed" and added, "the Carlos Gambino organized crime family was heavily involved."

The "advance fee" swindle, which the securities fraud artists began using in the mid-1960s, is well suited to the coal industry because coal operators need huge loans to buy land and equipment.

The con works like this: a businessman who cannot get a loan through a bank or a loan company turns to a private money broker like Davidson. The broker promises the businessman his loan, then collects from him a percentage of that loan in advance, anywhere from one to five per cent, depending on the size of the loan.

After the broker collects his advance fee, he vanishes. The businessman never gets his loan.

Davidson wasn't the only advance fee swindler interested in Adam's coal deals.

Alex Gaus, whom postal investigators consider the pioneer of the advance fee racket, was planning to purchase the same Pennsylvania mine Davidson said he bought.

Adams said he had never met Alex Gaus face to face but heard his name frequently from Rev. June Franklin Dennis.

Adams said he met Dennis, 48, a small, balding man with watery blue eyes, in the offices of MICI.

"He had a whole lot of properties, and I looked at a number of properties with him. We went all over the place, mostly in Kentucky. He knew a jillion people in the coal business," Adams said.

Coal apparently was a new field for Dennis, who got his master's degree in theology with a thesis on demon possession.

The diminutive Dennis owned a string of nursing homes in northern and central Kentucky. In 1974, he was driving a new Lincoln Continental and living in a $295,000 house in Williamstown.

Adams, during his trips through Kentucky coal country with Dennis, recalled Dennis speaking frequently of a certain "Brother Gaus."

Gaus "was supposed to be a big-money wingding, and he could get money to do anything. Dennis had some sort of working relationship with him," Adams said. "I'd put one of these packages together, and he'd say, "Well, we'll get Brother Gaus to look at this. He'll do something with it."

Dennis told Adams that Gaus trusted his judgment.

"Dennis presented Gaus a deal from which he made a lot of money and, therefore, when Dennis presented Gaus a deal, Gaus would trust him on it. That's the supposition that was put forth when we'd try to sell one of these coal properties Dennis and I were looking at," Adams said.

Adams said he and Dennis later became partners in a firm called the DAN Trust, which managed an Illinois Power and Light coal contract they had, but said that was unprofitable also.

Gaus acknowledged that he and Dennis worked together on many coal deals.

Dennis's career as a coal broker, though, was interrupted by the law.

A Grant County grand jury, charging unsanitary conditions, recommended closing his Christian Care Home for retarded children in Dry Ridge in October 1974. The same jury indicted Dennis for having sex with three retarded teenage girls. He was acquitted.

In March 1979, Dennis and his wife Bonnie were charged with willfully failing to file income tax returns for 1972 and 1973, during which Dennis made $302,113.

The Dennises were convicted, and Rev. Dennis was sentenced to two years in prison. His wife was given a probated sentence. Dennis was paroled from the federal prison in Lexington March 28, 1980.

Dennis' friend, Brother Gaus, was more than just a distant money-man who provided funding on various coal projects. When Gaus was released from federal prison in 1975, he immersed himself in the coal industry.

PART 10: ALEX GAUS JR.: PRAISE THE LORD AND PULL A SWINDLE
JUNE 11, 1980

Alexander Gaus Jr. waited backstage for his cue. The Rev. Jim Bakker, host of the *Praise the Lord Club*, beamed at the lights and cameras as he sang out an introduction.

"My next guest, from Arlington Heights, Ill. Is an investment banker with First Central Holding Co. Something *very* unusual happened in his life and he ended up—*in jail!* Is that right? *That's terrible!* We'll find out about it. Please welcome Alex Gaus to PTL!" Bakker trilled.

The studio audience burst into applause, and Alexander Gaus made his national television debut.

Gaus may have been a new face to the viewers of the nationally syndicated religious talk show, but the tall, 57-year old Flint, Mich., man was well-known to the FBI and the Securities and Exchange Commission.

They considered Alex Gaus one of the most notorious fraud artists in the country.

Gaus is the oldest son of Russian immigrants. He told the PTL Club audience his father was "a lay evangelist among the people." Young Gaus followed in his father's footsteps.

"At a young age, about 17, I accepted Jesus Christ as my saviour (and) was commissioned by the brotherhood to work as an evangelist," Gaus said. It was an experience he would draw on heavily in his later career.

But as a young man, Gaus found little money in church work. In the late 1950s he turned to business, working for a bank and taking college courses in finance, real estate and insurance.

That experience, too, would not be lost on him.

Gaus and the business world seemed at odds from the first. Between 1956 and 1966, he was sued 22 times, mostly for breach of contract. In 1957, he was convicted of passing worthless checks. In 1963, he was convicted of larceny.

About that time, Gaus began work on a scheme that postal authorities would later call "the foremost of his time," a sophisticated advance fee swindle. His 1963 conviction for larceny by conversion is a good example of how it works.

Gaus promised a Flint, Mich., couple he would arrange a $19,700 Veterans Administration home loan for them. For his work, he wanted $2,000 up front. Gaus never applied for the loan and spent the couple's money. For that crime, he was put on two years' probation.

He struck again in 1967, promising a nursing home in Janesville, Wisc., a $1.2 million construction loan. He got $6,000 in advance, but the loan never arrived. The same thing happened to a nursing home in Clinton, Wisc., which paid Gaus $5,000 for a $1 million loan. He was convicted of two counts of fraud in 1969.

Then, another side of the smooth-talking Gaus appeared, a darker side the enthusiastic *Praise the Lord Club* audience never got to see during Gaus' appearance.

In the spring of 1971, the Illinois Crime Investigating Commission linked Gaus with Chicago Mafiosi Dominick Santorelli, Paul (The Waiter) Ricca and Tony (Big Tuna) Accardo in a scheme to bilk three Chicago banks of almost $1 million.

The crime commission charged Gaus had attempted to get a $800,000 loan from the Gateway National Bank by using 10,000 shares of phony stock. That loan was to be used to buy Gaus a controlling interest in the bank. Santorelli, whom the crime commission claimed was an upper echelon Chicago mobster, had tried the same thing at two other banks with the same stock.

The stock was from a Florida firm called Picture Island Computers. Its president was Peter Francis Crosby. Crosby was convicted of a massive swindle involving Picture Island stock, a scheme to sell worthless securities supposedly backed by oil leases of Arctic wasteland.

No criminal charges were brought against Gaus and the other Chicago men.

Gaus told *The Kentucky Post* he attempted to "finance" the bank's purchase for another group but didn't try to buy it himself.

Gaus' projects with the Mafia didn't end there. By then, he was working on his most spectacular gambit: the Church of Christ Manors fraud.

He began working on the scheme in 1966, approaching several Church of Christ ministers and telling them he was a "government man." Gaus said the federal government wanted to give money to the churches for various welfare and housing programs. But there was one hitch, he told them. The Churches of Christ, with 10,000 independent churches, needed a strong, central organization to receive the federal dollars he said would be coming.

Gaus formed Church of Christ Manors Inc. in Washington, D.C., with three ministers as directors and himself as process agent.

Working with Gaus was Chicago mobster Lou (The Tailor) Rosanova, a former golf pro whose associates include the late Felix (Milwaukee Phil) Alderosio and Jackie (The Lackey) Cerone.

After Gaus set up Church of Christ Manors, he sent letters to churches across the country, telling them of the new venture, inviting to join and requesting copies of their financial statements.

When all financial statements were put under the umbrella of Church of Christ Manors, it looked as if Gaus' new organization had assets of more than $800 million.

Then Gaus began his "sting." He promised unwitting customers that, for a small advance fee, Church of Christ manors would loan them part of that non-existent money.

Soon, the scheme became too big for even resourceful Gaus to handle alone. A nationwide network of "brokerage houses" sprang up, all promising loans from Church of Christ Manors' seemingly endless money supply.

Running the brokerage houses were men like James (Jimmy the Bomber) Catuara and Frank (One Ear Frankie) Fratto, both named by the Chicago Crime Commission as "organized crime bigwigs;" William (Billy) Dauber, identified by the commission as an enforcer and hit man for South Chicago crime boss Albert Tocco; loan shark Guido (Weeds) Fidanzi and Charles and Louis Verive, identified as mob enforcers by the California Organized Crime Control Commission.

When none of the "loans" ever materialized, the federal government stepped in.

In February, 1972, Gaus, Rossanova, the Verives, Dauber, Fratto, Fidanzi, attorney Stanley Durka and eight other men were indicted on 41 counts of conspiracy, mail fraud, fraud by wire and interstate transportation of stolen money.

Gaus' Church of Christ Manors, Inc. had defrauded 70 people of more than $1 million in advance fees.

Gaus, Dauber and two Catuara employees were convicted of conspiracy and fraud. The remaining men were acquitted, with the exception of Fidanzi, who was murdered before the trail began. Fidanzi was rumored to have tipped federal authorities to Gaus' scheme.

"I didn't commit any sins, but I compromised," Gaus told his *Praise the Lord Club* audience in September 1977, but he refused to go into detail about the case. That "compromise" resulted in a 10-year prison sentence.

"The Lord commissioned me to a ministry in prison," Gaus explained. "God gave me a ministry there that most missionaries like to write home about."

But even before Gaus went to trail on that case, he and Stanley Durka—the Watseka, Ill. State's attorney indicted with Gaus—were cooking up another operation, this time in Kentucky.

Through a Delaware corporation called First Central Corp., a series of $50,000 debentures were issued on Sept. 20, 1972. A debenture is similar to a bond except that a debenture is not backed up by a mortgage or a pledge of assets. First Central issued 100 of the ten-year debentures.

The debentures were "validated" with the stamp of the West German Consulate in Mobile, Ala. Gaus said a man named Garet Van Antwerp III was the German consul who signed the bonds. Van Antwerp is also a convicted swindler, a disbarred attorney and a longtime associate of the self-styled insurance fraud king Stewart Hopps. Van Antwerp was convicted of a million-dollar bond fraud in Alabama [in] 1978.

The debentures were signed by Gaus and a Prestonsburg, Ky. coal broker named Lowell Robinson. Guaranteeing payment of the debentures was a company called First Central Holding Co. of Kentucky.

Stanley Durka incorporated First Central Holding in Frankfort three weeks *after* the debentures were issued. Its directors were Gaus, Robinson and Birmingham, Ala., man named John Simonetti.

A police intelligence report describes Simonetti as "a local organized crime figure in Birmingham."

Since First Central Holding existed solely on paper, it's hard to see how the company was in a position to guarantee payment of $5 million in debentures. Gaus himself, the company's president, was sent to jail shortly after the debentures were issued.

But Gaus said he knew little of the debentures, despite the fact that his signature appears on a copy obtained by *The Kentucky Post*.

Gaus told *The Kentucky Post* that the debentures were supposed to be held in escrow in a bank in Frankfurt, Germany. "The notes were withdrawn from the account," Gaus said.

They certainly were. So far, Kentucky authorities have turned up three debentures, which were sold in Holland and Switzerland.

It is not known how many investors purchased the $50,000 debentures or if any of them will be paid when they come due in 1982. This much is known, however: First Central Holding Co. is now out of business, and there is no listing for First Central Corp. in Wilmington, Del.

In 1972, First Central Holding lay dormant while Gaus was in Terre Haute, Ind., federal prison, pursuing his ministry.

"For 23 months, God opened the chapel every night, and I must have had the privilege of ministering to 30,000 convicted men. The guards were accepting Christ up and down the corridors," Gaus told his audience.

One member of Gaus' congregation was a burly, 32-year-old steeplejack named John Paul Kronquist, or Paul David Potter, depending on which name he was using. Brother Gaus got to like him.

Kronquist, a six-foot, two-inch, 230-pound Texan, was in jail for car theft, but he and Gaus had a lot more in common than their prison address. Kronquist's criminal record shows nine arrests and four convictions for either check fraud or obtaining money under false pretenses. He's also been convicted of firearms violations and forgery.

"He attended Bible class and chapel services in which we both participated," Gaus said of Kronquist.

Kronquist, who says he still owns 816 acres of coal property in Johnson, Breathitt and Magoffin Counties, knew the coal business. He said Gaus began pumping him for information toward the end of their stay in Terre Haute. "He already had that Kentucky corporation set up," Kronquist said.

That was Gaus' First Central Holding Co. which, at the time, was holding nothing but promise.

When Gaus and Kronquist got out of prison in the spring of 1975, Gaus made Kronquist president.

Gaus was paroled to a Dallas, Tex. company called Atco, Inc., run by a convicted felon named George Wesley Littlefield. It was about this time Gaus and Dallas accountant Archibald Barnhill entered the coal business.

Barnhill, who was convicted of fraud and stripped of his CPA license in 1976, is dead. He had done accounting work in the past for the late Mob boss Sam (Momo) Giancana. According to Kronquist, Barnhill was also Atco's accountant.

Atco's president, George Littlefield, is in prison for violating his parole by stealing a car. Gaus, though, said he was not actually employed by Atco. "I was to receive a fee for arranging a loan to Atco," he said. The $2 million loan was to enable Atco to go into the coal business. It was to come from a little-known bank in London, England, called Capital Funding Ltd. Merchant Bankers, Gaus said.

The relationship between Gaus and that bank is a curious one. Kronquist said he drew up Capital Funding promissory notes for Gaus while in Frankfort and had them printed at the Beechmont Press in Louisville for $65.

Kronquist said he didn't know if the bank even existed. Helping him with the language in the notes was Lance Kohler, a disbarred Lexington attorney. Kohler has had a checkered law career. He was suspended from the Kentucky Bar in 1967 for failure to pay his dues. He was convicted and jailed for assault and battery in 1970. And in June 1971, Kohler was arrested for selling two ounces of heroin to an undercover narcotics agent.

He was convicted, fined $20,000 and sent to jail for not more than 20 years. The following year, he was permanently disbarred.

"See, what we had, basically, was an organization of ex-convicts. George Littlefield had been in prison, Gaus had been there, and Kohler, of course, had been in the state prison," Kronquist said. And so had Kronquist. Gaus said he and Kohler were acquainted and had attempted to do business together, but said he knew nothing of the Capital Funding promissory notes.

He did, however, know something about Capital Funding. In a personal financial statement dated July 1, 1975, Gaus claimed Capital Funding owed him $30,000.

That same statement said Gaus, who had stepped from prison five months earlier, had a personal worth of $20.3 million and pegged his "100 percent ownership" of the one-room First Central Holding Co. at $19.3 million.

Gaus said the financial statement was used to get a loan from a New York bank to buy coal washing plants and tipples, but said the loan never went through.

The financial statement of First Central Holding Co. was even more eye-popping. It listed first year income of $202 million, which, if true, would have placed it among the top 1,000 corporations in the country.

Both financial statements were prepared by Joseph Borenstein, who represented Gaus in his attempted takeover of Gateway National Bank in 1971.

According to a police intelligence report, "Borenstein is a Chicago attorney whose client list includes Salvatore (Sam) Giancanna and various Las Vegas organized crime figures. He is currently under SEC investigation regarding limited partnership offerings with which he was connected."

With Borenstein's help, Gaus had the impressive financial statements he wanted. He went hunting for new coal deals.

And from an office in Newport, Ky., a coal broker named Paul J. Linnenbrink was running ads in the respected *Oil and Gas Journal*, looking for investors for coal ventures.

Gaus and Kronquist responded.

PART 11: BEHIND THE FAÇADE LIES OF A NETWORK OF CRIMINALS
JUNE 12, 1980

Alexander Gaus Jr. stepped out of federal prison in the spring of 1975 at the peak of the coal boom.

Gaus and fellow ex-con John Paul Kronquist revived First Central

Holding Co. of Kentucky, which Gaus had set up before he went to prison for mail fraud, and began scouting coal deals. There was a lot of money to be made in coal, and the two convicted swindlers wanted in.

So did Paul J. Linnenbrink of Newport, Ky. Since early 1974, Linnenbrink had been trying vainly to line up a big coal deal. What he needed, he decided, was to advertise.

In late 1974 he placed an ad in the *Oil and Gas Journal,* looking for people to invest in a coal venture in eastern Kentucky. Linnenbrink listed his address as Cherokee Oil and Gas Co., Ft. Thomas, Ky.

Cherokee wasn't exactly in Ft. Thomas. It operated out of the tax office of former Newport city manager Herman. C. Sorenson at 620 Monmouth St., Newport. Sorenson was president of Cherokee, and Linnenbrink was vice-president.

Linnenbrink, a bulky, sandy-haired man, said the response to the ad was tremendous.

The biggest deal came his way in late March 1975. He got a letter from a Bayonne, N.J., energy broker, who had a client with a 35 million ton coal contract but no coal to fill it.

That client was George Wesley Littlefield, a Dallas, Tex., coal broker convicted of theft and embezzlement.

George Littlefield also happened to be Alex Gaus' employer at the time. Gaus said when he was released from prison, he went to work for Littlefield at Atco Inc., attempting to get Atco a $2 million loan.

The loan was to buy land in western Maryland, which had the coal to fill the 35 million ton contract. Until the loan and the land purchase went through, Littlefield needed to get coal elsewhere. He and Gaus turned to Linnenbrink.

In early June 1975, Littlefield, Kronquist, and a man named Marion Leholmes (Tony) Braxton met Linnenbrink in Lexington.

"They all flew in on George Littlefield's Lear jet. They were dressed nice, and they talked a good line. They seemed real enough to me," Linnenbrink said.

Contracts worth tens of millions of dollars were haggled over and signed that day.

But Linnenbrink's clients were not international coal brokers.

They were all convicted swindlers. Their companies were little more than post offices boxes, not the trans-global corporations they might appear to be.

And even the Lear jet was only rented, Linnenbrink later discovered. It was all a façade.

And behind the façade a well-organized, underground network of ruthless con men who know one another, rely on one another's talents and work their complex schemes in collaboration. That network includes the Mob, as an examination of Tony Braxton's career will reveal.

In 1972, Braxton, 49, a dark-haired Dallas nightclub owner, was indicted on fraud charges in Texas. Five years later, he was convicted of fraud in Louisiana for an advance fee scheme there which was much like the racket Alex Gaus ran in Chicago 10 years earlier.

Braxton promised a New Orleans businessman a $500,000 loan through Braxton's Kentfield Corp. The loan was to help the businessman—who was unable get money elsewhere—expand his computer shops. The businessman gave Braxton $10,000 in advance. Less than a month later Braxton told him the "loan" fell through, and the $10,000 would not be returned. Braxton got four years probation for the swindle.

The financial statement of Braxton's Kentfield Corp. is another façade. It lists, for example, a $78,000 asset called Captain's Cove.

Captain's Cove, according to a confidential police intelligence report, is "a land development on Virginia's eastern shore consisting primarily of swampland." The man behind Captain's Cove, the report states, is New Orleans swindler Saul Siegel.

Siegel, a 60-year old Boston native, was convicted of fraud in 1977 for a complicated advance fee swindle that bilked an Oklahoma coal company of $48,000. He got 18 months in jail.

The police intelligence report identified Siegel as "a member of Carlos Marcello's La Cosa Nostra family" and said Siegel "specializes in bankruptcy fraud, particularly bankruptcy of coal companies."

Kronquist said he knew Siegel. "I'd say Siegel and Carlos may be friends," he said.

Mafia investigators say Marcello is the man who oversees all organized crime activity in the South.

According to a New Orleans police detective, the fat, balding Marcello and Siegel not only are friends, but business associates as well.

"When Siegel appeared in New Orleans, he appeared overnight in a real close relationship with Carlos Marcello, Mr. Organized Crime himself. They bought some property together in Shriver, La., in 1975. Siegel transferred it around a bit, and soon, it was owned entirely by Marcello," the detective said.

The police intelligence report stated: "Siegel is believed to be fronting for Carlos Marcello. It is believed that Siegel holds investment interests in trust for Marcello, and these interests are spread worldwide."

Marcello's name has been linked to a garbage hauling firm Siegel runs in Boston, Reclamation Services Inc.

The intelligence report also said one of Siegel's close associates in the coal business was the late Eddie H. Hammonds, whom the Kentucky State Police identify as the "former chief lieutenant for Meyer Lansky." Lansky is considered to be the financial wizard of the American Mafia.

The detective said the New Orleans police department arrested Siegel one night in 1976 for drunk driving, "and who do we find in the car with him but Tony Braxton."

According to the intelligence report, "Braxton and Siegel met Marcello in New Orleans in September of 1976, after which Siegel came to Kentucky. The Securities and Exchange Commission is concerned that (they) may be attempting to marshal assets as a prelude to a securities swindle involving coal companies."

The strings connecting Siegel and Braxton tie in several times to Lester Clifford Lee, a convicted felon, suspected hit man and would-be coal baron who was murdered in a Newport adult bookstore down the street from Cherokee Oil and Gas in 1978.

1. The intelligence report stated: "Hammonds and Siegel have spent a considerable amount of time in Harlan County, where they are associated with a Dr. Buttermore, who has extensive land holdings."

According to court records, Lester Lee was attempting to sell Buttermore's property. "In the event the Buttermore property should be sold, I personally would receive 50 percent of the profits," Lee stated in a deposition.

2. Listed in the intelligence report as a known associate of Siegel was a man named Haywood Clack of Monroe, La. The report said Clack was to supply coal mining equipment to Solar Coal Co., a firm Siegel owned in Harlan County.

Lee, in his deposition, said Clack served as his representative in showing the Buttermore property to interested buyers.

3. Braxton, in the Kentfield Corp. financial statement, listed as an asset a $1.4 million contract with Durango Coal and Leasing Inc., Louisville, and

the intelligence report stated Braxton met with Durango's owner, George Day, in Dallas on a number of occasions.

In the records of Lester Lee's Hy-Test Coal Co., an $11,000 transaction with a George Day is noted, and former Hy-Test vice president Ray Cumberledge confirmed that Hy-Test had a contract with Durango.

Alex Gaus said he also had business dealings with Durango and George Day.

And the connections between Lee and Gaus are even more numerous:

1. Both Lee and Gaus were in the Terre Haute, Ind., federal prison at the same time.

2. Both men dealt with an Alabama firm called Pawnee Mining. Pawnee was supplying coal for a contract Lee had with Turkey. Gaus said he also had a Turkish contract and said that Pawnee was supplying him with coal. Gaus later claimed to own Pawnee.

3. After Hy-Test went bankrupt, about 15,000 tons of coal belonging to Hy-Test were left sitting on the docks in Mobile, Ala. On June 3, 1976, that coal was purchased by Robert B. Kizziah, an Alabama coal broker who, according to Hy-Test trustee Jerry Truitt, "came up here to Lexington and sat through every one of the bankruptcy hearings."

According to Kronquist, his first coal-buying trip with Gaus in the spring of 1975 was to Alabama—to see Robert Kizziah.

Kizziah, through his Kenala Coal Co., had a multi-million dollar contract with the government of Egypt in 1976. Kizziah shipped the Egyptians coal that was little better than dirt and personally forged the coal testing reports to make it seem as if the coal was high-grade. He was convicted of mail fraud and sent to prison.

4. Kizziah's signature appears as a witness on several coal contracts between Gaus' First Central Holding Co. of Kentucky and a Pennsylvania firm run by coal broker Murray Friedlander.

Another Friedlander company, Commonwealth Western Corp., was under SEC investigation in November 1978, for alleged stock manipulation. The SEC subpoenaed Friedlander's records. In his address/telephone book were the names and phone numbers of Lester Lee's Hy-Test Coal Co., Robert Kizziah's Kenala Coal Co., John Kronquist, Paul Linnenbrink, Rev. June Franklin Dennis and Dominick Bartone.

Bartone, a convicted gun runner, signed several contracts with Lee's Hy-Test Coal Co. on behalf of American Concrete Builders Inc.

Bartone, reputed to be a top organized crime figure in Cleveland, is a close associate of Saul Siegel and Eddie Hammonds, according to the intelligence report.

Gaus said he and Rev. Dennis worked together on many coal deals.

5. On several of Gaus' First Central coal purchase contracts, First Central used a Louisville mailing address, even though its offices were in Frankfort. The Louisville address belonged to Gard Coal Co., with which both Gaus and Kronquist said they dealt.

In Hy-Test's books, a "Big H/Gard Coal Co." transaction was noted.

6. One of the incorporators of both The Big H Coal Co. and Gard Coal Co. was a Louisville man named Richard McDade. In Lee's deposition, he said: "Dick McDade's company is The Big H. If Lee buys any coal in this area, it comes through The Big H. Dick McDade."

Working in the offices of Gard Coal Co. was a disbarred attorney named Lance Kohler, who'd had his own problems with "The Big H," street slang for heroin.

Kohler was convicted in 1973 of selling two ounces of heroin to a narcotics agent.

Both Gaus and Kronquist said they knew Kohler and attempted to do business with him. And so did Paul Linnenbrink.

Despite the number of times Lee and Gaus had crossed paths, Gaus said: "I don't recall Lester Clifford Lee. I heard of Hy-Test Coal through (June Franklin) Dennis."

Dennis who, like Gaus, claims to be a minister, teamed up with Gaus in the fall of 1975. Dennis was recently released from the federal prison in Lexington after serving a sentence for tax fraud.

Gaus said he might know Tony Braxton, "My notes show Norman Braxton. Perhaps they were one and the same," Gaus said.

Gaus, however, crosses paths with several associates of Braxton, which in turn leads to the notorious swindler, Peter Francis Crosby.

In the telephone directory Gaus kept in the offices of First Central Holding Co.—a copy of which was obtained by *The Kentucky Post*—is the name of Alan Zalk, a Los Angeles man with a record of securities violations.

Zalk is also a director of Appalachian Energy and Coal Co., Jenkins, Ky. According to New Orleans police, that firm is controlled by Tony Braxton.

Another director of Appalachian Energy is Ben Harvey of Sanger, Tex. Harvey and Tony Braxton are friends, Kronquist said, adding that Harvey was office manager for Atco Inc., the company Gaus worked for when he was released from prison.

Ben Harvey is also a close associate of Peter Francis Crosby. Crosby told *The Kentucky Post,* "I gave Ben Harvey money, helped him with his expenses."

The incorporator of Appalachian Energy was Sam Clifford Gilbert, a Jenkins, Ky., man convicted of manslaughter in Perry County in 1967. At the time of his arrest, Gilbert said he was employed by Odom Construction Co. in Tennessee, owned by Hugh Odom. Odom's name and phone number appear in First Central Holding Co.'s address book.

Sam Gilbert's name and phone number were found in Crosby's possession when Crosby was arrested in Pineville, Ky., in December 1973.

Asked if he knew Gaus, Crosby replied: "The name rings a bell, but I've never met him. He's with the church, isn't he?"

Gaus was operating his notorious Church of Christ Manors fraud at the same time he was attempting to buy a Chicago bank using Crosby's phony stock.

Gaus said; "I think Peter Crosby is a myth. I have never met the gentleman."

First Central Holding Co. of Kentucky fell apart in late 1975, when Kronquist walked out on Gaus when they argued over a coal analysis report.

"The report had been forged, and that's when I decided I wanted out," Kronquist said. Kronquist is now dealing real estate with Tony Braxton in Dallas.

Linnenbrink said a similar incident prompted him to distrust Gaus. "I went and checked around about that 35 million ton contract he said Atco had, and I found out the contract didn't even exist.

"Then I had the Citizens Union Bank in Lexington run a check on First Central, and they told me they couldn't get any type of picture at all. It was all cloudy and nebulous," Linnenbrink said. He said his dealings with Gaus cost him $30,000 in expenses.

Gaus said he left Kentucky soon after Konquist did. He went to Dallas and set up First Central Holding Co. of Texas in May 1976. The incorporator was Gaus' longtime friend and purported Christian Brother, Archibald Barnhill, a Dallas CPA.

Two months after Barnhill incorporated Gaus' company, Barnhill was permanently enjoined from securities practice by the SEC for his part in a fraud involving a "secret" process to extract pure silver from low-grade ore.

Barnhill's co-defendant in that hoax was Charles W. Deaton, a con man who gained notoriety for his involvement in a scheme that bilked Vietnam POWs out of their back pay with phony revenue bonds.

A federal appeals court called the bond fraud "vicious and brutal. It is difficult to imagine how anyone could conceive a more diabolical scheme."

Also convicted in the revenue bond racket was Garet Van Antwerp, the Mobile, Ala., attorney Gaus said was the German consul who "validated" questionable debentures for Gaus' First Central in 1972.

Deaton and Peter Francis Crosby were charged with bank fraud in 1978 in connection with a coal company called Tri-State Energy, Inc. of Whitesburg, Ky. Crosby was acquitted, and Deaton was not tried, but is serving a 55-year sentence in Texas for the silver ore hoax with Barnhill.

When Gaus popped up in Texas with the "new" First Central Holding Co., Lowell Robinson, the Prestonsburg, Ky., coal broker who signed the First Central debentures, reappeared also.

Robinson introduced Gaus to Walt Aeschliman of Bluffton, Ind., and they formed the Central Investment Trust, a tax shelter program which promised investors they could take $12,000 and turn it into $84,000 through coal investments and tax write-offs.

Gaus circulated letters showing CI Trust and First Central of Texas with 28 million tons in coal reserves and a net worth of $225 million.

"Alex Gaus didn't have one contract. He didn't own one lease, and he never shipped one lump of coal," said Indiana Securities Commissioner Stephen Coons.

About 40 Wells County, Ind., residents poured $250,000 into Gaus' program. "The majority of them were affiliated with a church here," said Wells County prosecutor Everett Goshorn. "There were very strong religious overtones to his approach."

In December 1978, Alex Gaus was indicted on 18 counts of selling unregistered securities and fraud.

Gaus was on parole from his Church of Christ Manors conviction at the time, and his parole was revoked. He got out of jail this past February and has yet to stand trial in Indiana. Trial is set for July.

Gaus is still on parole, but parole officials are taking no chances this time. Under the terms of his parole, Gaus is forbidden to be self-employed; to sell securities, or solicit investments; to associate with investment advisors or to be "employed in any fashion or capacity including, but not limited to the following energy fields: coal, oil, gas, nuclear and solar."

Gaus shrugged off the strict parole limitations. "Let's just say I am gainfully employed, and God has opened doors the parole board cannot close," he said.

"Now that things are normalized to a degree, I believe the coal industry will be good to us. We are not planning to convert the world of coal, just earn as God pleases and provide funds for the furtherance of His work."

PART 12: COAL BOOM BRINGS SUDDEN RICHES AND SUDDEN DEATH
JUNE 13, 1980

It was a mid-July dawn in the mountains. A warm, gentle rain was falling as the killers parked their car and seized their rifles, just out of view of Bill Harvey Johnson's A-frame house, a mile outside of Jenkins, Ky.

Johnson, a rich coal operator, had just a few hours to live.

The gunmen slipped into the forest and crept to a vantage point on a hillside about 100 feet from Johnson's front porch. They lay down in the dense, wet underbrush and waited quietly.

Inside the A-frame, Johnson rose and dressed. He was a good-looking man with a well-built six-foot frame and sandy brown hair. It was Thursday, July 17, 1975, and Johnson thought he was going to work.

When he stepped into the drizzle about 9:30, the quiet mountain wood erupted with the crackle of rifle fire. A deadly hail of .22-cal. slugs slammed into his body. Johnson pitched face down on the damp porch, and two more shots punched into the top of his head. It was over in seconds. Thirteen bullets had found their mark.

The killers scrambled down the hillside and tugged Johnson's corpse off the porch, where it was visible from the road. Johnson was dragged behind a car, two large diamond rings were stripped from his fingers, and his pockets were rifled. The killers drove off. They have never been found.

Bill Harvey Johnson, 42, was one of a half dozen people who were killed in connection with the coal boom of the mid-1970s. Johnson's friends and police investigators say his killing may have been Mob-related.

"A lot of people I've talked to think organized crime may have had something to do with it, and I'm not too inclined to disagree," said Johnson's close friend and business partner, Marshall Clubb of Ashland, Ky. "Bill Harvey was all right until he started fooling with those criminals."

Johnson spent the last weeks of his life "scared to death. He was afraid of somebody," Clubb said.

Dean C. Stansbury, of Whitesburg, the former Kentucky State Police detective who investigated the murder, said: "They gave Bill Harvey a warning. They gave him a real big hint."

Stansbury said Johnson's house was burglarized several times before the killing. The last time, the intruders left behind a message.

"They took a .38-cal. bullet and just laid it on his bed," Stansbury said.

But before the last harrowing weeks, Johnson's experience in the coal business had been good.

In 1972, he was a lab technician at McDowell Hospital in Floyd County, moonlighting as a backhoe operator. Earthmoving led him into coal, and in 1973, he and Clubb formed Upper Elkhorn Coal Co. in Thornton, Ky.

The timing was perfect, and the money poured in.

"At one point there, we were making so damned much money it bothered me," Clubb recalled. For every ton of coal Upper Elkhorn sold, it earned a $30 profit. Wealth was something new to Bill Harvey Johnson.

"I hate to say this, but Bill Harvey was pretty damned stupid. And when he got this money all of a sudden, people were ready to take advantage of him," Clubb said. One incident stuck in his mind.

"One day I came to the office, and there were two or three motorcycles laying on the front porch of the office. Somebody had sold him two or three motorcycles. He'd buy anything. Stolen . . . didn't make a damned bit of difference, he'd buy it," Clubb said.

Investigators believe Johnson may have unwittingly bought stolen mining equipment, and that may have been one reason he was killed.

Two days before Johnson was murdered, a Memphis, Tenn., federal grand jury returned conspiracy and mail fraud indictments against nine people involved with a stolen coal loader which had wound up on Upper Elkhorn's property. One of the men indicted was Newport, Ky., energy broker Paul J. Linnenbrink.

Linnenbrink was vice president of Cherokee Oil and Gas Corp., which operated from an office at 620 Monmouth St. The office was shared by tax accountant Herman C. Sorenson, former Newport city manager and president of Cherokee.

Linnenbrink, who has served time for counterfeiting, said a former prison mate of his, Willis (Junior) Lindsey, called him in January, 1975, and said he had a $15,000 coal loader—which looks like a bulldozer with wheels—to sell.

"He said the owner of the equipment wanted to sell it and turn it in on an insurance fraud, so he could collect the insurance money. I told Lindsey I didn't want any Mickey Mouse deal like that, but if he had a bill of sale for it, I could find a buyer," Linnenbrink said.

Lindsey brought the loader on a flatbed truck from Memphis to Florence, but without a bill of sale.

"I told him the deal was off, that without a bill of sale, the guy (a local contractor) wouldn't buy it," Linnenbrink said. But the gruff Linnenbrink had another idea.

"I told Junior that if he needed the money, he could take the loader down to Letcher County and put it to work," Linnenbrink said. The loader ended up at Johnson's Upper Elkhorn Coal Co., which Linnenbrink and Sorenson were trying to sell for Johnson.

"I told Bill Harvey the history behind the loader, and he told me we could put it to work there, " Linnenbrink said.

A month later, Johnson called Linnenbrink at the offices of Cherokee in Newport. "He told me the FBI had been by about the loader, that it had been stolen two years before," Linnenbrink recalled. "He wanted to know what the hell was going on."

One week before the shooting, the FBI paid another visit to Upper Elkhorn Coal Co. The visit wasn't cordial.

"They leaned on (Johnson) real hard. They leaned on him to the extent that Bill Harvey was running around gathering evidence for his own defense," Stansbury said.

Clubb said Johnson was afraid the FBI would arrest him for being involved with stolen equipment, "I feel my partner was involved to some degree," Clubb said bluntly.

But investigators feel Johnson's frenzied evidence-gathering may have been misunderstood. When Linnenbrink, Lindsey and seven other people were indicted in connection with the loader on July 15, 1975, Johnson was not among them. Two days later, Johnson was murdered.

Lindsey and three others pleaded guilty to the loader theft. Linnenbrink was acquitted. Linnenbrink was questioned in connection with Johnson's murder. "I don't think Linnenbrink had anything to do with it," Stansbury, the investigating officer, concluded.

But the killing may have been related to the indictments, according to a West Virginia police intelligence report.

The report stated: "The officer has received information in which two white males out of northern Kentucky allegedly killed one white male by the name of Bill Harvey Johnson . . . who allegedly attempted to contact authorities reference (stolen equipment deals.)"

"The two subjects from northern Kentucky are involved in prostitution and are allegedly hit men."

The report was a product of an investigation into a stolen equipment ring operating in Mercer County, W. Va. Among the names mentioned in connection with the theft ring were:

1. William Glover, a partner in Great Plains Development Corp. with convicted swindler Saul Davidson, of Denver, Colo. Davidson and Great Plains had attempted to buy coal mines from Kentucky businessman Lew Adams. The West Virginia report stated a brothel in Bluefield, W. Va., was operating in a building owned by Great Plains.

2. Rev. June Franklin Dennis, a Williamstown man who later entered into a partnership with Adams. Dennis was recently released from prison for tax fraud.

3. Alexander Gaus Jr., a Mob-linked swindler from the Chicago area who signed contracts to purchase coal from both Dennis and Linnenbrink. The West Virginia report names Gaus as the "coordinator or the supervisor" of the stolen equipment ring.

4. Robert E. Bales, a West Virginia man now serving a nine-year sentence for coal-related fraud.

5. James Duncan, then an officer in the bankrupt Page Coal Co. of Lexington, Ky.

Another member of Page Coal Co. was a Columbus, Ohio, man named Larry H. Hunt.

Marshall Clubb said Hunt came to see him shortly after Johnson's murder. Clubb said Johnson, without Clubb's knowledge, had invested heavily in Page Coal Co. and another Hunt operation called Red Jacket Coal Co. The names of both Hunt and Red Jacket were found in the address/phone directory Alex Gaus kept in the office of his Frankfort-based First Central Holding Co. of Kentucky.

Clubb said: "Hunt wanted to borrow some money from me. I found out Bill Harvey had invested about a half million dollars in some foreign contract Hunt said he had. When I checked the contract out, I found it was a sham, non-existent."

Hunt had in his employ two former University of Kentucky football players, William N. (Billy) Mitchell and Robert (Hooker) Phillips. "That whole bunch is in trouble over some tax shelter operation they were running," Clubb said.

In December 1979, Hunt, Phillips and several other men were sued for $25.5 million in Columbus, Ohio, by 32 investors who claimed Hunt, through L.H. Hunt Enterprises Inc., swindled them of money they invested in his Randolph County Coal Program. A lawsuit gives only one side of a dispute.

Two days after the lawsuit was filed, Hunt, Mitchell, Phillips and four other men were charged by the Indiana Securities Commission with selling unregistered securities through their Energia Corp. The commission ordered a halt to the sales.

Hunt has since relocated in Lexington and is now under investigation by the West Virginia and Kentucky offices of the FBI, *The Kentucky Post* has learned.

Stansbury said "there is a good possibility" Johnson's death was linked to stolen equipment, but his investigation turned up other, more troubling business deals.

Stansbury said Johnson had been dealing with Dominick Bartone. Bartone, a reputed Cleveland organized crime figure, is a convicted gun runner who was then making inroads to the coal industry through Lester Clifford Lee, of Newport, a convicted felon and suspected hit man.

Marshall Clubb said Bartone had negotiated with Johnson about buying Upper Elkhorn Coal Co. in late 1974. Clubb, at that time, was in the hospital recovering from a heart attack. A friend of Clubb's went with Johnson to Columbus, Ohio, to meet Bartone.

The man, now living in East Point, Ky., is a former state policeman who agreed to be interviewed if his name was not used.

He said shortly after he arrived at Upper Elkhorn to help Johnson run the company, he got a phone call from a man named Lombardi in Cleveland. "He said he wanted to talk to us about buying Upper Elkhorn, and if we had what he wanted, we could make a deal," he recalled.

Johnson and he went with their wives to the Mark Inn in Columbus where the meeting was to take place the next morning.

Lombardi came to their motel room that morning about 10. "He said we would meet downstairs in the banquet room. We all got up to leave, and Lombardi said: 'No women.' We looked kind of surprised, and he said, 'Ain't no damned women coming to this meeting.' So our wives had to stay in the room."

Johnson, Lombardi and the ex-trooper went to the banquet room. "I looked around and thought: 'This is a hell of a place for a meeting.' The room could have seated 100 people, but there was just one table in the middle of this huge room. We sat down and waited."

After a few minutes, a sloppily-dressed Bartone ambled in, flanked by "two guys that could hardly get through the door. They looked like the Neanderthal twins. I'm about six feet, four inches tall and weigh 230 pounds, and I felt like a shrimp," he said.

Bartone called over a waitress and ordered breakfast. "I mean he ordered breakfast. We didn't have anything to say about it. Steak and eggs, everything."

When the dishes were cleared away, Bartone lit a cigarette and asked what Johnson had to offer.

"Bill took out some papers and handed them to Bartone. He glanced at them a little bit and gave them to one of the gorillas he had with him. He told us this guy was his accountant."

"This so-called accountant looked at the papers, scratched his head and grunted a few times. It was obvious neither one of them knew anything about coal," the man said.

Bartone explained he needed Upper Elkhorn because he had an "in" at US Steel and needed coal to fill a contract he had there. Then Bartone began talking of Jimmy Hoffa, the Teamsters Union boss who disappeared in July, 1975.

"He said he and Hoffa were friends, that they'd been in prison together. I thought: 'Oh Jesus, what have we gotten ourselves into?'"

Bartone asked the waitress over and settled the bill. "He pulled out a wad of $100s a show dog couldn't jump over and paid for breakfast. Then he gave the waitress a $300 tip," the man said.

After Bartone climbed into the back of his grey Mercedes limousine, the ex-trooper turned to Johnson and told him: "You'd better just forget you ever laid eyes on that bunch. People like that, they'll put you in a Biz bag."

But the impressionable Johnson didn't share his friend's uneasiness.

"All Bill Harvey talked about for weeks was Bartone. He kept saying: 'Oh, they're big wheels, they're big wheels.' I told him: 'You make a deal with these guys, and they've got a real poor retirement plan.' But he wouldn't listen."

Johnson may have met with Bartone in Lexington on another occasion, but the ex-trooper said the next he heard of Bartone was when Bartone was indicted in 1976 for bilking a Cleveland bank of $250,000.

That was the Northern Ohio Bank, which US Organized Crime Strike Force investigators said had been taken over by the Mob. The bank collapsed in 1975, costing the Federal Deposit Insurance Corp. $30 million.

Stansbury said correspondence from the Northern Ohio Bank was found in Upper Elkhorn's papers.

One of Upper Elkhorn's contract miners was THC Mining Inc., represented by Washington D.C. attorney James V. Brown, whose wife, Virginia May, was the chairwoman of the Interstate Commerce Commission.

In 1975, Upper Elkhorn had a $200,000 line of credit from two local banks, but Brown called Clubb and told him he could do better. "Brown told me he knew where I could get a $1 million line of credit, but it would cost me $5,000. I figured $1 million for $5,000 wasn't too bad a deal," Clubb said.

So Clubb and Brown boarded a private plane in Charleston, W. Va., and flew to Cleveland, where they met with Alexander Dandy, a Washington D.C. financier who was head of Cleveland Financial Services, a Northern Ohio Bank affiliate.

Dandy told Clubb that for $5,000, Cleveland Financial would, through the Northern Ohio Bank, lend Upper Elkhorn up to $1 million. But first, Dandy said, Upper Elkhorn's books had to be audited, and then it had to transfer its bank accounts to the Northern Ohio Bank. Clubb hedged on the last condition.

"I asked them for a financial statement, and they couldn't find one. There wasn't a financial statement to be found in that whole damned bank. Something didn't smell right. I told them I'd talk to Bill Harvey," Clubb said.

But he still paid Dandy the $5,000 to cover the expense of the audit. Soon afterward two men who said they were auditors came to Thornton, Ky., to examine Upper Elkhorn's operations.

"The auditors were packing guns," ex-trooper Stansbury said.

After that, Clubb said, he told Johnson he didn't want any further dealings with Cleveland Financial or the Northern Ohio Bank.

Within a month the bank collapsed. Dandy and Bartone were later indicted. Bartone was convicted of fraud and sentenced to five years in jail. Dandy pleaded guilty to transporting stolen money and was given a two-year sentence.

"I thank God I didn't put my money in that bank," Clubb sighed.

Despite Bill Harvey Johnson's frequent associations with mobsters and swindlers, Stansbury and Clubb believe Johnson was a simple country boy easily impressed by guns and money.

"I gave him a speeding ticket once, and then I heard back he was telling people he was going to have me bumped off. He'd say that about anybody who did something he didn't like," Stansbury said.

Said Clubb: "Bill would have loved to have been the head of the Mafia. He was that type of guy. But using their systems and their ways . . . it wasn't part of him."

"If he could have been Al Capone, with the title but not the crime, he would have loved it. I think Bill Harvey got in over his head."

PART 13a: "THE MAN WHO SOLD THE NORTH POLE TURNS TO COAL"
JUNE 14, 1980

Peter Francis Crosby scoffed when told that investigators of white-collar crime believe him to be the mastermind behind a score of frauds and swindles in the coal industry.

"That's just stupid," Crosby said from his home in New York City. "I have some very nice coal mines, actually three different mines. There's no need for me to engage in any type of illegal practice."

"Why would I jeopardize my freedom by swindling somebody when my father left me millions of dollars?" Crosby asked in a deep, reassuring voice.

If his father left him millions, they are no more.

Peter Crosby's fortune these days is a trust fund of $104,000, and that trusts has an $8 million IRS lien against it.

But Crosby has a history of exaggerating figures. It has landed him in jail, repeatedly.

Crosby, 56, a darkly handsome man with a powerful build, is the black sheep of a well-to-do New York family. His mother once owned the Mary Carter Paint Company. His brother James is president of Resorts International, a firm that owns the main casino in Atlantic City, N.J., and has others in the Bahamas.

In 1952, Crosby married a young actress named Denise Darcel and appeared ready to take up the reins of the family fortune. But something happened along the way.

Crosby took up the line of work he pursues today: "energy," he said. In August 1955, he and a man named Larry Rosen took out an ad in the *Wall Street Journal*, seeking control of a public corporation.

Rosen, also known as Paul Lawrence Rosenauch, was identified in Senate testimony as an associate of Anthony Coppola, nephew of Newport, Ky., gangster (Trigger) Mike Coppola.

One company that responded to Crosby and Rosen's ad was Texas Adams Oil Co. Within months, Crosby and his group had gained control of Texas Adams, using the company's own money, in a twisted scheme involving stock-for-stock swaps with bogus Crosby corporations.

After Crosby was at the helm, he began issuing millions of shares of worthless stock. He was convicted in 1960 of mail and wire fraud and sentenced to five years in jail. Paroled, he was sent back to jail for associating with known criminals.

But Crosby is best known as the man who sold the North Pole.

In 1971, Crosby claimed to have acquired the oil rights to millions of acres of frozen saltwater, most of it in the Bering Sea. He transferred his "ownership" of the sea into a shell corporation called Picture Island Computers.

He pumped out financial statements showing Picture Island owning the rights to one billion acres of Arctic oil property and valued it at $35 million. Then, Picture Island began issuing millions of shares of stock.

Picture Island's balance sheet also listed 5000 acres of California land sold to the company by an Arizona real estate broker named William Davidson. Crosby valued the land, which was paid for with worthless Picture Island stock, at $3 million. It was part of an Army artillery range.

Davidson soon showed up in Chicago with Scripture-quoting con man Alexander Gaus Jr., and the two were exposed by the Illinois Crime Investigating Commission for trying to buy out a bank with Crosby's worthless stock. (Gaus later turned up in Kentucky as head of Frankfort based coal company.)

Soon, Picture Island stock began appearing in the hands of swindlers across the nation: as collateral on loans, as stock to be traded for stock in legitimate businesses and, as in the case of Alex Gaus, to be used to buy control of banks and insurance companies.

In 1972, a federal grand jury returned conspiracy, mail fraud and securities fraud indictments against Crosby and six other men. Appointed to represent the men was New York attorney Daniel H. Greenberg, the attorney for Mob lord Carmine Tramunti.

But when the trail started, Crosby was nowhere to be found. He was tried *in absentia*. All of the men were convicted.

Crosby popped up in Kentucky, where he was operating under the names Carl Rich and Jim Ross. Kentucky authorities were tipped off by a conscientious phone company employee named Bernard Hill.

Hill, manager of Mountain Rural Bell in West Liberty, Ky., said Crosby gave him a $500 check to set up phone service for a Crosby company called First Kentucky Coal and Mineral. The check bounced, Hill said.

"We cut off his phone service, and he came down to the office just madder than hell. We've got a lot of shysters and crooks that moved down here with the coal boom, but this man was unusual. He wasn't like anything I'd ever seen here in the mountains before," Hill said.

When Crosby threatened to sue Hill for $1 million, Hill called the Kentucky Division of Securities. "They were very interested," he recalled.

Crosby and Steve Broady, a disbarred New York attorney, were arrested in December 1973, at the Stamper Motel in West Liberty.

Crosby was packed off to the federal prison in Lexington for two years, and Broady was charged with harboring a federal fugitive. The charges were later dropped, Broady said.

"Broady's got some sort of immunity. He used to be a CIA agent," said Marvin Stone, a disbarred Toronto attorney and associate of Crosby.

Broady, 76, denied any CIA connections. Broady said he was in Kentucky with Crosby "to keep him out of trouble and, if you know his record, you know that's a very hard thing to do. I had no financial interest in his Kentucky operation because interest in his business means trouble."

When the two men were arrested and authorities looked at the personal papers they had on them, they found the names of numerous coal brokers and coal companies.

Crosby had coal dealings, *The Kentucky Post* discovered, with many of the same men believed by investigators to be part of a nationwide network of confidence men and organized crime figures.

A confidential police intelligence report states: "Crosby is thought to be the head of a group of known swindlers who have attempted to fraudulently obtain coal mining operations and properties in eastern Kentucky (through) the use of fraudulent certificates of deposit in foreign banks, bogus coal purchase contracts, misrepresentations of their financial positions and fraudulent loans."

"That's not my style," Crosby retorted.

But Crosby's coal associates include:

1. Sam Clifford Gilbert, convicted of manslaughter in Perry County in 1967 and later foreman of THC Mining Inc., a contract miner for Bill Harvey Johnson's Upper Elkhorn Coal Co. Johnson was murdered in 1975. Gilbert's name and phone number was found in Crosby's possession. "Gilbert's name rings a bell," Crosby allowed.

2. Alexander Dandy, head of Cleveland Financial Services, an affiliate of the Mob-controlled Northern Ohio Bank, which collapsed in 1975. Dandy, convicted of transporting stolen money after the collapse of the bank, had attempted to get Bill Harvey a $1 million loan. "Dandy tried to get me some loans," Crosby said.

3. Alan Zalk, a Los Angeles man with a record of securities violations who is tied to some of Alex Gaus' coal ventures. Zalk is also associated with Dallas, Tex., con man Tony Braxton, an associate of New Orleans Mob boss Carlos Marcello.

4. Letcher White, a disbarred Manchester, Ky., attorney convicted of fraud this year in connection with a massive tax shelter swindle. White and West Virginia coal broker Garland Neeley, another Crosby companion, were seen in Charleston, W. Va., with Mob financial wizard Meyer Lansky two years ago, authorities say. Crosby said he tried to purchase River Coal Co. from White shortly before it was bought by the mastermind of the tax shelter swindle, con man Jerome Matusow.

5. Sinclair Robinson, a convicted New York securities cheat who worked closely with the late Alexander Guterma in Kentucky coal. Guterma is considered one of the giants in the field of securities fraud. "I went down to Alabama with Robinson," Crosby said.

6. Charles W. Deaton, an insurance fraud specialist from Dallas indicted with Crosby in 1978 for coal-related fraud. Deaton was also an unindicted

co-conspirator in the Northern Ohio Banks case. Deaton was convicted in a Texas fraud case along with Alexander Gaus' accountant. Deaton's name and phone number were found in Crosby's possession after his 1973 arrest in West Liberty. "I never had any dealings with him in the coal industry," Crosby said.

The police intelligence report continued: "In recent years, Crosby had developed even shadier friendships as supported by a reliable report connecting him to the loan sharking operations of Vincent DiNapoli, Robert Richard Schultz and Carmine Tramunti, all identified by the Justice Department as hard-core La Cosa Nostra figures."

"That's fantasy world they've built up," Crosby said.

Tramunti, Daniel Greenberg's former client, is now dead. "Poor fellow died in jail," Greenberg said.

Greenberg's name turned up as a director of a coal company called Global Coalenergy, a Nevada corporation registered in Kentucky in 1974. That was run by Crosby associate Marvin Stone, the disbarred Toronto attorney.

Greenberg, who in 1973 was suspended from practice for three months for mishandling a client's money, said he was unaware that he was a director in Global Coalenergy. "I'm going to have to ask Marvin about that," Greenberg said.

Another director of Global was Earl M. Maltby, an elderly man who is chairman of the board of the Royal Casino in Las Vegas. Maltby was also president of a Crosby-controlled company called Americoal Engineering Corp. Another Americoal director was Steve Broady.

Americoal had a branch office in Springfield, Mo., run by a Texan named Wayne Henson. Henson, now dead, had been in business deals with swindler Tony Braxton, the Marcello family associate, and John Kronquist, Alexander Gaus' Kentucky sidekick.

Maltby and Broady were also listed as directors of McNeil Coal Co. in Knox County, which Stone purchased in 1973.

Marvin Stone said he no longer owns McNeil Coal Co. When the price of coal rocketed in 1973, the owner, Dearl McNeil, decided to keep the mine, Stone said.

Stone said open warfare erupted in Knox County with Stone and Vincent, his 320-pound bodyguard, on one side and the McNeils on the other.

Stone said he was shot at twice and thrown in jail for allegedly passing

$135,000 in bad McNeil Coal Co. checks. Those charges, he said, were later dropped.

A similar thing happened when Stone attempted to purchase Blue Gem Coal and Land Co. in Barbourville, owned by the prominent Callihan family. That case wound up in court. Stone said he recently received a $300,000 settlement from the Callihans.

Greenberg said Peter Crosby tried to claim some of that money as his own, because he introduced Stone to the Callihans.

"I'm walking a little taller now in Knox County," the diminutive Stone said. He said he still operates coal mines in Tennessee but has sold his "extensive land holdings" in Knox County. "I'm not into coal much anymore," he said.

But the story is different with Crosby. "I'm active in every aspect of energy," he said.

Most recently, Crosby was indicted in New York on charges of conspiracy, mail fraud and making false statements to a bank. Court records show Crosby was involved with a Whitesburg, Ky., firm called Tri-State Energy, Inc.

"I don't think I've ever heard that name before," Crosby said when asked about it.

Tri-State was run by con man Charles W. Deaton. The company had a mine in Neon in Letcher County. On the strength of Tri-State's financial statement, Bankers Trust of New York loaned it $475,000 to expand its mining operations.

"They did a very little bit of mining for a short time, and then they closed up shop and went out of business. In the meantime, the bank had advanced substantial amounts of money on the representation that there were very valuable amounts of coal there and that they were actively mining it," said Rhea Neugarten, Assistant US Attorney for the Southern District of New York.

According to court records: "The scheme involved the use of false reports regarding Tri-State's coal mine, fraudulent sales contracts and misrepresentations that the stock which was pledged as collateral (on the loans at Bankers Trust) was unrestricted."

The stock, from an Alabama insurance company, was next to worthless. Ms. Neugarten, who prosecuted the case, said the stock was obtained for Tri-State by Peter Crosby, with the help of disbarred New York attorney William Hamilton.

Hamilton was also convicted of fraud in Crosby's Picture Island swindle.

Crosby told *The Kentucky Post* he did get the stock for Deaton, but said he didn't know what Deaton did with it.

Due to an error in drawing up the papers to extradite Deaton from West Germany, Deaton was not tried. He is serving a 55-year fraud sentence in Texas.

Crosby was acquitted. "They couldn't even get me on conspiracy," he chuckled. But three other men were convicted. Of the $475,000 in loans, Bankers Trust recovered $2,000.

Tri-State's coal mine was sold to Big H Coal Co., which had dealings with Alexander Gaus and Newport, Ky., hit man Lester Clifford Lee.

But Crosby takes umbrage at the suggestion that his dealings in Kentucky were less than honorable. Crosby said he and his "millions" provided much needed capital when coal was a forgotten stepchild.

"A lot of people saw an energy shortage developing, but we tried to do something about it," Crosby declared. "All I did was bring money in. McNeil Coal Co. (got) hundreds of thousands of dollars in cash. It didn't come from Kentucky."

McNeil is now out of business.

Crosby blamed his reputation on headline-hungry prosecutors.

"Once you become a whipping boy, it's easy to keep building on it from that base. You carry a cross for the rest of your life," he complained.

PART 13b: HOW TO BECOME A COAL MILLIONAIRE IN TWO WEEKS
JUNE 14, 1980

It's hard not to like "Rocky" Stone. A Canadian by birth, the 44-year-old Stone is a small, slender man with a quick wit and an easy laugh.

A charming conversationalist, he speaks with a polished diction. Former Gov. Louie Nunn, with whom Stone had some coal dealings, said of him: "I kind of liked him. I didn't know that much about him, but I heard some stories. And I remember he wore some real funny hats."

Stone used to be an attorney and "a pretty good one, I might add," Stone said.

He had a legal practice in Toronto and the Bahamas until he was disbarred after a fraud conviction.

Stone was sentenced to 30 months in jail, but his case was overturned on appeal, and he won in acquittal in his second trial. Now, he says, he is in the process of having his legal license restored.

In the meantime, Stone said he is content to fly around the country, dabbling in high-risk deals in energy and precious metals. He said he made his first million that way, scoring big on uranium stocks while still in college. "But I've dropped it several times since then," he said, chuckling.

Now, he said, he is "doing a gold mine in Colorado and a silver mine. I'm also dealing offshore in the Bahamas and the Cayman Islands."

But in the mid-1970s, Stone was "doing" coal. He said he held extensive coal properties in Knox County, Ky., and spent a great deal of time in Barbourville. Stone also spent two weeks in the Knox County jail, charged with a $135,000 check fraud. But Stone said it was all a mistake, and the charges were dropped.

In 1977, the Louisville *Courier Journal* referred to Stone as a "known swindler," a title he resents. "I have no affiliations with organized crime," he said primly.

Stone freely admits, however, some of his friends might fall into that category. He said his interest in their wheelings and dealings "is something of a hobby of mine."

"I know all the swindlers, known them all pretty well for about 10–12 years. I operated in the Bahamas, and all these fellows use it as a financial playground. You get to know them over the years, let's put it that way."

So, when Marvin Stone explained "from a con man's point of view," how a coal swindle works, he seemed to speak with some authority. He told one *Kentucky Post* reporter: "We'll go on a drive down to Knox County and I'll make you a millionaire . . . not overnight, but in about two weeks."

"You'll give me $2,000, and I'll go speak to one of the farmers down there, and I'll get you a coal lease, an actual property of 200 or 300 acres. I'll get a lease for 10 years. In addition, the lease will say that when mining commences, the lease will go even longer than that as long as you're mining coal. You'll pay that farmer $200 a month until you start mining," Stone said. That was step one.

Then Stone said he would go to a "friendly" geological engineer.

"I know several," he said.

"We'll go to the engineer, and you'll give him $1,000, and I'll show him how to write up an engineering report—properly. When he's done, you'll give him another $1,000. Now, you've got a beautiful report for $2,000 that looks like a million bucks. It's very pretty, in color, with maps and everything, and it says your land contains one million tons of coal," Stone explained.

"Now, nobody knows you've only put down $2,000 for that lease. And no one knows you've merely paid the engineer $2,000. What they see is a report with pictures saying you've locked in one million tons of coal for 10 years or longer," he said.

The beauty of the scheme, Stone said, is that "nobody in the world can tell you what those reserves are worth. Nobody can say. It's just a beautiful engineering report. As long as the coal stays in the ground, no one can tell what those reserves are worth. And the front pages of the newspapers say energy is great, coal is glamorous."

Next, Stone said, the con man would take one of his myriad of "shell" corporations—companies that exist only on paper—and write up a financial statement for that shell showing ownership of those million tons of coal.

"Since nobody can say what it's worth, you can put your own value on it. Say if somebody ever mines that coal, you would make five dollars a ton. So, on the asset side of the balance sheet, you would write down $5 million. Meanwhile, it's only cost you $4,000," he said.

White collar crime investigators say that financial statements of swindler-run coal companies are often puffed up with bogus coal purchase contracts, to make it appear as if the coal in the ground is already sold. Those contracts are often with other shell corporations, run by other swindlers.

From there, the only limit is the extent of the con man's imagination.

"You can go to a lending institution, and with that lease on your balance sheet, the banker might give you $100,000. Or you can trade it. You might swap that lease for control of a company. Or a guy needs a loan, he's glad to pay you $50,000 for that lease. You can do all kinds of things with a coal lease," Stone said.

In the past, Stone said, debts and notes from other shell corporations were used to pump up financial statements.

"But supposing you put coal reserves in it? That's another step down the line. These aren't illusionary, and that's the real attraction of the coal business. That's the real reason. Simply, it allows you to put assets in a shell. One step betterment in the shell game," Stone said.

Stone cited one instance in which an associate purchased a Mobile, Ala., record company using coal leases. Stone said the same man took over a Las Vegas casino in the same manner.

"He was a shell operator. Not a good one really, but his creativity was great. He's a rape and run artist. Take over a business, rape it and take the profits," Stone said.

Stone said a variation on the coal lease swindle is the use of mortgaged mining equipment on balance sheets. "You get a lease on the equipment from the owner, put it down on the balance sheet as unencumbered (mortgage-free) property, take them to a bank and use them for collateral," he said.

Another acquaintance of his used that ploy with great success Stone said. "He beat the banks for about three or four million dollars. He'd beaten about 10 or 12 banks for about $300,000 apiece using the same equipment. And he never got charged with anything because the banks were too embarrassed."

PART 14: GOOD OLD BOYS DABBLE IN DRUGS, 'DOZERS AND FRAUD
JUNE 16, 1980

In some ways the coal equipment swindlers were a breed apart.

Unlike the corrupt financiers, stock promoters, disbarred lawyers and crooked accountants who flocked to Kentucky during the coal boom, the equipment swindlers were just a bunch of good old boys.

Some had finished high school, others had not. They had grease under their fingernails and hailed from little towns in the South. But dollar for dollar, con for con, the equipment fraud ringleaders were a match for the Ivy League sharpers.

Their schemes were often complex as the paper blizzards churned up by Peter Francis Crosby and Alexander Gaus. At times, entire coal companies were bought to loot them of their heavy equipment. Bulldozers and loaders—often leased or heavily mortgaged—were shuffled through a labyrinth of dummy corporations and emerged as "new" equipment, unmortgaged and with different serial numbers. They were sold as if they belonged to the swindlers, and not to the finance companies.

Other scams were more direct. Bulldozers were often stolen outright and turned in as thefts on insurance claims. Sometimes, mining equipment was buried, well-greased and covered with tarpaulins, and turned in as stolen. The equipment was later unearthed and put back to work.

But there is a more sordid side to the stolen equipment swindles. Investigators believe some mining machinery has been shipped to equipment-hungry South American and traded for narcotics.

"What happens is that people steal the equipment from other people, or they steal it from themselves and turn it in as an insurance fraud, run it town to Tampa or Mobile and run it out of the country to South America," said Tom Krebs, Alabama Securities Commissioner.

Krebs said it's possible to make as much as 200 percent profit on a deal like that.

"Then they invest it in a boatload of narcotics, and it comes back into the country. So you take a $100,000 investment and turn it into $1 million," Krebs said.

In a confidential memo to the Justice Department in 1977, Krebs outlined an instance where a coal operator in Walker County, Ala., was selling stolen equipment and "making runs to California where narcotics are purchased." The drugs were brought back on Greyhound buses and taken to the coal company office.

"They are taken from that office to a strip mining pit where they are distributed to drug dealers by the drivers of the coal trucking firm," the memo stated.

And it's easy to dispose of a stolen piece of equipment. Investigators say there is an organized crime "pipeline" for stolen mining equipment that runs south from Toronto, Canada, through Chicago, to northern Kentucky, to Wise, Va., to Bristol, Va., to Albany, Ga. and finally to Tampa, Fla.

But not all of the equipment shipped to South America comes back as drugs. A London, Ky., equipment runner names J.R. Durham said he was happy to take his profits in cold hard cash.

"It's not a payoff with drugs. It's an organized crime situation where there are large contractors over there willing to pay $100,000 for a piece of equipment that sells for $50,000 over here. It's strictly money," Durham said.

James Randall Durham should know. He made a lot of money dealing stolen equipment.

By the time he was 19, he was a millionaire. He's 24 now and in federal prison for heavy equipment theft. But back during the coal boom, the world was rosy for J.R. Durham.

A dropout from Laurel County High, Durham bought a truck during the summer between his junior and senior years and began hauling coal in the Somerset-London area.

He advanced from truck driver to fleet operator in a matter of months. "Personally, I filed taxes on $1,127,000 in 1975," said Durham, a short, chubby man with an unruly thatch of thin brown hair. Durham said he had cash reserves of $700,000 and two homes in the Somerset area.

"I had three Lincolns, two or three different Cadillacs, pickups, Blazers and four-wheel drives," Durham recalled.

The homes and cars have been repossessed. The huge amounts of money have been spent paying off bookies and attorneys. Durham has spent the past three years behind bars.

"J.R. was a bad cookie when he was on the streets," said one Kentucky State Police organized crime investigator. "I reckon he was about as bad as they come."

It was tough being a teenage millionaire in a small town. "There was a lot of people who'd rather seen me walking than driving," he said.

Small-minded jealousy was the cause, Durham says, of his July, 1976, indictment for the murder of fellow coal operators Horace Gill and Curtis Murphy.

Gill and Murphy, two Florida road contractors inexperienced in coal and close to bankruptcy, were cut down in a shotgun ambush in December 1975, near a cabin on the shore of Lake Laurel.

Durham admits he was well acquainted with Gill and Murphy, had bought some of their coal leases shortly before the killings and was at the cabin the night they were murdered.

"I seen them killed, saw the whole thing, I've never denied that. But I didn't do it," Durham said.

A jury believed him and he was acquitted but has since been convicted of armed robbery and heavy equipment theft. Durham claims he was framed on the armed robbery charge, but admits to the equipment theft.

In that case, Durham rented two bulldozers from King Excavating in Burlington in 1977. The dozers wound up in Colorado, where Durham said a man named Vanis Ray Robbins had sold them for $37,000.

"I needed the money to pay off some gambling debts. They was into me for about $50,000," Durham says.

"They" was Robbins, a convicted gambler from Cincinnati. Robbins was also sent to jail on the heavy equipment theft. If Durham was eager to get Robbins off his back, it's not surprising.

Durham said he understood that Robbins had once stuck a revolver down the throat of a tardy debtor at Latonia racetrack. That kind of behavior got him indicted for extortion in 1974.

And when J.R. Durham was accused of gunning down Gill and Murphy, he accused Robbins of complicity. Robbins was arrested in Las Vegas, where he ran the Jackpot Casino. He was released when Durham recanted.

Defending Robbins was Burnside, Ky., attorney Lester Burns, who ran for state Attorney General in the 1979 Republican primary. Burns also had extensive dealings with fraud kind Alexander (Sandy) Guterma, who bought Mt. Victory Coal Co. from Burns in 1975. Burns later went on Guterma's payroll. Burns also represented Durham on the armed robbery charge.

Durham said he met Robbins through Burns, and that the three of them often played poker together in the back of Burns' law office. "I lost $30,000 in one game, and I quit fooling with them after that," Durham says.

But Durham didn't quit fooling with stolen mining equipment.

In January 1977, Durham and five other men set up a firm called Industrial Investors, Inc. in Middlesboro, Ky.

"Industrial Investors was more or less a fake company, a phony, buying up other coal companies," Durham said. "We had an office worth $40,000 and all of us were driving Lincolns and Cadillacs . . . one of the nicest looking fronts you could set up."

Durham recalled his former partners and smiled. "I knew they had a knowledge, and they knew I had a knowledge. Combined, we was *treacherous.*"

In April 1977, Industrial Investors placed two advertisements in the Louisville *Courier-Journal,* looking to buy heavy mining equipment or "companies associated with heavy equipment."

At least four unfortunate companies responded to the ads.

"We'd buy these companies, and within 30 days, we'd fire everybody, sell all the equipment, all the assets, drain the corporation for everything we could and then transfer the stock to someone else," Durham said. "We just wrecked them."

For example, Industrial Investors purchased a Knox County, Ky., strip mining operation for $10,000. Included in the deal were two heavily mortgages pieces of mining equipment, owned by Westinghouse Credit Corp.

The equipment was sold as if it was owned by Industrial Investors and funneled into the stolen equipment pipeline. Selling price: $101,000, a $91,000 profit.

Durham said he bought a Breathitt County, KY company for $100,000 and sold the equipment—which was only leased—for $300,000. "Beacon Leasing in Florida owned that equipment. They took a hell of a loss on it," Durham said.

When the monthly lease or mortgage payments stopped, the finance companies came to eastern Kentucky to repossess their equipment, It was nowhere to be found. Durham said several pieces ended up in Venezuela.

"All these companies flogged the FBI office all at once. They said: 'Hey! We've been ripped off!'" Durham said, laughing loudly.

The federal government didn't find it amusing. Durham and his five cohorts had defrauded three finance companies of more than $1 million.

Durham's partners were charged with multiple counts of conspiracy, mail and wire fraud. Durham was granted immunity and testified against his former partners. In March, all five were found guilty and given prison sentences ranging from five to 190 years.

But Durham said his group was just one part of "a network of crooks and crooked coal operators" flourishing in the stolen equipment racket. Durham said some of his equipment was sold to an Albany, Ga., company called Herco, Inc.

That equipment parts and leasing firm was run by Robert L. Herring. Durham said he sold Herring millions of dollars worth of heavy mining equipment. "Some of it was legitimate, other was illegal. Herring would buy or sell either way. He'd buy hot equipment along with legitimate stuff," Durham said.

Finance and leasing companies were also on the receiving end of Herring's swindles. One of the biggest losers was the giant National Acceptance Corp. in Chicago, stung both by Durham and Herring. Herring is believed by investigators to have bilked NAC of more than $9 million through hundreds of loans on stolen or non-existent equipment. Some estimates run as high as $25 million.

Herring is in jail on fraud and racketeering convictions. And it appears Herring shared his expertise in equipment frauds with other swindlers on the confidence ring.

The Kentucky Post learned Herring financed equipment for Durango Coal and Leasing Co. of Louisville, which had business dealings with swindlers Alexander Gaus Jr., Lester Lee and Tony Braxton. All three men have ties with organized crime, and all three men were dealing coal.

Another swindler for whom Herring obtained financing was Akiyoshi Yamada.

Yamada, 38, comes from a respected family of Japanese industrialists. A Harvard Business School alumnus, he was a "whiz-kid" stock broker in the mid-1960s, living in a $165,000 New York penthouse and tended to by a maid and chauffeur. But in 1969, he became a stock swindler.

Since then, Yamada has been enjoined against fraud four times by the Securities and Exchange Commission. A frequent "business" partner of Yamada is Arthur Baradelli, also known as Artie Gambino, cousin of the late New York Mob boss Carlo Gambino.

In 1972, Yamada pleaded guilty to three counts of securities fraud and was sentenced to two years in prison. In an effort to reduce his sentence, Yamada submitted 16 letters to the sentencing judge, all attesting to Yamada's civic-mindedness and good citizenship. The letters, purporting to be from Yamada's friends and associates, were all written by Yamada.

He was charged with mail fraud and obstruction of justice. An additional six months was tacked onto his sentence.

When Yamada got out of jail in 1974, he went into the coal business and began dealing with Robert L. Herring. Herring got Yamada loans from CIT Financial Corp. for Yamada's Southeastern Metallurgical Coal Co. in Alabama.

CIT now has two suits pending against Yamada for alleged failure to repay the loans.

Another associate of Yamada was Robert E. Kizziah, an Alabama coal broker who had business dealings with Alex Gaus and Lester Lee's Hy-Test Coal Co. in Lexington.

Herring's group was active in Kentucky, particularly in the Corbin area. Herring was indicted for theft by deception in 1978 in connection with a piece of equipment sold to a Leslie County coal operator.

When things got hot for Yamada in Alabama, he, too, moved to the Corbin and Barbourville areas. "Yamada was quite active in Kentucky for some time," said James C. Strode, director of the Kentucky Division of Securities.

Perhaps Herring's biggest Kentucky connection was a burly Thomasville, Ga., equipment dealer named James A. Shackelford. Shackelford, 42, ran the giant National Auction Co. in Atlanta, a nationwide dealer in heavy mining equipment. National Auction had a branch office in Corbin. J.R. Durham says he bought most of his equipment from Shackelford.

Today, Shackelford is under indictment in Alabama for grand larceny. He was allegedly involved in many of the fraudulent loans Herring obtained from National Acceptance Corp. Durham says Shackelford was introduced to him as a National Acceptance field representative.

Court records reveal one of Shackelford's closest business associates was attorney Paul Braden of Corbin, a former president of the Whitley County Bar Association.

Braden was vice president and attorney for a shadowy Panamanian company called Petroleum Refining Maritime Corp. (PRMC), a Shackelford firm that boasted worldwide oil and coal holdings, including Liberian and Moroccan oil refineries.

In a $10 million European stock offering dated Oct. 1, 1976, PRMC claimed ownership of both National Auction Co. and its affiliate, Shackelford Equipment Co., two firms PRMC claimed it "recently acquired."

The offering touted the tremendous business potential of Shackelford's companies and pegged their worth at $9.1 million.

Two months later, National Auction Co. and Shackelford Equipment were bankrupt. Their creditors found no trace of the millions PRMC raved about. National Acceptance Corp. filed claims for more than $2 million it lent Shackelford.

A suit filed by one of Shackelford's creditors charges that PRMC—with its Swiss banks—was nothing more than a hiding place for assets Shackelford slipped out of National Auction just before he put it into bankruptcy.

If PRMC was just a shell, though, it put on a good show. Kentucky Gov. Julian Carroll visited PRMC's Swiss offices during his well-publicized trip to Europe in September 1976, to open the Kentucky Department of Public Information office in Brussels, Belgium.

"He discussed PRMC putting up a coal gasification plant in Kentucky," a top state official told *The Kentucky Post*. "The man who set that meeting up was Jim Vernon, who was then head of public information for Carroll. It just so happens that Jim Vernon and Paul Braden are real good friends."

When Vernon, during his 1979 bid for the Democratic nomination for lieutenant governor of Kentucky, was sued for slander by opponent Bill Cox, Braden represented Vernon.

Vernon was the biggest public booster of the Carroll excursion to Europe, claiming it would entice European businesses to locate in Kentucky.

In PRMC's October stock offering—apparently printed just days after the Carroll visit—it was noted that coal gasification plants were being planned for Kentucky and that "preliminary discussions" had already taken place. PRMC proposed using $2 million of the $10 million raised by the stock offering to develop the plant.

The FBI estimates that heavy equipment swindles rake in about $150 million every year. And in Kentucky, state law makes it easy.

According to Durham, the key part of his fraud was that Kentucky has no title registration law which would enable a buyer to trace the ownership of a piece of equipment.

"The guys we sold that stuff to couldn't tell if it was stolen or not. You don't have to register nothing," Durham said.

Kentucky Supreme Court Justice Robert Stephens said Durham's point is well taken.

"There is no doubt in my mind that the problem of stolen equipment in the coal business has been magnified tremendously by the fact that we don't have a title law. We're the only state in the union that doesn't have one," Stephens said. During the coal boom, Stephens was Attorney General and pushed for adoption of such law during his tenure.

"The fact that there might not be enough money to set up a little registration system might be legitimate, but there's no excuse for not getting a bill passed or at least getting a plan developed until the money became available," Stephens said.

Asst. US Atty. Robert Trevey, the man who prosecuted Durham's partners, predicted similar scams will happen as long as Kentucky continues to do without a title registration law.

"I'm not saying it wouldn't happen with such a law, but it would be exceptionally more difficult," Trevey said.

The net effect of heavy equipment fraud is far-reaching. Not only are coal-producing mines made inoperable when equipment disappears, but finance companies—having been burned badly during the last coal boom—are now leery of lending money for coal ventures.

"We're not entirely happy in coal," said Stu Levy, attorney for the victimized National Acceptance Corp. "Now, we're very particular about who we lend to, and we check them out very carefully."

Durham laughed when he thought about the beating firms like National Acceptance took.

"The finance companies, they've been very well educated in Kentucky—the *hard* way," he chuckled.

PART 15: SWINDLERS HIDE IN TAX SHELTERS, AMBUSH UNCLE SAM
JUNE 17, 1980

Uncle Sam didn't intend to become the biggest dupe of the coal swindlers, but that's the way it turned out.

The Arab oil embargo of 1973 touched off an energy panic. In the midst of it, Congress rediscovered coal.

To lure private investors to the often-risky coal business, big tax breaks were offered. The idea was to give the coal industry a boost and to make America less dependent on foreign oil.

It was a fiasco.

Millions of dollars supposedly destined for American coal fields wound up in foreign bank accounts or bought gas-guzzling jets and luxury cars, for the coal swindlers.

The scheme centered on coal tax shelters. A tax shelter is usually an investment in a highly speculative venture—cattle-farming, movie-making or recording—businesses that require huge amounts of start-up money and often produce little in return for many years.

To make those kind of ventures attractive to high income investors, the government would allow big tax write offs.

The Tax Reform Act of 1976 closed the door on many favorite tax shelters, but coal ventures were left wide-open—on purpose. Lawmakers figured if wealthy taxpayers wanted to gamble on any industry, it should be coal. And the swindlers noticed.

Bushwhacking through the thicket of state and federal securities laws, they perfected a clever new fraud: the limited partnership coal scam.

A promoter with a piece of coal property would find up to 35 high-income investors. Each investor would buy a partnership "unit" costing, for example, $50,000. A $50,000 unit could be bought from the promoter for $10,000 in cash and a note for the remaining $40,000.

The notes were like IOUs. The investor would use his share of the profits from the coal venture to pay off the note. In addition, the notes usually contained a "no-recourse" clause. That meant the investor would not be billed or sued if the profits were insufficient to pay off the notes and the debts of the partnership.

The profits were always insufficient.

Making a profit would have been stupid because the IRS was allowing the investor to reduce his taxes by more than he actually spent

"They were just buying tax deductions," said Alabama Securities Commissioner Tom Krebs.

This worked well for high-income coal shelter investors, many of whom were physicians. The typical "Dr. Investor" in a 50 percent tax bracket got to subtract both the $10,000 cash investment and the $40,000 IOU right off the top of his income.

If $50,000 of Dr. Investor's regular income was "sheltered" in his coal mine, it escaped the 50 per cent tax bite, and he paid $25,000 less in taxes. Subtract his initial $10,000 cash investment, and Dr. Investor was $15,000 ahead.

"A man would be a fool not to take $25,000 for $10,000," Krebs said ruefully.

And what of the promoters? Their take was even bigger. If they rounded up 35 investors, their immediate income was $350,000. No questions asked.

Even before the coal tax shelters mushroomed, securities investigators saw them as a con man's paradise.

A 1977 police intelligence report stated: "Everybody makes money up front except for the investor who pays for it all. The potential for fraud and abuse should be obvious."

It was—to the coal swindlers. As an analysis written two years later by securities investigators observed: "Large profits coupled with easy and unregistered capital acquisition proved to be a lure for the organized crime connected swindler and con man."

Krebs said he and Kentucky Securities Director James Strode have examined roughly 750 limited partnership coal tax shelters since they began appearing in 1976.

How many of them were legitimate?

"Zilch," Krebs said. "None."

Said Indiana Securities Commissioner Stephen Coons: "Of the 30 or 35 I've seen that were registered in Indiana, there was something wrong with each one of them."

Krebs has refused to allow single coal shelter to be sold in Alabama. "They're a fraud. That's all they are. They're garbage. I'm not going to have them in Alabama," he said.

One of the biggest tax shelter frauds involved Aminex Resources Corp. It was based in Kentucky, but its investors came from across the nation. The deal began hatching in mid-1976 in a suite of offices on New York City's Park Avenue, home of Aminex.

Aminex was a relatively unknown public corporation at that time, but its officers and directors were impressive enough.

They included Robert Salisbury, a former economic consultant to the US State Department, Walter S. Mack, former president of Pepsi-Cola, Morgan Cramer, Jr., former chairman of Royal Crown Cola, and Andrew Lynn, former president of Yardley's of London, a huge cosmetics firm.

Walter Mack, though, had a business background that didn't appear on Aminex's promotional literature. In 1966 he and another man were charged by the Securities and Exchange Commission with filing false reports and violations of anti-fraud laws.

Mack's co-defendant was 60-year-old Jerome Matusow. According to a confidential police intelligence report "Matusow is known to have organized crime connections and has been linked to deals involving the Hazel Park Race Track (in Michigan) and the Detroit Mafia, stolen securities and business deals linked to Meyer Lansky."

Lansky is widely regarded as the financial genius behind the American crime syndicate.

The report continued: "Matusow is also reported to be, personal friends with Alexander (Sandy) Guterma and has been involved in deals with him in the past. Guterma has been involved in securities fraud activities for the past 20 years."

Despite Matusow's questionable background, he was made Aminex's president and chairman of the executive committee in June 1976. In exchange for Matusow's promise to locate coal mines to buy, Aminex gave him 53 percent of its stock.

Matusow worked quietly for four months, approaching owners of various coal companies in Kentucky and offering to buy them out. One of the first approached was Upper Elkhorn Coal Co., a relatively small operation in Thornton, Ky.

"He flew in in a Lear jet and told us he represented a company with a lot of money to invest in coal," said Marshall Clubb, Upper Elkhorn's owner.

Clubb was looking to unload the company. The summer before, Clubb's partner, Bill Harvey Johnson, was cut down in an ambush-style murder. The murder remains unsolved.

"Matusow looked at our financials and told us our cash flow wasn't big enough," Clubb said. But whatever it was, it was certainly bigger than Aminex's.

At that time, Aminex was barely alive as a corporation. In March, 1976, Aminex told the SEC it was doing so poorly that it was suspending salaries, cutting back on its phone use and doing is own tax returns "to maintain corporate survival."

But that was before the arrival of financial faith-healer Jerome Matusow. Matusow laid hands upon Aminex, and in a matter of months, it miraculously went from a total money-loser to a $90 million paper giant.

Matusow hooked up with a disbarred Manchester, Ky., attorney named Letcher T. White, a close associate of Peter Francis Crosby, the man who sold the North Pole.

Together, Matusow and White scouted sellers, flashing Aminex' paper assets.

On Oct. 12, 1976, Aminex bought six coal companies from Hazard, Ky., millionaire Andrew Adams. Aminex promised Adams $29 million, took over his coal operations and set up syndicated limited partnerships to raise the money to pay for the coal mines.

In all, they put together 15 limited partnerships.

Aminex raised $8.5 million in cash in three months, going from nothing to the third largest coal mining operation in eastern Kentucky. It owned 13 coal companies, 212 million tons of coal reserves and employed 300 miners, 250 truck drivers and 50 office workers.

That kind of activity couldn't escape notice, and the Securities and Exchange Commission started snooping. When it found out Matusow was involved, it launched a full-scale investigation.

In March 1978, the SEC accused Matusow and a New Yorker named Irwin Hyman of looting $1.24 million from the company, filing false and misleading financial reports, demanding kick-backs from brokers and falsifying Aminex's books.

Matusow, who was then living in Lexington, and Hyman pleaded guilty to wire fraud, filing false statements and interstate transportation of stolen property earlier this year. Hyman got three years in jail, Matusow got 30 months.

Aminex is now in bankruptcy, and Andrew Adams has sued to get back his mines.

The SEC turned to Letch White next. It accused him of falsely notarizing and forging signatures on the limited partnership documents. He pleaded guilty in February to wire fraud. On April 11, White was sentenced to 18 months in prison. He was already serving time for tax fraud.

According to Kentucky securities chief Strode, Aminex was unusual. "They were actually mining some coal. Most of these limited partnerships never mine anything," Strode said.Consider, for example, the SJ Minerals syndications in Boston. The SJ promoters raised $20,118,580 from at least 800 investors—including rock star Alice Cooper, starlet Margaux Hemingway, basketball pro Julius Erving and TV personality Allen Funt—to mine 11,000 acres of Wyoming land.

What the investors didn't know was that the mineral rights to 10,600 of those acres belonged to the federal government.

The SEC, in a civil fraud suit, is charging that most of the money went into the pockets of the promoters. And investigators say that at least three of SJ's principals "have been linked to land fraud deals in New England involving the Raymond Patriarcha La Cosa Nostra family."

The man who "sold" SJ the land was the same Huntington Beach, Calif., real estate broker who "sold" Peter Francis Crosby land for his Picture Island Computer swindle: Grant Kime. In the Picture Island swindle, the land was on an Army artillery range.

White-collar crime investigators found many of the same swindlers who worked stock frauds in the 1960s putting together limited partnerships in coal in the 1970s.

Alexander Guterma, Matusow's friend who bilked millions from public corporations in the early 1960s, put together several Kentucky limited partnerships shortly before his death in a plane crash in 1977. Strode said there "are millions unaccounted for in those."

Guterma's partner in those six tax shelters was accused of fraud by the SEC in April.

Guterma used the same law firm, the same corporate shell and the same mining consultant in his tax shelters that Jerome Matusow used in the Aminex swindle.

Peter Crosby also created a tax shelter, Maplewood Associates. Maplewood's corporate shell was located in the same Park Avenue office as Matusow's and Guterma's.

One of Guterma's officers, a New York accountant with a long history of fraud convictions, was Sinclair Robinson. Peter Crosby told *The Kentucky Post* he and Robinson had coal dealings together in Alabama.

Guterma and Matusow also used the same coal leases on occasion. Those leases were owned by two close associates of Scripture-quoting con man Alexander Gaus Jr., of Arlington Heights, Ill. One of those men, Dane Rowlette, had been the late Bill Harvey Johnson's contract miner.

Gaus is now under indictment in Indiana for fraud in connection with a limited partnership he sold there. He is alleged to have defrauded 40 investors of $250,000. Newport felon and suspected hit man Lester Lee's coal partner, gun runner Dominick Bartone of Cleveland, was named in a suit filed by the SEC in 1978. The SEC charged Bartone had siphoned $600,000 from a limited partnership he and another gun runner were operating in West Virginia. The millions drained from these tax shelters go to finance traditional organized crime activities like gun running, prostitution and narcotics trafficking, according to investigators.

Money from a Florida limited partnership went to make bail for a man caught smuggling marijuana into the country. That shelter was promoted by swindler Harold Audsley, who also worked with Peter Crosby in the Picture Island swindle.

Aminex put up bail and legal expenses for an Aminex employee who machine-gunned a union organizer to death in 1977.

And while Dominick Bartone was running his tax shelter, he was arrested for trying to smuggle machine guns to Cuba.

Despite the fact that state securities offices have identified at least 750 limited partnerships they believe to be crooked, prosecutions have been few.

Part of the problem is that investors who are swindled are reluctant to complain.

If a coal tax shelter is simply a sham without any real chance of making money, the IRS will disallow the investor's tax deductions. Investors risk losing not only their initial cash investment but all their tax write-offs if a tax shelter fraud is discovered.

With those ground rules, an investor won't complain if a promoter simply steals his money. "Actually, they're kind of sitting at home hoping we never come knocking at their door," Krebs said.

Indiana Securities Commissioner Coons said many investors are hostile to state investigators.

"Out of 38 or 40 people we interviewed in one partnership deal, the investors were uncooperative. They thought we were meddling in their business, and they couldn't see anything wrong. If they wanted to lose the money, that was their business," Coons said.

"Now I'll tell you something. When the IRS disallows their deductions—and right now they're auditing hundreds of returns with coal shelters in them—those same guys will be down here screaming, 'Why didn't you protect us!'" Coons said.

Another obstacle in the way of prosecution is the fact that investors in a single partnership can be scattered across the country.

"It's a totally diffused operation, and there's a reason for that," Coons said. "If you're going to have an effective prosecution, you've got to have all your players in one jurisdiction, not scattered in seven states. There's been a lot of thought involved in putting your accountant here, your promoter there and your attorney over here."

Congress' grand idea has proven to be a horrible mistake. It's been a field day for the swindlers. The profits are huge. The chances of being caught and convicted are slight.

Even if the swindlers are convicted, the penalties are minimal. To date, only three people have faced criminal charges in connection with coal tax shelters. The longest sentence has been three years.

According to Jim Strode, the result has been exactly the opposite of what Congress intended.

"Coal shelters have diverted millions and millions of dollars from legitimate Kentucky coal businesses, money that would have resulted in economic development," Strode said.

The estimated cash investment in these shelters is $750 million. The biggest loser is the US government.

"You figure the average tax write-off is five to one (five dollars written off for every one dollar actually invested), multiply $750 million times five and see what you come up with," Tom Krebs said.

It totals $3.8 billion in write-offs for rich investors. Figuring the investors were in the 50 percent tax bracket, that works out to an actual cash loss to the US Treasury of $1.9 billion.

To cut its losses, the IRS outlawed the use of the no-recourse notes and will now only allow deductions of money actually risked. But that hardly slowed down the coal swindlers.

"What they've come up with now are 60-year recourse notes that don't have to be repaid until 2040 or some such nonsense," Krebs said sourly. "It's still a fraud, and our duty is clear. We've got to stop it."

PART 16: MOB UNCOVERS RICH SEAM OF OPPORTUNITY IN COAL
JUNE 18, 1980

The mobsters and swindlers move around the Kentucky coalfields as if they own them. Many times, they do.

But during the coal boom of the mid-1970s, the industry was a whole new world to the Mob. And most coal operators had never heard of the mobsters who were moving into the coal fields.

To Stonewall Jackson Barker Jr., president of the sprawling Island Creek Coal Co., Dominick Bartone was a gruff-talking owner of an Ohio Cement company with $50 million to spend on mines.

To the Justice Department, Bartone was a convicted gun runner and a reputed Cleveland organized crime figure. The IRS knew Bartone as a tax-fraud artist.

Lester Clifford Lee represented himself to Ronald Reagan and Ohio State Sen. Donald E. Lukens as a serious businessman with a successful Lexington coal brokerage and an interest in Republican politics. To the FBI, Lee was "a hired gun" and "a notorious east Tennessee hoodlum."

Saul Siegel looked like a wealthy jetsetter and a multilingual financier to many in the coal business. To the New Orleans police department, Siegel was a bankruptcy fraud specialist and "a close associate of Carlos Marcello, Mr. Organized Crime himself."

The late Eddie H. Hammonds was a Louisiana banker to those who didn't know better. The Kentucky State Police knew him as "a former chief lieutenant for Meyer Lansky," the reputed brain's behind the American Mafia's finances.

Alexander Gaus Jr. had a reputation as a financier and a devout Christian evangelist. Gaus had a reputation with the Kentucky State Police as "a convicted swindler identified as being in the upper strata of the loan shark racket in Chicago."

Coal even brought the reclusive Lansky out of hiding. He was seen in West Virginia hobnobbing with two coal brokers, one of whom was in the process of executing the huge Aminex swindle.

Lansky also popped up at several Kentucky airports, according to one of Kentucky's chief law enforcement officials.

"When I found out Lansky had been here, my immediate reaction was: 'What's that SOB doing here?' He isn't here for his health or the scenery," he said.

According to Tom Krebs, an outspoken Alabama Securities Commissioner who's studied the problem for three years: "The nation has never seen the equal of this present conspiracy."

In some circles, Krebs is regarded as an alarmist, a man who sees gangsters under every lump of coal. Indiana Securities Coal Commissioner Stephen Coons said he, too, knows the feelings of not being believed.

"People say I'm out on a wild goose chase, hunting ghosts. I can assure you that people who threatened my life were not ghosts," Coons said.

When Coons and his staff began looking into organized crime coal connections, the reaction was swift.

Coons said two men tried to run over his eight-year old daughter on her way to school one morning. And there were phone calls.

"I started getting death threats as soon as it became known I was looking into coal frauds. During the worst of it, we got 55 phone calls in an hour and a half," Coons said.

Kentucky Post reporters Gary Webb and Tom Scheffey also got threatening phone calls during the course of this investigation. One 3 a.m. caller told Webb: "Don't park your car where you can't see it."

Eight coal related murders have occurred since Mob infiltration began in 1973. Three of those men had done business with Dominick Bartone.

The coal crooks moved quietly in the industry, buying coal mines, leases and contracts. They used front men whose names attracted little attention in law enforcement offices.

Bartone, for example, used a Springfield, Ohio, mortgage broker named Harold R. Fetter, a distinguished-looking man with a minor criminal record: seven arrests for check fraud and larceny, no convictions.

Alex Gaus—whose name is like the plague in the world of banking and finance—used a McKinney, Tex., man named John Kronquist in his coal dealings. Kronquist had a lengthy criminal record, but it wasn't nearly as flamboyant as Gaus'. While Gaus worked national fraud schemes, Kronquist confined himself to stealing cars or passing bad checks.

The mere mention of fraud king Alexander Guterma's name made Wall Street brokers shiver, so Guterma bought coal property through Louisville shopping center magnate John W. Waits, a man who wowed potential investigators with chatty phone calls to then-Gov. Julian Carroll. (Law enforcement sources say Waits, now living in Atlanta, has an an interest in the adult bookstore at 721 Monmouth St., Newport, where Lester Lee was killed.)

One theory why organized crime figures are attracted to the coal business is that coal operators deal in huge amounts of money, and money made from numbers running, prostitution and narcotics trafficking can be easily laundered in coal.

Barbourville attorney Beecher Rowlette, who said he made and lost hundreds of thousands of dollars in coal, said he ran into "these hoods and hooligans from New York and Detroit and St. Louis coming down here and laundering money in the coal business."

Rowlette, 29, said he went to Dallas, Tex., to obtain financing for a coal venture and found a man willing to invest $8 million up front and $12 million later.

"Come to find out, all I was going to be doing was laundering money, and then I found out where this money was coming from," Rowlette said.

When pressed for details, Rowlette chuckled. "What are you trying to do, get me to wind up in a lake with a cement overcoat?"

In Alabama, a coal miner slow in paying his equipment parts bill to the huge Herco equipment company got a phone call from Akiyoshi Yamada, a convicted swindler and a business associate of Herco's owner, Robert L. Herring of Albany, Ga.

According to an Alabama police report, Yamada reportedly told the coal miner to come up with the money he owed, "or Herring will have you taken care of. Don't you know Herring is financed by the Mafia in the Bahamas, and he will have you killed?" Yamada is quoted as saying.

There is no evidence to support a Herring-Mafia link, but it is known that Herring worked closely with fugitive financier Robert Vesco, now hiding in the Bahamas from fraud and illegal campaign contribution indictments. Herring has since been convicted of fraud and racketeering.

One man who was killed after extensive dealings with both Herring and Yamada was David Hill of Swainsboro, Ga. Hill's bullet-riddled body was found in an abandoned Virginia strip mine in December, 1977, two weeks before Lester Lee was murdered.

Shortly before his death, Hill had made plans to buy a coal company from Yamada, a former stockbroker with a history of securities fraud violations. Yamada's partner in several deals was Artie Gambino, cousin of the late New York Mob lord Carlo Gambino.

Several coal deals can be traced back to the organized crime families run by Gambino and New Orleans' Carlos Marcello. Marcello was indicted Tuesday on charges of racketeering, conspiracy, mail fraud and wire fraud for allegedly trying to influence the award of state insurance contracts.

One Marcello family member, convicted swindler Saul Siegel, owned a coal company in Harlan, Ky., and was quite active in the area. Marcello's close friend and personal banker, Louis J. Roussel, was also looking for coal properties in Kentucky.

Roussel, on the letterhead of Citrus Lands of Louisiana, Inc., wrote to Newport, Ky., energy broker Paul Linnenbrink on Feb. 28, 1975, requesting information about any coal properties Linnenbrink might have for sale.

Court records in Alabama said of Roussel: "Roussel's public record establishes a habitual disdain and contempt for law . . . he has testified falsely under oath, violated federal securities laws, violated federal banking laws."

In his letter to Linnenbrink, Roussel used the National American Bank in New Orleans as a reference. The Securities and Exchange Commission charged Roussel took over that bank illegally.

Another Marcello family associate, con man Tony Braxton, was involved in a Louisville company called Durgango Coal and Leasing. Braxton is believed by Kentucky authorities to own Appalachian Coal and Energy, Inc., in Jenkins, Ky.

But the involvement of the Angelo Bruno family in South Philadelphia is particularly direct.

On Feb. 8, 1979, agents of the Drug Enforcement Agency and the FBI raided the Bahia Mar Marina in Ft. Lauderdale, Fla.

They seized a 40ft. cabin cruiser named the *Danny Boy III,* a 1979 Buick, and broke into a nearby motel room where a drug deal was taking place.

The *Danny Boy III,* from which agents recovered cocaine and quaaludes, was registered to Bally Coal Co., a Kentucky mining operation in West Liberty. The Buick also belonged to Bally Coal Co., and Bally had rented the motel room.

One of the nine people arrested in connection with the drugs was a Pennsauken, N.J., labor leader named Ralph Natale. Natale's bodyguard, Frank J. Vadino of Turnersville, N.J., was also during arrested during the raid. At a bond hearing in the federal court in Miami, Vadino said he had been employed by Bally Coal Co.

Agents had been tipped to the drug deal by a confessed Mafia hit man named Charles Allen, who told the FBI he'd done contract killings and arson for Natale in the past.

Allen was nabbed on drug charges and agreed to go undercover for the FBI. Wired for sound, he and Natale discussed the sale of two shoeboxes full of quaaludes.

According to court records, Natale set up the meeting on Bally Coal Co.'s boat so Allen could introduce drug buyers to Natale's sources. The drugs were dispensed from the back of Bally's Buick and taken to Bally's motel room.

Court record state Natale is an upper echelon member of the Bruno crime family. In one taped conversation, Natale asked Allen to buy 10 automatic pistols to fit silencers the Bruno family had acquired because they feared "a gang war brewing between two factions of the Angelo Bruno family."

That gang war may have come to a head. "Don Angelo" Bruno, 69, was gunned down outside his South Philadelphia home March 21.

The exact connection between the Bruno family and Bally Coal Co. is obscure. It is known though, that Bally's president, Joseph C. Ripp of Broomall, Pa., and Ralph Natale are close friends.

The Kentucky Post called Natale's home in New Jersey and spoke to his 27-year old son Frank. Frank Natale was asked if his father had been involved in the coal business.

"A friend of his was, they were close friends. A Mr. Ripp," Natale said. Natale was asked if Ripp's first name was Joseph.

"Yes! I met Mr. Ripp once or twice," Natale said.

Ripp has not been charged with any crime relating to the drug bust, but according to a federal prosecutor in Miami, "He's awful close."

Two weeks before Ralph Natale was arrested for possession with intent to distribute narcotics, he was sentenced to 12 years in prison of arson, mail fraud, conspiracy and racketeering. At the time of his arrest, Natale listed his employer as John's Vending Co., the same firm Angelo Bruno said he worked for. John's Vending is owned by top Philadelphia mobster Raymond "Long John" Mortarano.

Natale, former head of the Jersey City Bartenders Union, mentioned coal in one of his recorded conversations with Charles Allen.

After speaking to someone on the phone about "contracting," Natale hung up and turned to Allen. "Kentucky," he whispered. "The mine's down there."

Ripp and Bally Coal Co. are also in trouble in Florida, where they were selling interests in a limited partnership based in Kentucky. The Florida Department of Banking and Finance enjoined Bally from selling partnerships in Florida because they were not registered with the state. Bally raised $420,000 from investors in one month.

And *The Kentucky Post* learned Ripp and his partner in Bally, former Delaware County (Pa.) commissioner Edward T. McErlean, are under investigation in Kentucky for alleged strip mining and state securities laws violations. Both men have been subpoenaed by the Kentucky Division of Securities.

According to documents from several securities commissions, Bally is just one in a string of coal companies run by Ripp, 37, and McErlean, 46.

The name of one company, Arthur Coal Co., turned up in investigator letters sent out by Century Coal Enterprises, a Peoria, Ill., limited partnership.

In a letter dated Sept., 5, 1978, Century Coal president David Van Dyke, an Illinois nursing home operator, told investors he was shutting down the mine in Grayson, Ky., because Century was not being paid by its customers. One of those customers was Arthur Coal Co.

"We entered into a contract with Arthur Coal Co., who professed a need for our coal to fill their orders. They were to pay us on Monday. They didn't, even though we had a clear written contract. Instead, they offered to 'help' us further by taking over our mine completely. If we didn't (agree) we would be shot, our legs would be broken, our office machine-gunned and my home fire-bombed," Van Dyke wrote.

Neither Ripp nor McErlean could be reached for comment. According to Kentucky officials, Bally and Arthur Coal Co's. recently reorganized and are now going by the name Arthur Group Leasing Inc.

Century said it was also having payment problems with Phoenix Fuels, an Ohio corporation run by Dominick Bartone's front man, Harold Fetter.

Fetter said Century "stole my coal" but refused further comment. Fetter also had contracts with a Hamilton, Ohio, firm called CB Coal Co. Phone records show 21 phone calls from Bally Coal Co. to CB Coal Co. in the fall of 1978. Fetter refused to comment on CB Coal Co., other than to say he "did some contract work for them."

There is also evidence the scandal-ridden Teamsters Union pension fund is being used to finance questionable coal ventures.

The Kentucky Post obtained transcripts of telephone conversations of an

Orlando, Fla., coal broker and small time con man named James Vincent Suarez. Suarez, 54, owned a company called Executive Mining Co. with a Charlotte, N.C., man named Parks Brantley. The following is from a conversation between Brantley and Suarez:

"Suarez: Yeah, but I got more news. I got a $5 million Teamsters standby loan! (giggles)

"Brantley: What are you drinking?

"Suarez: Nothing.

"Brantley: A $5 million standby loan?

"Suarez: What it amounts to is this. Bill is going to Luna Monday morning. Bill is going to tell them each (coal) washer is going to run $350,000 to $365,000 each. He is going to tell the greedy one he can have $15,000 off the top. Then what they do is go to a Teamsters bank and tell them that these people have been approved for the union for blah blah money and you are going to lend them the money, see."

"Luna" may be Donald E. Luna, who, according to a police intelligence report, "is connected to organized crime-controlled banks in Texas, Alabama authorities have reason to believe that much of the coal-related activity by organized crime figures is closely connected to Luna."

According to New Jersey federal court records, many of Ralph Natale's associates are former Teamsters bosses.

Those records state Natale has been partners-in-crime with Frank (Big Irish) Sheeran—recently acquitted of racketeering charges—and Louis (Buttons) Buttone. Buttone is former president of Teamsters Local 107 in Philadelphia and Sheeran is president of Local 326 in Wilmington, Del.

Hit man Charles Allen admitted killing one man in 1976, "at the direction of Frank Sheeran and Louis Buttone."

Allen also admitted to plotting with vanished Teamsters boss Jimmy Hoffa to murder AFL-CIO president Frank Fritzsimmons.

Hoffa's name came up several times during this investigation by *The Kentucky Post*.

Lester C. Lee, the convicted felon and suspected hit man who was once president of Hy-Test Coal Co. of Kentucky, Inc., told associates he had been a former Teamsters organizer and had been Hoffa's personal bodyguard.

Lee said he'd almost been killed by a dynamite bomb once while protecting Hoffa. Lee' claims could not be independently verified.

A month after Hoffa disappeared in July, 1975, Lee told Ohio State Sen.

Donald (Buz) Lukens, "Hoffa ain't dead. He's down in South America. Nobody's got Jimmy Hoffa."

"He seemed to know what he was talking about," Lukens said, adding Lee told him he had been a Teamsters organizer.

Cleveland mobster Dominick Bartone also has several Teamsters connections. Bartone was a close friend of murdered Teamsters leader John Nardi of Cleveland, who was blown up in 1977. One source stated Nardi and Bartone had plotted to run millions of tons of coal through the United Mine Workers strike in 1974.

Bartone also told people he and Hoffa were personal friends and had met while in prison together.

According to Bartone associate Harold Fetter, Bartone and Lester Lee met through mutual friends in the Teamsters Union. "Lee was heavily involved in the Teamsters Union at one time," Fetter said. Lee was also heavily involved with Bartone in coal.

The extent of Mafia control of the coal industry is something at which organized crime investigators can only guess. One thing is clear: there is definitely a presence lurking in the coal fields of Kentucky and surrounding states.

Said one former state policeman turned coal broker, "Don't let anyone tell you that Mafia stuff ain't for real. It damned sure is. They were coming out of the woodwork."

Even the garrulous Jim Suarez admitted as much, though reluctantly. In a conversation with a man identified only as Shannon, Suarez said, "Well, look. You and I understand each other but Pete, (unidentified) he starts with this Mafia crap and he's going to get hurt, he's nuts."

Replied Shannon: "Well, I don't ever talk about that, you know that. I might get drunk every once in a while, but I don't ever talk about the Mafia."

"Pitch for coal partnership: 'This is a real carrot'"

Of all the amazing deals of the coal boom, few could have topped the one offered in 1978 by Beecher Rowlette, then a student at Chase Law School.

For just $80,000, a limited partner in Rowlette's Hermitage Mining Co. would get "ownership of 872,500 tons of COAL!" the offering letter proclaimed, adding, "Your net profit, as you know, is $7,844,314."

An ad in the *Wall Street Journal* referred people to Rowlette's investor-finder

Virgil Bader of Matoon, Ill. Bader had a twenty-five-page packet of information about Rowlette and his coal. It contained maps, engineering reports, profit projections, and answers to such questions as "What is a tipple?"

The packet also gave answers to the question: who is Beecher Rowlette?

A brief biography told of Rowlette's astounding rags-to-riches story, tracing his meteoric rise from a coal conveyor belt mucker to a mine operator.

Rowlette wanted to work for himself. According to the offering, Rowlette struck out in two-and-a-half feet of snow with a borrowed tractor, a logging chain, a pickax, and a wheelbarrow and found a coal seam in December, 1977.

Rowlette's account concluded: "As of August 24, 1978, Simon Fork Coal Co. was running 1000 tons of coal a day."

After two years at Chase College of Law, Rowlette—who said he drove to Covington with his belongings in the back of a battered pickup truck— seemed to strike it rich.

In the spring of 1978, he and his wife Gloria and their four-year-old daughter Rebecca moved from a $200-a-month apartment at 2236 Hanser Dr., Covington, to a $200,000 Edgewood home at 3105 Hudnall Drive. Rowlette got four Cadillacs from Rockcastle Motors.

"A lot of people seemed to be under the impression I was worth a whole lot more than I really was," Rowlette, 29, said in a recent interview.

That impression was helped along by a two-page signed financial statement Rowlette included with the maps, studies, and other data in the Hermitage Mining investment packet. That statement claimed Beecher Rowlette was worth $85.6 million.

Under "Real Estate Owned," he listed River Hills Golf Course and valued it at $1.18 million. The 300-acre, 18-hole golf course in southern Campbell County was never Rowlette's "in the sense of deeds changing hands," he explained, but he said he had "an equitable interest" in the property while he was negotiating to buy it with other investors.

The deal fell through. The value of River Hills was not included as an asset on the statement. He did, however, list a $333,333 asset for his $10-a-share holdings of Blackacre Coal Co. Asked what a share of Blackacre would sell for today, Rowlette replied, "Zip."

"Blackacre's my child. It's my darlin' and it's in trouble now," Rowlette said, adding that he's holding onto it until the next boom, which he predicts in late 1981.

The coal reserves of Simon Fork are listed as assets worth $22.9 million. Blackacre's are valued at $42 million. "It may be good accounting principles, but it doesn't mean much. I've learned the only money that counts is what's in your pocket or in the bank," Rowlette explained.

Rowlette, in his financial statement, claimed he had an annual income of $1.3 million, but when it came time to tell the IRS what he earned, it was considerably less. In the past two years, Rowlette's income has totaled less than $45,000, he acknowledged.

His highest net worth, not in paper projections but "in dollar dollars," as he put it, was $200,000, "and that was only for a short time," he said. He said he's declared bankruptcy twice since then and is ignoring advice to do so a third time.

Rowlette said he does not know if any shares in Hermitage Mining were sold. There was a problem with the land the partnership laid claim to. It belonged to someone who never leased it to Rowlette.

Rowlette said he's still scouting coal, investors, and contracts and that he still gets investors through Virgil Bader. Bader claims to be a lay Methodist minister with a PhD in psychology and an MD in metaphysics, both from a mail order college in Indianapolis.

Rowlette described Bader as "likable" but "a little bewildered" and said he's had to turn back twenty investors sent to him by Bader this year alone.

Rowlette said he is annoyed when people come to him looking to invest money they've merely borrowed.

Bader did not get that message across in the Hermitage offer. Scrawled across the front page was the following message:

"This is a real carrot! Your banker will gladly loan you $150,000 when he sees the track record that will assure him a six-month payback! From then on, you have a free ride."

Rowlette said he found three Ohio investors last year who put up a total of $75,000. A rail strike and other difficulties caused that venture to close down. "I'm hanging in there until 1981. In my opinion, coal is the nearest thing to a sure thing we'll see in the 1980s," he said.

He predicted Blackacre would become "the Texaco of the coal industry."

But Rowlette is not going to be held down. Even if coal does not make him rich, he has other ideas.

He's toying with the possibility of running small Oklahoma banks or even taking off to Sri Lanka to become an export trader in tea and exotic woods.

PART 17: A COAL BOOM IS BUILDING, AND SWINDLERS ARE READY
JUNE 19, 1980

The signs are all around us. Coal is getting ready to take off again.

Coal is being touted as the panacea for energy-hungry America, and the government is cranking up programs to spur its use.

President Carter's energy policy calls for doubling coal production from the 1976 level of 665 million tons to more than 1 billion tons a year by 1985.

Congressional conferees this week approved a plan to provide $20 billion over the next five years to subsidize plants to produce synthetic fuels from coal and oil shale.

"That means roughly $40 billion because it's a 50-50 spread between the government and private industry," Sen. Wendell Ford, D-Ky., said.

Another bill pending in the Senate would provide up to $3.6 billion to promote conversion of oil-fired electric power generators to coal-fired.

And the coal export business "is probably going to double in the next few years," Sen. Ford said.

According to a new study by the Massachusetts Institute of Technology, *Coal— Bridge to the Future*, coal is the only fuel left to power the economies of the world.

"Even with the most optimistic forecasts for the expansion of nuclear power and the aggressive development of all other energy sources, as well as vigorous conservation, it is clear that coal has a vitally important part to play in the world's energy future," the report stated.

"Coal will have to supply between one-half to two-thirds of the additional energy needed during the next twenty years," the study concluded.

"We've got to have coal to preserve the security of this country," Sen. Ford said.

The growing demand for coal is likely to bring another "coal rush"— and golden opportunities for the swindlers. Although billions are earmarked for the coal industry, only a pittance is budgeted to fight coal crime.

For three years, coal-producing states clamored for federal help to curb the invasion of con men and mobsters. They were ignored.

Alabama Securities Commissioner Tom Krebs wrote a memo to the Justice Department in 1977, pleading for a federal Law Enforcement Assistance Administration grant to set up a federal and multi-state coal crime task force.

Krebs warned: "The risk of harm is so great that we cannot afford to gamble we are wrong. The question now is whether the Justice Department is willing to gamble we are wrong."

The Justice Department took the gamble, and the swindlers plundered the coal industry virtually unmolested. But the Justice Department wasn't the only federal agency to shrug off the threat of organized crime in the coal industry.

In May, 1976, officials of the Internal Revenue Service and the Securities and Exchange Commission met in Louisville with representatives of Kentucky, Florida, Georgia, Illinois, Alabama, Arkansas, Pennsylvania, and California. The states complained about the torrent of coal frauds and their inability to fight them on a state level because of budgetary and jurisdictional limitations.

"They didn't believe what we were telling them," said James Strode, director of the Kentucky Division of Securities. "They suggested we go out and make some cases to prove what we were saying."

They did.

The Alabama Securities Commission nailed coal broker Robert E. Kizziah for forging analysis reports on a huge foreign coal contract. Using information provided by the states, the Justice Department convicted Robert L. Herring, owner of Herco equipment company in Albany, Ga., of fraud and racketeering.

But Krebs said the job wasn't made any easier by the FBI.

"It appeared at times that the Louisville office of the FBI has hindered rather than assisted Kentucky authorities," Krebs charged in a memo to the Justice Department.

Krebs accused the FBI of nearly bungling the Herring investigation by interviewing Herring shortly after one of his employees was arrested by the Kentucky State Police for transporting equipment with altered serial numbers.

"Kentucky specifically requested Herring not be interviewed because Georgia (authorities) had obtained a court-ordered wire-tap for Herco. Within the week, FBI officials interviewed Herring. The phone conversation thereafter became so guarded as to be valueless to Georgia investigators," Krebs wrote.

Louisville FBI spokesman Phil Doty, in early May, told *The Kentucky Post* the charge was "an utter falsehood." Doty promised to rebut it "with some hard evidence." He never called back.

Despite the Herring and Kizziah cases, "help was not forthcoming," Strode said. Meanwhile, the multi-million-dollar LEAA grant Krebs had requested bogged down.

Strode and Jack Bunnel, then Kentucky securities chief, enlisted the aid of Kentucky Attorney General Robert Stephens. Stephens, now a justice of the Kentucky Supreme Court, said he went to Washington, DC alone "to raise a little cain."

Stephens said he was alarmed by what Strode and Bunnel showed him regarding organized crime activity in Kentucky. Stephens said he became convinced "the federal government was sitting on this thing and not recognizing the gravity and the dimensions of the situation."

Stephens said he was unsure his trip to Washington had any effect.

"The Justice Department was totally uncooperative in seeing the grant was expedited. Other federal agencies were not cooperating or were stopping it.," Stephens said.

The IRS and Justice felt that the states weren't capable or didn't have the resources or were impinging on their territory," Stephens said.

But Indiana Securities Commissioner Stephen Coons offered a different reason the LEAA grant was being stalled.

"The Justice Department tried like hell to get that grant scrapped because if it went through, it would be a great embarrassment to them. People would ask why the states were having to get this money and do the job themselves when, essentially, it was a federal problem," Coons said.

Finally, after three years of pleading and cajoling, the LEAA loosened its pursestrings last February and dribbled out $2 million.

That money is to be divided among Indiana, Alabama, Georgia, New York, Pennsylvania, Virginia, and Kentucky. Kentucky's share: $125,000.

The project is code-named Leviticus, after the third book of the Old Testament. It is to provide money for the states to hire more investigators to go after the coal racketeers.

But the money runs out next year, and there are no guarantees Leviticus will be refinanced.

One set of Leviticus indictments has already been handed down. Four people were indicted in March for a $3 million tax shelter fraud. One of them, miner Ernie Bush of Douglasville, Ga., is a close associate of swindler Akiyoshi Yamada.

Leviticus sources said the task force has already marked five other coal operations for prosecution, three of them in Indiana, one in New York, and one in Kentucky.

But is $1 million for one year really enough to chase the swindlers and the Mob out?

"We may well find that it's not adequate, but it's a lot more than we've ever had," Kentucky Attorney General Steven Beshear said.

Justice Stephens wasn't quite as cheery. Stephens said the money was "probably not enough. The coal industry is going to be very important in national energy policy and is going to continue to attract the con artists and the rip-off people"

Ironically, the more America depends on coal, the more its coal fields will attract criminal schemers. If legitimate investors are scared away, or if their funds are diverted by con men, the prospects for the country's most promising energy source are dimmed.

And the scent of billions of federal dollars will make coal even more attractive to the mobsters.

Law enforcement officials estimated that in three years the coal racketeers raked in $750 million from tax shelter scams and $600 million from heavy equipment swindles. How much was made from bogus international coal export contracts is anybody's guess.

No doubt Leviticus, if continued, will help investigators and prosecutors, but it is no cure-all. The coal swindlers are tough opponents.

James Vincent Suarea, a small time Florida con man, said this of his more adept brethren: "These guys, they've got minds like corkscrews, and all they can figure is big rip-off. They're not happy unless they're screwing somebody."

Marvin Stone, a disbarred Canadian attorney with long-standing friendships with the coal swindlers, said: "They're the best. They have a girl on each knee, Dom Perignon champagne and live in castles. As soon as they blow out of money, they go on to their next deal."

And despite Tom Krebs' distaste for the coal swindlers, he grants them their due. "They're brilliant people," he said.

Law enforcement is almost always outgunned and outmanned.

"The guys we're up against are usually attorneys and accountants and sometimes it's two years before we even find out what they've done," said Jim Strode. "By then, they've amassed such huge amounts of money that they can afford to hire the best lawyers and litigate these things forever. One guy can tie up an investigative team for years."

And Strode said Kentucky—the largest coal-producing state—is not equipped to deal with the coal racket, even with Leviticus.

"I think the state has to make an effort to develop capabilities within existing law enforcement agencies to deal with white collar crime. That doesn't exist right now," he said.

As a result, Kentucky, where, investigators agree the coal fraud problem in many ways is worst, has lagged far behind other states in prosecution coal-related fraud. "I can only think of one case," Strode said.

But it would be unfair to heap the blame for the unchecked wave of coal frauds on uninterested federal agencies and budget-conscious state legislatures. The judicial system, the press, and the public have also had a hand in making the coal racket such a lucrative business.

Historically, courts have been gentle with white collar criminals. In 1975, con men looted five times as much money from banks as did armed robbers, but only 16 percent of the swindlers wound up in jail, serving an average of slightly less than one year.

The stick-up men, by contrast, got jail terms in 90 percent of the cases, and the sentences were three times as long.

A three-year prison sentence may be a future deterrent to the stickup man who nets $5000, but for a swindler who loots $3 million from a coal company and stashes it in a bank in Switzerland or the Bahamas, eleven months in jail is a small price to pay.

Of course, that's only if the con man is convicted. Sophisticated swindles—as most coal frauds are—are prosecutors' nightmares. Trials can stretch on for months. Mountains of confusing and complex documents are involved, and the swindler puts on a good show.

"They've got the best credentials, and they bring in a flock of character witnesses all saying what fine citizens they are," Strode noted.

As Prof. John Conklin wrote in *Illegal But Not Criminal*: "The defendant in a business crime appears in court as a well-dressed and well-mannered citizen; the judge sees him not as a surly felon menacing the public safety, but as a fellow country club member who in a moment of weakness, strayed from the path and now knows it."

Many obvious cases of coal fraud never get before a judge or a jury.

"I think local prosecutors need to take a harder look at some of the coal-related complaints people bring into them. Usually, if someone claims they were cheated of money, the local prosecutor will take one look at the case and write it off as a civil matter," Strode said.

"They need to take a close look to determine if criminal activity is involved. Most of the time there is," he said.

Many times, complaints never reach the ears of prosecutors. Banks and other lending institutions—fearing loss of investor confidence—are notoriously loathe to admit they've been swindled. Therefore, they make excellent targets.

Marvin Stone recalled an acquaintance who "beat ten or thirteen banks of about $3 million or $4 million and he never got charged with anything because the banks were too embarrassed."

White collar crime also gets little attention from the news media. A grim murder splashed on the front page grabs more public attention than a business page account of an investor swindle, even though the swindle is likely to affect more readers.

Strode and Krebs seethe when they think of their futile attempts to generate media interest in coal frauds. "What the hell have you guys in the press been doing?" Krebs asked angrily when *The Kentucky Post* first contacted him.

Wrote Professor Conklin: "One reason for leniency towards business offenders is the absence of an influential and well-organized public demand for prosecution and punishment of business offenders."

Granted, it isn't easy working up public sympathy for multi-national banks or huge insurance and loan companies—usually the victims of the coal flimflams.

But the effect of just one coal mine falling into the hands of organized crime is devastating.

Miners are put out of work. Equipment is sold, and the proceeds finance drug expeditions. Active coal mines are closed, and the property is used to inflate balance sheets and financial statements of other Mob-run operations.

Those statements become tools with which to bilk banks and lending institutions of money which might have been loaned to legitimate coal mining ventures.

"We can't afford to let the Mafia get a toehold in the coal industry in Kentucky," said Attorney General Beshear. "We have to catch it before it becomes too widespread. If we don't do something, we could well wind up being held captive by a group far worse than the Arab oil sheiks."

Beshear strongly disagreed with those who suggest the organized crime problem ended with the coal boom of the mid-1970s. "It's still a serious problem, and it hasn't gone away. It's just not as visible as it once was because of the current coal depression. But these people are smart enough to realize that the coal depression is only temporary," Beshear, whose office supervises the Kentucky Leviticus team, said.

Strode concurred. "They're still heavily involved with the tax shelters. Heavy equipment theft is still a big business. As to what else they're into now, we probably won't know until the complaints start coming in," he said.

With the coal industry gearing up again, it's fair to assume the racketeers are doing the same. Only this time, they'll be more dangerous and even more difficult to catch.

For the past seven years, the coal fields have served as the training grounds for these Lear jet marauders. They now know the lay of the land. They know the language. They have already recruited their footsoldiers— attorneys, accountants, and engineers who aren't particular about what they sign.

They know which bankers will lend money for a fee. They know how to play on the greed and the fear of the investing public in an energy crisis.

The frauds that failed have given way to even more ingenious strategies. When the next coal boom hits, the law, the public, and the press will be up against better-organized crime. And the stakes will be much higher.

Whether or not anyone has noticed, the underworld crime heavyweights are in fighting trim for the next bout.

And, with billions in federal dollars as prize money, they're looking forward to it.

Editorials related to "The Coal Connection"

FOR COAL TO PROSPER, THE COAL CONNECTION MUST BE BROKEN

Something is wrong. The federal government is preparing to pump billions of dollars into the coal industry without taking adequate precautions to guard that money from the depredations of the coal racketeers.

Those racketeers feasted during the last coal boom. "The Coal Connection," a series by *Kentucky Post* Staff Writers Gary Webb and Thomas Scheffey, documented their successes in chilling detail.

The racketeers' methods included theft, murder and a dazzling array of swindles: advance fee schemes, tax shelter scams, stock frauds and other white-collar crimes.

Investigators and prosecutors were hard-pressed to keep up. For the most part, they didn't.

Now another coal boom is building, fueled by the federal government's desire to reduce our dependence on imported oil. On Thursday, the Senate approved by a 78–12 vote a $20 billion program to launch a synfuels industry that will depend heavily on coal.

"The sleeping giant is at long last beginning to awaken," Sen. J. Bennett Johnston D-La., said.

But the sleeping giant, like Gulliver, will awaken to find himself ensnared.

The coal racketeers have spun an intricate net. They know each other and work with each other. They have ties to organized crime, including the Mafia.

They can command vast resources of talent and money. Accountants, attorneys, engineers and other professionals will do their bidding for the right price.

The racketeers bilked the US treasury of an estimated $3.75 billion during the last boom, according to tax fraud investigators.

And what is the federal government doing to prevent it from happening again? Very little.

"Has the Justice Department been dragging its heels in the pursuit of fraudulent promoters who have infested the Appalachian coal fields?" asked the lead story in Friday's *Wall Street Journal*.

The story recounted the same complaints reported by Webb and Scheffey. Fraud investigators in Kentucky, Alabama and other coal states all said they don't have the resources to cope with the interstate threat posed by the coal racketeers.

Kentucky, the largest coal-producing state, has proven a particularly fertile field for the swindlers. James Strode, director of securities for Kentucky's Department of Banking and Securities, said there's been only one prosecution for coal-related fraud in the state.

The federal government is not solely to blame for that state of affairs. Said Strode: "I think the state has to make an effort to develop capabilities . . . to deal with white collar crime. That doesn't exist right now."

But the states can't do it alone. It's the federal treasury that the racketeers are raiding, and it's the federal government that is preparing to pump billions into the coal industry.

Kentucky's congressmen, especially Sen. Wendell Ford, have pushed hard for legislation like the synfuels bill. Ford called it a "milestone that . . . moves the synthetic fuels industry off the drawing board and into the mainstream."

Ford and his colleagues should push equally hard for a strong federal commitment to the fight against coalfield fraud. The stakes are immense. A coal boom is building and the swindlers are ready.

THE COAL CONNECTION

Coal is the pillar of our state's economy, though it's easy for northern Kentuckians to lose sight of that fact.

We're far removed from the strip mines and deep mines that make Kentucky the biggest coal-producing state in the nation.

Our only visible reminders are the coal trains that rumble through on their way north and the tows that ply the Ohio and Licking Rivers, barges full of cargo destined for the power plants strung out along the river bank from Pittsburgh to Paducah.

But the health of the coal industry affects us all. We got a grim reminder of that in the frigid winter of 1977, when a bitter strike in the coal fields threatened utilities' fuel supplies and brought fears of brown-outs or worse.

Coal is a fragmented industry with a history of labor strife, fast-buck operators and lax regulation. It's made-to-order for ambitious, ruthless hustlers.

Like Lester Lee.

Lee was far from the coal fields when he met his brutal end on Jan. 7, 1978, in a seedy Newport adult bookstore. But his wallet bulged with business cards of coal entrepreneurs—and money he'd looted from the coal company he destroyed.

The trail leading from the bookstore to the coalfields is an intricate one. It has fascinated *Kentucky Post* Staff Writers Gary Webb and Tom Scheffey, who have spent two years of their spare time following it.

The result of Webb's and Scheffey's work is an investigative series, "The Coal Connection" that starts today on Page One.

"The Coal Connection" will lead you through a rogue's gallery of sophisticated swindlers and racketeers, all of whom grabbed for a piece of the action when coal prices took off during the boom of 1974.

Law enforcement officials, undermanned and underfunded, proved no match for the fraud artists. Prosecutions for coal fraud have been few, convictions fewer.

The coal industry is in a slump, but it's due for a revival. Energy planners in Washington are counting on coal to ease our dependence on foreign oil, and Congress is prepared to commit billions of dollars to make that happen.

How much of that money will be siphoned off by the coal swindlers? As "The Coal Connection" makes disturbingly clear, top law enforcement officials have shown little interest in coping with the threat posed by the fraud artists.

That's a serious sin of omission. "The Coal Connection" touches us all. We ignore it at our peril.

I Create Life

Gary Webb and Maria Riccardi

Three-part series in the *Cleveland Plain Dealer* (November 1983)

INTRODUCTION BY GARY CLARK

A doctor had just developed the concept of surrogate parents. Childless couples were given the chance to have a child—through the artificial insemination of women who agreed to carry the baby to term—for a price.

It offered fresh hope for women who couldn't conceive.

There was also danger. Who were the surrogates hired to carry the child to term? What if they didn't want to give up the child at birth?

Gary and a friend and colleague, the late Maria Riccardi, dug in. Riccardi was smart and a fine writer; Gary was driven, probing, methodical, and focused.

It was the early 1980s. The story was about a new idea, a new way of helping the childless. The topic hadn't been thoroughly explored.

The story they produced revealed the sometimes frightening details of those surrogate arrangements, and offered insight and understanding. It also illustrated the range of Gary's work and his determination to help those who needed his help.

Gary was an expert at finding, researching, understanding, and using public records. But he was also a fine interviewer. People trusted Gary and knew he understood their problems. They opened to him. That illustrated Gary's humanity. Much has been made of his considerable reporting skills, and whether he was careful enough on the ill-fated "Dark Alliance" series. But before that, Gary was highly respected in the *Plain Dealer* newsroom and in the community of investigative journalists.

He had a sharp sense of humor. He could also be acerbic with those who tried to bluff him, and he could be sarcastic with editors and others who didn't share his drive to chase the bad guys. He believed in gay and women's rights. He loved music, working on home improvements, and his family.

He was inquisitive, loved to have fun, and would do anything for a friend. He could also find joy in things like a winter road-rally across snow-covered and icy northern Ohio back roads. The fact that the competition consisted of four-wheelers and we rode in his old Cadillac only added to the fun. It wasn't so fun when we realized the heavy Detroit monster could still hydroplane on ice-covered roads.

"Dark Alliance" defined Gary to his supporters and detractors. That series has been much maligned. But the post-mortem revealed a lack of editing support. Gary could be tough on editors. He also listened to and worked with those he trusted and respected.

What I remember most about Gary was his work ethic, energy, and drive. But I also remember him for his humanity. He was a tough hombre, but also sensitive and moved by the needs of the innocent or helpless.

Gary's suicide—after losing his job and after some of his colleagues in the investigative community turned their backs on him—wasn't just about the destruction of a fine reporter. It was also about the destruction of a fine man.

But Gary's legacy—a nearly thirty-year body of work partly reflected in this book—remains. Nobody can take it away from him.

In a small way, I helped Gary build that body of work. He was one of the best reporters I have known. He was a fine journalist and a fine man. I miss him.

□   □   □

ALL IS NOT WELL IN BABY CLINIC
NOVEMBER 6, 1983

Only seven years ago, Dr. Richard M. Levin was eking out a living performing abortions in a Connecticut clinic.

Today, childless couples from around the world flock to Louisville, Ky., to hear the 38-year-old gynecologist say, "I create life. I make babies."

Levin is president and founder of Surrogate Parenting Associates Inc., a three-year-old firm that finds women to bear children for infertile couples.

Appearances on television shows such as "Donahue," "Good Morning America" and "Today," and laudatory articles in dozens of newspapers have spread his name and brought him hopeful clients.

Recently, Levin got good news. A Kentucky judge decided Levin's activities are not prohibited by state law. Kentucky Atty. Gen. Steven L. Beshear, who had filled suit to close Levin's business, said he will appeal the ruling.

"Right now, it (the business of surrogate parenting) is a totally unregulated process. It's wide open to abuses, extortion. You're dealing with desperate people who are very venerable to unscrupulous types. Their desperation is being exploited by others to make a profit," Beshear told *The Plain Dealer*.

To many, Beshear's fears of abuse are justified:

- Some former clients said they gave Levin thousands of dollars for a child, and received only disappointment and despair in return. Two suits seeking total damages of more than $100,000 have been filed in the past year. Another couple is negotiating to get money back; others simply have written off their losses. Lawyers said more suits are coming.

- Former clients said Levin uses his Ivy League medical training as a major selling point of the program. However, he fails to mention he resigned from Harvard University Medical School's program shortly after being placed on probation.

- Two of his company's psychological consultants have left Levin's employ in the past two years, complaining of his ethics. They said he accepts women as surrogate mothers who have been diagnosed as mentally disturbed and unfit for his program. One former Levin surrogate is suspecting of shooting her three children, one of whom died.

- Levin's former corporate lawyer has sued him for $20,000 in unpaid legal bills and said Surrogate Parenting is fraught with legal hazards. Another former Levin lawyer ran into questions of conflict of interest by her actions in his program.

Levin denied anything is wrong with his operation, and said he is the victim of slurs and slander by competitors and others jealous of his success.

"There are too many nuts involved in surrogate parenting," Levin said. "I've just lost the flame, the desire I had when I started it."

Levin made surrogate parenting a hot topic for cocktail parties in early 1980, when he announced a woman he called by the pseudonym "Elizabeth Kane" was carrying a child for an infertile Louisville couple.

While Noel Keane, a Dearborn, Mich. lawyer, had been doing surrogate parenting for at least two years by then, Levin turned heads. He seemed tailor-made for TV. Flashy and articulate, he wears cowboy boots and gold chains, carries a gun and drives a red Corvette emblazoned with BABY4U license plates.

Levin, surrogate Kane and their lawyer, Katie Marie Brophy, hit the publicity trail, and reporters from around the world wrote lavishly about the dashing young gynecologist and his pioneering ways. Childless couples saw Levin as a miracle-worker who could give them what nature and adoption agencies couldn't: biological children in less than a year.

The process is simple. Levin—for a fee that started at $5,000, and is now $10,000 or more—finds for an infertile couple a woman willing to be artificially inseminated with the husband's semen. The husband and surrogate sign their own contract, specifying that for about $10,000, she will carry the child, then give it up. The infertile wife adopts the baby.

When "Elizabeth Kane" gave birth to a 7-pound boy on Nov. 9, 1980, and turned him over to the Louisville couple, Levin was triumphant. His untested program had worked flawlessly, and the ink flowed.

Levin's company was inundated with calls and letters from couples and prospective surrogates from as far as Italy, Sweden, Brazil and Australia. At a news conference after the birth, Levin predicted at least 100 more by 1981.

He was 97 short, according to former Levin surrogate Kathryn Wyckoff, who now operates her own surrogate-mother agency in Columbus.

Levin adamantly refused to give figures, saying reporters always get them wrong. Nor will he say how many surrogate candidates he has stored in his computer. He doesn't talk money, except to say that he isn't making any.

"Surrogate Parenting operates borderline black or in the red, and has since the day we started. I'm making nothing. I'm making zero. When I tell you that I could easily walk into court and file bankruptcy, I'm not kidding," he said.

Levin, his wife and four daughters live in a $110,000 Tudor-style home—"the only circular drive on the block," he said—on the outskirts of Louisville. He has a swimming pool, a $25,000 Corvette, a tricked-out van and $494,500 in other property in Jefferson County, Ky., including eight condominiums he bought in August.

None of that is attributable to Surrogate Parenting, he said, insisting the company drains money from his private infertility practice. He said he could make more money if he stuck to fertility pills and PAP smears.

The night before he spoke to *The Plain Dealer*, Levin said, he spent 10 hours waiting for a surrogate to give birth: "It was all wasted time. What did I get? Monday, I've got an operation that will make me $2,500 and it'll take an hour and a half. Now which do you think I'd rather be doing?"

"If I was making tens of thousands or hundreds of thousands of dollars, it'd be worth it. It's not worth it. I don't make my living as the surrogate-parenting doctor. It's a piece of the action, but that's all it is."

Directors of the 12 or so other surrogate-parenting companies that have sprung up nationally in the last two years say a piece of the action can be lucrative, because it isn't exactly a capital-intensive business.

In Levin's program, all expenses are paid by the adopting couple, including the medical, legal and subsistence costs. Couples also pay their own legal and travel costs and Levin's expenses—down to phone calls and postage stamps.

Cost of the entire process starts at $25,000, and packages of $35,000 and $45,000 are not unheard of.

What do couples get for the $10,000-plus fee they give to Surrogate Parenting?

"My time and talents," Levin responded.

According to former clients, Levin's talents are a major selling point. Lawrence C. Biedenharn Jr., a Duke University physics professor who has a suit pending against Levin, vividly recalled his first meeting with the doctor.

"We discussed his research, his ideas, his skills, how he though up these ideas, how he had done many, many things. It was a beautiful and very skillful sales job by a genuine expert at self-deification," Biedenharn said in a deposition.

Levin's resume is impressive: graduate of University of Louisville Medical School, internship at Johns Hopkins University, residency at Harvard, fellowship at Yale University. But his company's promotional literature doesn't include the footnotes to those laurels.

Levin resigned his residency at Harvard's Beth Israel Hospital in 1973, five days after he was told he was being placed on six months' probation. Records at Harvard reflect his superiors were displeased with Levin's "professional competence, fund of knowledge, depth of interest and growth. His motivation was clearly lacking. He often failed to appreciate the limits of his capabilities . . . potentially to the detriment of patients."

Levin returned to Louisville. He said he doesn't remember being placed on probation, and his Harvard teachers didn't really want him to leave.

"They asked me to reconsider. They wanted me to stay," he said. He said he resigned because he didn't like his department chairman, and his parents were going through a divorce in Kentucky.

After finishing his residency at the University of Louisville, Levin decided to give the Ivy League another crack.

A former Yale administrator recalled the day in 1975 when Levin showed up at Yale University Medical School and asked for a fellowship in reproductive endocrinology. Told Yale did not have the money to fund a fellowship for him, Levin offered to work for free.

"Maybe they were trying to tell me nicely to kiss of, but I didn't give them that opportunity," Levin said. He got his fellowship.

While studying ways to make infertile women pregnant, Levin supported himself by performing legal first-trimester abortions at Summit Women's Center in Bridgeport, Conn. He worked there a year.

"It was a job. It made the bucks. I needed to do my fellowship. There was nothing funny, or illegal or unkosher about it. It was real life. That's where the bucks were," Levin said.

Since he has become famous, Levin said, he has been hearing mumblings from Yale he doesn't like. During an interview with *The Plain Dealer*, Levin said several times he would sue all his former professors for talking about him.

One point made by many doctors is that Levin is not certified by the American Board of Obstetricians and Gynecologists. While certification is not mandatory to practice, most ob/gyns take their boards as a matter of course, and many hospitals will not grant staff privileges to uncertified doctors.

Levin said he passed the written part of the boards, but never found time for the oral part, which he said costs $1,000 to take.

"Why pay $1,000, study up, and waste all those hours?" Levin asked. "In reality, I can practice any frigging thing I want to as long as people are willing to pay the price. I can say I'm a plastic surgeon. All you need is that M.D."

Levin said the only reason anyone mentions that, or anything else about his background, is jealousy over his success.

A former professor disagreed: "It's not so much jealousy, but irritation at the way he's done things. There is a strong feeling among many people that he's very much motivated just for the dollar."

Adoption Pioneers Swap Harsh Words

They were jokingly referred to as the Batman and Robin of surrogate parenting.

For about a year, Dr. Richard M. Levin and his young sidekick, lawyer Katie Marie Brophy, made what seemed like an ideal team. Ambitious and opinionated, they saw themselves in the vanguard of a whole new industry.

But by the time Elizabeth Kane, their first surrogate, gave birth in November 1980, the two were feuding openly.

Brophy refuses to discuss her association with Levin, or its tumultuous end.

"I'm sick and tired of talking about Richard Levin," she said. "I don't give the man a second thought anymore."

Levin isn't as reticent. He calls Brophy "a louse" and stresses that he kicked her out of the program.

"I had to cut the cancer out," he said.

The final break occurred the day Kane terminated her parental rights in court and turned her son over to the adoptive parents.

"It was history in the making," Levin said. "This was the point that we'd been working to. It was my idea; the whole thing was my idea, and she (Brophy) told me the wrong time and place. When she cheated me out of being at the termination, I was livid." Kane confirmed Levin did not learn of the proceeding until it was over.

Levin said Brophy then formed her own company, Surrogate Family Services, and "snaked away" his clients, offering some the prospect of private adoptions: "You can have a baby immediately for this much.'"

Brophy and Levin met as patient-doctor in Levin's gynecological practice. When he needed a lawyer for his budding surrogate-parenting firm, he contacted her.

Brophy researched Kentucky adoption laws and copyrighted contracts she prepared for Levin. She acted as lawyer for both Levin and his organization, Surrogate Parenting Associates Inc., and when couples and surrogates came to Louisville, she represented them, too, Levin said.

Levin said he was stupid to allow Brophy to represent everyone, but she told him a letter from the Kentucky Bar Association had approved her unorthodox practices. The bar would neither confirm nor deny this.

According to Kentucky Asst. Atty. Gen. Joe Johnson, Brophy took the Fifth Amendment when asked if she ever had served as counsel for either

Levin or Surrogate Parenting Associates. Johnson deposed Brophy in connection with lawsuit State Atty. Gen. Steven L. Beshear filed against Surrogate Parenting Associates.

In a deposition in a pending suit by Levin's former lawyer, Jan Scholl, Brophy said she had neither represented nor been paid by Levin or his company.

In May 1980, Levin asked Scholl to do some research. Several weeks later, Scholl wrote Levin that Brophy's multiple representations were unethical, and she had misinterpreted the viewpoint of the bar association.

"Aside from ethical considerations, Ms. Brophy's presence invites litigation against you and Surrogate Parenting Associates Inc., particularly in the area of fraud," the letter said. "Compromise on this point is not possible."

Levin was wary of Scholl's advice, and disregarded it.

"Jan had an interest in replacing Katie as my attorney," he said. "I began to regard these attorneys with a very jaundiced eye."

The Kentucky Court of Appeals, however, raised the same complaint in a landmark adoption case involving Brophy last year. It called Brophy's representation of both the child's mother and the adopting couple "an obvious conflict" and termed her conduct in the case a "black mark . . . which we cannot overlook." The Kentucky Bar Association investigated Brophy as a result, but would not discuss the results of that investigation.

"I made her what she is," Levin said. "If it wasn't for me, she wouldn't have ever been on television or gotten her name in the papers. I had to insist she be allowed on the 'Donahue' show. They only wanted me."

Surrogate Firm Breaks Barren Couple's Hearts

It was the package Larry and Janet Tubelle had been waiting for.

Six months earlier, the middle-aged Los Angeles couple had given a $5,000 check to Dr. Richard M. Levin so Levin would find them a woman willing to bear them a child. They also had given Levin's lawyer, Katie Marie Brophy, a $2,500 check for legal services she was to provide them.

The Tubelles had handed over the money without second thought. They were desperate for a child of their own, which Mrs. Tubelle could not bear. They said Levin had told them his selection of surrogate mothers was choice.

"You got the feeling that you were in good hands, that he would screen all the people for you, rather than you putting an ad in the newspaper and getting somebody with problems. It all sounded wonderful," Mrs. Tubelle said.

Tubelle said he and his wife were "elated that finally someone was going to help us achieve our goal. We just jumped at the opportunity."

The couple watched the mailbox daily, and when the package from Surrogate Parenting Associates Inc. arrived, they eagerly ripped open the envelope and read the results of Levin's searched.

The woman was 25, a mother of three with an IQ of 127, blond hair and green eyes. Levin didn't give her a name, only a number: 30.

As the couple scanned the reports Levin had sent, their excitement waned. The psychologist who had interviewed the woman wrote, "Specific intellectual deficits—including social cause-effect reasoning—point to major psychopathology with depression and high anxiety disorganizing cognition and judgment. Personality and projective tests indicate an individual with a histrionic personality disorder."

The psychologist said he doubted the woman could successfully carry a child and, if she did, he didn't think she would give it up for adoption. The psychiatrist who had interviewed her agreed.

"Whether or not she would follow through with giving up the baby after the delivery is very questionable at this point, given the unconscious motivations for her participation in the program, as well as her poor impulse control and poor judgment," the psychiatrist reported.

Worried, the Tubelles called Levin and questioned him about the negative reports.

"He pooh-poohed it. He said, 'Don't go by that. This woman is terrific, she's just perfect for you,'" Tubelle said. He said Levin pointed out that the woman had beautiful eyes and would make them a pretty baby.

Meanwhile, lawyer Brophy had called and told them not to accept the woman under any circumstances. Levin told them not to listen to Brophy and urged them to accept the woman. Despite Levin's reassurances, the Tubelles rejected Surrogate No. 30 and asked him to find another woman.

Another Levin couple was less picky, Elizabeth Downs—No. 30—had a baby girl in May 1982, and gave her up to a couple who had contracted for her birth.

This past spring, Downs' three young children were shot with a .22-caliber pistol. One was killed, another crippled.

At a hearing in Eugene, Ore., during which the state took custody of

Downs' surviving children, she was named as a suspect in the shootings. No charges have been filed, but the investigation continues.

"Well, maybe we made a mistake with her," Levin said. Then again, maybe not.

"Any way you look at it, success is success," he said. "She performed according to her contract. A couple did get a baby. Maybe we were wrong, maybe (the psychiatrists) were wrong. As it turns out, it all ended up well."

Maybe for Levin. But the Tubelles paid about $10,000 in fees, transportation and other expenses and never got a child. Levin has refused to refund their money, saying he's still prepared to find them a surrogate—if they pay him another $2,500. He said the Tubelles owe him that much for the expense of Downs' screening.

"He wanted us to pay the expenses for a woman we didn't want," Tubelle said.

The couple has since gotten a child through a surrogate agency in California, and has given up on getting back their $7,500 in fees from Levin and Brophy. They say the expense of hiring a lawyer and suing Levin in Kentucky would cost more than they would recover.

"In retrospect, I suppose we were too willing to take the risk and to gamble. We wanted this child so much it made us very, very vulnerable," Tubelle said.

SURROGATE PROMOTER OVERRULED SCREENINGS

Dr. Richard M. Levin calls his computer "Einstein" and says it makes his surrogate-parenting program superior to all imitators.

Stored on Einstein's floppy disks are details of hundreds of women, any of whom can make an infertile couple's dreams come true.

For $10,000, Levin will flick Einstein's switch and taps its vast repository of doctors' wives, chemical engineers, nurses, school-teachers and housewives—all smart, pretty, scrupulously screened and eager to bear a child for the childless.

That's what Levin tells prospective clients at $400-a-couple monthly meetings in Louisville, Ky. The couples are given promotional booklets that call Levin's Surrogate Patenting Associates Inc. "a model throughout the world."

Court records, former employees and former clients tell a different story.

They say Einstein is nothing more than electronic Rolodex, Levin's screening process is minimal and the answers Einstein spits out can end up wasting thousands of dollars for Levin's clients.

Dr. Paul S. Mann, who gave psychological tests to Levin's surrogates for more than a year, said he was astonished to learn how little Levin knew about the surrogates before they were offered to infertile couples.

"To make this a game where everybody wins, you've got to be looking at more than just the biological availability of the mother," Mann said.

Mann, a Louisville psychologist, quit after learning the gynecologist had offered an Italian millionaire a surrogate Mann believed was mentally disturbed.

"She was a real space queen. You didn't have to be a professional person to know that this woman was unstable," Mann said. His report to Levin's company was blunt.

"Your client appears to present important risks vis-à-vis the surrogate program," Mann wrote on Jan. 5, 1981. "Pathological motivation and a history of immaturely promiscuous, histrionic behavior leads to a high level uncertainty as to her ability to sustain personal care appropriate to pregnancy. There is substantial question, due to psychopathology, as to whether or not she would in the end be willing to terminate parental rights."

Mann was appalled when he learned Levin had disregarded his advice.

"You wouldn't want this woman washing your dishes, yet Levin was saying this woman was fine. I really didn't know what happened to these people. I just assumed, stupidly, that if I said this person wasn't suitable, that was the end of that," Mann said.

The Italian millionaire wasn't the only person to whom that surrogate was offered; at least two other Levin clients were sent her profile. And she wasn't the only surrogate rejected by Levin's experts who later turned up bearing Levin's stamp of approval.

Sanford and Barbara Metzel of Denver gave Levin $6,000 in March 1981, along with a list of 16 characteristics they wanted in their surrogate. Among other things, the Metzels wanted a woman of above-average intelligence, no taller than 5 feet 7 and no older than 30.

It took Einstein almost a year to make a match. The Metzels got a 31-year-old woman who was 5 feet 10 and had an average IQ. Levin's psychiatrist and psychologist said the woman had no business being in Levin's program.

"Her personality is negatively marked by depressive conditions, paranoid trends and the likelihood of impaired ability in getting along with others. Should she ever identify the child she would carry as her own, it seems very possible that she would make moves to keep the child under her own protection," psychologist Dennis E. Wagner wrote Levin on Oct. 27, 1981.

It cost the Metzels $1,497 in screening fees to learn the woman Einstein had selected for them probably would keep the child. A Los Angeles couple was charged $2,556 for the information that their computer-matched surrogate—the woman Mann interviewed—was a psychopath.

Under the non-negotiable contract they sign with Levin's company, couples pay the cost of the entire surrogate screening process: psychological tests, legal counseling and all travel expenses of the surrogate and her husband to and from Louisville, including hotel rooms, meals, phone calls and cab fare.

"There's a limit to what we know about these people before we do the workups. We tell people that. We don't know these (surrogates). Many times we've never seen them. All we have is an application. We don't give out these surrogates with a Good Housekeeping Seal of Approval," Levin told *The Plain Dealer*.

The screenings can cost thousands, in addition to the $5,000 to $10,000 fee a couple has paid just to get Levin to turn on his computer.

"Certainly they (the couples) can't expect us to pay for it," Levin said. "Do you know what that would cost me? We decided early on that the cost of the product (the baby) should be paid by those for whom the product is being made."

Levin said if a couple pays for a screening and then rejects: the surrogate, he refunds the money if another selects her later. But he acknowledged that some couples have gotten no refunds, because no one else chose the surrogate.

"There's a certain element of crapshoot involved," he said.

The fact that couples must pay for the screenings is made clear in their contracts, he said. "They know that if the surrogate flies in here and drops dead . . . they have to pay for it."

If a couple is unhappy with their first surrogate, their contract gives them three more selections—provided they pay for three more screenings. If they can't make a choice after four surrogates, their contract ends and Levin keeps their money.

That clause protects Surrogate Parenting Associates from couples who can't be satisfied, Levin said, adding he's never had to enforce it.

In a lawsuit they filed against Levin to recover their money, the Metzels say he cut them off after they rejected his second surrogate and refused to send them another until they send him a few thousand dollars more.

The Metzels' second surrogate passed psychological muster. But Metzel, in a deposition, said she wanted close to $20,000, instead of the customary $10,000 surrogate fee. And, Metzel said, he learned the woman had breached an earlier contract because her couple couldn't or wouldn't come up with more money.

"That's one of the most delicate aspects of the contract: the willingness of the surrogate to surrender custody (of the baby). Obviously, it's an attempt at almost extortion," Metzel testified in his deposition.

The Metzels' suit is pending. Levin, who said the couple breached the contract, has countersued, claiming they owe him $12,500.

Louisville lawyer Jan Scholl warned Levin early that his causal procedures were leaving him open to lawsuits.

In May 1980, Levin asked Scholl, a close friend, to research the legality of his new business. Levin needed a quick opinion because his first surrogate was three months pregnant and he was getting new customers daily.

"It was pressing to understand whether what we were involved with was legal at the time so that I might bail out of the situation immediately," Levin testified in a suit Scholl later filed against Levin for non-payment of legal fees. The suit is pending.

Scholl became worried when he learned Levin was not screening the natural fathers, was screening surrogates himself and hadn't given any thought to what to do with a defective baby.

"Rich asked me one time, 'How much do you think I should charge?' He was looking for a price per unit, much like bottles of Coke or whatever, and the price per unit he was working with had no computation for the 5% to 2% defect rate that was statistically provable," Scholl testified.

Scholl advised Levin to hire more qualified people and let them do the work so they would be responsible if something went wrong. Specifically, he suggested Levin hire a genetics expert to do the sperm analyses on the fathers-to-be.

"Rich had no program for evaluating the biological father at all," Scholl said, adding Levin was not even testing the fathers for genetically transmitted diseases.

Levin never followed that advice. He said that would entail passing judgment on a couple and his philosophy does not permit him to "play God."

"Assuming they can afford the service, we don't tell anyone they can't have children," Levin said.

Levin listened when Scholl suggested he hire independent psychiatrists and psychologists to screen surrogates. But unless he agrees with their recommendations, they don't work for him long.

Psychologists Mann and Wagner said Levin complained their evaluations of his surrogates were too negative. Levin confirmed that.

"I was turning too many of them down," Wagner said, when asked why he no longer does screenings for Levin. "I was suggesting they might not be able to handle the stress and they (Surrogate Parenting Associates) said, 'Who are you to say?' I had to follow my ethics."

Levin said he believes the psychologists had built-in prejudices against his surrogates because they didn't like the concept. Mann, for instance, turned down every single surrogate he sent him, Levin said.

Mann said of 18 surrogates he interviewed, he rejected only eight. And, he said, it wasn't until he saw Levin in action that he began to question the program.

"This was supposed to be a non-zero-sum game where everybody was supposed to win. But when it became clear to me that these people couldn't care less about whether anybody won or lost, other than themselves, I quit," Mann said. "I felt like I had been co-opted into participating in an unethical operation, where the patient's needs were the last set of needs to be considered."

Mann said he once suggested to Levin that surrogates be given post-delivery counseling to see how they were coping with giving up their babies.

Dr. John P. Bell, a Louisville psychiatrist who screened surrogates for Levin for about a year, recalled making the same suggestion. Both said Levin showed no interest in the idea. Levin became irate when questioned about it.

"He (Mann) wanted to be paid for it!" Levin exclaimed. "If he was so concerned about these women, he should have said, "I'll do it for free." I can't believe some of these people. Everybody wants Levin to pay for everything!"

Mann offered another reason for Levin's reluctance.

"[He] didn't want to share his referral information with me or anybody because there are 80 zillion other gynecologists who can very easily do the same thing that he's doing. He was very possessive and very secretive when it came to his surrogates," Mann said. "Everything was on a need-to-know basis."

The secretiveness extends to the couples who, by contract, are forbidden to talk to reporters without Levin's permission. They also must promise they will not try to learn the identity of the woman carrying their child.

When Duke University physics Prof. Lawrence C. Biedenharn Jr. bumped into his surrogate in the elevator of a Louisville motel, Levin swiftly switched her to another couple.

At that point, Biedenharn and his wife had spent more than $5,000 bringing the woman from Michigan to Louisville for three artificial inseminations, and thousands more on their own travel.

Biedenharn, 60, said he pleaded with Levin to allow the surrogate to continue with the inseminations, but Levin was "totally obstinate."

"He was not terribly concerned about the ethics of the case . . . but the point he repeatedly emphasized to me was that I had damaged his rapport with one of his favorite surrogates," Biedenharn testified in a suit he filed against Levin.

Levin said the woman insisted on being switched because Biedenharn frightened her by "stalking" her to her motel room.

The Biedenharns spent more than $10,000 and did not get a child. They have sued for $105,000, and are attempting to get a child through a Columbus agency run by former Levin surrogate Kathryn Wyckoff.

"I have lost money. I have lost time. I have been made to suffer. My wife has suffered," Biedenharn said. "Richard Levin has caused me enormous anguish."

OHIO SURROGATE: "IT ALL HAPPENED SO FAST"

It took Ronda Price of Plain City, O., longer to get her supermarket job than to become a surrogate mother in Dr. Richard M. Levin's program.

Within hours of her arrival in Louisville, Ky., in August 1981, Price had been matched with a Portland, Ore., couple for whom she was to bear a child. The most Levin knew about her then was that she was married, had three children, appeared healthy and expressed an interest in being a surrogate.

"It all happened so fast, I really didn't know what was going on. Before I knew it, I was being handed contracts," Price said.

Price was sitting on the floor of her den, changing her son, T.J.'s, diapers. T.J., a blond blue-eyed, 5-month-old, googled happily.

T.J. is the result of Price's experience in Levin's Surrogate Parenting

Associates Inc. Five months ago in a Columbus motel, Price took him from the arms of the Portland couple and brought him home.

"Nobody's going to take you away from me," she told the baby, lifting him from the floor for a kiss.

Ronda Price is the nightmare of every couple who ever has given money to a surrogate-parenting agency. Even though she and other surrogates sign contracts with their couples, promising to give the child up at birth in exchange for about $10,000, the couples know the contracts are worthless if the surrogate keeps the baby.

While T.J. is only half Price's—the Portland man is the father—the mother usually prevails in court.

And the contracts the couples sign with Levin give no guarantees or refunds. In Price's case, her couple spent thousands without receiving a thing.

Their lawyer, Rupert Koblegarde, said he is negotiating with Levin to get their money back. Koblegarde said the would-be parents were "devastated. They are suffering intensely from the aftershock." That preys on Price's mind.

"Sometimes I think, my God, that poor couple. What I've done to them. I feel horrible for the love I feel for this baby. How am I ever going to tell him I took him away from someone who wanted him?" she said.

Price, 36, became interested in surrogate parenting after seeing Levin on television. She thought of bearing a child for an apparently infertile sister, but when the sister later conceived, her thoughts turned to other childless couples.

"I've always been a giving person. I thought I could give some couple the ultimate gift," she said.

Two weeks after filling out a surrogate-mother application form Levin had sent, Price, her three daughters and her husband, Tim, were on their way to Louisville.

After she conversed briefly with Levin, Price said, the doctor picked up the phone and called the Oregon couple.

"He said, 'I think I've found someone for you.' All of a sudden I was in. The whole time I was driving down, I was thinking of all the reasons they wouldn't want me. I wasn't ready for this to happen so fast," she said.

Levin told her what she would be paid, then asked her to step behind a curtain and remove her clothes. The examination was quick.

"He didn't take a blood test or anything. I've gotten more thorough examinations when I've gone in for a PAP smear," Price said.

She was handed a list of names—a psychiatrist, a psychologist and lawyer—along with the times she was to see them. That was part of the screening process, she was told.

The psychiatrists, Dr. Pran Ravani, interview her "for a whole 10 minutes maybe." She pulled out a copy of this half-page report and pointed to his diagnosis: "No mental illness."

"How did he know that from 10 minutes?" Price asked. Ravani listed her name on the report as "Wanda."

Psychologist Dennis Wagner impressed her. She said he interviewed her for several hours, and seemed conscientious. Wagner no longer works for Levin. Levin said he fired him because his reports were too negative.

The lawyer, who was supposed to advise Price on the legal ramifications of her decision, never showed up for the appointment, she said. She declined to name him.

Then she was on her way home. Price had gone from nervous applicant to full-fledged surrogate mother in one weekend.

Before she left, she was given one more name: Kathryn Wyckoff of Columbus. Wyckoff was another surrogate, Price was told, and should she ever need an understanding ear, Wyckoff was the one to call.

When Price began bleeding and cramping after her first artificial insemination attempt, she called Wyckoff in a panic. Wyckoff calmed her, and the two became close friends and confidantes.

While Wyckoff was six years younger than Price, she had been in Levin's program longer. Pretty and chipper, she often accompanied him on TV talk shows, extolling the virtues of the program and urging housewives like herself to give surrogate mothering a shot.

"I was the lady next door; the bright, attractive, college-educated woman who was there because she wanted to be there. I was the model surrogate," Wyckoff said.

For more than a year and a half, Wyckoff said, she followed Levin "like a little puppy dog. I would have believed anything he told me. I would have done anything for him." She often did just that, she said, leaving her three children with her husband and running to Louisville whenever Levin called.

Price also was making frequent trips to Louisville in 1981 and 1982. Her artificial insemination attempts weren't working, and she was beginning to think something was physically wrong with her.

"I was cutting out articles like this," she said, producing a newspaper clipping linking fertility to bad breath. "I couldn't understand why I wasn't getting pregnant. I was asking people, 'What if I stand on my head? What if I eat this or that?'"

Price's couple began running tremendous bills; she figures it cost them $200 a day just for her expenses during each three day insemination attempt, plus what they were paying Levin, plus what it cost them to fly in from Portland each month to give sperm samples.

"They must have spent thousands," she said.

Finally, on the eighth try in August 1982, Price got pregnant. Then her problems began in earnest.

By then, Wyckoff and Levin had split. After her third child, Wyckoff had been voluntarily sterilized, but Levin had surgically reconnected her Fallopian tubes to allow her to become a surrogate.

"I suppose it was silly to allow things to progress that far, but she really wanted to be in the program," Levin said.

Wyckoff maintained that she agreed to bear a couple a child for nothing, simply because she wanted the surrogate experience. In another interview, she said she was to receive a small sum for bearing that child. Levin said that is untrue.

"She initially said she was willing to do this for cheap or none, and I figured that was a good reason for a couple to accept a surrogate who's had an operation like this," Levin said. But, he said, after the operation appeared to be successful, Wyckoff asked the couple for $14,000.

"She went from cheap or none to the whole matzoh ball," Levin said.

Wyckoff denied asking for $14,000, but declined to say what her fee was to be.

In time, however, it became obvious Wyckoff was not going to get pregnant, because his operation had not worked, Levin said.

"She could not conceive, and you can no longer be a surrogate mother if you can't conceive. It's that simple," Levin said. He said he told Wyckoff he no longer had any need for her in the program.

Wyckoff was unspecific about why she left, but said Levin "hurt me terribly. Richard betrayed everyone in the program, and when I saw him for what he really was, I was crushed."

She denied Levin's contention she was infertile, and has said publicly several times that she had a baby as a Levin surrogate. However, Levin said Wyckoff never bore a child in the program.

Price said Wyckoff began calling her, often in hysterics, warning her not to stay in Levin's program.

"I would never have had a negative thought about this until Kathy started calling me and telling me all these terrible things about Levin and his program. She had me horrified. She said he had a gun and I'd be a dead woman," Price recalled.

Wyckoff was despondent over her failure to conceive, and Price said she felt sorry for her friend. Finally, she told Wyckoff she would help her promote the surrogate-mother program Wyckoff had started out of her Columbus home.

"I told Kathy I'd have this baby for her, that it would be our baby," Price said.

Wyckoff, mindful of how masterfully Levin had used the media to get clients, convinced Price to go public and strongly intimated in interviews that Price was a surrogate in her program. Levin was never mentioned.

For the first time in a long time, Price felt content. The pregnancy was coming along nicely, and she was looking forward to her role as being the Portland couple's savior.

Her doubts began when she felt the baby move insider her: "Up until then, it was like it wasn't real or something. Then the baby started kicking, and it was all downhill from there. I wasn't prepared like I thought I was."

Levin did not learn of her change of heart until the night Price was to be in Louisville so he could induce labor and deliver the baby. He had three births scheduled for that night, and *People* magazine had a writer and photographer on hand to record the event.

Price never showed up. The day before, she had given birth in Columbus to a 7-pound, 12-ounce boy.

Price and her husband were allowed to see the child and feed him. Price said Wyckoff encouraged them.

"She told me that you really can't say goodby[e] until you've said hello," Price said.

By the time the Portland couple arrived to claim their child, Price was a jumbled mass of emotions: "I started thinking about it as my baby."

Still, she knew how excited the couple was, how long they had waited for a child and how much money they spent getting to this point. She took the child to the motel where the couple was staying and handed him over.

"That was supposed to be the magic moment. When you gave the couple the baby and saw them as a family, you were supposed to realize that it wasn't your baby; it was theirs. Well, it never happened," she said.

Price left the motel room in turmoil, forcing herself to walk down the hall to the elevators. She got there and froze. "I just couldn't push that button. I couldn't leave without my baby."

She walked back to the room where the happy couple was cuddling the infant and told them, "That's my baby you have." The couple hasn't seen the boy since.

After the news got out that Price had kept the child, Wyckoff disavowed any connection between the recalcitrant mother and her program, Association for Surrogate Parenting Inc. She blamed Price's decision on Levin, and said she had only been doing her friend a favor by saying Price was in her program.

As for Price, her indecision still gnaws at her.

"Sometimes I want to call them and tell them to come get him," she said. "I wish sometimes he was a colicky baby who kept me up nights. But he's such a perfect baby."

While she steadfastly avoided reporters when the news broke—she left her house once in the trunk of a car, with the baby in a picnic basket, to avoid being seen—Price said she wants other women to know her experiences:

"I want surrogates to really think before they do this. I've got the baby, but I'm still suffering. I feel guilty that he brings joy into my life.

"The other surrogates I know who have given up their babies live for the letters they get from the parents. They live in this dream world that someday they'll see their baby again. I don't know if there's ever a happy ending for a surrogate."

Doctoring the Truth
Gary Webb

Series in the *Cleveland Plain Dealer* (April 7–13, 1985)

INTRODUCTION BY GARY CLARK

Gary Webb had an unmistakable voice. It was confident, and usually tinged with a wry humor that could easily move to sarcasm.

It was a different voice, quiet but still friendly, that spilled from the phone in my office one day in 2003. I was the managing editor of *The Denver Post*, and Gary got right to the point. He asked whether *Post* editor Greg Moore and I would consider hiring him. We had worked with Gary about two decades earlier in Cleveland. He was one of the best reporters I had ever worked with. He was smart, dynamic, tough, focused, and driven. He had also been largely unemployed since leaving the *San Jose Mercury News* after the crushing fall-out from his "Dark Alliance" series.

I offered a bit of hope. I said we would talk about it. And Greg and I did talk about it. We were excited about the possibility; we also talked to an ethicist at the Poynter Institute for Media Studies who said Gary's hiring would have to be explained to the newsroom. But he also said that it was absolutely fair to give someone another chance.

It didn't work out. The *Post*, like most major newspapers, would instead start to shrink its staff and news report as declining revenues brought hiring freezes, buy-outs, and lay-offs.

He was incredibly disappointed, and so was I.

Gary was the type of reporter that gave newsrooms swagger. He routinely produced big, hard-hitting investigative projects, stories that a newsroom — and a newspaper — took pride in. He was relentless. He used documents and interviews to carefully expose those who took advantage of the innocent or, worse, failed in their duty to protect the innocent.

"Doctoring the Truth" was one of those stories. The Ohio Medical Board, like all state medical boards, was supposed to protect the public. Instead, Gary found a medical board that largely operated in secret and that was hobbled by cozy relationships with doctors repeatedly accused of malpractice, or those addicted to drugs or alcohol. From the blunt opening sentence to the authority of writing based on months of careful work, it was excellent investigative reporting. It was also public service reporting at its best and remains an example of why the public needs good newspapers and courageous reporters.

□   □   □

UNSAFE M.D.s FREE TO PREY ON PUBLIC

They sell drugs, they steal, they rape and they kill. They circulate freely among an unsuspecting public, virtually immune to prosecution. Perceived as society's most respected members, they prey on society's most helpless—the sick, the elderly and the mentally ill.

They are the dregs of Ohio's medical community. Among their ranks are physicians who write prescriptions for people they have never seen and physicians who charge insurance companies for operations not needed or not performed. Some ensure a busy practice by turning their patients into drug addicts. Others leave patients maimed or dead from surgery that exceeded their capabilities or that they performed while under the influence of drugs or alcohol.

The only thing between you and them is the State Medical Board of Ohio and, as a six-month *Plain Dealer* investigation shows, that's little comfort.

The medical board's job is to protect the public from that minority of physicians who abuse their licenses and their positions of trust and from those too incompetent to treat patients. Instead, the medical board has compiled and appalling record protecting the reputations and livelihoods of the state's medical outlaws:

- Board officials hide many physician crimes from the public through the use of secret hearings and deals negotiated privately with the offending doctor. Most board members are unaware of what transpires in these clandestine tribunals because they have been advised by the board administrator and board lawyers not to attend and not to examine the records.

- The board has refused to release any information regarding its closed-door proceedings, but hundreds of pages of secret board records show medical board officials have ignored crimes including drug abuse, illegal processing of drug documents and sexual abuse of patients. Over the past 10 years, the board had conducted nearly 1,100 secret hearings, while holding only 308 public hearings.

- The board has allowed dozens of doctors convicted of felonies such as drug trafficking, insurance fraud, forgery, theft, sexual assault and drug abuse to remain in practice with little more than a lecture. Part of the reason for that is the way the board and the Ohio attorney general's office chose to prosecute physician-felons in board hearings, which are stacked heavily in the physician's favor.

- The board has allowed dozens of physicians with serious alcohol or drug problems to remain in practice—even perform surgery—while they are undergoing treatment, withdrawal and psychotherapy. Although state law requires the board to suspend the licenses of addicted doctors, the board rarely does so. Drug addicts are frequently given back their federal drug licenses within months of coming out of drug treatment programs. Time after time, these doctors have gone back to the bottle or needle, with little or no response from the board.

- The board has allowed doctors diagnosed as suffering severe mental problems to remain in practice for years while their cases wended their way through the board's cumbersome and backlogged hearing process. Even though the board was given the power in 1982 to obtain a summary suspension of a doctor's license before a hearing, the board has pursued that option only once, then only because of a public outcry.

- The board makes little effort to police the profession for incompetent or negligent practitioners, and investigators say they rarely are asked to look into malpractice claims or complaints. Unlike those in most states, Ohio hospitals and insurance companies have no obligation to report disciplinary actions or malpractice judgments. As a result, those physicians are almost never disciplined, even for repeated acts of incompetence or negligence.

  When the Ohio Legislature proposed in 1980 that the medical board be required to investigate malpractice, the board members objected strenuously and the requirement was dropped.

- The board routinely refuses to act against a physician convicted of a crime until the doctor has exhausted all appeals, allowing convicted felons to continue practicing for years while their cases drag on in court. The board rarely conducts its own investigation of the crime, allowing doctors who escape felony convictions because of legal technicalities or plea-bargain agreements to sometimes avoid disciplinary actions entirely.

- Even when a physician has repeatedly violated the law, the board seems loath to pull a license, and members worry that the physician will be unable to earn a living. Historically, Ohio has lagged far behind the rest of the nation in the number of disciplinary actions it has taken. In the last 14 years, only 13 doctors have had their licenses revoked. By contrast, the State Board of Pharmacy, which licenses about half as many people, revoked 10 pharmacists' licenses last year alone.

- While ignoring some physician crimes, the board has assigned its small staff of six investigators to dig up evidence against nurse-midwives, physician's assistants, health food stores, chiropractors, acupuncturists, masseuses, manicurists and other suspected of practicing medicines without a license. The nurse-midwives, particularly, have accused the board of harassing them through the use of secret hearings, which for years were conducted by an obstetrician.

- The board is beset by internal management problems and poor morale among its staff, particularly among its investigators, who feel the board is against enforcement. Turnover in the legal department is high, which severely hampers enforcements efforts. Board employees say the board's administrator, William J. Lee, is ineffective and weak and has misdirected the board's priorities.

Board Secretary Dr. Henry G. Cramblett, who has been a board member for 15 years, acknowledges some of those problems.

"I know we do not have enough disciplinary actions in the state of Ohio. I know that. But we do not have enough staff. We simply can't reach all the cases," Cramblett said. "We try to do the best we can do with the resources we have."

Board Administrator Lee blames nearly all of the board's failings on a lack of resources, saying the board is woefully undermanned and underfinanced. Lee said the board, because it lacks an adequate number of investigators and lawyers, could not do the job the public expected and often could not act on the information it had.

All of the board's critics agreed that the investigative staff was too small to do a proper job, but they said the problem had more to do with priorities and attitudes than with dollars. The board has received steady budget increases over the past 10 years but has hired only one additional investigator in all that time.

In terms of manpower, the medical board is the largest of the state's 18 regulatory boards. It is the only agency empowered to police the 27,469 M.D.s, osteopaths and podiatrists in Ohio. State and local medical societies and associations have no power over a doctor's license. Their only authority is over the doctor's membership in the organization.

Like most of the other state regulatory boards, the medical board is autonomous, responsible to no one. The governor appoints the 11 board members, nine of whom, under state law, must by physicians. In addition to its disciplinary functions, the medical board is responsible for testing and licensing medical school graduates and making sure licensed physicians keep up on their continuing medical education.

"I think if you were to name one of the six best medical boards in the country, Ohio would come up, on balance, on all the things we do," Board Secretary Cramblett said. "The Ohio board, certainly since 1970, has never licensed a physician with fraudulent credentials as far as I know, and that takes a lot of effort."

But its disciplinary record is where the board falls down. In 1980, the Ohio board was ranked 30th in the nation in terms of the number of disciplinary actions taken against physicians. By 1982, the board had fallen to 40th, according to a recent study in the *New England Journals of Medicine*.

Most of the medical board's skeletons are closeted from the public through the use of "informal meetings," held on the average of 100 times a year. While there is nothing in the law to permit those secret hearings and while board members and the board's own lawyers have privately questioned their legality, the board's official position is that they are a vital part of its investigatory process. Many regulatory boards in the state do not hold such hearings, saying they have been advised they are illegal.

"I asked Ray (Bumgarner, the board's chief counsel) once what statutory authority we had to hold these things, and he finally admitted we didn't have any at all," said a former board vice president, Dr. Jerauld Ferritto. "I don't know why they hold them, and I *heard* some of them." Bumgarner could not be reached for comment.

In addition to the board's secretary, others in attendance at the secret hearings usually include one other board member, the board's administrator, one or more board lawyers and a stenographer. The doctor, who is given little idea why he has been ordered to appear, is permitted to bring his own lawyer.

Michael Falleur, who served as a medical board lawyer in 1980 and 1981, said the informal hearings were part of the reason he quit the board.

"I'm not sure there is any statutory provision that permits those informals," said Falleur, who sat in on many of them. "I started seeing some things that I felt were very wrong."

J. Stephen Teetor, another former medical board lawyer, said he wasn't as worried about the legality of the secret hearings as he was about their appearance.

"I never felt that uncomfortable with them, although I was always real big on the fact that these problems should have been decided at (public) hearings and not behind closed doors. You run the risk of someone saying you're trying to cover up problems internally," Teetor said.

A former medical board secretary, Dr. Anthony Ruppersberg, unwittingly confirmed that during a secret hearing in May 1982. When told by a doctor's lawyer that a prosecutor wanted the minutes of the hearing, Ruppersberg replied, "Notes taken at the meeting were never exposed to the outside, and the purpose of the meeting is to clean up things on the inside."

Jerry C. McDaniel of Columbus recently retired after 17 years as a medical board investigator. "The informals have been put to good use on occasions, but they should not be used to gloss over felonies, and they have been," he said. "They have been abused. I've been in informals where the principals involved should have been before a judge, not another doctor."

"It just seemed like those informals were deliberately abused," said a former board member. "If the doctor had pals on the board or he was prominent in his community . . . they handled his case informally."

EXAMPLES

- Dr. Nathan D. Belinky is Mahoning County coroner. The medical board has been aware for more than a year that he has been overprescribing hard drugs to some patients. Board record show a number of his prescriptions were written for women living at the address of a Youngstown brothel. Belinky appeared for a secret hearing Sept. 5, 1984, to discuss his prescribing practices, board records show. Belinky said he agreed to cut down on his prescribing and said only one of the patients he was questioned about was a prostitute. The board took no action.

■   Dr. David Pixley is president of the Adams County Medical Society. Board records show Pixley was writing Dilaudid prescriptions for known drug addicts and continued writing them after he was told by the board that his patients were addicts and had criminal records. Pixley appeared for two secret hearings and negotiated a consent agreement in March 1983, promising not to give addictive drugs to people unless they were dying of cancer or suffering from intractable pain.

■   Dr. George M. Shadle is chief of the Office of Safety and Health of the state Bureau of Preventive Medicine. Shadle surrendered his federal narcotics license in September 1981 because of improper prescribing of controlled substances, and he appeared for several secret hearings during 1981 and 1982.

■   Dr. Paul J. Matrka is a former president of the medical staff of Mount Carmel Medical Center in Columbus and was under investigation in 1982 by the board for writing false prescriptions for the drug Demerol. Matrka admitted it during a secret hearing in November 1983 and admitted taking the drugs himself. He said he was in pain from back surgery. Board member Dr. Leonard L. Lovshin, who presided at the hearing, "stated he would rather have this matter remain on an informal basis" and the board investigators were told not to report Matrka's admission to the Upper Arlington police or the state pharmacy board, who had been assisting in the investigation. No action was ever taken.

Rep. John R. Kasich, R-12, of Westerville, said those were the kinds of abuses he was trying to prevent when, as a state senator in 1982, he pushed through a bill requiring the board to file a quarterly public report listing all the cases that had been closed and the reason they were closed.

"What I was concerned about was that Dr. X, who was a powerful doctor, was doing something that was a violation of the law, and the investigation was dismissed during an informal hearing, while at the same time they were charging people for practicing medicine without a license," Kasich said. "The only ones against the bill was the medical board."

Six months before Kasich's bill became law, the board met and discussed ways to get around it, records show. One board member suggested that investigations never terminated, so the board wouldn't have to disclose them on the quarterly report.

When the law first went into effect in August 1982, the board had only 94 cases classified as pending. It now has 374 "pending" cases, but internal board records show nearly all of those cases have been "pending" for two to five years.

While the board claims its secret hearings are used to investigate violations of state law, records of those hearings show that's often where the investigation ends.

Dr. David M. Schneider, a Cincinnati ophthalmologist, was called in for a secret hearing on Feb. 10, 1981, because the board's investigators had learned that Schneider had written bogus prescriptions for Dilaudid and Percodan, powerful painkillers widely used on the street.

According to the minutes of that meeting, Schneider admitted he had a drug addiction. When asked if he was taking drugs he had prescribed for others, he refused to answer because of the possibility that criminal charges could be brought against him. Writing false prescriptions for those drugs is a felony under state law.

"Dr. Ruppersberg then informed Dr. Schneider that the purpose of this meeting was to clarify some problems concerning his medical practice and that the board was not trying to get something to incriminate him. Dr. Schneider then stated that he wrote the prescriptions in other people's names and used the medications himself," the minutes state. No action was ever taken.

The minutes of a secret hearing with Schneider on Dec. 30 1981, noted Schneider "uses drugs to open up and get high." He was asked to voluntarily surrender his federal drug license but refused, and, again, no action was taken.

In another secret hearing, Dr. Victor E. Badertscher of Delaware, Ohio, admitted on May 19, 1983, that he had written narcotic prescriptions for himself to sustain his addiction to drugs, a violation of federal and state narcotic laws. The board's only action was to suggest he surrender his license and seek drug treatment. His license was returned seven months later.

Badertscher is now a defendant in a malpractice suit that alleges he addicted one of his patients to drugs.

And Dr. L. K. Wallerstein, a Toledo general practitioner, had an intriguing explanation for why he was buying huge quantities of the drug Talwin, a street substitute for heroin, when he appeared at a secret hearing on June 23, 1977.

"Dr. Wallerstein stated that he was buying drugs for the Cuban underground. He has been doing this for years. The drugs are picked up by men, ID unknown, who come in from out of state. They are supposed to be taken to a Dr. Sanchez in Miami for medical supplies for a Cuban force. Formerly gave cash but couldn't afford it so began giving drugs," the minutes of that meeting state. The board took no action.

Three years later, the board found Wallerstein guilty of prescribing addictive doses of Talwin to one of his patients. He was put on probation. The board later learned Wallerstein was shipping large doses of the drug Stadol, similar to Talwin, to the government of Haiti, but did nothing.

A month after *The Plain Dealer* requested records pertaining to Wallerstein, the doctor was formally charged by the board with, among other things, supplying drugs to the Cuban underground—nearly 7 ½ years after the board first became aware of it.

Patricia Good, head of compliance for the Cleveland office of the Drug Enforcement Administration, said her office was never contacted about Wallerstein's Caribbean adventures. "I think we should have been told," she said in a recent interview.

"The medical board is great for covering things up," investigator McDaniel said. Surprisingly, most of the board members have little or no idea what lurks in the board's secret files. They're not permitted to see them. Dozens of consent agreements have been signed, dozens of licenses have been surrendered and hundreds of secret hearings have been held without their knowledge, records show. Former Board President Dr. Oscar W. Clarke was on the board for a year before he even knew about secret hearings, board records show.

Asked how board members could assure the public it was being protected when the board itself didn't know what was going on in the secret hearings, board consumer member Carol Rolfes said, "We can't."

Board members who inquire are told by the board's lawyers and board Administrator Lee that they are better off not knowing, because they would prejudice themselves against the doctor involved if the case later came up at public hearing. The full board makes a final decision on punishment following a public hearing.

"For all intent, you've got two medical boards in the state of Ohio," former board lawyer Falleur explained. "You've got the one that the board members are on, which meets for a few hours a month. Then you've got this subterranean board, which was run by Bill Lee and Dr. Ruppersberg." (Ruppersburg is now dead.)

In 1980, three board members complained that things were going on behind their backs, board records show.

Dr. Joseph P. Yut "advised that he does not like something being done in his name without him knowing about it, and what he is asking for is an awareness of what transpired at these informal meetings," board minutes state.

Board member Ferritto warned his colleagues, "The newspapers will later discover that action is being taken in the board's name without the board having any knowledge about it. Dr. Ferritto stated that the board members cannot defend themselves from the newspapers if they have no idea what is going on in these meetings."

So far, the doors to the secret proceedings have remained closed to the public and to board members. Last December, *The Plain Dealer* filed suit to make the minutes of the secret hearings public and to release records pertaining to the secret negotiation of consent agreements and voluntary surrenders of medical and drug licenses.

The board is vigorously fighting that lawsuit. But since *The Plain Dealer* first requested those records, the number of secret hearings held has fallen to its lowest point in seven years, record show.

HOW OHIO TOOK CARE OF DR. DAYO

A lot of people don't seem to want Dr. Mateo P. Dayo around.

Since his 1981 conviction on drug charges in Ohio's rural Meigs County, the US Immigration and Naturalization Service has been trying to deport him as an undesirable, and Mississippi medical board refused to give him a license and he was kicked off the staff of Pleasant Valley Hospital in Point Pleasant, W.Va.

Yet Dayo has been allowed an unfettered practice in Ohio, thanks to the State Medical Board and the behind-the-scenes maneuverings of an assistant state attorney general.

"It's a crying shame the way this case was handled," said Gary Wolfe, former chief investigator for the Meigs County sheriff.

Dayo's case is also a good example of how the medical board looks the other way when a physician commits a crime.

In early 1980, the State Pharmacy Board got complaints that Dayo, a 44-year-old family practitioner from the Philippines, was stopping in southeastern Ohio drugstores and getting prescriptions filled for vials of injectable Demerol. Demerol is a potent painkiller and widely abused narcotic.

Wolfe said ". . . [The pharmacists] got suspicious because the prescriptions were not in Dayo's name but he was paying for them himself. He said he was making house calls." Dayo's private office is in Pomeroy, O.

When Wolfe contacted the predominantly elderly patients for whom the Demerol was prescribed, many gave him statements that they had never gotten the drug.

"I had seven, clear-cut, fully documented felony cases against him," Wolfe said. Writing false prescriptions for Demerol is a felony under state law.

Wolfe notified the medical board in July 1980. The board called Dayo in for a secret hearing five months later.

According to the minutes of that secret hearing, Dayo admitted what Wolfe already knew, that a number of the prescriptions were phony. Dayo said he had used the Demerol in his office for other patients, a violation of state and federal drug laws.

Despite Dayo's admission, the board's lawyers maintained there was no evidence of wrongdoing.

"I would prefer (sic) not attempting to make a case out of the information discussed at the informal. Such a procedure, I believe, would defeat the objectives of the informal conference process," board lawyer David Wenger wrote Board Administrator William J. Lee in March 1981.

Meanwhile, Assistant Attorney General Jeffery J. Jurca, then assigned to represent the medical board, kept Dayo's lawyers supplied with information on the medical board's investigation.

Jurca, at the request of Dayo's lawyer, Michael R. Szolosi, poked through the board's investigative files and assured Szolosi that the medical board would take no action against his client.

According to Szolosi's records, Jurca told him exactly what the board was investigating, where the investigation stood and that the Meigs County Sheriff's Department and the State Pharmacy Board had supplied the medical board with the information on Dayo.

Jurca told *The Plain Dealer* he did not reveal any confidential information.

"Finally, Jeff suggested that to the extent any further investigation was warranted, it would be appropriate for him to notify me so that we might attempt to resolve the matter through the informal process of the board rather than through a formal hearing," Szolosi wrote on April 27, 1981.

"That was Mike's idea," Jurca said.

But the Meigs County grand jury spoiled their plans. In July 1981 Dayo was indicted on one count of writing a false prescription. As part of a plea-bargain agreement, he pleaded guilty to a misdemeanor charge of falsification, was given a $750 fine and a year's probation.

With Dayo's conviction, the medical board was forced to issue a formal citation, but waited nine months to do so. By the time of his public hearing in January 1983, Dayo had a new explanation: He had mailed all the Demerol to his mother-in-law in the Philippines who was dying of cancer.

Grand jury transcripts show Dayo testified that he had given most of the Demerol to his patients, and Jurca acknowledged he had read the grand jury transcripts. He also acknowledged reading the minutes of the secret board hearing, during which Dayo also said he had given the drugs to his patients.

Jurca said he couldn't recall if he had asked Dayo why he was now telling the board the Demerol had been shipped overseas.

The public hearing was curious in other regards as well. The only witnesses were Dayo and his wife, who met privately for 30 minutes with Dr. Henry G. Cramblett, the board member hearing the case. No records were made of those talks. Jurca didn't call a single witness.

At the conclusion of his meeting with the Dayos, Cramblett announced that he was putting Dayo on probation for a year, a deal worked out earlier between Jurca and Szolosi.

The medical board in July 1983—three years after it first became aware of the case— unanimously approved Cramblett's decision.

Szolosi said Dayo did nothing wrong and that the Meigs County sheriff's office was out to get Dayo. He said Dayo suffered a number of heart attacks since then and had not been practicing.

Former deputy Wolfe sees the situation as one of doctors being above the law.

"I've sent people to the state penitentiary for doing exactly the same thing Dayo did," Wolfe said.

MISLEADING THE PUBLIC

How much information can you, as a patient, expect to get from the State Medical Board if you fear you doctor is a drug addict, an alcoholic, an ex-convict, or has a history of mental problems?

Chances are, if you get any information at all, it will be false.

Over a period of several months, *Plain Dealer* reporters called the medical board and asked for information on seven physicians known to have been the subjects of disciplinary actions.

In dealing with government agencies, reporters are often given greater access to information than other citizens. Sometimes the reverse is true. To keep either of those situations from happening, the reporters did not identify themselves.

There was no problem obtaining basic information on the seven doctors selected. Board employees quickly provided the doctor's current address, the year he was licensed, his license number and the year his license expires.

But when asked, "Has this doctor ever had any disciplinary problems or has any action ever been taken against his license?" the responses were either untrue or the information was refused.

DR. EDWARD G. SEYBOLD
TOLEDO, CARDIOVASCULAR SURGEON

On April 29, 1980, Seybold signed a consent agreement with the board admitting "that he has excessively used controlled substances and that he has prescribed these controlled substances for himself . . . his wife, and other members of his family." Seybold also admitted "that he has written prescriptions for controlled substances in the name of Frieda K. Jackson, knowing that Frieda K. Jackson had died."

The reporter was told: "He's OK."

DR. JAMES L. REINGLASS
CANTON, NEUROLOGIST

On August 30, 1983, Reinglass entered into a consent agreement admitting "that he has excessively used controlled substances during the years 1977 and 1978, and that questions have been raised concerning his possible use of controlled substances during late 1982 and early 1983." Reinglass agreed to continue drug treatment and to undergo random urine screening, but told the board last August that he was no longer going to abide by the agreement.

The reporter was told: "His license is current and valid." Further information was refused. Two months later, Reinglass was cited for drug addiction.

DR. BUD E. QUINTANA
MASSILLON, SURGEON

In 1980, the Michigan Board of Osteopathic Medicine put Quintana on probation for three years for writing false prescriptions for the hypnotic drug Quaalude, which he took himself. The Ohio board took no action, but called him in for secret hearings.

In August 1982, Quintana surrendered his federal drug license to the medical board after he was dismissed from Massillon Community Hospital for drug abuse.

In November 1982, he was formally charged by the board with writing false prescriptions for the drugs Lomotil, Valium, Demerol, Quaalude, morphine and Stadol and with taking most of them himself. The case was handled through secret hearings.

Nearly two years later, Quintana secretly negotiated a consent agreement, in which he promised to go into drug treatment and to submit to biweekly urine screenings.

The reporter was told: "His license is current, and we do not have any derogatory information."

DR. ALBERT D. MCERLANE
CINCINNATI, GENERAL PRACTITIONER

In 1968, McErlane was convicted of a drug-related felony and lost his federal drug license. The board put him on two years' probation. For three months in 1970, he was a patient in Longview state psychiatric hospital, suffering from alcoholic pyschosis, acute brain syndrome and delerium tremens.

McErlane surrendered his license in 1981 because of alcoholism. He also was injecting himself with the addictive painkiller Talwin. The board gave back his medical and drug licenses the next year. McErlane has appeared for numerous secret hearings over the years and entered into a consent agreement. Board records show he was drinking as recently as November and is now in charge of a county-owned clinic in Bainbridge, a small town near Chillicothe.

The reporter was told: "His license is current and valid. We cannot give you any more information than that."

DR. KEITH R. GASPICH
WHEELERSBURG, FAMILY PRACTITIONER

In 1978, the board discovered Gaspich was personally using large quantities of the painkilling drug Demerol. Gaspich appeared for several secret hearings between 1979 and 1983 and was in drug treatment programs for his Demerol addiction.

The reporter was told: "We do not have any derogatory information."

DR ROBERT W. FINCH
DAYTON, INTERNAL MEDICINE

In 1981, Finch surrendered his license in exchange for the Dayton police Organized Crime Unit's agreeing not to prosecute him on drug charges. Finch was accused of supplying amphetamines to drug addicts. The same year, Finch was sued for allegedly addicting one of his patients to Quaalude and amphetamines. Finch settled out of court. The board returned his medical license after three months, and in May 1982, as a result of a consent agreement, Finch was given back his federal drug license provided he use it only in a hospital setting.

The reporter was told: "There is no derogatory information."

DR. RAYMOND A. MOREHEAD
PORTSMOUTH, THORACIC SURGEON

In 1982, the Florida medical board filed charges when Morehead was caught stealing morphine from the hospital where he worked. He surrendered his Florida license and came to Ohio in 1983. He admitted to the Ohio board in public and secret hearings that, in addition to morphine, he had also abused amphetamines and Quaaludes and was a heavy drinker.

Morehead was given an Ohio license in November 1983, and he signed a consent agreement promising to continue his drug treatment program and to submit to a random urine screenings.

The reporter was told: "There is no derogatory information on Dr. Morehead."

All information above was obtained from the medical board's own records, most of which are public.

Board lawyer Lauren Lubow explained that there had been a misunderstanding between the records and enforcement departments over what was public information. She said Board Administrator William J. Lee had ordered a written policy put into effect that would prevent that kind of misunderstanding from happening again.

The policy: Callers who want disciplinary information must now leave their names and phone numbers, and the board will get back to them.

While a consent agreement is a public record, the board sometimes promises the doctor involved that it won't tell anyone above the agreement unless asked for it specifically. But of the six physicians above who signed consent agreements, only Finch's contained that clause.

Board Administrator Lee was asked how that was in the best interest of the public, since the average citizen isn't likely to know consent agreements even exist.

"Well, I don't know," Lee replied. "I don't particularly favor that clause."

BOARD PROTECTS ADDICTED DOCTORS

> *It's a proud moment, knowing you were able to help one of your own.*
> —Dr. Evelyn L. Cover, former president, State Medical Board

The woman was worried.

She had heard the State Medical Board was thinking of returning Dr. Ronald M. Gustin's medical license, so she wrote and begged that not be done.

"I have personally witnessed him so drunk on the street that he was unable to walk without holding on to parking meters and telephone poles, and I have seen him so drunk in the corridors of Highland District Hospital that he stumbled, banked off walls and staggered uncontrollably," the woman wrote.

She also told the board Gustin had been freely prescribing hard drugs. "I cannot tell you how many of his patients we have seen who are hooked on Darvon, Percodan, barbiturates, tranquilizers, etc.," she wrote.

But the woman wasn't telling the medical board anything new. The board knew the 60-year-old Hillsboro general practitioner had been drinking heavily since 1963 and had been hospitalized several times for alcoholism.

The board also knew that, in 1976, Gustin slipped into the Highland hospital pharmacy and frequently slugged down shots of paregoric, and opium-based diarrhea medicine. Gustin had prescribed himself and his family more than 15 quarts of the addictive potion in one six-month period.

In late 1977, Gustin gave up his license and checked into a Chillicothe hospital. After three weeks of treatment, he told the board he was ready to resume his practice.

"I believe that if you give his license back he will soon be right back where he was . . . drunk, narcotized and endangering patients again. I'm willing to risk my job to prevent the kind of heart-rending abuses I have seen," the woman wrote, on Jan. 25, 1978.

Nevertheless, the board members voted unanimously to return Gustin's medical and drug licenses 11 weeks later.

But the woman's prediction was correct. Gustin began prescribing himself drugs again and, in 1980, sold an undercover medical board investigator a Quaalude prescription made out in the name of a woman Gustin had never seen.

Caught, Gustin handed over his medical and drug licenses for the second time in 28 months. The board gave them back less than a year later and Gustin is still in practice.

Gustin's story is not uncommon. The secret and public files of the state medical board are full of similar or worse tales.

"There are doctors in this state that shouldn't be practicing, just because of their own use of drugs or alcohol, but that was the kind of case the board thought better to handle [from the] inside," former board lawyer Michael Falleur said.

Records show the medical board and the Ohio State Medical Association (OSMA) have collaborated to keep the public in the dark about physicians who are addicted to drugs or alcohol, in apparent violation of both the Controlled Substances Act and the Medical Practice Act.

The state's Controlled Substances Act requires the board to suspend the licenses of drug-addicted doctors but records show the board often ignores that law. Instead, it hides drug addiction cases through the use of secret hearings and secretly negotiated agreements. Records of those secret hearings show that such physicians are told the board will take no public action if drug treatment is sought.

"It's been the opinion of counsel that that (suspension) provision is either unconstitutional or not mandatory," Board Administrator William J. Lee said.

Pharmacy Board Administrator Franklin Z. Wickham said his board has suspended licenses under that law before and has had never run into any legal problems because of it.

The law states: "Any practitioner . . . who is or becomes addicted to the use of controlled substances shall have his license or registration suspended by the board . . . until such time as (he) . . . offers satisfactory proof . . . that he is no longer addicted."

Enforcing that law would mean placing the name of a drug-addicted physician on the public record, something the board tries to avoid. In February 1984, records show, the board and representatives from the state medical association's Impaired Physicians Committee worked out a plan to keep most of those cases from ever becoming public knowledge.

Board Secretary Dr. Henry G. Cramblett told the OSMA officials that "everything was in place for the board and the committee to work together," Cramblett, with the board's approval, told the OSMA that it was not necessary to tell the board about a drug—or alcohol-imparied doctor unless the doctor refused to seek treatment.

If that happened, Cramblett suggested, the OSMA should notify only the board's secretary. The secretary convenes the secret hearings, the records of which the board claims are confidential.

"If it came to the board first, the board would have to go to disciplinary procedures right away," Cramblett reminded the OSMA officials.

But Dr. William H.L. Dornette, a nationally recognized expert in the field of medicine, said patients had a right to know if their physician was or had been addicted to drugs or alcohol.

"It's part of informed consent, part of a patient's right to free choice in medicine," said Dornette, a former Clevelander who holds both a medical degree and a law degree and is a past president of the American College of Legal Medicine.

Dornette said the close relationship between the board and the OSMA's impaired physicians programs was unhealthy and possibly dangerous for the public.

"The interests of the board in theory, are totally adverse to the interests of the OSMA and their (impaired physicians) program. If they start getting buddy-buddy on that issue, then there are a lot of potentialities for patient injury," said Dornette.

Pharmacy Board Administrator Wickham said it was nice that the medical associations wanted to help their members, but said from a standpoint of public protection their programs presented serious problems if it meant regulatory boards were not being notified of practicing alcoholics or drug addicts.

"Until they are no longer addicted, I don't believe they should be in practice at all," Wickham said.

One of the medical board's secret addicts was Dr. Bharat Kelotra, a Warren surgeon whom the board and Trumbull Memorial Hospital allowed to practice even while he was undergoing methadone withdrawl treatment in mid-1980. Kelotra was taking massive does of the addictive painkiller Demerol, records show.

Kelotra, 40, has two malpractice suits pending against him, one of them resulting from a surgery performed just weeks after he started on methadone. The patient, who underwent surgery for a bleeding ulcer, died of complications after the surgery. Kelotra is fighting the suit. He said he no longer had drug problems.

While the Medical Practice Act requires physicians to report possible violations of the Act to the board, physicians commonly ignore that law and the board has never taken any action to enforce it.

Though mandatory reporting laws are intended to help the board identify problem doctors and are supported by the American Medical Association and Federation of State Medical Boards, to which Ohio belongs, the law is openly opposed by many of the board members, the board's administrator and the board's chief counsel. They say it is too strict and impedes treatment.

Lee said no one had ever been cited for violating the mandatory reporting statute because the board had never been notified that a violation had occurred and he said he didn't have any personal knowledge of any violations.

But it's hardly a secret in the medical community that many doctors flout the statute.

"It is probably honored more in the breach than in the observance," board member Dr. Deirdre O'Connor acknowledged.

"With that kind of a law you become a threat to the physician and we see ourselves as a physician's friend," said Dr. David L. Farrington, an official with the OSMA's Physician Effectiveness Program. Asked how the OSMA could just ignore a state law, Farrington replied, "You play dumb. Nobody does anything about it anyway. If you wanted to enforce it, you'd have every physician in the state in jail."

More often than not, the board places the rehabilitation of alcoholic or addicted doctors above the safety of the public. Board members have publicly said that moving such doctors from practice would jeopardize their "recovery" by exposing their addiction to the public and interfering with their income and self-esteem.

"You have to have what I would call tough love," Board Administrator Lee said.

Board member O'Connor, director of an alcohol and drug treatment program in Toledo, said, "I think physicians in recovery are very fragile and I think they need nurturing and not knocking down. If a businessman is allowed (to stay in business while recovering), why shouldn't a physician?"

Medical-legal expert Dornette replied, "Losing your money is not the same thing as losing your health or your life. You can sue a lawyer who steals your money and you can recover in kind, but you can never sue and get back your health."

Board records show that medical and drug licenses have been returned because the board members felt it would be "therapeutic" for the physician to practice medicine again, or because the physician was having financial problems.

Last August, board consumer member Carol Rolfes angrily reminded her fellow board members that the board existed "to protect the public, not to worry about a doctor's financial solvency."

The board allows doctors with long histories of drug and alcohol abuse to practice with little board supervision. While the board says that its investigators keep such physicians under surveillance, the investigators regard that term as a bad joke.

"You know what 'under surveillance' means? It means that next time I'm in their area, which could be six months or longer, I might stop by his office if I have the time. It sure as hell doesn't mean what the board members think it means and it sure as hell isn't any protection for the public," one veteran investigator said.

There are only six investigators for the entire state, yet internal board records show the board had 66 doctors under surveillance last July.

Probationary periods for alcoholic or addicted physicians normally run only year or two, even for longtime abusers. Moreover, the terms of probation are mostly self-enforced.

"A lot of this program is inherently dependent on the good faith execution of the physician," Board Administrator Lee admitted in 1982. If a physician is required to submit reports of urine tests, the board frequently allows the physician's partners to administer the tests. Urine sampling is often discontinued if the physician complains of its expense or inconvenience.

If the board requires a physician to seek drug or alcohol treatment as part of his probation, it is normally left up to the physician to decide what kind of treatment he wants.

"Treatment covers a lot of territory. It can be anything from going to see your friendly psychiatrist, who happens to be your drinking buddy, to real honest-to-God treatment that has a statistical base for good long-term results," said Dr. William J. Kennedy, of Newark, O., director of two widely known impaired physician programs. "To just say, 'Get some treatment' is ridiculous. I think that is where the licensing board has trouble."

In Oregon, as in other states, doctors with drug or alcohol programs are put on strict reporting probation for up to 10 years before the board allows unrestricted practice.

"I don't know how an alcoholic or a drug addict can be rehabilitated after only a year or two. Those kinds of problems don't just go away after a short period of time," said David LaDuca, chief investigator for the Oregon medical board. "We feel that someone who's into alcohol or drugs needs very close supervision over at least a five- to seven-year period before we feel confident in letting him out on his own."

Told that Ohio's board often gives drug addicts their narcotic licenses back within months of coming out of treatment programs, LaDuc said, "What? Are you serious? Holy mackerel, I've never heard of that before."

Board member O'Connor summed up her feelings on the topic last year, saying, "The board doesn't need to feel responsible if it turns an impaired physician loose and that physician has a relapse."

Medical-legal expert Dornette disagreed. "There are lawsuits against parole boards for turning people loose early who then go out and commit mayhem and I think it would be very nice if some lawyer in Ohio got a hold of one of these cases and sued the medical board," he said.

Board member Dr. Leonard L. Lovshin said two years ago that "some board members do believe that alcoholism and drug dependency is a disease and that those with that philosophy know that chances have to be taken."

But too often the board takes unnecessary chances, and frequently at the public's expense.

EXAMPLES

■ The medical board was aware in 1980 that Dr. Earl T. Hoffman, an Akron anesthesiologist, was addicted to the painkiller Percodan and was writing false prescriptions to obtain the drug, but did nothing until 1982 when he was cited for drug addiction. Hoffman agreed to seek treatment and the board dropped the case. He was asked to leave the treatment program five weeks later and was reported to the board as being "a psychopathic personality and not a good candidate for rehabilitation."

The board let Hoffman practice for another 17 months before it took action. It ordered his license suspended for a minimum of six months in March 1984 but when he appeared before the board for the verdict, Hoffman confessed that he had written more false prescriptions for Percodan.

The board responded by cutting his minimum suspension in half. "The honesty he showed . . . deserves some consideration. Suspending him from a method of earning a living would be going against Dr. Hoffman's efforts to recover," board member O'Connor said.

Two days later, Summit County authorities charged Hoffman with deception to obtain dangerous drugs, a felony, and he pleaded guilty. Three months ago, he was cited for practicing medicine without a license.

■ Dr. Victor Strauss, a Cincinnati cardiologist and an associate professor at the University of Cincinnati medical school, surrendered his medical license in 1975 because of a history of alcoholism. Strauss appeared before the board in 1978 and asked for his license back.

". . . Dr. Strauss should be given a chance." Board member Lovshin said, and the board agreed unanimously.

Strauss continued drinking and surrendered his license again in 1979. The board gave it back again at his request in 1981.

Board investigator Charles F. Young went to Strauss' apartment in August 1983 and found him standing in the yard "completely nude except for a pair of shoes and a green sun visor . . . Dr. Strauss looks like a derelict," Young's report stated.

Later, Young spoke to Dr. Charles Kiely, whom Strauss said was his personal physician. "(Kiely) advises that Dr. Strauss is very unkempt and is an embarrassment to the medical community. He further advises that Dr. Strauss steals food from the (hospital) cafeteria and must think no one is aware of it. Dr. Kiely also advised that in his opinion, and some of the other doctors, Dr. Strauss does not have the mentality to function as a physician," Young's October 1983 report to the board stated.

Strauss told Young that he was treating patients in his rubbish-strewn one-bedroom apartment. Strauss still has his license.

■ Dr. Harry H. Hillier, a Springfield pediatrician, came to Ohio with a long record of drug abuse. The Oregon medical board in 1979 put him on probation for 10 years because of his addiction to codeine and he entered a psychiatric hospital. In 1981, his license was suspended because he was again on drugs.

Six months later, the State Medical Board unanimously granted Hillier an Ohio license and he set up practice in Branesville (Belmont County). He was arrested within weeks for breaking into a pharmacy and stealing drugs. Hillier surrendered his license and pleaded guilty to breaking and entering, a felony.

Ten months later, the board gave back his medical license and his federal drug license was returned last year.

"Dr. Hillier is one of the board's success stories . . ." board member Lovshin declared in 1983.

One critic of the board's handling of addicted and alcoholic doctors is former board secretary Dr. Joseph P. Yut, whose term expired last month.

Last April, Yut sharply reminded his fellow board members that "this board is an enforcement and licensing agency, not a rehabilitation agency."

Yut said that while it was commendable the board members wanted to reclaim fallen colleagues, they were forgetting about their main purpose.

"The board has to recognize why it is here, and it must establish priorities. This board's job is to enforce the Medical Practice Act. The board has had to rush through that job to rehabilitate physicians who can be better handled by the experts in the field of rehabilitation," Yut said.

Former Board President Lovshin disagreed with those comments.

"It is party of the board's job to rehabilitate. The physicians are coming to the board as a form of treatment," Lovshin told Yut.

But as the case of Dr. Thomas Lamott Haynes shows, it is one of the most peculiar brands of treatment ever devised by a consumer protection agency.

Haynes, an emergency room physician at St. Alexis Hospital in Cleveland, started his treatment in 1976, when he first applied for his license. At the time, he had been a drug addict for two years and had been kicked out of two hospitals because of drug abuse.

The board issued him a probationary license in February 1977, which he used to get a job in the emergency room of Barberton Citizens Hospital.

Five months later, Haynes began abusing the addictive painkiller Talwin.

"Dr. Haynes disclosed that he did not feel capable of quitting his habit on his own at this point in his life . . . When it was suggested that his hospital remove his access to Talwin, Dr. Haynes stated that he would find some way to procure it," the minutes of the February 1978 board meeting state.

The board didn't ask him to turn in his license; board member Dr. Peter Lancione ". . . reminded the board that action of that nature would be taking a physician out of an emergency room where he was needed," board minutes show.

Instead, the board waited five months and held a formal hearing on the matter; Haynes continued seeing patients and was on drugs most of the time, records show.

Haynes was put back on probation in October 1978 and was back on Talwin within three months. Again, the board allowed him to practice until his hearing in August 1979.

"I was totally out of control," Haynes told the board, saying he would take large doses of Talwin any time he felt like it. He also admitted for the first time that he was addicted to alcohol.

Haynes asked the board to let him keep his license, pointing out that he was still seeing patients at Barberton Citizens Hospital "despite their being aware again and again of my continued use of Talwin."

The board went along, but before that decision was even typed up, Haynes was on drugs again. His license was indefinitely suspended in November 1979. Haynes came back nine months later, swearing he would never again touch drugs. He told the board that if his license was returned, Baberton Citizen Hospital would give him his old job back.

Board member Dr. Jerauld Ferritto had heard enough.

"Dr. Ferritto stated that he couldn't let this man go back into practice. Dr. Ferritto stated that although everyone is recommending that his practice will be therapeutic for Dr. Haynes, he wonders about the board's wisdom in allowing Dr. Haynes to practice on the public again," the board minutes state.

Ferritto was outvoted and Haynes' license was returned in August 1980, on the condition he have his urine tested daily. That requirement was lifted nine months later at Haynes' request.

". . . Dr. Haynes appears well on the way to successful rehabilitation," board member Lovshin declared in May 1981.

Within three months, Haynes began taking drugs from the Barberton hospital emergency room. This time, he was seeing patients while under the influence of the narcotic Nubain, which is 10 times stronger than Talwin. Haynes was asked to surrender his license but refused and checked into another drug treatment program.

Haynes asked the board five months later to let him keep his license, saying he had a job in the St. Alexis emergency room. Yut and Ferritto demanded that Haynes be charged but the other board members disagreed.

"Dr. Lancione stated that he did not think the board would accomplish anything by keeping Dr. Haynes out of practice. Dr. Yut said the board would accomplish keeping him away from patients should he fail again," the board minutes state.

In September 1983, Haynes asked for his federal drug license back. Yut again objected, calling Haynes a flagrant abuser who couldn't be trusted.

But Board President Dr. John Rauch worried that if the board refused, Haynes would become so despondent he would start drinking or taking drugs again.

". . . Dr. Haynes has remained drug free and the board is obligated to help him stay that way," Rauch said. The board returned Haynes' drug license and discontinued his urine screenings at the same time, after he complained they were "an inconvenience and an expense."

Haynes is now completely off probation.

EX-CON, ADDICT KEEPS HIS LICENSE

Paul and Nancy Cannon were repainting the bathroom of their newly rented home in Madeira, Ohio, when they found a secret compartment concealed in the bathroom wall.

They reached in and pulled out 32 empty bottles of Percodan and five empty vials of vials of Demerol, highly addictive prescription drugs. They also found several hypodermic syringes and a few pieces of rubber tubing.

The Cannons didn't realize it but they had found the stash of Dr. Paul K. Yankow, former tenant.

The bathroom has some more history the Cannons probably didn't know about. It was one of the last places Marilyn Ashworth Miller ever saw before she killed herself with a drug overdose—drugs Yankow had given her.

Miller's sister, Yvonne M. Hodge, thinks more people ought to know about Dr. Yankow. Hodge says her sister would probably be alive today if it wasn't for him.

"It absolutely amazes me that he still has his license," Hodge said.

In his few years of practice in Ohio, Yankow, 42, of Cincinnati, has compiled an impressive record as a criminal and a drug addict.

He was convicted in Butler County of receiving stolen property in 1978, after police found drugs in his apartment that he had stolen from the Miami University pharmacy. Yankow had been working at the university's student health center, coming there from the student health center at Kent State.

He later admitted he had been involved with drugs since at least 1971, when he was kicked out of his residency program at Akron General Hospital because of drug abuse. He was kicked out of a Georgia military hospital in 1978 for the same thing.

The board cited him in 1979 because of the criminal conviction but did nothing, deciding Yankow had been successfully rehabilitated after two weeks of hospitalization.

"I'm not as bad a guy as I used to be, I think," Yankow told the board.

"The board has made Dr. Yankow a new man," former board consumer member Walter H. Paolo declared.

But board investigator Charles F. Young decided to keep his eye on Yankow anyway. He checked with Mercy Hospital in Cincinnati, where Yankow was then working, and when Yankow found out, he complained angrily to the board because the hospital was unaware of Yankow's drug addiction.

The board apologized and board member Dr. Leonard L. Lovshin worried that "a physician's rehabilitation could be jeopardized by careless contacts such as this," the board minutes show.

Eleven months later, Marilyn Miller killed herself.

Court records show Miller, 38, had been living with Yankow for about a year and they were planning on marriage. After an operation in early 1981 left her suicidally depressed, Yankow began bringing her large quantities of the anti-depressant drug Elavil.

Shortly before her death, records show, Miller locked herself in the bathroom of their house and threatened to take her life. Yankow told police he took the Elavil out of the bathroom after that, but put it back a few days later because she seemed better.

Within two weeks she was dead of an Elavil overdose.

"The possibility of suicide in depressed patients remains until significant remission occurs. Potentially suicidal patients should not have access to large quantities of this drug," the Physician's Desk Reference says of Elavil. Yankow then began writing dozens of phony prescriptions for the drugs Percodan and Demerol, addictive painkillers which he took himself. The Cannons found those empty bottles and vials in the bathroom of their new house in June 1982.

On Jan. 5, 1982, Yankow was arrested by Cincinnati narcotics agents and indicted on two counts of illegal processing of drug documents. Paolo's "new man" surrendered his medical license and pleaded guilty to the felony charges.

Yankow then asked the court to allow him treatment in lieu of conviction, saying he was a drug addict at the time of the crimes. Under that program, if an addict receives drug treatment the court will consider dismissing the conviction.

Yankow appeared before the medical board in June 1983 and asked for his license back but the board refused. Yankow requested a hearing and by the time it was held, six months later, he had completed drug treatment and the court had dismissed his conviction.

As usual, the board hadn't done an independent investigation of Yankow's crimes and the board's lawyer, Assistant Attorney General Scott Lavelle didn't call any witnesses during the hearing. Lavelle's entire case consisted of the now-meaningless court records of Yankow's dismissed conviction.

Hearing officer Dr. Peter Lancione concluded the board had to give his license back because ". . . the record is totally void of any independent evidence showing the specific acts serving as the basis for the criminal charges against Dr. Yankow."

Since then, Yankow has settled two malpractice cases out of court. Both of those cases involved ailments Yankow allegedly failed to diagnose, even though evidence showed they were apparent in the patients' X-rays.

Miller's sister has filed a $3.2 million malpractice suit against Yankow, charging that his negligence in supplying Miller with unlimited quantities of Elavil resulted in her death.

"I feel like if Paul Yankow would have gotten my sister the proper medical attention and if he had not left her with all those pills, she may be alive today. She trusted him because he was a doctor," Hodge said in a deposition.

Yankow could not be reached for comment, but has denied the allegations in Hodge's suit.

Last October, Yankow again complained to the medical board that investigator Young was bothering him. He said Young mentioned to a receptionist at Kreindler Medical Center in Cincinnati, where Yankow now works, that Yankow was on probation with the board.

The board apologized to Yankow and instructed its chief investigator to "take appropriate action" against Young.

Shortly after that, Young asked for disability retirement. He declined to comment.

DR. CAUL: JUNKIE TO MEDICAL CHIEF

The Ohio Department of Mental Health has kept the story of Dr. David Caul under wraps for years.

Caul, the former medical director of the state mental hospital in Athens, first walked through its doors as a patient. He was also an ex-convict and a drug addict, records show.

The department, which once deleted references to Caul's addiction from public records, still doesn't have much to say about him. Neither does the State Medical Board, which has had Caul in for several secret hearings over the years and, records show, is investigating him again.

Caul is no longer with the Athens Mental Health Center. After the president of the hospital's medical staff threatened to report him to the medical board, Caul stepped down as medical director in 1983. He was then given a $40-an-hour contract to serve as a consultant for several multiple personality patients, including William S. (Billy) Milligan, the Columbus man who made legal history when he was cleared of three rapes at Ohio State University because he was diagnosed as having multiple personalities.

Caul, a psychiatrist, was the hero of the 1981 bestseller, *The Minds of Billy Milligan*, written by a friend, Daniel Keyes, an English professor at Ohio University.

Medical board records show Caul, 63, has had drug problems since at least 1953, when he pleaded guilty to federal drug charges in Louisiana and was committed to a federal hospital. He came to Ohio after his release and between 1956 and 1964 he was off and on drugs several times, using both morphine and methadone.

Caul checked himself into the Athens mental hospital on Jan. 12, 1965, a week after the State Medical Board charged him with gross immorality because of his drug abuse.

He had been off drugs only a month when the hospital hired him as a staff physician.

The board allowed Caul to keep his medical license on the condition that he practice only at a state medical hospital. "This is a long record. His rehabilitation is very questionable," one board member noted at the hearing.

In 1979, Caul was appointed medical director of the 1,450-bed Athens mental hospital, a position that put him in charge of the hospital pharmacy. Soon after, he was back on drugs.

This time, the medical board took no public action but called him in for a number of secret hearings and suggested he seek drug treatment. In February 1981, Caul was admitted to Riverside Hospital in Columbus.

Although the medical board took no action, Dr. Sami Michael, a psychiatrist and president of Athens hospital medical staff, decided he had had enough.

He asked hospital Supt. Dr. Sue Foster in May 1982 to review Caul's appointment, saying his drug addiction and mental condition were causing serious problems for patients and the staff.

While concluding the hospital was in need of "improved psychiatric leadership," then-commissioner of Mental Health and Forensic Services, Dr. Howard Sokolov, said he found no basis for disciplinary action against Caul.

"I believe you found from your investigation that Dr. Caul is in need of treatment. He has had a serious drug-related problem for some time and the problem impairs his professional judgment. He has involved nurses in administering the drugs to him, and while is the medical director, he has full access to a wide range of drug intoxicants," Michael wrote Sokolov on Sept. 15, 1982, demanding that the department take action.

Caul said he did not have access to the pharmacy.

"As you are also aware, several questions regarding sexual overtures to patients were brought to your attention in the investigation. This also creates a very serious situation in the hospital while Dr. Caul continues to administer to patients."

Caul declined to comment on that, citing doctor-patient confidentiality.

Michael reminded Sokolov that, as licensed physicians, they had a duty to notify the medical board.

"I would prefer to keep this controversy in the department. However, I cannot ethically ignore serious problems at the Athens Mental Health Center while the department does nothing with the hope that the problem will resolve itself," Michael wrote.

Sokolov told Michael to hold off. "I hope that in the very near future this will be resolved in a manner satisfactory to all involved," Sokolov wrote.

Caul retired as medical director in March 1983, but remained on the active medical staff and was given a contract to act as a consultant on multiple personality cases.

While his reappointment to the staff came up at a medical staff meeting in October 1983, Michael objected and mentioned that the staff had not been given any information on Caul's "health status." Supt. Foster ordered that statement deleted from the meeting minutes. In a recent interview, she said she did that because it was not pertinent, but refused to discuss any other details of Caul's tenure as medical director, saying it was not public information.

The next month, Michael notified the medical board.

Edward M. Valentine, then the medical board's chief investigator, spoke to the mental health department's security chief, Joseph Zisler, who conducted two internal investigations of Caul between July 1982 and June 1983.

"He advised that in regard to the alleged sexual misconduct with a patient by Dr. Caul at the center, the female involved . . . was a patient for a short time in 1978. Further, that Dr. Caul and (the patient) did have a short affair in 1980," Valentine's Feb. 8, 1984, memo to Board Administrator William J. Lee stated.

Caul terminated his consulting contract on March 2. Three weeks later the medical board subpoenaed the patient files of Milligan and one woman from the Athens hospital. Supt Foster refused to honor the subpoena and the board did not pursue the matter, she said.

The board has taken no further action. Caul said he has been drug-free since 1981 and is now in private practice.

BOARD GOES EASY ON DRUG DEALERS

The connection had been made and the deal was going down. The dealer and the buyer, who was a police informant, were cryptically haggling over the price of the drugs.

INFORMANT: *That's 90, that's 94. Doesn't the Rs (Ritalin) sell for—what? Six or seven dollars on the street?*

DEALER: *Well, she has the whole solution, she sells people by the thousands. That's why the small quantities will do the . . .*

INFORMANT: *OK, how much does that come to . . . three scripts of 30 for $500, R?*

DEALER: *Three scripts of 30 for $500, T (Talwin). I'm running out of Ts this week . . . all they want is Ts. Just some new kick going on out there.*

Moments later, the Columbus police rushed in and arrested Dr. Mary Joy Groom on charges of trafficking in drugs and writing false prescriptions for the stimulant Ritalin and the painkiller Talwin. She made bail and fled from a 36-count indictment.

The Missouri state police caught her on a back road near Unionville on Feb. 23, 1982.

While a state trooper and Groom's parents, who were in the car, watched in horror. Groom pulled out a .38-caliber Charter Arms Undercover Special and killed herself with a shot to the stomach.

Columbus police said that while she stood a good chance of being convicted, she stood a better chance of keeping her medical license.

The State Medical Board says putting physicians such as Groom out of business is one of its top priorities, but the board's record over the past few years is less than convincing. Narcotics detectives and county prosecutors say the board often creates more drug problems that it solves.

"As far as I'm concerned, the medical board is nonexistent. They don't even make an effort to do anything. They exist out here in name only," said Warren narcotics detective Sgt. Thomas Stewart.

Columbus narcotics detective Sgt. James Dempsey, who heads a unit that deals solely with the illegal use of pharmaceutical drugs, said the board failed to realize the problems it caused by falling to act quickly against drug-dealing doctors when they were identified, and by failing to adequately discipline them once they were caught.

"The guy on the street might have 30 or 40 pills to sell at one time. The doctor can sit behind his desk and spew them out by the hundreds and thousands, which is what Joy Groom did. She put more than 30,000 pills on the streets," Dempsey said. The Columbus police had notified the board of Groom a year earlier.

Sgt. James Veres, acting chief of narcotics for the Cuyahoga County Sheriff's Department, said, "To me, a doctor is in the same position as a public official and if a public official is convicted of a felony, he can never again hold public office. I think the same should be true with a doctor, but the medical board, they won't do anything. I'll be honest, I try to have as little to do with the medical board as possible."

Records show the board rarely revokes the license of a convicted drug criminal and board members have, on occasion, justified it by saying the doctor has already had paid a heavy price by being embarrassed in the newspapers. Only 13 licenses have been revoked in the past 14 years.

"In my opinion, a doctor convicted of a drug-related felony should never be allowed to practice medicine again. Most of these people, they're writing prescriptions knowing full well they're going to be used illegally or sold on the streets. (They are) absolutely no different than your run-of-the-mill drug pusher," Dempsey said.

The Ohio Supreme Court, in a recent landmark decision, agreed.

"A physician who flagrantly disregards his sworn professional obligation by allowing large quantities of dangerous drugs to enter illicit channels is no less a criminal than the layperson on the street who sells the same," Justice Robert Holmes wrote last December.

The case involved Cincinnati general practitioner Dr. Daniel H. Sway, who is accused of giving an addicted prostitute drugs in exchange for sex. Sway was indicted on 17 counts of aggravated drug trafficking in November 1982. Sway's lawyers argued that Sway was not selling drugs by writing prescriptions, but the Supreme Court said it was the same thing and ordered him to stand trial.

The medical board has been aware of the Sway case for 2 ½ years, but has taken no action. The board had Sway in for a secret hearing in August 1982 and asked him to surrender his drug license, but he refused. The prostitute gave the board a statement in September 1982 admitting she had sex with Sway in exchange for prescriptions.

Assistant Hamilton County Prosecutor William E. Breyer said his office had asked the medical board at least twice to act.

"The impression we got from them was they wouldn't act unless there was a conviction. I personally think they have a duty to investigate doctors and they ought to conduct their own investigation to find out if there is any substance to the charges and they ought to act on it," Breyer said.

"The bar association routinely investigates and suspends attorneys from practice, not because they were convicted of a crime, but because of the way they were conducting their practices."

The Supreme Court said it was "patently clear from the facts" that Sway had violated the medical practice act, even if he was not guilty of drug trafficking.

Over the past few years, the board has permitted numerous doctors who were found guilty of drug-related crimes to continue practice:

DR. DAVID H. BLACK
AVON LAKE

Convicted in 1981 of 16 felony drug counts for supplying Percodan to people he knew were addicts and convicted criminals. Black's license was suspended for 60 days but he was serving a 90-day jail sentence at the time and could not have practiced anyway.

DR. JOSETTE W. BIANCHINE
COLUMBUS

Convicted in 1982 of seven felony drug counts for writing prescriptions for people who told her they were going to sell them on the streets, including an undercover policeman who asked for five prescriptions as payment for putting linoleum in her office. The board put her on probation.

DR. IVAN CZNORYJ
PARMA

Indicted in 1977 on eight felony drug charges after selling prescriptions to undercover police for the addictive tranquilizer Quaalude and the addictive diet pill Preludin. He pleaded guilty to one count. The board put him on probation—four years later.

DR. DONALD B. FRANKMANN
CLEVELAND

Pleaded guilty in 1981 to a felony count of forgery after forging hospital records to conceal the fact that he had taken drugs from Cleveland Clinic to feed his addiction. The board put him on probation.

DR. MARTIN J. GUNTER
CUYAHOGA FALLS

Found guilty of drug abuse in 1983 after police discovered he was supplying prostitutes with narcotics in exchange for sex. Gunter, a psychiatrist, agreed to seek psychiatric treatment and, as part of his deal with prosecutors, was allowed to withdraw his pleas and the charge was dropped. The board took no action.

DR. GEORGE E. KACHELE
CINCINNATI

Pleaded guilty to one felony drug count in 1981, after he forged prescriptions to feed his 35-year-long addiction to the sedative drug Nembutal. He surrendered his license, but it was returned seven months later.

DR. KENNETH P. LEVISON
DAYTON

Convicted in Kentucky in 1964 of six felony drug charges and sentenced to 160 years in jail after police found he was writing prescriptions to drug addicts in exchange for sex, stolen suits and electrical appliances, and cash.

He served four years in jail. In 1973 he was granted an Ohio license. In 1981 he was convicted in Dayton of two felony drug counts for prescribing Dilaudid for a known drug addict and he voluntarily surrendered his license. He is now requesting its return.

DR. ROBERT J. MCCONNELL
DAYTON

Indicted in 1981 seven felony drug charges after police learned he had written and cashed false prescriptions for the addictive painkillers Dilaudid, Demerol and Talwin and supplied the drugs to a suspected dealer who would show up at the back doors of McConnell's office. He pleaded guilty to two felony drug charges and surrendered his license. The board gave it back less than a year later.

DR. FREDERICK L. MUGASHE
TOLEDO

Indicted in Seneca County in 1981 on seven felony drug charges, Mugashe pleaded guilty to reduced charges during his trial. Mugashe was accused of writing false prescriptions for Demerol even after he had surrendered his federal drug license to the medical board. Three months ago, he pleaded guilty to a felony drug charge in Toledo for writing more phony Demerol prescriptions. The board has been aware of Mugashe since 1979, but he still has his license.

DR. PAUL H. NORTON
CLEVELAND

Pleaded guilty in 1983 to 11 drug felonies, a theft felony and five forgery felonies for writing narcotic prescriptions for addicts and then filing phony insurance claims. He served an 18-month jail term, but he still has his license.

DR. PETER SAMAME
CLEVELAND

Indicted by a federal grand jury in 1974 for illegal distribution of Quaalude, Samame pleaded guilty to a reduced charge and the board suspended his license for 90 days. Last October, Samame was arrested again and charged with nine felony drug counts for selling prescriptions to undercover police. He recently pleaded guilty to three felony counts. The board has taken no action.

DR. DONALD M. SHAPIRO
DAYTON

Pleaded guilty to five felony drug counts in 1981 after police found he was writing false prescriptions for Demerol and taking them himself. The board handled the case through secret hearings.

DR. GEORGE SMIRNOFF
CLEVELAND

Indicted in 1977 on felony charges of trafficking in Quaaludes and pleaded guilty to a reduced charge in the middle of his trial. His license was suspended for 60 days.

DR. RUDOLFO STOCK
WEST VIRGINIA

Pleaded guilty in 1981 to federal felony charges that he supplied Preludin to female addicts. One of the women later sued Stock and won, testifying that he forced her into prostitution and also forced her to bring him other women he could have sex with. He was sent to jail for six months, fined $20,000 and his West Virginia license was suspended for five years. The board put him on probation and ordered him to restrict his Ohio practice to a state hospital.

DR. FERRUH UNALAN
WARREN

Convicted in September 1983 on two misdemeanor drug charges after a Warren police informant bought Talwin prescriptions for herself and for a detective who was sitting outside in the car monitoring the conversation. A year later, Unalan's license was suspended for 30 days.

The California medical board, one of the most aggressive in the country, does not operate that way.

"If it is a felony concerning drug diversion to the streets, we would revoke (a doctor's license) almost automatically, without even thinking very hard about it," said Linda McCready, chief of external affairs for the California board.

One thing that infuriates Ohio police and prosecutors is the State Medical Board's steadfast refusal to act until a doctor's conviction is upheld on appeal, no matter how far the doctor appeals it. That allows convicted drug dealers to remain in practice for years after their convictions.

The board's slavish reliance on the criminal courts to prompt disciplinary action is puzzling, prosecutors say, because it is far easier to take away a doctor's license than it is to put him in jail.

While guilt beyond a reasonable doubt is required to convict a doctor of a crime, the medical board can revoke a doctor's license on the basis of "reliable, probative, and substantial evidence," a lower burden of proof. Prosecutors say cases they wouldn't dare to take to a jury would easily revoke a license, but since the board won't act until a conviction is obtained, many drug-dealing doctors go unpunished.

"We ran into a situation down here where the medical board wouldn't act until the prosecutor did, and the prosecutor wouldn't act unless the medical board did," said Mansfield police Capt. Wayne Cairnes. "So everybody stood there looking at each other and nothing ever happened."

Board Administrator William J. Lee said the board waited to discipline a doctor until his appeals were exhausted because if it took away a license and the conviction was overturned, the doctor would have lost his license for nothing.

But Lorain County Prosecutor Gregory White, whose office is probably the most aggressive in the state in pursuing drug-dealing doctors, said if a criminal conviction was overturned it was usually due to a legal technicality and should not concern the medical board.

"That doesn't mean the doctor didn't do what was alleged, it just means the court thought the prosecutor or the judge or the policeman or jury made a mistake," White said.

Part of the reason for the medical board's leniency with convicted criminals is the way the cases are presented at the board hearings. An assistant attorney general represents the board during hearings but the cases are prepared by the board's own lawyers.

As with many state medical boards, only one board member is present at the hearing and he acts as the hearing officer, or judge. The other board members rely on the hearing officer's recommendations and his written synopsis of the hearing when deciding on the appropriate punishment.

An analysis of hearings involving criminal physicians shows that the evidence presented to the hearing officer and, ultimately, to the board, is often heavily weighted in the doctor's favor.

While the doctor spends hours presenting his side of the story and often brings friends, colleagues and dozens of letters from adoring patients, the medical board's case normally consists of a piece of paper showing the doctor was convicted of a crime.

The police who investigated it, the victims or witnesses are almost never called to testify and the board does not conduct its own investigation. Further, previous disciplinary actions or admissions made in secret medical board hearings are rarely brought up.

(Board lawyer Lauren Lubow said the board was unaware until a reporter pointed it out that a Youngstown doctor it was accusing of quackery for prescribing sugar pills as a cataract cure had been found guilty of the same thing in 1978. The case did not surface at the doctor's 1984 hearing.)

What results is an appearance that a pillar of the community was unjustly persecuted for one mistake.

"It's an extremely rare occasion where you charge someone with one innocent little violation," Columbus detective Dempsey said. "Most of the time, it's dozens and dozens of crimes and the doctor pleads guilty to one count. The problem is, the board just looks at that one count and doesn't consider the fact that there were perhaps 100 other instances that he didn't plead to or wasn't indicted on. You know, we just don't pick these doctors' names out of a hat. If he's arrested, it's because there have been a lot of problems."

Board Administrator Lee said it was not necessary to go into the details of the crime because conviction of a crime was sufficient to justify disciplinary action.

"If you want to open up the whole case and bring the detectives in, you run into problems and dangers of, you might say, getting the conviction overturned in the administrative law proceeding," Lee said. The attorney general's office makes the final decision on how to proceed in those cases, Lee said.

Robert Tenenbaum, a spokesman for the attorney general's office, denied that and said, if the medical board wants more information presented at those hearings, "all they have to do is tell us. The final decision rests with them."

Regardless of whose decision it is, the case of Dr. Rodger L.M. Taylor, of Dayton, is an example of how that policy works in practice.

In 1977, Taylor and two other men were indicted on 30 counts of writing false prescriptions and trafficking in Quaaludes. Prosecutors charged that the trio ran a lucrative operation writing phony Quaalude prescriptions, cashing them at a friendly pharmacy and then selling the drugs on the streets.

"During our investigation, the police department was able to determine that over 5,000 fraudulent prescriptions had been prescribed by Dr. Taylor through one pharmacy.

Our investigation covered only a two-year period; however, we were able to determine that this illegal act had been occurring since 1973," former Dayton Police Chief Grover W. O'Conner wrote the board.

"It is estimated that the fraudulent prescriptions written by Dr. Taylor represented well over $1 million in illegal drugs being placed on the street."

Taylor pleaded guilty to four felony charges in the midst of his trail. Montgomery County Common Pleas Judge Rodney M. Love sentenced him to jail for 2 to 20 years and fined him $20,000, noting that in one month Taylor had processed 530 prescriptions for more than 15,900 Quaaludes.

In sending Taylor to jail, Love said he spoke for "the hundreds, yes, thousands . . . subjected to methaqualone addiction . . . who many have resorted to crime because of these prescriptions."

Taylor surrendered his medical license and spent a little more than a year in jail. When he got out, he asked for his license back, saying he was innocent of the charges he pleaded guilty to and he had not deserved a jail sentence.

"The (guilty) plea was not at my suggestion. The attorneys suggested it. Plus the fact that I am looking at a jury that is very possibly prejudiced because they were all white. Second, I heard the police get on the stand and blatantly lie." Taylor testified at his August 1980 medical board hearing.

Taylor testified at length, claiming the prosecutors had tricked him into pleading guilty, and that the judge had treated him shabbily. Taylor's wife testified that her husband's lawyers had done a lousy job. Two of Taylor's friends testified they did not believe the charges against him and Taylor brought dozens of laudatory letters, including one from Dayton's mayor and another from State Rep. C.J. McLin, D-36, of Dayton.

The medical board's lawyer, Assistant Attorney General Jeffery J. Jurca, presented a court document showing Taylor had pleaded guilty to writing four illegal prescriptions, and rested his case. He called no witnesses and told the hearing officer that it was not necessary to get into the details of why and how those four-prescriptions were written.

"Dr. Taylor had paid his debt to society in full and deserves our honest consideration," the board's hearing officer ruled, and he recommended Taylor's license be restored. The board agreed. Last year, it restored Taylor's federal drug license.

"I'm not especially happy with the fact that somebody who was as involved as I *know* (Taylor) was is back practicing medicine and dispensing drugs," Love said. "We lawyers are sometimes pretty lax in who our members are but, by God, the doctors are worse than we are."

A PAPER BLIZZARD IN YOUNGSTOWN

If you want to get a rise out of the Strike Force detectives in Youngstown, mention the State Medical Board.

The way the detectives see it, the medical board was indirectly responsible for putting more than 500,000 pills on Youngstown's streets between 1982 and 1984.

Until six months ago, Youngstown's Dr. Edward L. McIver ran what narcotics agents say was the biggest prescription drug mill in Ohio, at least since Dr. Leonard Faymore of Lorain went to jail. McIver's mill started within days of Faymore's closing down.

McIver's operation was so efficient he was often able to sell more than 2,000 prescriptions a month, records show, even while he and his entire office staff were under indictment for drug trafficking.

"The thing that was amazing to us is that they were so wide open about it. It didn't make any difference that they were all under indictment," said Det. George Pavlich.

It didn't make any difference to the medical board either.

"They didn't do s—," Pavlich groused.

Youngstown police and the State Pharmacy Board began investigating McIver, a former Eagle Scout and star quarterback on a football team at North High School, in November 1981 and informed the State Medical Board of the problem a few months after that.

"The (Drug Enforcement Administration) people we were working with told us not to depend on the medical board because we weren't going to get anything done that way. They were right," Pavlich said.

Pavlich's men and their informants made numerous undercover buys from McIver. In April 1982, they arrested McIver and one of his "patients," who had walked out of McIver's office with 70 prescriptions in the names of 70 different people.

McIver was indicted the next month on charges of aiding and abetting drug trafficking. Pavlich said his department figured that would be enough to get the medical board moving. It wasn't.

McIver's prescriptions continued to blow around Youngstown like a paper blizzard: One month after his arrest, records show McIver sold prescriptions for 2,550 tablets of Demerol, 1,470 tablets of Desoxyn, 10,960 tablets of Percodan, 12,450 tablets of Quaalude, 1,680 tablets of Talwin and 232 ounces of Tussionex, all highly addictive and widely abused drugs.

Youngstown police collected a pile of McIver's prescriptions, and punched them into a computer.

"When we finished putting all the scripts on the computer we came up with 619 different names. We picked 329 names at random from the computer printout and of those 329 people, we found 159 of them had criminal records with our office alone," Pavlich said.

Still there was no word from the medical board.

"They were the only ones that could do anything. We'd arrested the guy and gotten him indicted but as long as he still had his license, there wasn't anything else we could do," Pavlich said.

"We had sent them all the prescriptions, given them everything we had. There was no reason they couldn't have done something."

Meanwhile, the detectives concentrated on McIver's runners, the handful of ex-convicts who, police said, sold McIver's prescriptions on the streets.

"The runners would come into McIver's office every morning with their orders—so much Perc, so many Ritalin, so much Dilaudid—and a list of names they wanted the scripts made out in," explained Patrolman John Perdue, who frequently sat outside McIver's office and monitored the transactions.

Perdue said the list were then taken to the law office of lawyer Timothy O'Neill, where he, his wife, Alice Marie, and secretary, Linda Booker, would type up the prescriptions and send them back to McIver.

"Around 3:30 in the afternoon, the runners would come back with the money and they'd be given the scripts. Then the runners would go out, and they had a number of street corners where they'd meet their junkies and sell them the scripts," Perdue said. "It ran pretty much like a Sears store."

In 13 months, police say, McIver sold 13,314 prescriptions. At $35 a prescription, which is what Perdue said the runners were paying, that comes to nearly $466,000.

The prescriptions were selling on the streets for $75 each, but police say McIver did not get involved in that $1 million business.

In December 1982, lawyer O'Neill's office was raided. Police found 3,000 pre-printed prescriptions for Percodan, complete with McIver's signature, and $4,000 cash. Alice O'Neill was sitting at a typewriter banging out a prescription when the police came in.

O'Neill, his wife, secretary Booker, and McIver's office manager, Curtis McCullum, were arrested and indicted on drug charges.

But Pavlich and his men had another year to wait before the medical board acted.

It finally filed charges on Dec. 7, 1983, but to the amazement of the police, McIver was allowed to keep his medical and drug licenses pending a formal hearing.

More prescriptions than ever started showing up. In one month last spring, records show McIver sold 2,116 prescriptions for more than 42,000 doses of narcotics. His prescriptions were showing up in pharmacies across the state.

Finally, the medical board decided to get McIver's license suspended.

Under Ohio law, if a physician's practice represents an immediate danger to the public, the board can ask a judge to suspend the doctor's license before a hearing. The board had that power since August 1982, but had used it only once.

Board lawyer Beverly Yale drafted a petition and collected affidavits for a restraining order and took the papers to the attorney general's office, which represents the medical board in court. Yale asked that they be filed in Mahoning County Common Pleas Court.

Assistant Attorney General Simon B. Karas, chief of the attorney general's administrative agencies, refused.

Asked why, Karas said, "I think your question is really inappropriate." He said he could not comment due to the lawyer-client privilege.

McIver continued practicing and continued writing prescriptions. His four associates were found guilty in July 1984 of drug charges and each was sentenced to 1 ½ years in jail. But the prescriptions kept coming.

In October 1984, the Youngstown police arrested four runners in McIver's parking lot. McIver closed his office the next day.

"I think he finally figured out we weren't going to let up," Pavlich said. "It's too bad, in a way, because we were ready to slam-dunk him."

Meanwhile, McIver still has his license. The medical board has had two days of hearings on the charges it filed more than a year ago. More hearings were scheduled for January but were snowed out and no further hearings have been scheduled.

McIver's criminal charges are also still pending. He could not be reached for comment, but has denied the charges.

BOARD LEAVES POLICE FRUSTRATED, ANGRY

Mansfield police Lt. Philip Messer doesn't mince words.

"The State Medical Board is a big waste of the taxpayer's money, in my opinion," Messer said.

Dayton police detective Robert Clemmer said the same thing. "They're worthless."

Messer and Clemmer speak from experience. In 1980 and 1981, the Dayton and Mansfield police departments began intensive efforts to curb the flow of pharmaceutical drugs into the streets of their cities.

Mansfield's "Operation Script" identified eight physicians who were determined to be the source of 80% of the drugs winding up on the streets, Mansfield police Capt. Wayne Cairnes said. Dayton police put together a list of 10 doctors and convicted five on drug felony charges.

While the State Medical Board was given the names and the evidence against all 18 physicians, the result was that one Mansfield doctor was allowed to retire and two Dayton physicians voluntarily surrendered their licenses.

The police were left frustrated, disgusted and angry.

"It was a waste of time," said Dayton detective Charles Gentry. "Even if you convict the guy, you know he's going to get probation because judges won't send a doctor to jail. That leaves the medical board. If they don't act and pull their licenses, then we haven't accomplished a thing."

One Dayton surgeon, Dr. Suhkdev R. Singla, was selling prescriptions for the powerfully addictive drug Dilaudid to an addicted prostitute he was visiting at a Dayton brothel called Sherry's.

When Gentry and Clemmer went to Singla's office to question him, Singla denied it. But he handed them an envelope containing $1,000.

Singla was indicted in 1981 on one count of bribery and three counts of writing false prescriptions. He pleaded guilty to bribery, received a suspended jail sentence, and the drug charges were dropped.

The medical board put him on probation.

Another Dayton physician who was involved with the same prositute was Dr. Ronald S. Kahn, a family practitioner. Kahn admitted to the board in a secret hearing that he had been giving the prostitute and her friends addictive drugs in exchange for sex and he voluntarily surrendered his license. Kahn was convicted of two felony drug charges.

Two months after Kahn gave up his license, he asked for it back.

"Dr. Kahn is a valuable member of the medical profession," board member Dr. Leonard L. Lovshin declared, and Kahn's license was returned. A month later he was seeing 65 to 80 patients a week.

"You know, if an average person did some of this stuff, they'd be gone forever," Gentry said.

Mansfield detective Sgt. Robert Mortimer said, "You can go out and bust the cokers and the dopers and the junkies and bring them into court, no problem. You move uptown and start messing with doctors, though, and everybody backs off."

Dayton ophthalmologist Dr. Gaston Bouquett was indicted on 24 counts of illegal processing of drug documents as a result of the investigation. Police records show Bouquett was writing numerous prescriptions for Dilaudid for patients who told Clemmer and Gentry they had never received the drugs.

But after Montgomery County Prosecutor Lee Falke discussed the case with powerful State Rep. C.J. McLin, D-36, of Dayton, a new prosecutor was assigned to the case, and a new grand jury dropped the charges.

Gentry said Falke admitted to him that political pressure from McLin was the reason the charges were dismissed. Falke did not return phone calls.

Medical board lawyer David Wenger drew up a citation accusing Bouquett of prescribing drugs for non-medical reasons and for two other violations of the Medical Practice Act, but Board Administrator William J. Lee ordered the citation killed, board sources said.

Recently, Lee said Bouquett was still under investigation, but refused further comment. Internal board records show Bouquett's case has been "under review" by the board's legal staff for four years.

Two other physicians identified in the Dayton probe, Dr. Max Blue and Dr. Arthur Schramm, are also still "under investigation" by the board, and internal board records show they have been for three to four years.

Sources said Lee also killed citations against four Mansfield physicians after a two-hour meeting in August 1983 with representatives of the Richland County Medical Society.

Captain Cairnes said he was initially encouraged by the medical board's response. Of the eight cases they turned over to the board, Dr. J. Harold King, Dr. Samuel A. Lerro, Dr. Gordon F. Morkel and Dr. Nagin Ranchod were quickly cited for excessive prescribing of addictive drugs and prescribing drugs for non-medical reasons.

While the police were happy, the local medical community was outraged.

"The citations were coming down just as they'd promised," Cairnes said. "Everything was on track. Then some members of the local medical society went to Columbus and met with Bill Lee and then everything stopped. No more cases."

"The reason, they told us, was that they had other cases and couldn't concentrate just on Mansfield. But we haven't heard back from them since." That was nearly two years ago.

Lee denied that meeting had anything to do with the citations being halted, but refused to say why they were stopped. He said the cases are still under active investigation.

Of the Mansfield doctors cited, King retired, Morkel and Ranchod secretly negotiated consent agreements, and Lerro's case is still pending.

The remaining physicians, Dr. Barbara A. Reed, Dr. Donald W. Dewald and Dr. Donald L. Dewald have been under investigation by the medical board for improper prescribing since March 7, 1983, internal board records show. Dr. Milton C. Oakes has since died.

Mansfield police say they've learned a valuable lesson.

"Don't waste your time going to the medical board, that's what we learned," Messer said. "You can bust street dealers day after day and we got 54 drug trafficking convictions as a result of the investigation, but if you don't get the source you've wasted your time."

Captain Cairnes, chief of the department's Special Investigation Unit, said, "This sort of discourages you from making these kinds of cases a priority item. I can't justify spending investigative time when I get results like this."

MD GOT MORE PILLS THAN HOSPITALS DID

It's easy to miss the medical offices of Dr. Reuben Richardson. They are in the basement of his house, a modest brick ranch on a side street in the Cincinnati suburb of Wyoming.

But to federal and local drug agents, Richardson's tiny basement office is hard to overlook.

According to a confidential 1984 Drug Enforcement Administration report, Richardson bought 44% of all the methamphetamine sold to Ohio physicians in 1983. He was also the biggest single purchaser of amphetamine and the stimulant Ritalin, and ranked second to a Cadiz (Harrison County) doctor in the purchase of the addictive painkiller Percodan.

It is an interesting assortment of drugs for someone who advertises himself as a child specialist. Amphetamine and methamphetamine, commonly called speed, are primarily used for weight loss in adults, though they can also be prescribed for severe behavioral disorders in children. Some states have banned their sale because of the high potential of addiction and abuse. Percodan, an opium derivative, is not to be given to children.

To visualize how much amphetamine and methamphetamine Richardson purchased in 1983, consider this: He bought 1,047 grams of methamphetamine. All the hospitals in the state bought a total of seven grams, DEA records show.

Richardson bought 2,155 grams of amphetamine. The most amphetamine sold by the state's busiest pharmacy amounted to 595 grams. Mt. Sinai Medical Center in Cleveland bought 97 grams.

Richardson bought 345 grams of Ritalin. Kaiser Foundation Hospitals bought 134 grams.

The State Medical Board has been aware of Richardson's drug purchases for more than eight years, records show. He appeared for a secret hearing on Nov. 30, 1976.

The minutes of that hearing show Richardson "admitted to ordering two million (diet pills) over the past two years. Dr. Richardson says he knows some of his patients are selling their medication to others and when he finds out he stops seeing such patients immediately."

The board did nothing. From 1977 to 1979, DEA records show, Richardson dispensed 1,243,220 diet pills to his patients. Richardson could not be reached for comment.

"He can account for all the pills he buys," said one Cincinnati police official. "He's had a couple of drug audits done. Now, whether it's good medicine to be giving people that much speed, we can't say. That's the medical board's job."

Therein lies the problem. Law enforcement officials can act only if there is evidence the doctor is pushing drugs. If the physician is simply over-prescribing, police are powerless, no matter how reckless or dangerous the physician's practices are.

"There's a fine line between legitimate medical practice and drug pushing and you have to be able to demonstrate very clearly the doctor stepped over that line," said Lorain County Prosecutor Gregory White, who put drug king Dr. Leonard F. Faymore out of business.

While the State Medical Board is supposed to bridge that gap and protect the public from doctors who don't know or care that they are turning their patients into drug addicts, it often fails to meet that responsibility, a six-month *Plain Dealer* investigation shows.

The board's standard punishment for overprescribers consists of requiring the doctor to submit periodic reports showing the amounts and kinds of narcotics he prescribes. In the most flagrant cases, the doctor's drug license is taken away for awhile. Rarely does the board remove the doctor from practice.

In effect, doctors too incompetent or unwilling to intelligently prescribe narcotics are still allowed to make life-and-death decisions affecting their patients.

Medical board consumer member William W. Johnston disagrees with that approach, but on a board dominated by physicians, Johnston's opinion is in the minority.

"(The other board members feel) you can't take away his right to practice. You can restrict, restrict, restrict, but *surely* you're not going to make him pump gas. Frankly, my attitude is a little different. If the guy is that bad, then maybe he ought to be pumping gas," Johnston said.

Medical board Administrator William J. Lee doesn't see it that way.

"The doctor's judgment may still be perfectly fine in terms of his ability to practice medicine," Lee said, adding that he can't recall one case where a physician who surrendered his drug license was later found to be incompetent in other aspects of medicine.

But Dr. William H.I. Dornette, former president of the American College of Legal Medicine, agreed that a physician's inability to rationally prescribe narcotics says a lot about his overall medical aptitude.

"It's a difficult question for the board to decide, but my gut reaction is that the board should protect the public, not the doctor," Dornette said.

The board, however, thinks many of these cases are the fault of the patient, not the doctor.

"In many instances the primary problem is the people coming and trying to get drugs from the doctor," Lee said. Medical board member Dr. Deirdre O'Connor agreed, saying many doctors are "duped or terrorized" by their patients into overprescribing addictive drugs. If that's true, Ohioans are among the most cunning patients in the country.

DEA records for 1983 show that while Ohio ranked seventh in population, it ranked third in per capita consumption of Quaalude (no longer on the market), fourth in amphetamine consumption, fifth in secobarbital consumption (used in sleeping pills), and sixth in methamphetamine consumption.

Ten percent of all amphetamines sold in the United States are sold in Ohio.

Not surprisingly, the toll in human suffering is high. DEA records show that, between July 1983 and August 1984, the addictive painkillers Demerol, Dilaudid and Percodan hospitalized 211 people in the Cleveland area alone, compared to 77 hospitalizations due to heroin and LSD.

Heroin killed two Clevelanders during that time; Valium, a commonly prescribed tranquilizer, claimed 15 lives. Seven people died from codeine, six from Demerol and five from secobarbital.

But while heroin dealers are quickly packed off to jail, little happens to doctors who dole out addictive or fatal does of dangerous drugs.

Take Dr. Allan R. Korb.

In 1978, the medical board got a complaint from an angry father who said the drug Korb had given his daughter, Cindy, had put her in Mt. Carmel Hospital for three weeks because of a drug overdose.

Korb, a Columbus psychiatrist, had prescribed a strange brew of addictive tranquilizers, amphetamines and painkillers for the girl over an eight-month period—840 doses of Quaalude, Dexamyl and Percodan. A week after she got out of the hospital, Korb gave her more Quaalude and Percodan.

The board had Korb in for a secret hearing on May 10, 1979, and asked him about his prescribing practices:

"Mr. (Jeffery J.) Jurca (a board lawyer) asked Dr. Korb is he could explain the fact that on January 8, 1978, he wrote a prescription for 60 Percodan and then on Jan. 9, 1978, he wrote another for 60 Percodan, both for . . . (the same patient)." Dr. Korb stated that he couldn't explain that.

Mr. Jurca asked if it were possible to prescribe Percodan to a patient over a period of 2 ½ years on a regular basis without the patient suffering some sort of side effects from the medication, Dr. Korb stated that would be possible.

"Dr. (Anthony) Ruppersberg (then board secretary) felt that Dr. Korb had justified his actions and felt that no further action was warranted at this time."

Nobody asked why Korb had given addictive drugs to a patient who had just suffered a drug overdose. Nor did they ask him about Ola Jane Barr, who had died three weeks earlier because of Korb's drugs.

Barr, 42, was found dead on April 22, 1979, after accidentally overdosing on Placidyl, a sleeping pill Korb was giving her even though she was suffering from chronic depression and alcoholism. Placidyl is known to worsen depression, especially if combined with alcohol.

"I kept telling him he was giving her too many drugs, but he said he was the doctor," Barr's husband, Darrell, said. "I would write messages to him on her medical charts telling him what she was doing with the drugs, so my wife wouldn't know, but he didn't pay any attention to it."

Darrell Barr, who owns a barbershop in Greensville (Darke County), said his wife was referred to Korb after she suffered a nervous breakdown. Korb prescribed her "just a ton of things . . . Quaalude, Placidyl, Elavil, Valium, I can't remember all the stuff he was giving her. Miltown. She'd always run out way sooner than she was supposed to and she'd call Dr. Korb and he'd phone the pharmacist and order her more drugs.

"I tried to keep the drugs away from her the best I could, I really did. I was poking pinholes into the Placidyl to get the medicine out but that didn't work because she'd just call up and get some more. I never want to have to live through something like that again."

In March 1982, the medical board's lawyers went scurrying for their secret files on Korb after John Martin Combs filed suit in Franklin County Common Pleas Court.

Combs, who was Korb's patient from 1979 to 1981, accused Korb of addicting him to Quaaludes. It wasn't the first time Combs had seen Korb. Six years ealier, evidence showed, Combs had been hospitalized for drug addiction and Korb was his psychiatrist.

When asked why he gave Quaaludes to a patient whom he had already treated once for drug addiction, Korb testified that he couldn't remember why Combs was hospitalized in 1973.

"No past history was taken . . . no present history was taken . . . no diagnosis was made, no plan of treatment was indicated or followed, nothing occurred but the passing of drugs," Combs' lawyer, Stanley L. Myers, said at the trial.

"You'd go in for five minutes, talk to him, and he'd give you Quaaludes," Combs' other lawyer, Philip Q. Zauderer, said. "I don't know how many people he hooked that way, but he hooked Marty and Marty had a hell of a time getting out of it. When Korb finally cut him off, Marty had to go buy them in the streets and got busted twice."

A panel of arbitrators found in Combs' favor and Korb settled the suit for $25,000. The medical board, which reopened its investigation after Combs sued, has done nothing since and Korb is still practicing.

The medical board did take some action against Dr. James K. Smith of Columbus, but only after it was too late.

The board began receiving complaints about Smith's generous prescribing practices in 1977, but did nothing.

In June 1979, a counselor at a Columbus drug treatment center reported to the board that a 68-year-old woman named Edwina Weyer had come to him to kick her addiction to Placidyl and Valium. She told the counselor that she was seeing Smith "and all he did was write prescriptions for her. According to her, the doctor was also giving out prescriptions to other people that just asked for them."

Her longtime friend, James Bennett, went with Weyer to see the counselor that day.

"She had been to other doctors and they cut her off and then she found

Dr. Smith. She said she could go there any time and get drugs any time she wanted them," Bennett said. "She wanted to get off the drugs and she was scared. She used to get confused and fall down when she was on them."

Four days later, Weyer fell in her beauty shop and hit her head. She died of a massive brain concussion.

On Aug. 8, 1979, board records show, Columbus narcotics detective Sgt. James Dempsey informed the board Smith was writing numerous prescriptions for controlled substances. The board investigated but took no action.

Kimberlee S. Hall, 25, was the next to die.

After looking into the circumstances surrounding her death, Kimberlee's grandfather, Fred L. Hall, went to the Columbus police and said if they didn't arrest Smith, he'd have him killed.

"I said it then and I'll say it again because I'm 75 years old and there's nothing they could do to me. I told them that if they didn't take care of that guy, I'd pay someone to have him taken care of. I think it's a terrible thing that they allow such creatures to practice medicine," Hall said.

Kimberlee Hall had just had an abortion and was deeply depressed when she went to see Smith in September 1982, records show. Smith prescribed Valium and Placidyl, despite warnings in almost every medical text that those drugs should not be given to depressed patients because of the danger of suicide, and should be used with caution in patients prone to addiction. Kimberlee Hall had a history of alcoholism, records show.

He prescribed her 175 tablets of Placidyl in 73 days, in the largest dosage available. On Dec. 4, 1982, she overdosed and was in a coma for 10 days before she died.

"I wish Dr. Smith could have seen what Kimberlee went through those last 10 days. She was a beautiful girl. To look at her was just horrible. I've never seen anyone in that state," Hall said.

Eight months later, Smith voluntarily surrendered his medical license. The board made no finding of wrongdoing and Smith is free to ask for his license at any time.

"Would they (the board) have acted properly and brought Smith in earlier, it's possible this young girl would be alive today," Sgt. Dempsey said.

Dr. George D. Smith of Middletown is another physician still in practice despite the board's being aware for almost 10 years of his bizarre prescribing habits.

Smith signed a consent agreement in 1981 promising not to prescribe nine different addictive drugs. Smith said he was released from that agreement in 1983.

On Nov. 4, 1983, a 27-year-old addict named Dana Patrick went to see Smith for the first time, complaining of back pain. Smith gave Patrick an injection of the addictive painkiller Talwin, a muscle relaxant, and 40 tablets of methadone, a drug used to help heroin addicts kick their habit. Smith said he saw nothing wrong with prescribing methadone for back pain, saying the drug had legitimate medical uses.

By the next morning, Patrick had taken 27 methadone pills and overdosed. He died four days later. The autopsy revealed numerous needle punctures in Patrick's hands and feet.

Accompanying Patrick to Smith's office that day was another first-time patient, John Gregory, 41, of Hamilton. Gregory got a prescription from Smith for the amphetamine Obetrol, one of the drugs Smith was forbidden by the board to prescribe, along with Valium and Placidyl.

Gregory died six months later after smashing his car into a tree on Main Street in Hamilton. The autopsy revealed high blood levels of alcohol and Dalmane, a sleeping pill. Records show Gregory was receiving the Dalmane from Dr. Daniel H. Sway of Cincinnati, who has been under indictment since 1982 on drug felony charges.

Board records show Middletown Hospital officials have complained to the medical board about Smith's prescribing habits, as has the Warren County Council of Alcohol and Drug Abuse and the Warren County sheriff. Those complaints say Smith is prescribing drugs to known addicts and known drug dealers, including people that have been convicted of heroin trafficking and prescription forging, and the pills are being sold on the streets. Smith said he was unaware of that.

The board has had Smith in for almost a dozen secret hearings since the mid-1970s and internal board records show Smith has supposedly been under investigation for improper prescribing since 1981. It has never taken any public action.

Here are some physicians in northern Ohio whom the board has accused of overprescribing:

DR. DEMETRIO M. CERAMELLA
NEW PHILADELPHIA

In five months, Ceramella prescribed 3,060 tablets of Darvocet—an addictive painkiller known to worsen depression—to a severely depressed woman with a history of suicide attempts. On Feb. 6, 1983, four days after she received her 32nd Darvocet prescription, she died of a Darvocet overdose. Ceramella, who testified that the woman had been his patient for several years, said he was unaware of her previous suicide attempts, even though her autopsy report noted she had numerous scars on both wrists and forearms. Carmella destroyed her medical records after her death. Evidence at his hearing showed he had other patients on Demerol and Percodan for two to three years. DEA records show he was one of the leading buyers of amphetamines and methamphetamines in northern Ohio in 1983. Ceramella was cited by the board in January 1984 and his license as revoked a few weeks ago.

DR. RAMON PLA
CLEVELAND

Between 1979 and 1982, Pla prescribed 67,854 doses of controlled substances, including 60,140 Quaaludes. In 1979, Pla was prescribing an average of 113 Quaaludes a day. The board accused Pla of selling an undercover narcotics agent Percodan, Quaaludes and Preludin, knowing she was three months pregnant. Pla was indicted on drug charges in 1982 but the charges were dismissed. He was cited by the board in 1983 and his case is still pending.

DR. BORIS FIYALKO
NORTH OLMSTED

In 1978, Fiyalko sold a board investigator Quaaludes. The investigator said he told Fiyalko he was having a party and was tense. Evidence at Fiyalko's 1984 hearing showed he had three patients on Percodan for up to nine years, knowing one of them was addicted. He also had 12 patients on amphetamines for up to eight years, even though some of them gained weight during his diet treatment, and three patients on Quaaludes for between five and seven years. The board suspended his license for 30 days and ordered him to surrender his drug permit, but he sued and the board's ruling was recently overturned.

DR. ANTHONY J. NAKHLE
CLEVELAND

Nakhie, former physician for the Cleveland Police Department, surrendered his license in August 1983 while a patient in Cleveland Clinic for drug addiction. Records show Nakhle has appeared before the board for several secret hearings to discuss both his addiction and his prescribing practices. Since 1972, three of his patients have accused him of improper prescribing of drugs, court records show. One suit alleged Nakhle gave an alcoholic patient and injection of barbiturates which, combined with the alcohol in his blood, killed him. Nakhle settled that case for $15,000. He paid an addicted Cleveland man $20,000 last March in an out-of-court settlement and a third case is pending. Nakhle, who is now under indictment on drug and insurance fraud charges, recently asked for his license back.

NEED DRUGS? NO SWEAT

I'm not a particularly svelte person, but then I'm far from obese. At a height of 6 feet and a weight that fluctuates between 168 and 172 pounds, I weigh what I should.

Dr. Antonio M. Valbuena and Dr. James F. McKeever didn't think I needed to lose weight. They told me so. But they went ahead and prescribed me addictive diet pills anyways.

To find out how difficult it would be to obtain controlled drugs from physicians, I made appointments with two doctors with reputations as generous prescribers. Valbuena is on the West Side, near Rocky River. McKeever, an osteopath, is in Euclid. They were suggested to me by narcotics agents familiar with their prescribing practices.

None of the drugs I was prescribed were taken and despite the fact that I gained weight during the "diet" plans, the drugs continued to flow.

Valbuena has had previous troubles with the State Medical Board. In 1977, the board suspended his license for 90 days for writing prescriptions for Dilaudid (synthetic morphine) for a man he'd never seen. Internal medical board records show the board has been investigating him for improper prescribing since June 1981, but has taken no action.

McKeever has had no formal disciplinary action taken against him by the board.

I called Valbuena's office Sept. 25, 1984, and asked for an appointment, telling the receptionist that I wanted to lose some weight.

"Well, you know he is not writing for Preludin anymore," she told me. Preludin is an amphetamine-like diet pill that is widely abused on the streets and a drug Valbuena is known for prescribing.

I told her it didn't matter, and she informed me that Valbuena would give me no drugs on my first visit and would take a blood test that would cost $35. An appointment was made for Sept. 27.

"You don't look like you need to lose any weight to me," Valbuena told me when I appeared for the appointment. I told him that was a matter of opinion.

He put me on the scale and, fully clothed, I weighed 171 pounds.

"So, you weigh about 180 now, right?" he asked, and wrote that on my chart. He then took my blood pressure and remarked that it was high. He took it again and again commented that it was high.

"Has anyone ever told you that you have high blood pressure?" he asked. I told him that no one had. "Well, it is very high," he said.

He then listen to my heart and commented that it was pounding rapidly. He checked my ears and eyes, listened to my lungs and checked my legs for varicose viens.

"So you want something to control your appetite? Well, I'll give you something here." He wrote me a prescription for 100 tablets of the drug Plegine, an amphetamine-like drug closely related to Preludin.

Plegine is a federally controlled substance and not recommended for patients with even mildly high blood pressure, because the drug tends to elevate blood pressure and increase heart rate, according to several medical texts.

The Physicians Desk Reference says Plegine and other similar drugs are generally ineffective for treatment of obesity beyond a few weeks because the body quickly develops a tolerance to their effects. The drugs are also habit-forming.

No blood test was taken and I paid him $35. He told me to try drinking diet soft drinks and come back in a month.

By my next visit my weight had increased by five pounds, but Valbuena commented that I had lost six pounds. He again remarked on my high blood pressure, but gave me another prescription for 100 Plegine and asked me if the pills were working.

I told them they weren't and it seemed like I had developed a tolerance to them. He said he would give me something stronger next time.

The next month, my weight was the same. Valbuena chided me for not losing weight and wrote me a prescription for 30 tablets of Adipex-P, a controlled drug similar in action to Plegine. He took my blood pressure, again commented that it was high, and sent me on my way. I was out of his office within five minutes.

McKeever's operation was a litter slicker than Valbuena's, but the result was the same. My blood pressure was taken, my blood was drawn, an electrocardiogram was taken, a urine sample was collected and I was carefully measured and weighed, tipping the scales at 178 fully clothed. The examination cost $90.

"You don't look like you need to lose any weight," McKeever commented. "According to my charts, your weight is just right."

I told him I felt fat.

"Well, it's your money," McKeever shrugged. He handed me some diet books and three packages of pills—28 tablets of phendimetrazine (the drug used in Plegine), 28 tablets of phentermine (the drug used in Adipex-P) and 28 tablets of levothyroxine sodium, a drug for patients whose thyroid glands don't produce enough hormones.

According to the Physicians Desk Reference, small doses of thyroid hormone are useless for weight reduction with normal thyroid glands.

"Larger doses may produce serious and even life-threatening manifestations of toxicity, particularly when given in association with sympathomimetic amines," the PDR says. Phendimetrazine and phentermine are sympathomimetic amines.

Four weeks later I returned wearing a pair of heavy boots, I weighed 179. McKeever looked at my boots and wrote my weight down as 172 pounds.

He took my blood pressure and walked back over to my chart. "One hundred and sixty over 90, same as last time. Anyone ever told you you have high blood pressure?"

"Is that bad?" I asked.

"That's pretty bad," McKeever said. "I'm going to have to give you something to slow you down."

I left his office with a package of 28 phenobarbital tablets, an addictive controlled substance drug and a package of 28 hydrochlorothiazide pills, a drug designed to lower blood pressure by increasing the output of bodily fluids.

And despite his concern for my blood pressure, he also gave me the diet pills and thyroid hormone.

The topic of my blood pressure was all but forgotten when I returned in February. McKeever, in fact, didn't even examine me; that was left to his medical assistant, who asked if I wanted "the nerve medicine." I told her I did, but didn't want the other pills because I was urinating frequently.

McKeever stopped in the doorway of the examining room and said his medical assistant told him I had gained weight.

"This is supposed to be a weight *loss* program, ya know," McKeever said with a laugh. "She also tells me you're going to the bathroom a lot. I told her to tell you that's because you're full of piss!" He guffawed.

I walked out of his office 10 minutes after I came in, with two packages of diet pills and a package of thyroid hormone.

In six visits to the two doctors I had obtained 426 pills and capsules of controlled drugs, along with another 112 pills for my heart and thyroid gland.

Last month, I underwent a complete physical and there were no problems noted with my blood pressure, my weight or my thyroid gland.

GALION'S PRINCE OF PRESCRIPTIONS

Of all the horror stories in the files of the State Medical Board, few are more chilling than that of Dr. William Chauncey Manthey, a general practitioner and health commissioner for the town of Galion.

When the board in 1982 cited Manthey for overprescribing addictive drugs to 210 patients, howls of protests went up from the citizens of the Crawford County city. The board was swamped with letters from Manthey's patients, all attesting to his kindness, decency and medical knowledge.

But it's doubtful many of his patients made the trip to Columbus to read the mountain of transcripts from Manthey's medical board hearings.

And it's certain Harold R. Mercurio didn't.

Mercurio's wife found him dead one morning in December 1980, surrounded by empty bottles of Seconal, an addictive sleeping pill Manthey had been prescribing him for six years. Two months before the fatal overdose, Manthey had prescribed 120 capsules in 10 days, knowing that Mercurio was grieving over his mother's death.

It wasn't the first time Mercurio, 47, had taken an overdose of sleeping pills. Manthey's records showed his patient had been hospitalized for a barbiturate overdose in November 1976.

But instead of making sure Mercurio never got his hands on the drug again, Manthey began prescribing even more—doubling the dosage, in fact.

Those facts so astounded the medical board's expert witness, Dr. John J. Winsch, of Newark, O., that Winsch called Manthey's actions "reckless and ill-advised" and said Manthey demonstrated "a flagrant disregard for the danger" of suicide.

"I simply cannot imagine a similar practitioner so doing, or so prescribing that medication again, ever, for such a patient. I cannot imagine how a conscientious physician, especially one who was forewarned by a previous episode, could subject a patient to this kind of a risk," Winsch testified.

The medical board's hearing officer, board member Dr. Oscar Clarke, of Gallipolis, was also troubled. Clarke suspended Manthey's license for 30 days.

Had the problem been limited to just one patient, Clarke's ruling may have been understandable. But Clarke also found Manthey guilty of dozens of other violations of the Medical Practice Act, including:

■ Prescribing Seconal regularly for three years to a woman who was suicidally depressed over her husband's death.

■ Prescribing sleeping pills for a woman he had diagnosed as suffering from narcolepsy, a rare disease that causes one to suddenly fall asleep.

■ Prescribing Percodan, a narcotic painkiller containing aspirin, for two years to a patient with a gastric ulcer. Winsch testified, "To employ a medication with aspirin in it to treat pain in a patient with an ulcer is like trying to put out a fire by throwing gasoline on it. This is literally a life-threatening thing to do." Manthey said he wasn't aware of the ulcer at the time he prescribed the drugs, but his own medical records showed he was.

■ Prescribing Percodan regularly for five years to a woman who had previously abused drugs, knowing that the woman was also getting sizable quantities of Percodan from another doctor. The other doctor had told Manthey the woman was addicted and he was trying to get her off the drug.

■ Prescribing amphetamines for four years to a patient who had a drug problem and was diagnosed as a schizophrenic. Winsch testified, "That would probably be one of the worst things to subject a patient to and would have worsened the (schizophrenic) condition." Manthey said it was more important for the patient to lose weight, but despite being on amphetamines for four years, the patient gained weight.

- Prescribing amphetamines regularly for four years to an obese patient with severe asthma and chronic lung disease, a practice Winsch called "particularly dangerous." The patient was also receiving Percodan. Manthey said he saw nothing wrong with those practices.

- Prescribing Seconal and Percodan to a woman who, Manthey's records showed, suffered four convulsions during a 1975 hospitalization, which were diagnosed as being due to barbiturate withdrawal. Despite that, Manthey continued to prescribe Seconal and Percodan until 1981. "To give a barbiturate to a patient who had a convulsion caused by a barbiturate is simply irrational," Winsch testified. Manthey said he was prescribing the drugs to control her convulsions.

- Prescribing Quaalude, the addictive painkiller Demerol, and the amphetamine-like drug Preludin to a patient with a history of alcohol abuse. In addition, Manthey's own records show the man had forged one of Manthey's prescriptions, was hospitalized for an infection caused by a dirty hypodermic syringe and that Manthey had advised him to go into a methadone treatment program. Even after that, Manthey continued to prescribe Quaalude and Preludin. Manthey testified that he had no knowledge the patient was a drug abuser.

- Prescribing amphetamines and barbiturates at the same time to four patients for periods of up to five years. Winsch testified that it was "just ridiculous" to "mix uppers and downers in a patient because the dangers are so well known as to be one of the first things taught to avoid to medical students." Manthey said he didn't see any problems with it.

"To find the guy guilty of all those things and let him walk with only a 30-day suspension gives you an idea of the mentality around this place," one board lawyer said disgustedly. "We had . . . (Manthey) cold."

Despite the board's order, Manthey hasn't lost a minute from his busy practice and is still in good standing on the staff of Galion Community Hospital.

John C. Imhoff, president and chief executive officer of the hospital, said he was of the opinion that no disciplinary action was warranted in Manthey's case. Imhoff acknowledged, however, that neither he nor anyone else in the hospital's administration had ever read the hearing transcripts.

Manthey later sued the medical board in Crawford County Common

Pleas Court, saying his suspension was unjustified. Last December, a local judge threw out the board's ruling. The judge said much of the evidence against Manthey had been improperly obtained and that he hadn't gotten a fair hearing.

The board is planning an appeal.

BOARD OVERLOOKS MALPRACTICE SUITS

The members of the State Medical Board were up in arms. The legislature was going to make it a duty for the board to investigate malpractice.

"The board should educate the legislators that malpractice suits do not necessarily mean that there has been bad medical practice," two-time board President Dr. Henry G. Cramblett said during a board meeting in May 1980. "There are many malpractice suits filed that are not legitimate. The board is against this section of the bill because it gives the connotation that malpractice claims mean bad medical practice, and that isn't always the case."

Board member Dr. Leonard L. Lovshin said he "would like the word 'duty' removed and placed with the word 'option.'"

Board member Dr. Joseph P. Yut said he "would just as soon do away with this whole section."

The board, which is supposed to protect the public from substandard medical care, got its wish, with some help from the powerful Ohio State Medical Association.

The only section of Ohio's Medical Practice Act that deals with malpractice suits is a meaningless clause that says: "The state medical board may obtain information . . . from courts and other sources concerning malpractice claims against physicians."

The board's attitude puzzled Kirk B. Johnson, general counsel for the American Medical Association's Special Task Force on Professional Liability and Insurance.

"There is no question that a state medical board has a duty to investigate a physician when it appears that a physician has an unusual number of bad claims against him," Johnson said. "I don't know how a rational person can say there is no correlation between incompetence and repeated malpractice claims."

But in Ohio, unlike most states, gross negligence, professional incompetence or adverse malpractice judgements are not grounds for disciplinary actions. The Federation of State Medical Boards, to which Ohio's board belongs, recommends using those criteria as grounds for discipline. Medical-legal experts have recommended it since the mid-1970s as one way to hold down the cost of malpractice insurance.

The board's only power in that area deals with a physician's "failure to conform to minimal standards of care" as defined by similar practitioners in similar circumstances. That is the legal definition of malpractice.

Dr. William H.L. Dornette, a former Clevelander and a past president of the American College of Legal Medicine, said Ohio's statute is an excellent excuse for not looking into malpractice.

"In theory that should work, but in practice it doesn't. If it was applied literally, you'd be hauling all sorts of people before the board. So, the excuse for not applying it is obvious. It's vague, and it's too broad," Dornette said.

The AMA task force recently recommended, as part of a nationwide effort to control the cost of malpractice insurance, that state boards play a greater role in finding and disciplining incompetents.

But a six-month *Plain Dealer* investigation shows the State Medical Board makes little effort to do so. The board's investigators said they were rarely instructed to investigate malpractice judgments or complaints of poor medical practice.

"I don't recall more than one or two occasions where I was asked to look into a malpractice suit," said former board investigator Jerry C. McDaniel, who recently retired after 17 years as a medical board investigator. "I've seen more malpractices stories in the newspaper than I was ever asked to investigate." Other investigators confirmed this.

"As far as the board is concerned, there is no such thing (as malpractice)," one current investigator said. "I've never been asked to give them a report on a malpractice suit."

Cramblett, now the medical board's secretary, denied that and said investigators hadn't been doing their jobs.

Former board lawyer Michael Falleur said the board placed little emphasis on that area, preferring to concentrate its limited manpower on cases of overprescribing, or trying to get drug-addicted or alcoholic physicians into treatment.

"As far as the next echelon goes, people who were just plain old bad doctors, we didn't have time for," Falluer said.

Some board members interviewed said they didn't view malpractice as one of the board's more pressing issues.

"There are so many other problems out there," board member Dr. Deirdre O'Connor said. "I think it would be nice to be able to look at somebody's record, but I'm not sure it would prove anything. Some of that stuff is taken care of at the local level."

O'Connor is right, because that's how the medical board handles the problem.

It routinely turns over cases of substandard care to state and local medical societies, which have no power over a physician's license. The most they can do is expel the physician from the organization. Medical societies also have no obligation to investigate the case, no obligation to inform the board of their findings and do not publicly disclose any disciplinary actions they take against their members.

Records show that of 207 cases of substandard care the medical board has dropped since 1982, only 12% were dropped because they were groundless or lacked sufficient evidence of a violation. Eighty percent of the cases were closed by passing them on to medical societies or other organizations.

Board Administrator William J. Lee said that was done only when it was felt the problem was not severe enough for the medical board to become involved. "It's a judgment call," he said.

Board Secretary Cramblett said that would no longer happen. "When you're talking about minimal standards (of course) that is what we're all about. I talked to Bill Lee about this the other day. I don't want anything going out (to medical societies) while I'm secretary that has to do with minimal standards. This concerns me."

The board refused to release copies of its closed complaints, and *The Plain Dealer* is suing to gain access to them.

Since 1977, the board has brought charges against only a handful of physicians for incompetent or negligent medical care. Despite Lee's contention that serious allegations are always acted upon, internal board records show that is not the case.

Ten years ago the board was receiving complaints from physicians alleging that Dr. Donald S. Pritt, a West Virginia podiatrist with a practice in southern Ohio, was performing unusual and excessive surgical procedures in his office resulting in foot deformities, secondary infections and, for one elderly patient, gangrene.

The West Virginia medical board filed charges against Pritt on 1979 and revoked his license 17 months ago, ruling that Pritt's surgeries had resulted in patient injury and needless suffering.

Pritt can still treat Ohioans. The Ohio board just filed charges six months ago and has yet to schedule a hearing.

Cincinnati gynecologist Dr. Meyer J. Fleischman has been the subject of three complaints alleging substandard medical practice since 1979, records show. But the board has taken no action, despite being informed by one of its investigators that Fleischman's medical offices were unsanitary and his medical records consisted of a few scraps of notepaper rolled up with a rubber band and stored in a broom closet.

Last year, the board received a complaint from a woman who said Fleischman's office was filthy and that he had given her a vaginal examination with dirty instruments. Another woman complained that she had seen him for nearly a year for infertility problems and that he had finally recommended a hysterectomy. She saw another doctor and later became pregnant, the complaint said.

Fleischman said those complaints were ridiculous and untrue. He said he was interviewed by a medical board investigator about "some medical cases that were cleared up." He declined to be specific, saying, "It's a private thing between the board and myself. But everything was resolved to everyone's satisfaction."

Some believe physician dominance of the board is the reason so few negligence or incompetence cases are taken up. There are only two non-physicians on the 11-member board.

Former board lawyer Falleur said he sensed board members were queasy about passing judgment on another doctor's abilities or mistakes. "It was almost a 'There but for the grace of God go I' attitude," he said.

Dr. Sidney A. Peerless, a Cincinnati plastic surgeon, resigned last year after only a few months on the board. Peerless said lack of time was the main reason, but said part of it had to do with uneasiness over judging another doctor's faults.

"I found it very difficult to be a judge," Peerless said.

Even on those rare occasions when the board does act, its punishment is often slight.

Dr. Hart Guonjian, a North Canton pathologist and former chief deputy coroner for Stark County, was found guilty of substandard care in 1983 for pronouncing a traffic accident victim dead despite being told by paramedics that the man had vital signs and a pulse and could be seen breathing. Guonjian ordered the paramedics to take the man to a funeral home.

The paramedics refused and a complaint was filed with the board. Guonjian was also cited for accusing a patient at Mansfield State Hospital of faking a back injury and pulling her to her feet.

"He pulled her legs over the edge of the table and was lifting her up, trying to get her to stand. The entire time, she was screaming at the top of her lungs. She had tears coming out of her eyes," a witness told the board.

The board ordered Guonjian to limit his practice to pathology.

Board lawyer William J. Schmidt said cases of substandard care were hard for the board to prove, because it is difficult to find a physician willing to testify against another.

"You'd be surprised how many times a doctor will tell you on the phone, 'This man ought to be in jail, this man shouldn't be practicing, this man should lose his license,' but when they get up on the stand they say, 'Well, this isn't the way I'd do it, but I can't really say there is a violation,'" Schmidt said. But many cases never get that far because the board never learns about them.

Twenty states require insurance companies or physicians to report when they lose or settle a malpractice case, and 32 states require hospitals and medical societies to report sanctions against members. Those laws are supported by both the AMA and the Federation of State Medical Boards.

Ohio has no laws like that, and the board has never asked for them. The last time an attempt was made to introduce such legislation was 1981, and the bill's sponsor said he got no support from the medical board.

Today, dangerously incompetent physicians can bounce from one Ohio hospital to another and those so inept no hospital will have them can set up private practices without the board ever finding out. They can leave a trail of malpractice judgments behind them without the board ever being told.

The board recently began requiring physicians to disclose hospital and medical society sanctions on their license renewal applications, but if a physician lies, there is no way for the board to learn that.

"A reporting requirement is a pretty good mechanism for locating a physician who may be incompetent. And there are incompetent physicians out there," Johnson of the AMA said.

Officials with other state medical boards said such laws had been useful in weeding out incompetent doctors.

David LaDuca, Oregon's chief investigator, said, "We'd probably miss a lot of (enforcement) cases if that information wasn't being sent to us. It helps, believe me."

Linda McCready, chief external affairs for the California medical board, said her board gets about 400 reports a year from California hospitals. "There are some real gems in there. Every once in a while, you really hit paydirt."

Board Administrator Lee said he was not opposed to those laws, but said the board couldn't afford them.

"That's one of our arguments to the legislature, that we need more resources to do that kind of thing, particularly in the area of failure to meet minimal standards [of care], excessive surgery and that type of thing. I don't think it is [being ignored], but I don't think it is being looked at as much as we would like to look at it," Lee said.

But the board told the Office of Budget and Management last year the problem was barely being investigated at all.

"Time available for extended investigations on such matters as fraud, improper surgery is almost non-existent. Provisions . . . which were enacted to better protect the public from unqualified, unethical or incompetent practitioners have been little, or never, used," the board told the OBM.

Lee said, "It doesn't do any good to get that information if you don't have the resources to do anything about it."

"Oh, that's hogwash," said State Rep. Dean Conley, D-32, of Columbus, who introduced the malpractice reporting bill and has been involved in medical board legislation for years.

"If their sole reason (for failing to investigate) is that the legislature does not give them enough money and resources, then I question seriously their internal management abilities," Conley said.

Lack of resources also doesn't explain the board's reluctance to pursue investigations into malpractice judgments, since most of the board's work in those case has already been done.

Proven cases of negligence, incompetence and unnecessary surgery that have been fully documented and professionally prepared are lying in county courthouses across the state, gathering dust.

The information on Dr. Raymond F. Rooney, a Berea surgeon and former chief surgeon of Bay View Hospital, was collected in one afternoon at the Cuyahoga County courthouse:

■ Between 1969 and 1971, the American Osteopathic Board of Surgery twice refused to allow Rooney to take his certification test in surgery, citing poor surgical judgment, lack of ability in heavy abdominal surgery, unjustified surgery and excessive and unjustified mortalities. The surgical board noted that 52 of Rooney's patients died after surgery between 1967 and 1971.

Rooney sued the AOBS for libel and said in a deposition that one of the AOBS surgeons who negatively evaluated him was "out in the hall grabbing some nurse's behind" instead of observing Rooney's surgery. Rooney received a $35,000 settlement, but the AOBS stood behind its findings.

■ In 1975, a jury ordered Rooney to pay $508,000 to a Sheffield Lake woman who was needlessly sterilized when she was 16. Evidence at the trial showed Rooney had misdiagnosed a uterine mole as being cancerous and performed a hysterectomy, even after a pathologist told him the results of a biopsy were inconclusive. Tests showed the mole was not cancerous and that Rooney had removed healthy organs.

Rooney appealed the verdict and later settled the case out of court for around $120,000.

■ In 1976, Rooney was sued for $8 million by the parents of a 16-year-old boy who, the suit alleged, was needlessly castrated by Rooney. The suit said Rooney missed an obvious diagnosis that could have saved the boy from castration. Rooney made "a sizeable settlement" out of court, the boy's lawyer said.

■ In 1977, Rooney's staff privileges at Bay View were revoked by the board of trustees, which expressed concern over surgical audits that concluded Rooney had a lack of training in gynecological surgery, showed poor technique and a lack of justification for urological surgery and kept miserable surgical records.

A panel of doctors appointed jointly by the hospital and Rooney disagreed with those findings but the hospital board revoked his privileges anyway. Rooney, in a lawsuit against the hospital that was later dismissed, said he was fired because he was critical of the hospital's administrator.

- In 1979, Rooney paid a $120,000 settlement to a Sheffield Lake woman whose husband died following surgery for the removal of gallstones. Evidence in the case showed the man's abdominal cavity had been closed with stitches to which he was allergic, which caused the stitches to dissolve. Rooney reoperated to close the wound and allegedly punctured the man's intestines by accident. He then stitched that puncture with the same stitches that had dissolved before. The man's intestines later split open, and he died.

The board of St. John-West Shore Hospital recently refused to grant him full staff privileges, Rooney's attorney said, and Rooney is contemplating legal action against the hospital.

The medical board has never taken any action against Rooney, and it is possible the board is unaware of the lawsuits. Rooney declined comment.

The board is aware of the string of malpractice suits against Medina County Coroner Dr. Andrew J. Karson. In May 1981, *The Plain Dealer* reported that Karson had been sued for malpractice 14 times in 10 years. He settled six of those cases out of court and paid a judgment in another.

At the time, the board said it was investigating. Internal board records show the legal staff has been preparing a case of substandard care against Karson since September 1981, but no action had ever been taken.

The board's attitude about malpractice suits was never more evident than when Dr. Arthur O. Charpentier Jr. of Newcomerstown made one of his regular appearances before the board in 1982. Charpentier, a drug addict, complained to the board members that a patient's widow who was suing him for malpractice was trying to drag his drug addiction into the case.

The board didn't ask Charpentier anything about the lawsuit, which alleged he had failed to diagnose heart problems in a man who died of a heart attack three days later.

Instead, the board members "asked Dr. Charpentier if his attorney has been able to keep irrelevant matters out of the trial." Charpentier settled the suit out of court.

Dr. Rein Siiner, an Akron gynecologist, has been sued six times since 1981. Four of his patients have alleged the same thing, that Siiner punctured their uteruses during abortions. Another patient charged he left a sponge in her abdomen. Two suits were dropped. Two were settled, and two are pending.

Internal board records show Siiner has been under investigation since 1983 for alleged inability to practice due to his use of alcohol. No public action has ever been taken.

"I think in cases where a judgment call has been rendered, the medical board has an obligation to take some action," said William W. Johnston, a Columbus lawyer who formerly represented physicians in malpractice actions.

Nothing stirred up more complaints about board inaction than did the case of Dr. George P. Gotsis of Lorain.

"I'll give you an idea how long it took the board to do something about George Gotsis," said Assistant Lorain County Prosecutor Jonathan Rosenbaum. "My father was president of the Lorain County Medical Society, and I remember him complaining about Gotsis when I was like nine or 10."

Gotsis' record of incompetence and unnecessary surgery stretches back to the 1960s. In 1973, he was kicked off the staff of Lorain Community Hospital, and his chief of staff at the time termed Gotsis' professional conduct "criminal."

His colleagues testified that Gotsis was "an absolute disaster as a surgeon" who showed "contempt for the patient." They said they had never seen so careless and inept a surgeon in their lives.

The medical board took no action for six years. In 1979, based on an exhaustive investigation by Medical Mutual into Gotsis' insurance claims, the board charged that the infection rate among Gotsis's surgical patients was unacceptably high; 30 of his patients had severe post-operative infections in one six-month period, which was attributed to poor surgical technique and unsanitary operating conditions.

Gotsis blamed the infection on his patients, whom he described as alcoholics, drug addicts, prostitutes and psychotics who didn't know how to keep themselves clean.

It was the first and, so far, the only time the board has cited a physician for a pattern of incompetence or negligence. Medical Mutual officials said it was done only because the insurance company handed the board a fully documented case and pressured it to act.

"The record as a whole shows a surgeon willing and anxious to operate at every opportunity with little or no regard for the medical necessity of the surgery," board member and hearing officer Dr. Joseph P. Yut ruled.

"In light of the extent and the seriousness of these faults, the hearing officer cannot escape the conclusion that the continued practice of surgery by George P. Gotsis, M.D., constitutes a danger to the health and safety of the public," Yut ruled. He ordered Gotsis' surgical license revoked, but allowed him to keep his medical license, which meant Gotsis could continue treating patients.

Yut's conclusion came nearly three years after the board hearings had ended and Gotsis, a proven public health hazard, had been in the operating room the entire time.

"The board's response . . . discourages you from even working up cases like that," one Medical Mutual official involved in the Gotsis case complained. "One of the great fallacies in this state is that the medical board protects the public."

As it turned out, the board ruling was moot because by the time it was issued Gotsis had already been taken out of practice by the police.

In February 1983, he was sent to jail for selling drugs to undercover agents who told him the drugs would be sold on the streets. Gotsis is currently serving a 5 to 25 year sentence.

The board cited Gotsis again for the drug convictions, but last June he voluntarily surrendered his license, and the board dropped the case without making any finding of wrongdoing.

Gotsis' lawyer, James Burge, said his client had every intention of going back into practice once he gets out of jail.

"He would have to be readmitted to practice," Burge said. "He gave up the license voluntarily, and . . . (the board) accepted it on that basis."

CLINICS ACCUSED OF FOOTLOOSE SURGERY

If the Family Foot Care Centers of Cleveland have done nothing else, they have put food on a number of malpractice lawyers' tables.

Records show that since 1982, 125 suits have been filed against the eight-clinic podiatric chain. Last year, they were being filed at the rate of more than one per week and 10 have been filed so far this year.

The US Postal Service and the Financial Investigations Department of Blue Cross have been investigating the clinics since 1983, looking into allegations that patients have been subjected to needless foot surgery simply so the clinics could generate insurance billings. Last year, one of the podiatrists involved, Dr. David Tarr, pleaded guilty to mail fraud charges. The investigation into the chain's owner, Dr. Rustom Khouri, and several other podiatrists is continuing.

"It's the first time a doctor has been criminally convicted of performing unnecessary surgery," said William Huston, director of Blue Cross' financial investigations department. "It was a precedent-setting conviction."

In an affidavit filled in support of a search warrant, postal inspector Robert G. Baumann said that since 1980 Family Foot Care Centers has "operated a systematic scheme to defraud patients and insurance carriers" by performing unnecessary surgeries and billing insurance companies for them.

But Huston, Baumann and the Northeast Ohio Academy of Podiatric Medicine say they have had little contact with the State Medical Board.

"It really is amazing. I have been very surprised by their lack of response. You're talking about surgeries that are being performed which are absolutely not needed. They [the board] have to realize what is going on up here and why they haven't shown more interest, I don't know," Huston said.

One official with the academy, who asked not to be identified, said "We have sent so much material down there [to the board] you wouldn't believe it, but they haven't done a damned thing. For the last year and a half our academy has been ready to assist the medical board if they needed information from us."

Asked if the board ever requested any information from the academy, the official replied, "Never, never. I mean, here we've got how many lawsuits against . . . [Family Foot Care]. It's incredible."

Baumann, who has all the patient files, said the board has never asked to see them. "We would be happy to provide them," he said.

But just public records on file at the courthouse raise disturbing questions about Khouri's operation:

- While Family Foot Care's podiatrists represented only 1% to 2% of the podiatrists served by Blue Cross, in 1982 and 1983 they received between 20% and 30% of all the money the insurance company paid out for podiatric services. The podiatrists were also the top billers in the state for Medicare payments in those years. Family Foot Care also performed more than 60% of all surgeries costing more than $400, but less than 1% of those operations costing under $40.

- Former employees have said that nearly every patient that walked through the doors was told he needed foot surgery, whether that was the case or not, and that reluctant patients were sent to other Family Foot Care podiatrists to receive "second opinions," which always confirmed that surgery was required.

  "Patients would sometimes come out white as a sheet after finding out all of the medical problems that were described by the doctors," one former employee office manager told the postal inspectors.

  "The object was to do as much surgery as possible whether it was needed or not," former Family Foot Care podiatrist Tarr told the postal inspectors. "Dr. Khouri professed the goal of each podiatrist . . . should be to perform at least 20 tendon procedures on each patient, in addition to additional surgery that may or may not be actually needed."

- Former employees and postal inspectors said foot surgeries were performed without any diagnostic tests being taken and that surgical results and medical records were faked or altered to persuade insurance companies to pay off the claims. "As a general matter, tendon surgery was performed before the X-rays were even developed and before the results of blood tests were received," one former employee stated. Tarr told postal inspectors the podiatrists were to pretend they had performed surgery by making a tiny incision and putting surgical staples in the foot. The stables were removed after a photograph was taken for the insurance company. "Dr. Tarr subsequently advised . . . that the deliberate alteration of patient charts was a common practice at Family Foot Care Centers and would be done after patient charts had been called for relating to civil suits filed by former patients concerning allegations of malpractice and unnecessary surgery by Family Foot Care physicians," a court affidavit stated.

- Undercover investigators paid 46 visits to clinics in 1983 and on 19 occasions they were told their feet needed major corrective surgery. The investigators had their feet examined by other physicians prior to the undercover visits and none of those physicians indicated surgery was needed, records say.

Last January, Khouri sold the chain to Dr. David Keller, who changed the name to American Foot Centers.

"To my knowledge, it's the same group. No one was fired or left the employment. As for Dr. Khouri, they won't say if he does or does not work there anymore. To my knowledge, he still does work at least one of the locations," Baumann said.

Keller denied that.

"I have different doctors. The staff is basically the same, but most of the doctors are not here anymore," Keller said. He said Khouri has had nothing to do with the firm since late February. Khouri could not be reached for comment.

MALPRACTICE? WHAT MALPRACTICE?

The Franklin County courthouse is just a stroll from the offices of the State Medical Board but, as far as the board is concerned, it could be on the moon.

For years, the details of Dr. Frederick Elder Jr.'s unhappy career as an orthopedic surgeon have been public record, available to anyone just for the asking. But since the State Medical Board doesn't consider malpractice suits worthy of its attention, it never asked.

So when the board received a complaint about Elder in April 1984, the board's chief investigator, John W. Rohal, went to the board's files and came back empty handed.

"There is no previous enforcement record on . . . Dr. Elder," Rohal wrote on May 8, 1984.

Had the board been checking the courthouse records, Rohal would have known that three Columbus hospitals either revoked or suspended Elder's surgical privileges between 1977 and 1982. The hospitals didn't tell the board, but in Ohio they are not required to do so.

The board also would have known:

- In 1980, six orthopedic surgeons assigned by Columbus' St. Anthony Hospital to observe Elder's operations found that his spinal surgeries posed "a definite hazard of serious injury to patients." The hospital revoked his surgical privileges.

- At crucial points during complicated surgeries, Elder had become disoriented, confused, and unable to function. Doctors testified that Elder would dawdle at the operating table and mumble incoherently for long periods of time, significantly lengthening the surgeries and increasing the danger for the patient. Sometimes the anesthesiologist or the operating room technician would show Elder how to finish the operation.

- In a six-month period in 1979, more than half of Elder's spinal surgery patients at St. Anthony suffered life threatening complications. Further, the hospital found little indication the patients needed surgery and in some cases, Elder's own tests showed surgery was unwarranted.

- At Grant Hospital, an in-house audit of two years' worth of back surgery cases revealed that 85% of Elder's patients suffered abnormal or unusual complications. Nurses and doctors testified that Elder's patients lost more blood, took longer to recuperate, and were in more pain than other patients. The audit also revealed slim medical justification for many of those surgeries.

"I must say, universally . . . [the surgical technicians] all liked Dr. Elder as a person, but they conveyed the feeling they were frightened to assist Dr. Elder in surgical procedures," Dr. J. Mark Hatheway, chief of orthopedics at St. Anthony, testified in 1980. "They were afraid that the patient was going to have major complications during the surgical procedure."

Between 1971 and 1978, Elder was sued eight times for malpractice, settling several of those cases out of court.

During a malpractice suit involving a case at Grant Hospital, an arbitration panel hearing the case last April ruled in the patient's favor and cited Elder's behavior as one reason.

"Dr. Elder, throughout his testimony, was confused, unable to deal with his own hospital notes, out of touch with hospital procedures, uncertain about what had occurred . . . and uncertain of what responsibilities were carried by nurses and others. Dr. Elder was himself notice of his own incompetence," the panel ruled.

The case involved a 58-year-old waitress who ended up with a clawed and useless right hand after one of Elder's operations. Despite numerous complaints to Elder that her hand was giving her intense pain, Elder did nothing, testimony showed.

"He told me . . . that I was a crybaby," the waitress testified.

The arbitration panel awarded her $225,658 and also found Grant Hospital negligent for allowing Elder, 58, to continue performing surgery there.

"His demeanor and ability to respond appropriately to hospital procedures put the hospital on notice of his condition every day he was on the premises at Grant Hospital," the panel decided.

Elder did little better at St. Anthony, records show.

Terry Scott Burchett, an operating room technician at St. Anthony, told a hospital committee in 1980 that Elder had fouled up three surgeries he had assisted on. Once, Elder put a metal pin in a patient's leg backwards; another time, he used the wrong screws to set an arm fracture and the third time he cut open a patient to search for a missing surgical sponge, Burchett said.

"The sponge wasn't in the patient. It was underneath the (operating) table," Burchett testified.

The medical board first became aware of Elder when the lawyer for one of Elder's relatives reported him as being an alcoholic. It turned out that Ohio State Medical Association's Impaired Physicians Committee already knew that.

Board lawyer Thomas Prunte spoke to Dr. Ransom Williams of the OSMA's committee on May 22, 1984:

"Dr. Williams informed me that Dr. Elder is definitely impaired and substance dependant. Dr. Williams also recounts that Dr. Elder took X-rays that came back blank, rendered an 'interpretation' from them and prescribed a treatment plan based on the 'findings,'" Prunte wrote in a memo to Rohal.

In a recent interview, Elder said he had never been contacted by anyone from the medical board. He said he still was actively practicing and seeing patients daily. He declined further comment.

MENTAL ILLS NO BAR FOR DOCTORS

Bohumila Slabochova lived in a nightmarish world of violent delusions.

When she came home from work, she found that strangers had been living in her house and wearing her clothes. When she went to sleep at night, doctors and nurses would sneak into her home and let black men rape her.

The police wouldn't believe her when she told them the builder of her condominium was trying to kill her with nerve gas, or when she reported that the tenant upstairs had murdered his mother.

"I am certain that she has schizophrenia, paranoid type. This week she told me she had delusions and hallucinations regarding black people. Although her delusions and hallucinations subside, her judgment is impaired. She has had two known episodes of overt emotional illness," psychiatrist Dr. Frank Gelbman wrote in February 1976.

"I repeat, at the present time it is my opinion that Dr. Slabochova should not be practicing medicine in the Youngstown Hospital Association," Gelbman concluded.

Dr. Slabochova practiced medicine in northeastern Ohio for another eight years, thanks to the Ohio State Medical Board.

In 1982, the State Medical Board received a complaint that Dr. Kenneth J. Langlois, a general practitioner in Milford, O., had engaged in sexual relations with a female patient over a 15-month period and was supplying her with 12 different kinds of drugs.

Board records show Langolis admitted to a board investigator that he had sex with the woman four or five times. The board has had that report since March 30, 1982.

It has taken no action against Langolis. Langolis said he did not have sex with the woman and denied admitting it to a board investigator.

In 1983, a Canton woman sued Dr. Myron E. Puterbaugh, chief of Radiation Oncology for Aultman Hospital, for $5 million, claiming Puterbaugh had raped her during an examination at the hospital. She was undergoing radiation therapy for cervical cancer.

Her lawyer also charged Aultman Hospital with negligence: "Had Aultman Hospital exercised appropriate credential and investigatory procedures, it would have known that Dr. Puterbaugh had previously manifested unprofessional and unethical conduct towards female patients in Tuscarawas County, where he was prior to coming to Aultman Hospital," the suit stated.

Canton police investigated and believed the woman's story. The case was submitted to a grand jury, but no indictment was returned. Puterbaugh's former partner was lined up to testify about the previous incidents. Puterbaugh denied the allegations but settled the suit out of court. The

State Medical Board has never taken any action against him, and he is still department chief at Aultman. He could not be reached for comment.

Dr. Atlaf Hussain of Columbus was convicted in 1980 of a felony count of forgery for fraudulently billing the state Medicaid program for office visits that did not occur and for lab tests that were not performed. In exchange for his not being prosecuted on additional charges of forgery, theft and perjury, Hussain resigned from participating in the Medicaid program.

The next year, he was indicted on charges of trafficking in Quaaludes, after police charged he gave a prostitute drugs in exchange for oral sex, which was performed in his office while police listened on the prostitute's concealed transmitter. Hussain pleaded guilty to a reduced charge. He secretly negotiated an agreement with the board to give up his license for a year, and the board agreed not to cite him for having sexual contact with the prostitute.

Hussain is still in practice.

Psychotics. Sex offenders. Thieves. Not exactly the kind of physicians you would expect to find in practice in Ohio, unless you were familiar with the workings of the State Medical Board.

"Things that would land you and me in jail for the rest of our lives, the board won't do anything about," said one medical board investigator. "They say those things don't have anything to do with whether or not the guy is a good doctor. Does the medical board protect the public? No. In my opinion, it does not."

A six-month *Plain Dealer* investigation of the medical board confirms the investigator's statements. Records show physicians have committed crimes that, in most professions, would spell the end of the offender's career. But in Ohio, it seems there is almost nothing a doctor can't do and still remain in practice.

Overbilling or stealing from insurance companies and state welfare programs counts for nothing. Board records show those misdeeds rarely even rate a citation.

EXAMPLES

■ Dr. Richard J. Fiorini, of Campbell, overbilled the state welfare department $194,419 between 1972 and 1980, auditors found. The audit findings said

Fiorini had charged the state for blood tests he didn't do, hospital visits that couldn't be verified, surgeries he didn't perform and emergency room visits done by other doctors. Fiorini also double-billed for services he had rendered, the audit said. Internal board records show the board has been investigating the case for more than two years. No citation has ever been issued.

- Dr. Joseph A. Fogarty Jr. of Youngstown, overbilled the state welfare department $71,184 between 1972 and 1979 for obstetrical services, surgery and office visits. He double-billed for 488 separate services, and billed for 2,150 urinalyses that were never done, auditors said. The auditors also said Fogarty had billed the welfare department for tests that had been done by the Ohio Department of Health for free. Internal board records show the case has been under review for nearly four years. No citation has ever been issued.

- Dr. Burt E. Schear, of Dayton, overbilled the state welfare department $55,578 between 1972 and 1979, audits found. Auditors found Schear was double-billing and charging the welfare department numerous times for the same blood tests. Internal board records show the case has been under review for almost four years. No citation has ever been issued.

- Dr. J.W. Washington, of Dayton, was found by the state auditor to have overbilled the Ohio Welfare Department nearly $60,000 for services that were never performed, services that could not be verified and double-billing. According to internal medical board records, the case has been under review for close to three years. No citation has ever been issued.

Lula A. Anderson is chief of the Medicaid fraud division of the attorney general's office. She said, "There really is no ongoing relationship with the medical board. Our relationship with the pharmacy board is much closer."

Anderson said the pharmacy board investigators were granted permission to regularly review the investigative files of the Medicaid fraud unit. The medical board, she said, has never asked.

"We would have no problem with allowing them to do that," she said.

Board members have said publicly that simply because a physician is a swindler or a thief doesn't mean he should be taken out of practice, or even reprimanded.

Former Summit County Coroner Dr. Anastasius H. Kyriakides was convicted of theft in office, a felony, in 1983, for illegally profiting from the purchase of valuable coins found in a dead man's house. Another charge of tampering with evidence was dropped after the conviction.

Board President Dr. John Rauch, himself a county coroner, was the hearing officer and heard doctor after doctor testify that Kyriakides was a wonderful physician with impeccable credentials. The president of the Summit County Medical Society urged Rauch "to base his decision on Dr. Kyriakides' record as a physician, and not on his alleged civil folly."

Rauch let Kyriakides—a convicted thief who can no longer hold public office—off without so much as a reprimand, stating, "It is apparent that the conviction and concurrent media attention focused on Dr. Kryiakides by a community he has served for many years have been sufficient sanction for the crime of which he was convicted."

Rauch's ruling sparked an angry debate by the board members, Dr. Joseph Yut wanted Kyriakides' license suspended for six months, stating Kyriakides "was convicted of a dishonest act, which was as dishonest as selling amphetamines."

Rauch pointed out that Kyriakides "was not reprimanded by the Masons, his church or the medical society." The board compromised on a one-month suspension.

In 1979, Dr. Francesco Michienzi of Sandusky was convicted in federal court of one count of mail fraud and one count of making false statements, after being indicted on 60 counts. Prosecutors accused Michienzi of intentionally defrauding the federal government through inaccurate and misleading billings for Medicaid patients. He was sent to jail for five months and put on probation for five years.

The board proposed suspending his license for two years, but relented after hearing Michienzi's lawyer say, "Dr. Michienzi has been punished enough for a crime that did not involve any harm to patients. The quality of care Dr. Michienzi provides to the community was testified to and his ability as a physician was not questioned at trial."

Board member Dr. Jerauld Ferrito suggested putting Michienzi on probation. "Dr. Ferrito stated that he makes this motion because he finds nothing in his reading of the transcript that reflects on Dr. Michienzi's technical ability to practice medicine," the board minutes state. Michienzi was put on probation.

William H. Huston, director of Blue Cross/Blue Shield's Financial Investigations Department, doesn't believe the argument that a convicted criminal can still be a good physician.

"It's a violation of a trust. You've got a health-care practitioner whose actions have reflected on the medical community adversely, and whether it's directly related to a patient or directly related to an insurance company, it still involves his practice. I think [the medical board] should react to the situation," Huston said.

"Can a person be a good doctor and be a thief? Yes. But I think you have to look at a real clear definition of 'a good doctor.' Can a policeman be a good policeman and still be a thief? . . . It's a question of integrity. I wouldn't want to go to a doctor I knew was involved in unlawful conduct," Huston said.

Most people would also feel uncomfortable going to a physician who is mentally ill, but the board's handling of those cases is no more expedient than its handling of crooks.

The board began getting complaints about Dr. Gary L. Reed, a Columbus surgeon, in 1980. Columbus police that year reported Reed was abusing drugs. No action was taken.

Early one morning in April 1982, Columbus police Patrolman James F. Burns was sitting in his cruiser alongside Interstate-70. While Burns watched in disbelief, Reed zipped by in a car with only three tires on it, sparks flying.

Burns gave chase, and Reed's car jumped the median and headed the wrong way down the other side of the interstate. He then swerved back and came to a dead stop in the middle of the highway. Burns and Columbus police Patrolman Irvin Reichgott pulled Reed out.

"He stated the Reynoldsburg police and the mayor had a plot out to kill him. He stated . . . to me that he was going to have me assassinated if I didn't let him go," Reichgott later testified. "I made the statement to officer Burns, I said, 'Jim, this guy is nuts.' This was just obvious to me that there was something mentally wrong with him."

Said Reichgott: "I'll be perfectly honest with you . . . this was the worst, worst case of driving under the influence of anything I have ever seen in my entire career up to this point. I have never seen anyone in the state this gentleman was in. I have never in my career seen anybody that bad."

The following month, James W. Sharps, a paramedic for the Truro

Township Fire Department, was called to Reed's office, after Reed reported he'd been poisoned. Sharps found Reed on his examination table, complaining that a woman had slipped heroin into his coffee the night before.

The paramedics, after examining Reed and taking an electrocardiogram, said there was nothing wrong with him.

"He grabbed the EKG and started reading it and started explaining he had elevations and depressions, but when we checked it further, he was reading the EKG upside down," Sharps later testified. That incident was reported to the State Medical Board the next day.

Two months later, the board scheduled two secret hearings for Reed, the purpose of which, board lawyer William J. Schmidt testified, was "to get Dr. Reed to voluntarily submit to a psychiatric evaluation. He refused and was cited by the board."

The board cited him for being unable to practice due to mental illness in November 1982, four months later.

Reed was examined in January 1983 by Dr. Ralph F. Henn, a board appointed psychiatrist. Henn diagnosed Reed as suffering from "amphetamine induced delusional disorder" and "mixed personality disorder with antisocial, narcissistic and borderline traits."

Henn wrote, "It is my opinion that this risk is unacceptable to the public and that without a serious commitment to intense exploratory psychotherapy the risk cannot be expected to diminish. It would therefore be my recommendation that his license be suspended until such time as he has established an effective therapeutic alliance with a licensed psychiatrist."

The board let Reed keep his license for nearly two more years while his case dragged through the board's hearing process.

While the board has the power to ask a judge to summarily suspend a physician's license until a hearing is held, that was not done. In fact, the board has exercised that power only once since 1982.

Board Administrator William J. Lee said the board didn't have enough money or lawyers to seek summary suspensions and said proving a physician is a danger to the public was very difficult.

Reed continued to treat patients. A Reynoldsburg woman who went to see him for treatment of high blood pressure complained to the board in December 1983 that "Dr. Reed was very rude and verbally abusive toward her. He told her that he did not care whether or not she liked the way he treated her."

Reed was arrested again in early 1984 after a gas station owner accused him of refusing to pay for gasoline. In the trunk of his car, police found 53 used hypodermic syringes, bloody cotton balls and empty vials of drugs. He failed to show up for his hearing on that charge and was arrested in his medical office by Reynoldsburg policeman Steven R. Baughn, who later described Reed as looking like Howard Hughes.

"Dr. Reed had not shaven for I would say between a few days and a week. He smelled as if he had not taken a bath in about a month. He was sitting at a table in his office, and there was a glass ashtray probably a foot or better in diameter, just heaped full of cigarette butts, and he was just sitting there," Baughn said.

Reed physically attacked deputies when he was taken to jail, refused to sleep on a mattress, refused to shower and became infested with crab lice. Reed's lawyer said it was a form of protest.

"He would call deputies for no reason, and excuse my language but this is a quote: 'M—, I don't have to do what you tell me to do. I'm a doctor,'" one jail worker testified. The petty theft charge was later dropped, and Reed has sued Reynoldsburg.

The board found Reed had "an unquestionable inability to practice medicine" and ordered his license revoked in October 1984, nearly four years after it received its first complaint. Reed has filed suit to overturn that order.

"We've had a lot of patients calling us asking us to please get his license back because he's such a wonderful doctor," Reed's lawyer, Peter Beagle, said.

It took the board even longer to get Dr. Slabochova out of practice.

In June and July 1977, the board received letters from two Youngstown psychiatrists who pleaded for action.

"It is my opinion that Dr. Slabochova should be in psychiatric care because of the tremendous mood gyrations and the delusional thought patterns that she is having at times," Dr. R.S. Boniface wrote.

Dr. Frank Gelbman, who examined her at the request of Youngstown Hospital Association, told the board that Slabochova had accused other physicians of raping her, and accused a doctor and his nurse of running a prostitution ring.

"I urge the Ohio medical board to take immediate action. I repeat, many local physicians are concerned both for Dr. Slabochova and her patients," Gelbman wrote.

Nearly a year later, the board put her on probation. Within months, she was seeing 40 to 50 patients a day.

In August 1979, she was cited by the board for prescribing addictive drugs for non-medical reasons and being unable to practice because of mental illness. The board made no decision in the case for almost two years, and she practiced the entire time. It found her guilty of improper prescribing and put her on probation again. The mental illness charge was dropped.

Four months later, Slabochova called police in Boardman and told them the man in the condo upstairs had killed his mother, because she heard a loud thump. The same day, she told her neighbors that the builder of her condo was trying to kill her by poisoning her food and water, tampering with her car and pumping nerve gas under her door.

In August 1981, she drove her Cadillac to the police department to report that someone had tried to bomb her car and pointed out what she said were bomb blast marks on the front wheel and bumper. It was mud.

The next month she ran screaming from her house and banged on neighbor Joe Jabanchick's door, yelling "The gas will get me!" Jabanchick said Slabochova went back to her condo, came out wearing a surgical mask and gloves and scrubbed down her driveway and sidewalk for four hours with Murphy's Oil Soap, explaining that the water would carry the poison gas back to the builder's home.

Slabochova reported some of those events to the medical board in October 1981. She also explained that an addictive cough syrup she was prescribing her patients in huge doses was composed of "resin, pineapple juice and codeine." The board went into closed session and decided "that there be no further discussion of this case pending further information being supplied to the board." The board took no action for an entire year.

In October 1982, Slabochova was cited for the third time for being unable to practice because of mental illness and for prescribing massive doses of the cough syrup Tussionex for non-medical reasons. She was allowed to keep her license pending a hearing, which didn't take place for six months.

The board accused her of overprescribing addictive drugs to 161 patients, most of whom received Tussionex, which sells on the street for $25 a shot glass. Slabochova admitted some of her patients were heroin addicts and one was receiving Tussionex because "it was the only thing keeping him from the needle." Most of the other patients, she claimed, were suffering from bronchitis and laryngitis. Her office records showed that sometimes she saw 48 "bronchitis" cases in a single day.

In one month, Slabochova prescribed 9,208 ounces of Tussionex, which led the board's expert witness, Dr. Jack Schreiber, to comment: "I tried my best to estimate what I would use seeing 30 to 40 patients a day for the same time period. That's 200 ounces, as opposed to 9,200 ounces. That amount just staggers my information and belief."

The board found her guilty again of overprescribing addictive drugs and being unable to practice because of mental illness, more than a year after the citation was issued. It ordered her license indefinitely pended, but suggested she reapply in six months. The board's hearing officer, Dr. Henry G. Cramblett, said he "worded his order in such a manner to offer some encouragement to Dr. Slabochova."

"That woman is a known nut and has been for years," said former Youngstown police detective John Rinko, who investigated Slabochova's prescribing practices. "I don't know how many times I tried to get the medical board to do something about her. I finally just quit calling." Slabochova hung up when called for comment.

"DIABOLICAL" PLAN GOT FIANCÉE HOOKED

The judge and the court referee were running out of epithets to hurl at Dr. Edmund Barry Eisnaugle.

Judge Craig Wright, then a Franklin County Common Pleas judge and now a justice on the Ohio Supreme Court, used "outrageous" and "evil."

Referee Stewart Roberts called Eisnaugle's conduct "reprehensible," "fraudulent," "malicious," "corrupt," "wicked," "depraved and diabolical" and "evil."

Roberts concluded that Eisnaugle "was guilty of gross negligence . . . committed the torts of assault and battery . . . probably committed felonious assault . . . probably committed various felonies of corrupting another with drugs" and recommended that the case be referred to the county prosecutor and the State Medical Board for "appropriate action." That was in December 1983.

Eisnaugle, who told police he was kicked out of the Air Force 14 years ago after being diagnosed as a paranoid schizophrenic, still has his Ohio medical license and said he's surprised people speak of him uncharitably.

"The things that a lot of people say are right. I deserve a good chunk of it. I did some pretty bad things," Eisnaugle said.

The jurists were discussing a lawsuit Eisnaugle's former fiancée, Brenda Fike, had filed against him in 1982, which accused Eisnaugle of knowingly addicting her to the painkilling drug Demerol. He did that, referee Roberts found, to force her to bear his children.

Eisnaugle "desired to control . . . [Fike], body and soul, and to use her for his own purposes and to serve his own needs. To accomplish this evil objective . . . [Eisnaugle] purposely and knowingly created a drug dependency within . . . [Fike], all the while deceiving her with promises of love, marriage and care," Roberts ruled.

Eisnaugle said that was not true and said Fike was not his fiancée. He said Fike was hired to take care of his son and he never gave her drugs.

Fike, who met Eisnaugle in 1980 while she was a patient at Grant Hospital in Columbus, was soon hopelessly dependent on Eisnaugle for her Demerol injections, which he steadily increased both in strength and frequency.

"I couldn't do anything. I was just more like a vegetable throughout that time," Fike testified.

When Fike had a hysterectomy against Eisnaugle's wishes, Fike said he threw her out of the house. Her addiction raging, she forged three of Eisnaugle's prescription blanks, was arrested and convicted of a felony.

Finally, she locked herself in a room for two weeks to kick her habit.

"It was the worst thing I ever went through. The nausea, the vomiting, the fever, the hot and cold sweats; it was a nightmare. It was just the worst thing you could ever imagine going through. I went into fits of violence where I would just scream and it was—no one can actually imagine it. It was worse than being sick when I had the pain, the abdominal pain," Fike said.

Said Eisnaugle: "It's a very sad story and I continue to feel sorry for that girl."

Had the State Medical Board been doing its job, Fike might never have met Risnaugle.

The *Plain Dealer* obtained records showing complaints against Eisnaugle as early as 1977. "It has been rumored in the past that this doctor might have a problem with drugs. It's not that he isn't a good physician, only that he might need help before someone is hurt," one patient wrote in 1979.

The patient's allegations were true. Records show that in 1978, Grant

Hospital asked Eisnaugle to enter a methadone withdrawal program to cure his addiction to the narcotic painkiller Percodan. In 1980, he underwent drug treatment at Grant for several days.

Records show that in May 1981, board resident Dr. Evelyn Cover and Dr. Perry Ayres, then an official with the Ohio State Medical Association, reported to board Administrator William J. Lee that Eisnaugle had mental problems, was allegedly supplying drugs to motorcycle gang members, was addicted to Percodan and was possibly on amphetamines as well. At the time, Eisnaugle was working in the emergency room of Mercy Hospital.

Columbus police also had him under investigation for drug dealing.

A board investigator and a Columbus narcotics detective went to Eisnaugle's home on June 24, 1981, and asked him to give up his license, which he did. Records show Eisnaugle admitted to the investigators that he was addicted to Percodan and Percocet.

Two days later, he hired former medical board lawyer Terry Tataru, who informed the board that Eisnaugle was withdrawing his voluntary surrender.

Despite a state law requiring the board to suspend the licenses of drug-addicted doctors, the board made no effort to do so. Instead, Eisnaugle was allowed to check himself into another drug treatment program, this time at Harding Hospital. Three days later, he checked himself out. "In the view of the psychiatrist involved, I was successfully rehabilitated at that point to go back into practice," Eisnaugle later testified.

Eisnaugle now says that was a mistake and said the medical board should not have given him his license back at the time.

"I erred. I was wrong. The medical board, I really think, has to take . . . [a hard line] approach because that's the only way some people can get help. Voluntary programs don't work. Until you're put in a position where you don't have a choice, most drug addicted people won't take advantage of what's there," Eisnaugle said. Eisnaugle was back on drugs soon after his release from Harding.

"We jumped right back in with Percocet, slightly stronger than Percodan, then Percodan, Biphetamine and Dilaudid," he testified later. "It was usually every four hours, which is five to six [pills] a day and it got as high as 50 pills a day."

He moved to northeastern Ohio, got a job in the emergency room of Warren General Hospital, and bought a $250,000 colonial mansion with a three-car garage on two acres of land.

On April 19, 1983, he was arrested by Warren narcotics detectives and charged with trafficking in the drug Dilaudid, a synthetic morphine that sells for around $45 a pill on the streets. Warren police estimated Eisnaugle dealt about $12,000 worth of the drug, using phony prescriptions.

Eisnaugle pleaded guilty to illegal processing of drug documents, a felony, on September 1983 and was sentenced to a year in jail. At his sentencing, during which he admitted he was a drug addict, he informed Trumbull County Common Pleas Judge David F. McLain that he had recently applied for staff privileges at St. Elizabeth Hospital in Youngstown.

"Did they ask you if you were a drug addict?" McLain asked.

"Oh no," Eisnaugle replied.

"I'm just sort of astounded that . . . you sort of expected St. Elizabeth Hospital to hire you to practice medicine there," McLain said. He ordered Eisnaugle to begin serving his jail sentence within three days. Eisnaugle appealed the sentence and his case is still pending.

The medical board cited him in March 1984 but no action has been taken yet.

Asked if he was surprised that Eisnaugle still had his license, Trumbull County Prosecutor Dennis Watkins said, "I think it's almost incredible."

Court referee Roberts said, "It upsets me that nothing has been done about this. I've been in the courtroom for nine years and probably done a couple hundred trials and I was as affected by this particular situation as I ever have been."

Brenda Fike won her lawsuit against Eisnaugle last year, after Eisnaugle failed to respond to the suit. He said he was never notified of it. Fike was awarded $208,000 but her lawyer said she hasn't seen a penny of it yet because no one has been able to locate Eisnaugle. Eisnaugle said he is spending his time these days counseling drug-addicted physicians and others and is working to improve drug rehabilitation programs in Ohio.

"[I work] all over northern Ohio. I have met and taken part in counseling some of the people you've written about. It's a horrible problem . . . much worse than people realize," he said.

BOARD LET FELON HAVE 3RD CHANCE

Dr. Arnold H. Kambly was already a two-time loser when the State Medical Board gave him a third chance in 1982.

It didn't take him long to become a three-time loser.

Kambly, a psychiatrist, was convicted in Michigan in 1977 of obtaining money under false pretenses by billing the government for $16,025 worth of appointments and examinations he never conducted. At the time, Kambly was director of a long-term psychiatric treatment center for adolescents. He pleaded no contest to a felony and was fined $2,500.

That same year, the Michigan medical board charged Kambly with having sexual relations with a woman patient he was supposedly treating for marital difficulties. In 1980, the Michigan board suspended his license for a year.

The Ohio board cited Kambly in 1978 based on the Michigan conviction, but at Kambly's request, took no action for three years, preferring to wait until Kambly had appealed the conviction and the conviction was upheld.

Kambly, who at that point was a felon and was prohibited from practicing medicine in Michigan, practiced in Berea and Toledo the entire time. The board finally held a hearing on the charges in April 1981. Kambly testified that his conviction was due to politics and that the charges were cooked up by a mentally disturbed patient. He maintained that he did nothing wrong and that the Michigan attorney general hadn't really wanted to prosecute him, but was forced to by the newspapers.

No mention was made of Kambly's sexual contact with a patient and the board's lawyer, Assistant Attorney General Jeffrey J. Jurca, told the board's hearing officer that the Michigan board's suspension was not pertinent to the hearing.

Kambly's license was ordered suspended for six months, over Kambly's indignant protests that he had "been unfairly treated."

His license was returned on June 1, 1982, and Kambly set up a practice in the Fallen Timber Medical Center in Maumee.

Kambly began double-billing insurance companies.

Maumee police detective Douglas Brainard said in one case Kambly was charging Metropolitan Life for treatments rendered to a young boy and his sister, even though the sister wasn't his patient.

"The sister was driving her brother to the office and waiting there to drive him home. Kambly told the girl she didn't have to sit in the waiting room and he invited her to wait in his office. Then he charged the insurance company for two sessions," Brainard explained. He said he turned up three separate cases of that happening.

Kambly was indicted on one count of grand theft by the Lucas County grand jury on Dec. 23, 1982. On July 25, 1983, Kambly permanently surrendered his Ohio license as part of a plea-bargain agreement and the charge was dropped.

"The judge wouldn't have accepted the plea bargain if it didn't include a permanent surrender of Kambly's license," Brainard said. "The medical board gave him back his license after the first incident in Michigan. We knew enough about the medical board to insist that he give his license up forever."

Kambly still has his Michigan license but is now living in La Jolla, Calif. He could not be reached for comment.

SUIT THREATS SCARE MEDICAL PANELISTS

The State Medical Board can be tough when it wants to be.

In October 1983, it gave one of its $260-a-week clerical workers a 15-day suspension without pay for repeatedly showing up a few minutes late to work. Considering the infraction, the loss of a half-month's pay counts as one of the stiffer disciplinary actions the board has ever taken. But with its licensees, many of whom make well in excess of $100,000 a year, the medical board can be a real pussycat.

Two months before they suspended the tardy clerk, the board members had before them the case of Dayton psychiatrist Dr. Oreste T. Chiaffitelli, a felon and an admitted drug addict who wanted back the license he surrendered after his conviction on drug charges. Chiaffitelli had been without his license only five months when he requested its return.

The board had him examined by psychiatrist Dr. Ralph Henn. He reported Chiaffitelli had lied in order to obtain a suspended jail sentence, was now blaming his felony on seeing too many black welfare patients, had been abusing amphetamines for years and, in Henn's opinion, lacked the most rudimentary knowledge of psychotherapy.

Attached to Henn's report was a confidential memo to the board, which said Chiaffitelli had tried to bribe him to get a favorable report.

"Reinstatement of Dr. Chiaffitelli's license, even with prescribing limitations, would not adequately protect the public," Henn concluded.

The board members voted unanimously to return Chiaffitelli's license, after his lawyer promised a lawsuit if they did otherwise. The board is now in the process of trying to take the license away again. Chiaffitelli, through his lawyer, declined comment.

"'Lawsuit' was the magic word," former medical board lawyer Michael Falleur said. "All you had to do was say the word 'lawsuit' and you'd see nine doctors grab their throats because they hated to see their names on lawsuits. They swallowed their tongues when they saw that. They'd think of the annuities and the Cadillacs going out the window. I saw that group of people cringe so often when they thought they were going to get sued."

Falleur said many lawyers who deal with the board were aware of that. The former board lawyers, Terry Tataru and David W. Wenger, are now representing errant doctors before the board.

"If someone ever called me up and said, 'Hey, I think I'm going to get cited by the medical board, what should I do?' unfortunately, I would tell them to send the board a copy of a complaint for harassment and see if they cite you then. More than likely, the board would back down, just because you threatened to file suit," said Falleur, now in private practice in Columbus.

While the board officials said the board's problems were due largely to a lack of staff and money, a six-month *Plain Dealer* investigation has found that is only part of the problem. Records and interviews with the board members, board observers and current former board employees show:

- Serious doubts about the leadership of the board. Those interviewed said board Administrator William J. Lee was ineffective and weak and that many of the board's delays were caused by his inability to make a decision. Board lawyer Lauren Lubow said the legal staff often waited for weeks and months for decisions from Lee on enforcement cases. "Sometimes you never hear back at all," she said. During the research for this series, several board members privately expressed concerns about Lee's abilities and several said they wanted him removed from his job, but said they were hampered by the fact that Lee is a civil servant, one of the few board administrators in the state who is. On Thursday, however, the board asked Lee to resign.

- Misplaced priorities in the enforcement and legal divisions. While some doctors, known to be dangerous overprescribers or sex offenders were allowed to practice unhampered, board investigators and lawyers said their time was often consumed with mundane and meaningless tasks, or spent pursuing physicians who practices were not dangerous, merely different from the standards of the board members. Board investigators have also been instructed to look into nurse-midwives, health food stores, physician's assistants and others the board believed were practicing medicine without licenses.

- A lack of differing viewpoints among the board members and a lack of consumer-oriented board members. While the board oversees the practices of masseuses, mechanotherapists, physician's assistants and nurse-midwives, none of them were represented on the board. Out of 11 board members, only two come from the ranks of the public the board is supposed to protect. The rest are doctors.

- Legislative mistrust of the board's motives and management abilities. Legislators interviewed agreed that the board was underfunded, but said they were not convinced increased funding would solve any of the problems because it might not be wisely spent.

The board's last three audits have been highly critical. Auditors complained of weaknesses in the board's financial operations that "could lead to significant waste or misuses of state funds," "indiscriminate use of debit vouchers," and an "absence of meaningful internal controls and careless bookkeeping." And in one off-the-record finding, one auditor told the board he had never seen such poor morale before.

Many believe the board's problems are due in large part to board administrator Lee, who has set board policy since 1970. Lee makes $42,000 a year as the medical board administrator. He is a former assistant attorney general.

Former board lawyer Falleur described Lee as "the kind of a guy you wouldn't mind for a neighbor because he's such a friendly, well-meaning person. But he's a very, very weak office manager. He doesn't command the respect of the first person there."

Former board lawyer Sherry Cato, now in private practice in Dayton, agreed.

"I didn't have as much concern over the board members themselves. I have a problem with the internal management. I think you need an energetic administrator. A bright, energetic administrator."

Both Falleur and Cato said that perception was not lost on legislators when Lee appeared to plead for more money.

"If I was in the legislature and I saw him sitting at the table asking me for money, I certainly would have some second thoughts," Falleur said. "It's true, the board doesn't have the staff or the funding to do the job it is supposed to do, but then who would fund Bill Lee?"

One ranking House Democrat who has been heavily involved in medical board legislation in the past said, "There is no doubt about it. The legislature does not trust . . . [Lee]. He has not been very professional in his administration of the medical board. The board has done a very sloppy job."

Legislators said other regulatory boards seemed to make use of their budgets than the medical board. The State Board of Pharmacy was frequently cited as an example of how a regulatory board should function.

While the pharmacy board has a smaller budget and fewer personnel, its ration of disciplinary action far exceeds those of all other boards. The reason: Of the pharmacy board's 24 employees, 10 of them are field investigators. Although the medical board has 33 employees, only six of them are working in the field and there are nearly twice as many doctors as there are pharmacists.

"Most of our budget goes to the field staff," said pharmacy board Director Franklin Z. Wickham. "We are enforcement-oriented and always have been."

Law enforcement officials across the state sing the praises of the pharmacy board, saying it is an aggressive, no-nonsense agency that doesn't hesitate to seek arrests and indictments of drug-dealing pharmacists and physicians. Records show that many of the medical board's enforcement cases result from pharmacy board investigations.

Medical board Secretary Dr. Henry C. Cramblett said he didn't know why the pharmacy board had more investigators than the medical board.

Medical board administrator Lee said a lack of money had prevented his board from increasing its investigatory and legal staff and said that alone was responsible for nearly every problem the board had in disciplining errant doctors.

Lee said the effects of inadequate funding show up in the board's failure to investigate allegations of negligence or incompetence, its failure to issue investigatory subpoenas—a relatively new power the board was granted to beef up enforcement—and its failure to seek immediate suspensions of dangerous physicians.

"In order to get on a case, you've got to have enough personnel, and you can't spread so thin that you can't go for it. To do it the way it should be done, I could use 40 investigators and 12 attorneys without any problem at all—more than that," Lee said.

Lee has been making that argument for nearly a decade. Some legislators no longer believe it.

"I am not at all sympathetic to the argument that because we can't get what we want, we can't do our job. Those are excuses," said State Rep. Dean Conley, D-32, of Columbus, who is one the subcommittee considering the board's request for increased funding.

"They very well may need more resources, and in this budget that we're doing now, we may give them more resources, but that is not a reason not to be doing the job properly," Conley said. "The other boards generally do a good job of policing their profession. And I will say this: They don't use the argument that they're not getting enough money as an excuse not to do their jobs. I guess if you can't manage properly, you blame it on anything you can."

While Lee said the legislature had remained deaf to his pleas for more funding, records show that isn't exactly true. Since 1976, the medical board's budget has been increased an average of 17% every budget period, going from $1,228,201 for 1976-1977 to the current recommended budget of $2,575,709 for 1986-87. The board's budget increases have averaged higher than what the rest of state government has received for the same period, records show.

"Keep in mind that the last few years the state has been in a budget crunch and that a lot of people haven't gotten any increases at all," Conley said.

William J. Shkurti, director of the Office of Budget and Management, said, "The medical board's budget has been increased pretty dramatically over the past few years. The argument I would make is that when you don't have all the resources you need, you've got to be able to set priorities."

"The board always asks for a huge increase in staff every budget period. Then, whenever they get questioned by the legislature or the press on why they aren't doing this or that, their answer is, 'Well, look at all the staff we asked for and didn't get,'" Shkurti said.

Shkurti said the board's presentation during its recent budget hearings was less than convincing. His office scaled back a number of the board's requests as a result.

"We asked them the same thing we asked the other boards. What are your priorities? What are you doing with the money you have now? And what is your justification for these increases? It was very difficult to get that information," Shkurti said. "They were unable to justify much of what they had asked for. That's not saying they don't need it, but we're dealing with taxpayers' money, and we need some justification for spending it."

Despite a 109% overall increase in its budget, the board has only hired only one additional investigator since 1976.

State Rep. John D. Thompson Jr. led an effort three years ago to improve the medical board's operations after a 1980 series in *The Plain Dealer* reported many of the same problems.

"They [the board] had me convinced that their problems were all financial, and I made more money available to them," said Thompson, D-16, of Cleveland. "We gave them money to hire more investigators . . . (but) they built a little empire over there for themselves at the expense of the state. They went and got larger quarters, more equipment, more office staff, but they didn't increase the investigative staff."

The investigators say that was not an oversight. They blame the problem on what they perceive as an anti-enforcement attitude among some board members, the administration and the legal staff.

"They don't want you to go too far. Most of the time, I get the feeling that they'd be happy if I never found anything," said one veteran investigator. "This is the most screwed-up board in the state. It operates more for the protection of the doctors than it does for the public."

OBM Director Shkurti said that in the late 1970s, the board's problem was "they had a bunch of old-line doctors who didn't believe in regulating other doctors, so will was much more of a problem than resources. The board has changed somewhat since then, but I still think that is a concern."

When Thompson proposed in 1980 that the board be given the power to summarily suspend a dangerous physician's license prior to a hearing— a power many state medical boards have—the board members themselves objected, records show.

Dr. Oscar Clarke, who was later elected board president, announced that he "has a great distrust of regulatory boards and added that when they are given excessive powers, the public regrets it." Board member Dr. Joseph Yut, later elected board secretary, agreed. "Any more power than . . . [the board] already has might possibly be misused," he said.

In a 1981 memo, board investigator Charles A. Eley, then acting chief investigator, made several suggestions to Lee on ways to improve the board's investigative abilities "to better serve the people of this state."

Eley suggested investigators be given fake IDs to use in undercover investigations, that the license numbers of cars used on investigations be purged from motor vehicle records, that the board provide money for undercover drug buys and wireless transmitters, and that the investigators be better trained and better educated.

"I have concluded from the nature of your memorandum that perhaps it is not our investigators currently in the field who need additional education, but rather the sender may need counseling upon how to attain goals and objectives," Lee wrote Eley. "I was unimpressed with the memorandum."

Lee said he thought Eley should have consulted his superiors before sending the memo.

Said an investigator with another regulatory board: "I don't think it's so much of a problem of their investigators not being any good. The problem is, they won't let their investigators investigate."

The board's lawyers direct the investigations from Columbus and use the investigators primarily as errand boys, investigators complain.

One investigator said, "When I get a complaint, I have to send it to Columbus and wait to hear back. Most of the time I never do."

The board's legal staff has also objected to that procedure. In 1981, the board's chief counsel, Ray Q. Bumgarner, wrote Lee: "The legal staff is becoming involved in enforcement actions at too early a stage. I would advocate that matters not even be presented to the legal staff unless or until it is determined . . . that the case merits formal action. Investigators, I believe, know best how to investigate."

Bumgarner's memo also complained that the board's lawyers were being forced to spend too much time preparing board meeting agendas, handling correspondence, licensing cases and preparing draft legislation.

"I felt that too often we were chasing things we didn't need to chase when there were more important and serious things to do," former board lawyer Falleur said. "It crossed my mind a lot that we were doing things just so we could have some impressive statistics, so the board could say we handled 250 complaints in this period of time rather than saying we handled eight complaints, even though those eight complaints were people like Romano Barney and Thomas McCarthy (two physicians with long histories of overprescribing addictive drugs)," Falleur said.

One thing the board's critics all agree on is that no matter how much money the board receives, it won't affect the board's outlook on medical discipline, which historically has been weak.

"I don't think you can ever solve a problem by throwing money at it," OBM Director Shkurti said.

The medical board has been and still is dominated by doctors, the majority of whom have been private practitioners. As a result, the board's actions have generally reflected their views.

One of the board's long-time battles has been to keep consumer representatives off the board, and the physician members have actively lobbied the legislature to keep the number of lay members to a bare minimum.

Until 1975, there was no consumer representative and the first one was Walter A. Paolo, an elderly political crony of then-Gov. James A. Rhodes.

"Wally was a heck of a nice guy but, frankly, his purpose on the medical board was to get a free dinner," Falleur said. Paolo left the board in 1983.

Following a *Plain Dealer* investigative series on the medical board in 1980, the legislature put another consumer member on, over the strenuous objections of the board members, who fought the issue for two years.

The physician members argued then, as they had in the past, that consumers did not possess the necessary medical knowledge to make decisions affecting physicians. (That argument was later turned against one of its proponents, Dr. Jerauld Ferritto, when another board member suggested that Ferritto, a podiatrist, didn't have enough medical knowledge to be the board's vice president).

The addition of consumers has also been labeled as "fiscally irresponsible" and a move that would "result in inefficiency."

Ferritto also charged it "would establish something that should never be done legally, that is, establish a special-interest group on the board."

But some suggest the physicians, not the consumers, are the special-interest group on state medical boards.

Claiming a necessity of medical expertise may be no more than a mask for providing physicians with "a sympathetic tribunal," Giles R. Scofield wrote in *The Journal of Legal Medicine* in 1979. "Although such expertise is clearly required, this does not compel the conclusion that representatives of the medical profession should be drawn from a limited area of the medical community, or that their expertise should dominate the board's decisions. The system suffers from an infestation of self-interested members of the medical profession."

One of the most aggressive medical boards is in California and a committee made up of five physicians and two consumers decides disciplinary cases; the full board is made up of 12 physicians and seven consumers.

"We get pretty nifty public members. These folks are sharp, they are intensely interested in what is going on and they are not afraid to speak out. They do not become the captives of the physicians," said Linda McCready, chief of external affairs for the California board. Past presidents of that board have included a venture capitalist and a black woman who formerly worked for the United Auto Workers. No consumer has ever been president of Ohio's board. The most powerful position on the Ohio board is that of secretary, but consumers are forbidden by law from holding that job, something board consumer member Carol Rolfes thinks is unfair. Rolfes is a retired nurse.

"What we're talking about is the need for a balanced board, if expertise is needed, it can be sought out," she said. "My head is in a different place simply because I am not a physician and I don't have a professional or potential economic stake in what we do."

Rolfes said she often had felt frustrated by the lack of kindred spirits on the medical board, and said the public would be better represented if two more consumer members were added to the board.

"I think the board would be more balanced," Rolfes said.

Board Secretary Dr. Henry G. Cramblett said he was not opposed to adding more consumers—although records show he had historically been one of the most vociferous opponents—but said the board probably couldn't afford to enlarge its membership.

"My response to that is, decrease the number of physicians," Rolfes said.

Harris S. Cohen, a former public health official with the federal Department of Health, Education and Welfare, wrote in 1980 in *The Journal of Health Politics, Policy and Law*:

"That the professions have an important role to play in licensure goes without saying, but that they should virtually monopolize the process of licensure raises serious public policy issues. Numerous policy considerations are brought to professional boards where the public's interest is not necessarily the same as the private interest of the regulated profession."

Frequently, the medical board has stood shoulder-to-shoulder on many issues with the Ohio State Medical Association, the lobbying group that represents Ohio's physicians, particularly on the issues of consumer representation, alcoholic and addicted doctors, and investigating malpractice.

Board records show the two consumer members now on the board have been the sternest disciplinarians in recent years.

Board consumer member William W. Johnston, a Columbus lawyer, said he is referred to as "the hanging judge" because of his belief that felons should not be allowed to practice medicine in the state, a belief shared by Rolfes. That stance has provoked many disagreements from the other board members.

Asked why, Johnston said, "Because Carol and I are the only non-physicians on the board." Despite their attitudes on discipline, the two consumer members have had only a minor impact on the board's decisions because they are always outnumbered. Johnston said the physician members, because of their outlook, often cannot bring themselves to revoke a physician's license.

"I think that for someone who's been through 12 years of high school and four years of college and four years of medical school and two years of residency, their life will not end if they can't practice medicine. There are other jobs out there, but the other board members don't see it that way, and that's where we have the arguments," Johnston said. "I guess that's when they would say I wouldn't know because I'm not a doctor, not a member of the fraternity."

Last October, longtime board member Dr. Peter Lancione wondered at a board meeting "if the board gains anything by revoking a license." The year before, Lancione had recommended letting a New Jersey doctor who had been convicted of manslaughter, conspiracy and 37 drug-related felonies keep his Ohio license.

Board secretary Cramblett said more licenses were not revoked because the board has been advised that revocations are hard to uphold in court.

In 1980, a *Plain Dealer* investigative series showed that the board's discipline was weak, that it lacked an adequate number of investigators and an adequate number of consumer members and that it poorly monitored addicted and alcoholic physicians.

The series also pointed out that state laws did not require hospitals or insurance companies to report malpractice judgments and disciplinary actions and that the board didn't have the power to summarily suspend licenses or issue investigatory subpoenas.

The legislature, led by Thompson, responded by increasing the board's budget, adding another consumer member and giving it the power to seek summary suspensions and issue subpoenas.

Thompson said the board's improvement since then had been negligble.

"Back then, on a scale of one to 10, I gave the board a zero. Now, I think I would give them a 2," Thompson said. "The board is still not doing its job, and I think it's about time we brought them into the 20th century."

Thursday, Thompson was appointed by House Speaker Vernal G. Riffe Jr., D-89, New Boston, to head a five-man committee to investigate the practices of the board and make recommendations to the legislature.

Thompson said he would hold extensive hearings and would subpoena records and witnesses before his committee.

Said Thompson: "We're going to do the whole thing."

BOARD GOES AFTER THE SMALL STUFF

The State Medical Board accused Akron podiatrist Dr. Kenneth C.A. Parker of being crazy because, among other things, he advertised and offered free foot examinations.

In 1979, the board publicly charged him with being unable to practice because of mental illness and forced Parker to undergo a psychiatric examination to prove his sanity. Meanwhile, it has never taken any action against Cleveland podiatrist Dr. Stuart Abrams, who

- Admitted in a secret hearing in 1979 that he had written narcotics prescriptions for himself and his wife for non-medical reasons, a felony under Ohio law;

- Has had a longtime drug problem, which the board is aware of and has done nothing about, despite a state law requiring it to suspend the licenses of drug-addicted doctors;

- Admitted in court in 1983 that he had written 132 false narcotics prescriptions for a mob-linked gambler to pay off gambling debts, after he and the gambler were indicted on 93 counts of drug trafficking and other drug felonies. Abrams pleaded guilty to obstructing justice;

- Was a partner with Columbus podiatrist Dr. Donald Plotnick, a twice-convicted criminal whose latest conviction was for setting fire to a man who Plotnick believed had reneged on a drug deal.

While board officials say they don't have the money or manpower to go after every doctor like Abrams, they apparently have the resources to investigate doctors like Parker, whose offenses included putting his name in bold-faced type in the Yellow Pages, offering free foot examinations, and sponsoring a radio show called "Footprints of Jesus." The board dropped its charges when a board-appointed psychiatrist found no evidence of any mental problems.

"It was uncalled-for harassment," said Parker, a devout fundamentalist Baptist. "They figured if you advertised, you must be crazy. This was back when nobody advertised. Now, everybody does it. But they put me through so much craziness that it was simply unbelievable. The thing of it was, I wouldn't go along with the program. I wouldn't be one of the boys. And the medical board is still investigating me."

Medical Board Administrator William J. Lee bridled at the suggestion that the board allowed dangerous physicians to run free while it focused its limited investigative powers on those it perceived as competing with organized medicine.

"That's the argument we've gotten over in the legislature and I don't think that can be backed up by facts. There have been some investigations, but to say that that has been our primary thrust, I would not agree. The people who are complaining that we are going after the little limited practitioner are in error," Lee said.

But former medical board lawyer Michael Falleur didn't remember it that way.

"They used to climb all over those lower-income clinics because they'd have a physician's assistant see someone with a cut on his finger instead of an M.D. They thought this was just tragic. Given the limited funding and manpower the board has, going after people who were giving free treatments seemed a little bit strange."

Falleur said Lee and former board secretary Dr. Anthony Ruppersberg, who set the investigatory agenda, were referred to by board employees as "Batman and Robin. They were out there making the world safe from people who were giving foot massages and meanwhile there were dozens and dozens of cases of really bad practice that no one was doing anything about."

Dr. Donald Williams, a family practitioner in Cincinnati, said he was ordered to appear for a secret hearing several years ago because the board questioned the activities of a medical assistant Williams employed.

"It still irritates me to this day to think about it," Williams said. "They claim they don't have the time to get around to everybody, but if they've got the people and the time to devote to that, they surely ought to have the time to devote to the people who really are the bad actors and need to have their licenses revoked."

Internal board records show that from late 1983 to mid-1984, the board was investigating or had assigned to its legal section:

- 97 cases of illegal practice of medicine by chiropractors, masseuses, mechanotherapists, nurse-midwives and others, including such organizations and programs as the Dayton Free Clinic, the Dyna-Slim diet plan, electrolysis centers, the Herbalife nutritional program, and several nurse-midwife and nurse-practitioner groups.

- 10 cases of improper use of physician's assistants.

- 11 cases of misleading advertising.

Those same records show that the board—out of more than 500 active investigatory and legal cases—was investigating only seven cases of unnecessary services or surgery. Six of those cases were against podiatrists and osteopathic physicians.

Sung Bok Hsu, a Korean woman who has oriental food stores in Columbus, was ordered to appear for a secret board hearing in 1979 and was accused by Lee of the illegal practice of medicine.

Her crime: attributing medicinal value to ginseng tea.

"Mr. Lee advised her that our problem was to protect the public and that was all he had to say. Mrs. Hsu wondered why she had been brought here to be psychologically intimidated," the hearing records state.

Lately, the board has been concentrating on certified nurse-midwives, nurses who deliver babies. Home births and alternative methods of birth have been increasing over the years, much to the dismay of organized medicine and the medical board.

One of its favorite targets is Columbus nurse-midwife Maria Eversole. Records show that the board has been calling her in for secret hearings since 1981 and, in 1983, an investigator was assigned to look into 25 home births Eversole had done. Her lawyer, Fred Gittes, complained that she was being harassed and would sue if it didn't stop.

"Home births are not illegal per se. Nor does a physician have to be present for a registered nurse-midwife to deliver a baby. Mr. Gittes' argument may very well have merit if there has in fact been no complaint in this matter," board lawyer John C. Albert advised the board's chief investigator in a memo.

Internal board records show there were no complaints; the investigation was prompted by former board secretary Ruppersberg, an obstetrician, now dead.

But investigations of nurse-midwives continue. Cincinnati lawyer Marilyn C. Reece represents several in southern Ohio, one of whom was called in for a secret hearing last April and accused of the illegal practice of medicine for fitting a diaphragm and showing women how to detect breast cancer. Another one of Reece's clients is an obstetrician who employs a nurse-midwife in his practice and he too was called in for a secret hearing, she said.

"It was a real interesting Star Chamber process," Reece said. "They were called in, cross-examined, told . . . [the board] had secret informers that said you were doing such-and-such and they wanted it stopped or they were going to pull their licenses," Reece said.

"Now, what is someone who is a small practitioner going to do? How is a nurse-midwife who is making $6,000 to $8,000 a year going to fight them? They can't. The board in my opinion is harassing them," Reece said. "They are jealous guardians of the medical monopoly." Reece, in a letter to a state senator, also questioned the legality of the secret hearing process.

Butler County coroner's investigator Thomas Marsh said, "I've dealt with all the boards sometime in my career, either as a policeman or a coroner's investigator, and all of them do a good job, all of them except the medical board. The only ones I can ever get them to move on are people doctoring without a permit. They move very quickly on those people."

STATE SENATOR IS AT HIS DOCTOR'S SIDE

State Medical Board lawyer William J. Schmidt says people who criticize the board should remember one thing:

"We are charged with regulating the most powerful, wealthy group in the state. Some of the people we've gone after are the personal physicians and personal friends of some of the people across the street [at the Capitol]. They can bring a lot of pressure to bear," Schmidt said. That was evident during the board's deliberations over the license of Youngstown's Dr. Skevos M. Zervos.

Zervos was accused by the board in 1979 of overprescribing addictive drugs to 183 patients. Evidence at his hearing showed Zervos had been giving some patients hundreds of doses of amphetamines and tranquilizers at the same time for months.

One of Zervos' patients, who Zervos acknowledged was addicted, was driving from Cincinnati twice a month to receive Percodan, an addictive painkiller, from Zervos. He said he was giving another woman habit-forming stimulants "because it seems to give her some energy to do some work around the house."

The board hearing officer found Zervos had risked addicting his patients by carelessly prescribing "illogical" amounts of drugs, with little medical justification. He recommended Zervos surrender his federal license to prescribe Schedule II narcotics for two years.

On April 9, 1980, the board was to decide on the hearing officer's recommendations. Sitting in the tiny board room was State Sen. Harry Meshel, D-33, of Youngstown, then president of the Senate and one of the most powerful politicians in Ohio.

Meshel didn't say a word during the meeting, records show, but he hardly had to. Zervos' lawyer made sure the board members knew where Meshel stood on the matter:

"Dr. Zervos makes house calls and will often take on patients when others have given up. He named Senator Meshel as one of Dr. Zervos' patients whose life he saved," the board minutes state.

The board's lawyer recommended the board not consider the case then, because only four of the board members had read the transcripts of the hearing. One board member asked that the matter be tabled for another month.

But board member Dr. Peter Lancione, whose brothers include a former speaker of the Ohio House and a former chairman of the Franklin County Democratic Party, wouldn't hear of it.

"Dr. Lancione stated that, since several of the visitors to the meeting are present regarding Dr. Zervos, the board should take action now and not wait," the minutes state.

Board Vice President Dr. Jerauld Ferritto asked the hearing officer if he was willing to amend his findings to allow Zervos to keep his federal drug license. The board's lawyers left the room.

Finally, after furious negotiations, Zervos' lawyer asked the board to table the decision and the board agreed. Later in the meeting, some board members said they had been so embarrassed by the affair they were thinking of getting a new vice president.

The next month, Lancione announced that he didn't see anything wrong with Zervos' prescribing practices and the board voted not to take away Zervos' drug license. He was put on probation for two years, and told that he must appear before the board every three months.

Three months later, the board decided to extend those appearances to every six months and six months later, board member Dr. Henry G. Cramblett wondered "if continued probation was necessary . . . Dr. Zervos' ability to practice was never questioned, only his prescribing practices."

Zervos complained that his probation was causing the state Industrial Commission to doubt his medical reports in worker compensation cases, which caused board member Dr. Leonard Lovshin to announce that he "is sympathetic with the problem that Dr. Zervos must be facing with his Industrial Commission reports."

The board drew up a consent agreement to take Zervos off probation, but at its next meeting, Zervos' lawyer said he advised Zervos not to sign it.

"With a new agreement on record, the matter would again be released to the newspapers and the publicity would be worse than staying on probation," Zervos' lawyer told the board. The board went along with Zervos' wishes.

Caltrans Ignored Elevated Freeway Safety

Gary Webb and Pete Carey

San Jose Mercury News (October 19, 1989)

INTRODUCTION BY PETE CAREY

Gary found a promising lead for this story in some documents that the state highway agency had made available to the media—the name of a retired engineer who turned out to have some helpful information. As Gary described it later, he found the man sitting on the front porch of his home in Sacramento and introduced himself as a reporter. "I was wondering when you'd come by," the man said, meaning someone from the press. Although I've been critical of Gary's crack cocaine series, working with him on this story was a pleasure. The *San Jose Mercury News*' detailed and extensive coverage of the Loma Prieta earthquake won the newspaper's entire staff a Pulitzer for general news reporting.

□   □   □

STATE IGNORED NIMITZ WARNING:
275 FEARED DEAD AS DAMAGE COSTS SOAR INTO BILLIONS
OCTOBER 19, 1989

State officials have known for more than a decade that Oakland's Cypress Street Viaduct, which collapsed in Tuesday's earthquake, had an outdated design that made it vulnerable to such shock waves.

But Caltrans officials said they doubted that the bridge's concrete support columns would collapse like they did—and they offered a variety of explanations about why the columns were not reinforced.

As the dust settled from Tuesdays's murderous earthquake, it quickly became apparent that the collapse of the Oakland highway was the single deadliest event of the quake.

Investigators are focusing their attention on the failure of dozens of support columns separating the upper and lower decks of the viaduct.

And Gov. George Deukmejian called for an investigation of the collapse.

"I had assumed that the freeways were . . . constructed with adequate standards so that they would be able to withstand a quake of this severity," he said.

In 1977, the viaduct was retrofitted with a cable linking its road decks together. But it was the four-foot thick concrete columns—and not the road decks—that gave way Tuesday.

Officials acknowledged that a 1987 quake in Whittier clearly showed the need for reinforcing the columns, which were built without the spiral steel reinforcements used in current bridges.

J. David Rogers, a Pleasant Hill engineer who studied the viaduct in 1975, said it was clear that the structure could not make it through an earthquake like Tuesday's—a north-south temblor shaking the structure along its entire length.

When those supports snapped, more than a mile of concrete roadway collapsed onto the lower duct of the bridge, crushing as many as 250 homeward-bound commuters.

State and federal highway officials Wednesday gave a variety of explanations why the columns on the 32-year-old structure—one of California's first double-decker freeways and a known earthquake hazard—hadn't been reinforced.

Dean Carlson, a top Federal Highway Administration official, said reinforcement work was imminent. After an Alameda press conference, state highway department structures chief James Roberts said research was under way and work was slated for 1991.

But several other top Caltrans offices told the California Transportation Commission Wednesday afternoon that the agency was nowhere near starting such work, since the technology to do it hasn't been developed yet.

"We hadn't started because we don't have the technical knowledge, nor does it exist in the world, to tell us how to retrofit," said William Schaefer, chief engineer for the Department of Transportation. Schaefer said the only elevated highway bridges in the state scheduled for column reinforcement are of a different construction than the Cypress Viaduct.

Viaduct not on retrofit list

Records of the Transportation Departments 1988–89 bridge reinforcement project schedule show that the Cypress Viaduct isn't on the list. However, the Embarcadero Viaduct in San Francisco—which is similar in construction to the Cypress and is a few years newer—is. It is scheduled to receive $75,000 worth of support column reinforcement this year.

The Embarcadero sustained heavy damage, but did not collapse. When asked why that bridge was on the bridge reinforcement project list if the technology doesn't exist to fix it, Caltrans officials said they thought experimental work was under way there.

It was clear that the state's top bridge and highway engineers were caught flat-footed by the Cypress Street Viaduct disaster.

"If you had asked me two days ago, I would have told you that our best conclusion is that an earthquake involving the Cypress Viaduct wouldn't have resulted in the catastrophe that it did," said Caltrans spokesman Jim Drago.

Top Caltrans officials said the department's earthquake-proofing plans were based on the results of the 1971 quake in Silmar, during which bridges built like the Cypress Street Viaduct suffered the least amount of damage. The most damage resulted from road decks tearing apart. As a result, the only retrofitting that had been done to the Cypress bridge involved lashing the roadway together with steel cables to prevent the road pieces from separating. That work was done in 1977, the last time the bridge had undergone a detailed seismic safety analysis, said James Gates, a senior structural engineer at Caltrans.

Once an engineering showpiece

The highway, opened July 1957, "went from being a showpiece of engineering to being a different kind of showpiece were we took classes of engineers out there" to study its problems and weak points, Pleasant Hill engineer Rogers said.

Rogers said his 1975 study found that the worst problems with the bridge were the support columns, which taper from top to bottom and lack spiral steel reinforcement now commonly used in column construction.

The Pleasant Hill engineer said his engineering professor in reinforced concrete design, Jerome Raphael, took the earthquake safety issue up with Caltrans officials.

"I remember at the time talking to Raphael. He talked with them directly. [He said] that they realized this viaduct had serious possibilities of problems in a major quake, of 6.5 and up lasting more than 25 seconds, because the structure is so long and the north end is built on old estuary deposits, bay muds and gravels."

In 1956–57, when the Cypress Street Viaduct was built, engineering knowledge did not include the use of spiral steel in support columns.

Rogers, after inspecting the bridge on Wednesday, said the viaduct collapsed under the quake in a sort of "zipper failure from south to north."

The Bay Bridge, which saw a 50-foot section of its upper deck drop onto the lower deck, also received deck reinforcement under Phase I of the highway department's earthquake project. But Gates confirmed that the section of the bridge that collapsed had not been strengthened with steel cables.

No need was 'apparent'

"It wasn't apparent that there was a need (for deck strengthening) at that point," Gates said. "We're still looking at why that decision was made."

Chief Caltrans engineer Schaefer said he suspects the soil upon which the north end of the bridge rests will wind up being the culprit, as it is old fill dirt that is notoriously unstable in earthquakes.

"The Cypress bridge, I hate to say the word anomaly, but it does stick out as strange. There's something that's not right here. Bad soils. Liquefaction, maybe," he said.

RETROFITTING PUSHED ASIDE BY NEW CONSTRUCTION
OCTOBER 30, 1989

Early one February morning in 1971, the earth moved beneath the San Fernando Valley for a dozen seconds, and a freeway considered modern at the time collapsed in rubble. At rush hour 18-years later, much of the same thing happened to Oakland's more antiquated Cypress Street Viaduct.

The collapse of the Cypress structure Oct. 17 quickly revealed that the state's seismic retrofit and research program had been given a low—sometimes almost non-existent—priority amid its ambitious multibillion dollar program of building new freeways and maintaining old ones.

While the mechanism behind the collapse of the Oakland viaduct may not be known for some time, the San Fernando and Oakland freeway disasters have striking similarities. In each case, the chief culprit seems to have been a hinged joint. In 1971 the joint was in the freeway deck and in 1989 in the freeway column.

And in each case, there has come a cry for more research into ways to protect the freeways from such devastation.

High-level state officials say money needed for seismic safety always has quickly been granted. Caltrans says it had a prudent reinforcement program. But some engineering consultants and former Caltrans engineers complain that retrofit and seismic research was the last in line for maintenance money.

What happened to the seismic safety effort? How was the urgency that characterized state efforts in 1971 lost? Why was the state so slow to reinforce its concrete columns? Here is a look at the developments of those 18 years.

Beginning in 1971, the federal Department of Transportation gave money to an effort, undertaken in part by the Earthquake Engineering Research Center at the University of California, Berkeley, to find out what had caused the collapse of the curved freeway bridge and how to prevent it from happening elsewhere.

UC Professor William Godden, who co-directed the studies conducted at the Berkeley center, recalls, "There was a lot of money for research on curved bridges at that time, and there was a lot of urgency. Mind you, the same may happen right now."

One finding of the post-1971 studies was that the roadway joints needed reinforcing and that restraining cables linking together slabs of curved, elevated roadways would prevent a repetition of such a collapse.

A second finding—this by other engineers—was that the freeway's columns needed reinforcing. Steel jackets were designed for such columns, but unlike the restraining cables, Caltrans waited nearly 16 years to install them on pre-1971 freeway structures.

In the August 1978 issue of Bridge Notes, then-chief design engineer Oris H. Degenkolb wrote that the 1971 earthquake had pointed out a number of deficiencies in bridge design—among them that the superstructures were not properly tied to columns and that bridge columns were not adequately reinforced.

In the same article, Degenkolb noted: "Methods of retrofitting columns to make them earthquake resistant are being investigated, and a developmental contract will be let in the near future for trying out some of the schemes. All bridges that might require column retrofitting are currently being identified."

As it turned out, Degenkolb was about nine years ahead of his time. As

California Department of Transportation officials have admitted in recent days, the contract Degenkolb spoke of has not still not been let, and records show that the process of identifying the bridges that had the most critical column dangers wasn't done until 1987.

When asked why, Caltrans officials point to layoffs and other "financial crises" that have buffeted the $3.3 billion agency.

Retrofitting put on back burner

A more precise reason is that earthquake retrofitting became a backwater project in the sprawling highway department. The agency turned its attention toward building more and bigger superhighways and relieving congestion nightmares.

In 1976, citing a shortage of funds, Caltrans let go of its entire seismic design unit as part of a layoff that cut the agency's staff. Older engineers had to be trained to take over the seismic unit.

Adriana Gianturco, then director of transportation, says her administration recovered within a year and from then on concentrated on the maintenance of existing roads. She argues that the Deukmejian administration has concentrated on glamorous new road projects instead.

"Our approach, which was fixing up existing roads, had no glamour and sex appeal," Gianturco said. "What is glamorous is building new roads, where you can cut a ribbon. Nobody cuts a ribbon on a repaired pothole."

The first phase of the three-phase retrofitting program sputtered along from 1971 to 1976 with minimal funding. Only 291 bridges were retrofitted during that time, at a cost of $7.4 million. Funding picked up in the late 1970s and early 1980s but dwindled down to nothing in 1986.

Over the 17-year span of the first phase, 1,261 bridge decks were retrofitted with steel hinges and steel cables, a process engineers say is pretty simple to do. Caltrans spent an average of $3 million a year on the task, about one one-thousandth of its $3 billion annual highway budget.

While the projects served to keep bridge decks from sliding off in a quake, Caltrans did nothing to reinforce the columns that held up those bridge decks, or to conduct the kind of detailed examination that might have led to spotting other weaknesses in the Cypress and other structures.

On a list of proposed joint research projects that Caltrans gave to

Japanese engineers in 1985, research into reinforcing columns was at the end of the line.

Candid letter from engineer

And in an unusually candid letter to a Palo Alto engineer in 1988, Caltrans' chief bridge engineer, James E. Roberts, said of the column-strengthening program: "This is a program which has been given intermittent attention as time permitted among our ongoing daily bridge design duties for the past 10 years. Retrofitting is one minuscule part of our highway program."

Former chief of design engineer Degenkolb said in an interview last week that funding for the construction of the improvements was constantly a problem. The reason: Bridge collapses hadn't killed enough people.

Degenkolb said Caltrans had a "rule of thumb" that 5,000 people were going to die on California's highways each year, and money was allocated to high-risk areas. Bridge collapses had only accounted for two deaths, Degenkolb said, and that's what officials at Caltrans headquarters looked at when dividing the money.

"You see these reports saying 10,000 deaths will result from an earthquake, and people forget when they read them and that these aren't going to be people that are going to be imported from outer space. They are us. People forget that," he said.

By the time Degenkolb retired in 1981—a decade after the San Fernando quake—less than half of the most dangerous bridges in the state had been retrofitted under the first phase of the program.

What turned the earthquake program around was the 1987 temblor in Whittier. It was then, records show, that Caltrans engineers remembered how serious the column problems were.

In assessing the failure of the columns of the Interstate 5–Interstate 605 separator bridge, Roberts wrote: "The columns were on the verge of total failure and surely would have failed in an aftershock, which occurred two days after the main shock."

That separator bridge was a multicolumn bridge—like the Cypress Street Viaduct.

Bosses were warned

To gain funding for the column project, Roberts, a taciturn, crew-cut engineer with years of experience in the upper echelons of the Caltrans bureaucracy, warned his bosses that fatalities could exceed 100 and damage run into the millions from bridge collapses if the program was not sped up.

The department, along with Gov. George Deukmejian and the California Transportation Commission, quickly approved $64 million to be spent on 767 old bridges.

A research contract was let, with results due this year or next, and the first work was scheduled for 1990. The Cypress Street Viaduct wasn't scheduled to be fixed for another few years. While UC-Berkeley experts say column reinforcement alone would not have prevented the Cypress structure collapse, they say a close examination would have disclosed the viaduct's flaws.

"The best insurance policy for the future is ongoing research money and money for both studying old bridges and buildings and retrofitting them," observed Godden. "If you don't buy that insurance, you are going to be caught in the economic disaster we are now."

Good Cop Bad Cop
The Thin Blue Line
Gary Webb

San Jose Mercury News (September 16, 1990)

INTRODUCTION BY JEFF KLEIN

True investigative reporters are rare. In the US, perhaps ten per generation, tops. Like virtually all of his colleagues, I recognized Gary as this rare creature the moment I met him. Gary was happily compelled to expose abuses of power. Working as his editor was a pleasure and an honor. In "Good Cop Bad Cop," he shows how the badge of authority combined with the cloak of official secrecy can allow society's sworn protectors to transform into brutal predators.

The rare, resolute investigative reporter deserves protection. Gary's gifts and zeal were well known throughout the newsroom. He loved finding liars in high places and truth-tellers in low ones. He was a hard-ass, but an unpretentious one eager to talk with anyone who might help him understand: "What's goin' on here?" Gary frequently dropped his g's. His informality put me at ease, just as his perspicacity kept me on edge.

The gritty, detail-filled exposés Gary pursued took time and hence money, both of which were hoarded by management. Yet because Gary repeatedly delivered the goods, he was gradually given more freedom. Editors of various departments, myself included, competed to get stories from Gary. He was a star.

If "Dark Alliance" failed to meet the *Mercury News'* standards, as the paper retrospectively claimed, that fault lay with the paper. They had the power to add all the caveats, clarity, and weasel words they wanted prior to publication. In fact, under pressure the *Merc* surrendered Gary to the media's top capos, who were humiliated by their complicit cloaking of the CIA and the Contras. Gary was an honest Internal Affairs investigator turned on by the police brass. This was a crime of the highest order, as menacing to society as any that Gary exposed.

□   □   □

One was an introspective do-gooder who "just wanted to help." One seemed to delight in brutalizing helpless people. Both were Deputy Kevin Wise.

Still slightly inebriated from Mexican beer and tequila chasers, Eric Johnson steered his 1984 BMW into a darkened industrial park on Sacramento's south side and headed back to work.

It was 2:30 in the morning. He had to make a quick call to check on a computer networking problem his employer was having and he could call it a night.

Johnson's squat gray sedan raced past the silent warehouses and low office buildings. A stop sign flashed by. Then another. Suddenly, there was a carnival of multicolored lights dancing in the darkness behind him.

Deputy Kevin Wise, a brawny veteran of the Sacramento County Sheriff's Department, ordered Johnson out and searched the BMW before announcing his findings: Eric Johnson—if that was his real name—was a burglar on his way to a break-in, driving a stolen car.

Johnson, a lanky, 24-year-old network analyst, frantically protested that the car was his and that his wallet was in his office, right across the street.

Johnson's story was an obvious lie, Wise decided. A grating, maddening lie.

The 230-pound deputy slammed Johnson against the patrol car and forced his head back with a massive forearm. The muzzle of a semiautomatic Glock pistol was jammed under the analyst's quivering chin.

"Why are you lying to me, motherf—?" Wise muttered. "Tell me the truth or I'm going to blow your brains out."

Johnson heard the pistol click, as if it was being cocked, and he threw his arms over his eyes, waiting helplessly for the lawman to put a nine-millimeter hole through his head.

For Stacy Inman, a low-level prosecutor in the Sacramento district attorney's office, it had been another frantic morning. She scanned the file of a drunken-driving case her boss had passed on to her; the arresting officer would be stopping by to give her a rundown on the testimony he would give at the morning's motion hearing.

She did a double-take when Deputy Wise ambled into her office, his eyes hidden behind sunglasses and his muscular 6-foot-2 frame covered by a tight black T-shirt and Levi's. Inman made a mental note to apologize to the judge for the deputy's unseemly get-up.

As they went over the details of the arrest, Inman noticed that the deputy seemed hazy on the facts.

More than once she sensed he was seeking suggestions on what to say in court.

Inman's fears were soon realized. When Wise took the stand, the motorist's attorney began attacking him with blunt questions: Had Wise drawn his weapon and placed it at the defendant's throat? Had Wise shoved the driver against the top of the car and pointed a weapon at him?

It never happened, Wise said.

"And you haven't perjured yourself here today, have you?" the attorney asked.

"No, sir."

The judge swiftly upheld the legality of Eric Johnson's arrest.

Inman stormed out of the courtroom and found Wise in the hall.

"What the hell was that all about?" she demanded.

Wise assured her that he had not pulled his gun, and that he had no idea why Johnson's attorney was asking such outlandish questions.

Deputy Wise was standing beside a busy thoroughfare two weeks later, trying to break off one of Randy Scherer's fingers.

A few minutes earlier, Scherer had improvidently waved his middle finger in the rear window of his pickup truck, to show annoyance with the headlight-flashing driver on his tail.

It turned out to be Deputy Wise, hurrying to a hot call, an assault with a deadly weapon reportedly in progress at a nearby apartment complex.

Scherer's gesture made Wise so angry that he disregarded the assault call and, hitting his emergency lights, pulled over the battered, primer-gray pickup to give its driver a lesson in highway courtesy.

With his left arm, Wise picked up the skinny, 5-foot-6 Scherer by the neck and toppled him into the truck bed. He then punched Scherer in the chest a few times, pulled him back out, and with a heavy police boot ground one of Scherer's unshod feet into the sharp gravel. (A print of the deputy's Vibram-soled boot was clearly visible on Scherer's white sock when the shaken 20-year-old arrived home to tell his mother of the encounter.)

Punctuating his lecture with rabbit punches to Scherer's chest, Wise told the young cabinetmaker to thank God he'd flipped off a police officer and not some roving psychopath.

"I could have been a group of Hell's Angels, f—head! They'd take you out in this field and f—ing bury you!" Wise shouted. He invited Scherer to "flip me off again" and when Scherer refused, said: "Well, I'll put a gun to your neck and blow your head off. How would you like that?"

Seizing the first two fingers of Scherer's right hand, Wise told him to make a choice: Which finger did Scherer want broken off and shoved up his nose? Wise pulled the fingers apart like a wishbone; Scherer dropped to one knee in pain.

Across the well-lighted street, restaurant workers Michael Denny and Scott Seo stared out the window of Boss Hawg's Bar-B-Que in disbelief.

"We were just amazed about how much power that officer had over the driver of the truck," Denny later told an investigator from Internal Affairs. "It could have been us. It could have definitely been us."

Despite nine years of hardening, Wise walked into the district attorney's trap like a trusting spaniel. It wouldn't dawn on him for more than a week that his meeting with Deputy D.A. Steven Cilenti had been a set-up.

Wise was warmly welcomed by Cilenti, who ushered him into an office festooned with mementos from Cilenti's years as a Redding police officer. Seeing he was dealing with a fellow cop, Wise relaxed and the two men made small talk about police weaponry, a subject Wise relished.

"I carry a Glock," the patrolman announced, referring to his plastic Austrian-made sidearm. "The only problem with it is it's the one Jan Zeboski shot that kid with. Some people say that it's real, real easy to shoot people with because it's like carrying a .45—hardly any trigger pull . . . So I mean—shoot/don't shoot situations . . ."

Cilenti's eyebrows shot up at the mention of Deputy Jan Zeboski's name. Two weeks earlier the rookie patrolman had gunned down an unarmed 15-year-old boy who'd surprised him in a dark schoolyard. The killing had touched off anguished protests from the black community, and Cilenti's office was investigating the shooting.

Uh-oh, Cilenti thought. This guy's impressed because he has a gun that killed someone.

The prosecutor steered the conversation to the topic he'd called Wise to discuss: Eric Johnson's drunken driving arrest. The case was coming up for trial, Cilenti reminded him, and the prosecutor's office wanted some assurances that there were no land mines waiting out there. "Let me say this to start with, OK?" Cilenti said. "I've been there. I've been on the street and I've had my butt kicked a few times and kicked a few myself, OK? You make mistakes."

Replied Wise: "I'm going to tell you the truth on this."

After listening carefully to the deputy's innocuous version of the arrest, Cilenti dropped his bombshell: Eric Johnson's attorney had come to see him, claiming he could prove Wise lied under oath because he had the whole arrest on tape.

"I said, 'Yeah, like your guy had a recorder, right? My officer never found no damn recorder.' He said, 'No, I've got it on video.'"

The guard at Johnson's workplace, Cilenti went on, had noticed the flashing lights, trained a remote-controlled video camera on the scene, and, recognizing Johnson, flipped on the recorder.

The defense attorney had given him a copy of the videotape, Cilenti said, but the picture was so blurry that it was hard to tell what was happening.

"Let's assume what he said was right," the prosecutor proposed. "You jerked this guy out of the car and at some point you stuck a gun in his face or something like that. Does that ring any bells?"

"No," Wise said, then amended his answer. "I've done that before to people, OK? But it's not like I've done it so many times that I've mixed up the pictures." Wise repeatedly insisted he had not drawn his gun.

Cilenti then led Wise to a conference room where a videocassette player was waiting. The monitor flickered on, showing the Chevrolet patrol car neatly framed between two trees.

The silent, black-and-white tape was crystal-clear and it unerringly replayed the events of that evening six months earlier.

"This is weird watching this," Wise said, as he saw himself spin Johnson around and shove him back against the car. He supplied a running narration for Cilenti's benefit: "'What are you doing to me, f——head? What are you lying to me about?' It looks like I pulled a gun, but . . ."

"It looks like it's under his nose," Cilenti remarked. "Right there. See the shine off the barrel? . . . What is going on?"

"It's either my flashlight or my gun. It might be my gun."

"Let's back it up again. Is that your gun? Did you pull your gun?"

"Well, yeah, it sure looks like it," Wise admitted. "That's me on the tape, I'm not going to hide from it. They got me. They got me. That's every police officer's nightmare, to be caught on tape doing something wrong."

Cilenti played the tape again, but Wise didn't need any more convincing.

"I couldn't justify that if the guy was Charlie Manson," Wise said heavily. "I'm done and I hate to say that, but I'm cooked. I just wanted to be a cop, you know. I just wanted to be a cop. Sometimes in my over-zealousness, I've done stuff. I've gone over the line before."

"People do that all the time," he told Cilenti, cursing his luck. "I'm the one. One in a million. On videotape."

"Put it this way," said Cilenti, who was wearing a hidden microphone. "You're not in a good way."

Outside the conference room, two officers from Internal Affairs were waiting to take Wise away. He resigned from the sheriff's department a week later, citing medical reasons, and was arrested on felony charges of police assault and perjury.

"Cops always spill their guts," Cilenti said later. "Always."

THERE WAS NO TRIAL at the urging of his attorney, Wise pleaded guilty to assaulting Johnson and entered a no-contest plea to lying under oath; the county paid $50,000 to compensate Eric Johnson for his night of terror. The assault charge involving Randy Scherer was dropped. In late June, Superior Court Judge Fred K. Morrison sentenced Wise to probation, plus 364 days in the Sacramento County Jail.

Deputy District Attorney Frank C. Meyer, who prosecuted the case, believes the patrolman got off too lightly.

"Cops hold a very special position in our society," Meyer said. "That's why, when you find one that abuses the position, you need to hammer that guy."

Meyer said the D.A.'s office learned of another incident involving Wise after news of the deputy's arrest hit the papers. The purported victim was Delroi Laniere Hill, an 18-year-old whose girlfriend's mother called the police after Hill took liberties with her daughter's blouse during a drinking session in a parked car.

Hill claimed that Wise, two years earlier, had handcuffed him, put him in the back seat of his patrol car and told him: "We're gonna blow a nigger's brains out and you're the one." He said Wise drove down a dark road, opened the car door and encouraged him to run away, saying it was his only chance to live.

Wise then bashed him on the head with a metal flashlight, splitting open his scalp, Hill said. The teen-ager surreptitiously smeared his blood on the seats and windows of the patrol car so "they would find the blood and use it as evidence against Wise if he killed me."

Sacramento County Sheriff Glen Craig, former commissioner of the California Highway Patrol, said Wise's crimes were some of the worst he's ever seen.

"I don't know of any more serious offense by a police officer than what I saw on that tape," Craig said. "To use the color of authority to browbeat an individual with a weapon pressed against their chin . . . I've never heard of anything like that in my 35 years of law enforcement."

"Guess what?" Wise said. "I've seen that stuff on a nightly basis."

KEVIN WISE, the youngest of five children, came to police work from a comfortable middle-class life in the Napa Valley. Both parents were accomplished professionals: His father was an electrical engineer for the federal government, designing missile guidance systems, and his mother taught retarded children.

Both talked "about ideals a lot . . . I'm sure I was one of only a few kids at 10 discussing morals and ethics, the way our family did," Wise told his psychotherapist last year.

One of his older brothers, Roger, is a former *Mercury News* reporter and now an Episcopal clergyman in Berkeley. Another brother is a school administrator in Panama and another is a counselor in an Oakland halfway house. Wise's parents envisioned their youngest son as a lawyer, and he worked as a law firm clerk for more than two years.

"I wanted to help the public. I was socially conscious to a certain extent and I wanted to do what I could to help. I mean, that's what I put down on my first application," Wise said.

He dropped out of college a few hours shy of a degree to enter the police academy and, like the rest of his class, was sent off to guard the county jails and courthouses until a position opened up on road patrol.

It was in the cellblocks where Wise began his metamorphosis.

His "do-gooder attitude pissed off fellow officers," he later told a psychologist. After a few months and some heart-to-heart talks with veteran jailers, Wise said, he "woke up."

"You can only get lied to or spit on or vomited on so many times and then you have you ask yourself why you're doing it," he said.

The inmates would soon come to regret his change of heart.

Wise developed a reputation as a hard-ass deluxe and, because of his size, was frequently called on to break up fights and subdue unruly convicts. Among the other guards, he became known as "Crazy Kevin," and racked up a string of inmate complaints for brutality and excessive force.

One psychologist, years later, described Wise's transformation as evidence of a "headlong collision of values. Although he wanted to be of help . . . he appears to have done a substantial about-face and became a polar opposite."

Wise disputed a psychiatrist's contention that he enjoyed intimidating prisoners: "Because I'm good at something doesn't mean I enjoyed it." In fact, he said, he hated jail duty, which he described as cold, damp and depressing. He said he believed it is "basically inhumane to keep people behind bars." After three years in the jail, he contracted tuberculosis, probably from an inmate, and became severely depressed.

By the time his turn arrived for road patrol, Wise's training officers were openly wondering if the hulking deputy was mentally fit to be turned loose on the general public.

One supervisor, Patty Butler, contacted the chief deputy to tell him that Wise had been talking of "blowing somebody away" and was "preoccupied with weaponry." She said she had an impression that Wise was "looking for an opportunity to act out some of his fantasies."

Roger Wise recalled a disturbing change in his younger brother. "He had an obsession with guns which I really saw as unhealthy. I did the San Jose police beat and the Santa Clara police beat [as a reporter] and I've known a lot of cops who were like that. That's what I saw in Kevin."

Wise was sent to psychologist Joseph R. Newton, who found the deputy to be a tactless loudmouth who liked to be the center of attention—but not crazy.

Still, Wise probably would do things he would regret, Newton said. "Wise's dramatic, rather uninsightful interactions with other persons would be particularly onerous to members of minority groups," he warned.

The psychologist's advice: Leave Wise in the jail for another three to 12 months, send him to psychotherapy and keep an eye on him. If his troubles persisted, Newton said, "grave questions could he raised regarding his suitability for being a sheriff's deputy."

Wise was sent out on solo patrol almost immediately.

"I never saw that report," Wise says. "I was told it was better if I just went out on patrol and kept my mouth shut."

By all accounts, Wise's first two years on the road were placid, even rewarding. His beat was an easy one, the evening shift in the slumbering south Sacramento suburb of Elk Grove.

"I loved it. I was out there helping people. I wasn't dealing with bad people. Drove around, talked to people," Wise said. Two psychiatric evaluations done during that time turned up no problems.

Then Wise made a decision that would ultimately lead to his ruin.

Despite his idyllic descriptions of life in Elk Grove, he asked for a transfer to Rancho Cordova, a far rougher suburb. He was placed on the graveyard shift, working the streets after midnight, which he described as "a battle-field . . . It's robbery and fights and spousal fights and drunks and drugs, gang fights. I liked it because it was hard work. I just didn't like the people."

His psychiatric reports say Wise's mental state began deteriorating after his reassignment. He lost interest in his thrill-seeking hobbies—auto and motorcycle racing, sky-diving and rock-climbing—cut off his friends, and holed up in his house during his daytime off-hours, unable to sleep and existing on a diet of candy bars and Gatorade.

He broke up with his live-in girlfriend, and walked away from his house and all his furniture. He moved out of the county and became a virtual recluse, sometimes refusing to show up for work because he was afraid he would "lose it."

Wise said he soon came to "mistrust everybody . . . I kept dealing with people that would either lie to me, cheat me or try to fight me. I never minded the bank robbery or the burglaries in progress or the car thefts or the gang fights. Those are calls you can go into and everything is black and white. The calls where you have to deal with people and their emotions . . . those were the calls that took it out of me."

It got so bad, Wise said during a civil deposition, that "I couldn't tell who was on the right side and who was on the wrong side. Sometimes it's plain. Sometimes it's not plain at all. That's when the lies and innuendos and stuff come in."

Wise's inquisitor didn't accept that. Obviously, he asked Wise, an 85-year-old woman who gets her purse stolen is the good person and the purse-snatcher is the bad person, right?

"I don't know," Wise replied, "I don't even think about that stuff any-more."

WISE AND HIS SUPPORTERS argue that he was just as much a victim as his unfortunate detainees.

The stress of nine years of police work, they say, drained Wise of sym-pathy, compassion and understanding, and turned an articulate and naïve cadet into a thug who no longer cared about right and wrong.

Prosecutor Meyer thinks those claims are nonsense. "I don't think he was in any more of a stressful situation than any other cop is in," Meyer said. "He played a real macho tough guy. He was trying to intimidate these people and throw his weight around and he got caught."

Prosecutors said that even after Wise resigned, he kept up his bizarre behavior, issuing a general death threat against anyone in the D.A.'s office involved in the case. The prosecutors were advised to obtain permits for concealed weapons, and at least one did.

Cilenti, now in private practice as a criminal defense attorney, reluc-tantly concluded that Wise "derived pleasure from it. I've thought about this a lot and I think Kevin got some kind of a rush out of it. I hope I'm wrong, but that was the only conclusion I could ever come to."

A psychiatrist for the county, Dr. Ralph Biddle, administered a battery of tests last year and wrote a 78-page report concluding that Wise had serious mental problems—a schizoid personality disorder—long before he donned the khaki-and-green uniform of a deputy sheriff.

"Mr. Wise brought his problems to his employment, and his employ-ment was simply a passive stage upon which his basic personality characteristics unfolded and evolved," Biddle wrote.

Wise argued that Biddle's conclusion was pre-ordained since it was ren-dered as part of a stress claim Wise had filed against the county to collect worker's compensation. "He's the county's boy," Wise said of Biddle. "He always finds that the problems were longstanding. That way, the county doesn't have to pay the claim."

But Wise's own psychologist, Grant L. Hutchinson, agreed that Wise had psychiatric difficulties, concluding that his patient was essentially two people struggling against each other—one helpful and humanistic, the other hostile and aggressive. That struggle became unmanageable when Wise transferred to the crime-ridden Rancho Cordova area, Hutchinson wrote. In his assessment, the psychologist didn't let the system off the hook.

While Wise was a jailer he was able to express his aggression "in a confined and restricted setting," Hutchinson wrote. ". . . On patrol, however, he was left to his own devices . . . His work as a deputy sheriff struck him in his Achilles' heel."

Sheriff Craig—who suspects Wise is laying the groundwork for a negligence suit against Sacramento County—said that while many officers suffer from stress and burnout, "violence is not a usual manifestation." He said Wise could have easily gotten a stress-related transfer, but never asked for one.

"My experience has shown that people just don't acquire violent tendencies," Craig said. "In most cases, they're present under the surface. When you look at excessive force, brutality and citizens' complaints, it's a small percentage of the people who get most of the complaints. It's a very small percentage . . ."

"How many Kevin Wise incidents have you ever heard of?" Craig went on. "It's extremely rare. We probably spend more time and money to try and make sure these things don't happen than any other profession out there anywhere."

Michael Langer, who heads San Francisco's Police Office of Citizen Complaints, said the precautions aren't enough. "It isn't fair to give somebody a police car and a star and a gun and turn them loose on the public and let them wreak havoc," said Langer, a police officer for 25 years. "They're out there to protect the public and serve the public and not to beat the crap out of them."

The public has to take Sheriff Craig's word for the infrequency of police brutality. Thanks to persuasive lobbying and hefty contributions by police leagues and associations, the inner workings of a police department have been classified as official state secrets. Until recently, simple statistics about the frequency and outcome of public complaints were confidential. Even now, unless the case results in criminal charges, the public is unlikely to realize there was ever a problem.

While other states have begun to question the wisdom of keeping police misconduct quiet—Ohio's Supreme Court, for example, recently ordered all internal affairs case files publicly released—California has been moving in the opposite direction, making its security apparatus even less accountable to the public.

Langer said there is no good reason for the secrecy that surrounds police disciplinary proceedings. "Why should police officers have a right to privacy that is greater than any other person?" he asked. "How does that protect the public?"

As a result of the smothering secrecy, society's faith in its police agents is literally blind. Yet it is so intense that anyone who dared to challenge Wise's version of the truth was suspected as a liar and a criminal.

Even when the videotape of Eric Johnson's arrest was played for him, prosecutor Meyer acknowledged, he thought it might have been staged.

"Cops have one of the toughest jobs there is, but at the same time, they get a special consideration: If a cop says something happened, most people are gonna believe the policeman," Meyer said.

Delroi Hill said that when he threatened to report the beating to the authorities, Wise scoffed and said, "It won't do you any good." Even his lawyer, he said, told him it would be "safer" to drop the matter.

All three prosecutors who worked on the case agree that the only reason Wise isn't still on the streets, heavily armed and looking for trouble, is because of a freakish accident of technology. Had Eric Johnson's arrest not been videotaped, Wise would not have been charged with anything, they acknowledge.

"All we would have had in that case was another person making the usual allegation of police brutality," Cilenti said. "We would have said: 'Sure, put him on, who's gonna believe him?' And I can tell you that kid [Johnson] would have been convicted of DUI and Kevin would have been right back out where he was. And by doing that we would have said, 'Kevin, it's OK.'"

Wise also contends the tape is the only thing unusual about his case—hard evidence in the hands of the public that couldn't be swept under a rug of official silence. He said other not-so-public crimes by deputies, including unjustified shootings, sex crimes and thefts from inmates, had been covered up or handled with quiet resignations.

Sheriff Craig hotly denied it and warned against taking the word of "a convicted perjurer."

(A few weeks after the interview with Craig, the sheriff's department arrested an employee on charges of embezzling $367,000 from inmate accounts, one of the cases Wise had mentioned as evidence of a cover-up. The alleged thefts had been going on for at least five years, sheriff's office officials acknowledge; they could not explain why they had gone undetected for so long.)

Wise said he holds the sheriff's department partly responsible for not recognizing or caring that he was having mental problems, but he also blames himself.

"This job takes probably more strength than I have and that's something I don't like admitting. I just couldn't do it anymore. You have to give something of yourself to people, either the bad guys or the good guys, whether you're helping them or hurting them. Each thing you do on that job takes something from you. Sometimes you get something back . . . but a lot of times people don't really care and your supervisors don't care and you get nothing back in return and pretty soon you're used up."

IT'S HARD TO LOOK AT WISE'S PRESENT situation and say he's not suffering for his crimes.

At 35, when most men are entering the most productive years of their careers, Wise is unemployed and disgraced, a convicted liar sitting in a prison he once guarded. He lost his house and surrendered his boat to pay off legal bills, which are still coming in. Wise figures he owes lawyers nearly $20,000.

Worse, his legal troubles are spilling into the lives of three people who didn't even know him when he was a deputy: his wife, Joy, and her two daughters, ages 6 and 10.

Wise met Joy a month after his arrest and married her four months later. Now, as a result of the conviction, her ex-husband demanded custody of the girls. "He's saying she picked a crazy cop and it's bad for the girls," Wise said. "When I focus my anger, I focus it on him."

Wise's cell is right next to someone he once arrested, and another inmate recognized him across the exercise yard, 200 feet away. Wise worries that his reputation as a jailhouse ass-kicker might plague him now that he's not wearing a badge and gun.

During a recent telephone call from the jail, Wise complained that a transfer arranged by a friendly deputy to a minimum-security work camp was nixed. "The orders came down from the sheriff that I'm to be punished instead. Good old Craig. He says I gave a black eye to law enforcement."

Roger Wise, shortly to be ordained as a priest, is philosophical about his brother's predicament.

"I kind of hoped that someday he'd stumble, something would happen before someone got hurt. He liked that power and that authority so well I figured something like this was going to happen. There are a lot of cops like that, too many who have slipped through the system," he said.

Former prosecutor Cilenti agreed that the Wise case reveals a giant hole in the fabric of law enforcement, a calamity for which there is no fail-safe system and no protection.

"What makes it so dangerous is that this is a person who acts with the authority of the people behind him, who can stop you anywhere, day or night, come into your house, take you to jail," Cilenti said. "The potential is there for a great deal of harm."

"The ideal police officer," Wise said, "would be like Robocop, unemotional, but he wouldn't be there to provide the heart that some people need out on the street. You have to have compassion in this job, but you can't have compassion in this job. I mean, it's . . . damned if you do and damned if you don't."

DWB (Driving While Black)

Gary Webb

Esquire (April 1999)

INTRODUCTION BY MARK WARREN

It was a late summer evening in 1998, over dinner at a fancy New York restaurant where the waiters really dote on you, that my boss, *Esquire* editor in chief David Granger, and I presented Gary Webb with the Pulitzer Prize he had earned for the "Dark Alliance" series that he had published in the *San Jose Mercury News* exactly two years previous. That the honor was long overdue was obvious, and to say that the oversight was egregious is no small understatement. Even as the tortured separation from his newspaper was still being negotiated (for reasons that the profiles in courage who ran the paper had never found the words to articulate), the CIA's own inspector general had earlier that summer largely validated Webb's findings. Big news, you might think! But all the major newspapers from coast to coast—from the *Washington Post* and *The New York Times* to the *Los Angeles Times*—had somehow neglected to cover this seismic news, at least not with the same vigor they had put into savaging the "Dark Alliance" series two summers before.

I will never forget that when the *Merc* published the series and the CIA had emerged from the shadows to take the unprecedented step of issuing a strongly worded denial, those same pillars of American journalism had simply taken the Agency's word for it. Yes, official denials are always to be heeded, because as we know they are always true. And I.F. Stone, Webb's north star, spun madly in his plain pine box.

And so it was that by the evening of our private award ceremony at the Four Seasons, Gary Webb, certainly one of the greatest investigative journalists of his time, had, at age forty-three, been shunned and abandoned by his profession, and all the mewling cowards in it.

But the good cheer in the room! For Webb was undaunted and unbowed, and the evening was such a buoyant and inspiring celebration of the very idea of noble journalism—*Investigate the bastards! All the bastards!*—and the wine—

selected with solemn purpose by Granger—flowed freely, even though Webb was really a Maker's Mark kind of guy.

Okay, so I lied. We presented no haughty prize to Gary that night, as it wasn't ours to give, and what the fuck's a Pulitzer anyway, really? But we did bestow a small token of appreciation to Gary on behalf of the profession to which he had devoted his life, and might have actually given him something better: an assignment.

The talk had turned to stories that we might do together—which had been the whole purpose of the dinner in the first place—and Granger excused himself to the men's room. Gary mentioned that he had found work with an investigative committee of the state assembly in Sacramento, and that through this work he had discovered a secret federal program, administered by the Drug Enforcement Administration, by which the Agency had taken to training law enforcement agencies nationwide in the art and science of racial profiling. Probable cause for pulling somebody over reverted to what it had been in the bad old days of Jim Crow—being black. The program was called Operation Pipeline. For decades, overwhelming anecdotal evidence notwithstanding, state and local governments had denied that black people were more likely to be suspected of crimes solely on account of their race, and here Gary Webb had given the lie to that assertion, revealing in the process that not only was it a lie, but there was a federal program—applied in forty-eight states, paid for by taxpayers (of all races, presumably)—whose business it had been to institutionalize such profiling. And had been doing so since 1986. It was an explosive story. "Holy shit, David," I said to Granger as he returned to the table. "Gary, tell him what you just told me." And just like that, Gary Webb got the assignment that returned him to the ranks of working journalists.

"Driving While Black" was published in the April, 1999 issue. It contains groundbreaking reporting and its writing is riveting. But the whole profession of journalism seemed so determined to erase Gary Webb that on publication the story was manifestly ignored. Nineteen months later, in late November 2000, I received a call from Cynthia Cotts, who was then a columnist for the *Village Voice*. The New York Times, it seems, had just published a blockbuster story about racial profiling. The *Times* was running it prominently and in several parts. It contained explosive revelations about a federal program, administered by the DEA, called Operation Pipeline. Cotts noted that it was indeed a big story, but that it wasn't news: Gary Webb had broken the story more than a year and a half earlier in *Esquire*. In their account of Operation Pipeline, the *Times* pretended not to know this, and gave Webb no credit whatsoever for his pioneering work.

Thinking back to our dinner together—can you tell in that moment whether what seems like a glorious new beginning is just a pause in a man's decline? No, you can't. Because as God is my witness, it was a new beginning, the next chapter in the life of a man dedicated to fearless journalism, to poking a stick in the eye of power. Except here's the part where we—where I—also abandoned Gary Webb. Over the next couple of years, he and I would talk regularly about stories, many stories. But for a thousand good and a couple not very good reasons, nothing came of our talk. We talked about a regular investigative column. As the 2000 election approached, we conceived of covering Bush and Gore not as the herd typically covers them, but by thoroughly and pitilessly investigating them as only a hawkeyed investigative reporter could—and as anyone who presumed to ask for such power deserved—issuing our findings in a series of reports. Again, nothing. And then, over time, Gary and I simply lost touch. And so we of course, never said a proper goodbye.

□   □   □

You may have noticed that many of the motorists pulled over on the side of the highway are black or Hispanic. You may have attributed this to some kind of unspoken law-enforcement racism. You may be surprised to learn that it's the result of a federal program. Called Operation Pipeline. Your tax dollars at work.

"Oh, God, help me! Oh, my God! Oh, no no no! Oh, God, help me! Help me, God! Help me, God! Please, God, save me! Oh, God! Oh, my God!"

Our instructors call him the Screamer. We are not told his name, which is just as well. That added bit of humanity would make his debasement all the more difficult to watch. Judging from the enthusiasm of the California Highway Patrol officers who are training us, the Screamer promises to be a high point of sorts in our lessons. Several times during this morning's classes, when the lectures have dragged, one or another of our uniformed instructors has called out from the back of the classroom, "Play the Screamer!" And so, eventually, they do.

As the video equipment is being readied, a sergeant briefs us on what we are about to see: a tape of an actual search made by an Operation Pipeline team in rural Arkansas. The tape will demonstrate several things, we are told, not the least of which is the effectiveness of the training we are receiving. We will see with our own eyes just how well Operation Pipeline works.

The television monitor flickers on and we see a smeary black-and-white shot of a gangly man in a checkered shirt. He is standing by a car, alongside some highway in the boondocks, trailer trucks roaring by. On the tape, it is the dead of winter, overcast and blustery, and the man keeps brushing long strands of hair from his eyes as he nervously answers questions from the two Arkansas state troopers towering over him. He is nobody, some jobless hillbilly plucked from the traffic stream by two cops who have been specially trained—like us—to spot suspicious characters.

The troopers give the man the once-over and tell him they want to search his car. He reluctantly agrees and is shoved into the backseat of their unoccupied prowl car, behind the dash-mounted video camera, and from then on, we watch through his eyes as the Pipeline team searches his car.

When the trunk lid pops open, the man begins to whimper. When one of the troopers reaches in and tosses a black plastic garbage bag onto the hood of the patrol car, he lets loose with piercing off-camera shriek.

"Help me! Help me, God! Help me, God! Please, God, save me! Oh, God! Oh, my God!"

He keeps it up, alternating between wails and moans, for what seems like an eternity, gibbering at the visions he is conjuring of his near future. Just when he seems finished, when it seems certain his lungs can take no more, he starts up again, screaming even louder than before. *"Oh, God, save me! Oh, sweet God, please! Please save me!"*

"Now, look, look," our instructor says excitedly, pointing at the screen. "The troopers are finally gonna hear him!"

As a gut-wrenching howl erupts from inside the patrol car, one of the cops looks up slowly from the Screamer's trunk and gives the camera a puzzled glance. Comedy.

The classroom explodes with laughter.

CURTIS V. RODRIGUEZ is a San Jose lawyer. He looks far younger than his forty years, has a couple kids, owns a house, drives a nice car. He's a prime example of an emerging army in California: educated urban professionals who happen not to have white skin.

Last June, he and a friend, fellow attorney Arturo Hernandez, drove Rodriguez's Mazda Millenia to Merced on a mundane legal task: taking pictures of a client's house. On their way through the windy Pacheco Pass, in the mountain range separating the Pacific coast from the dusty farms of the San Joaquin Valley, they saw some cars that had been pulled over and were being searched by California Highway Patrol officers. In every instance, it seemed, the car's driver was a dark-skinned male.

On the way back, hours later, they saw more. One after another, every couple of miles.

"After seeing the third car in a row—same deal, driver is a dark-skinned Latino and the cops have them standing off on the side of the road—Art and I looked at each other and said, 'Do you believe this?'" Rodriguez says. "It was obvious whom they were stopping. It's not like there are that many dark-skinned Latinos on the road, but that's all they had. Art got the camera out and started taking pictures of the stops, because we figured no one would believe us."

Hernandez began snapping away, getting photos of a fourth car whose dusky occupants were being questioned by the roadside. As the Millenia whizzed by the fifth such vehicle, a highway patrolman looked up and saw Hernandez with the Olympus. Soon, the Mazda's rearview mirror was filled with the chrome grille of the trooper's hard-charging Crown Victoria.

"I'm driving like a saint," Rodriguez recalls. "I'm going under the speed limit, straight down the middle of the lane. There's nothing he can do to me. But he turns on his lights and pulls me over. He walks up and tells me I was weaving, which is a total lie because I was driving that car like it was on rails."

The trooper then told Rodriguez he wanted to search the Mazda, and Rodriguez scoffed. To hell with that, he thought. I didn't go to law school for nothing. No way, he told the officer, am I consenting to a search. I know my constitutional rights. Art and I are criminal lawyers. The Fourth Amendment protects us from this kind of nonsense. If you want to search the car, get a warrant. Otherwise, just give me a ticket and let me go.

The trooper was unmoved. He looked at the two attorneys calmly and ordered them out of the vehicle. "I'm in fear for my life," he informed them in a monotone. "The passenger made suspicious motions, which gives me the right to search your car—for my own safety." Rodriguez's license and registration were taken back to the cruiser, where a drug dog sniffed at them indifferently. Not surprisingly, the search turned up nothing.

Rodriguez was dumbfounded. "The whole thing was about as illegal as you can get. He had no cause to pull me over. He had no reason to search my car. He knows I'm a lawyer, and he goes ahead and does it anyway! So the thing I'm wondering is, what happens to the people who aren't lawyers?"

What sometimes happens is this: They get frisked, and sniffed by dogs, their luggage gets dumped out and pawed, on occasion their cars are towed away and dismantled back at the police station. Other times, their vehicles are taken apart on the spot. If they're lucky, they are simply left standing alongside the road, frightened and mystified, holding an expensive traffic ticket they didn't deserve and wondering why, out of all the cars on the highway, the police came after them.

In most cases, it can be summed up in two words: Operation Pipeline. Like tens of thousands of other innocent motorists, Curtis Rodriguez had been sucked up and spit out by one of the federal government's more secretive antidrug campaigns, a giant vacuum cleaner of a program financed by the U. S. Drug Enforcement Administration and run by hundreds of state and local police agencies across the country. Over the past thirteen years, Operation Pipeline has been waging an expanding and largely invisible war on the nation's highways against "mules," people who haul cash and drugs for dope dealers. In its time, Pipeline has scored some impressive victories. But as with any war, it has left considerable collateral damage in its wake: legions of law-abiding motorists who have been ticketed, interrogated, and searched simply because they looked or acted funny—or happened not to be white.

"It isn't just blacks and Hispanics, though they do seem to be the majority," says Utah attorney W. Andrew McCullough. "In my experience, any motorist who looks different is a candidate for getting pulled over by these folks."

Complaints of racially motivated traffic enforcement are nothing new, of course. But in the last couple of years, these complaints have become louder and more persistent. Some legal experts, such as constitutional-law professor David A. Harris of the University of Toledo, believe we are in the midst of a "national epidemic of race-based traffic enforcement."

That perception has been strengthened by recent civil-rights suits filed in Maryland and New Jersey and statistical studies done in North Carolina and Florida proving that on some highways, the traffic laws have been enforced far more stringently against dark-skinned drivers. Because of these documented cases of roadside racism, Democratic congressman John Conyers of Michigan was able to persuade the Republicans in the House last year to pass a bill requiring traffic police to record the race of the drivers they stop so that the phenomenon could he studied nationwide, but the measure died in the Senate. Last September, the California legislature overwhelmingly passed a similar bill—sponsored by Senator Kevin Murray of Los Angeles, who himself had been subjected to a questionable search—only to see it vetoed by Governor Pete Wilson.

For the most part, police characterize these cases as isolated lapses in judgment by rogue officers or insensitive police commanders who've sent out the "wrong signal" to the troops. But what no one has seemed to notice so far is the thread that connects many of these seemingly unrelated cases: this unheralded federal program called Operation Pipeline.

I ended up inside Pipeline last summer as an investigator for the California legislature after hearing stories from law-enforcement sources about special CHP units that were pulling Latino motorists off the interstates on a whim and rousting them in an effort to find guns, cash, and drugs. What was happening on California's highways, I discovered, was happening across the country—methodically and with increasing frequency.

Operation Pipeline has helped give rise to a new catchphrase in the minority community: DWB, Driving While Black, or Driving While Brown. Yet few outside of law-enforcement circles have even heard of Operation Pipeline.

The DEA, Operation Pipeline's federal sponsor, doesn't talk about it much, which is odd, since the agency considers Pipeline to be "one of the nation's most effective drug-interdiction programs."

But with 301 police commands in forty-eight states now participating in Pipeline in some fashion—from the tiny Picayune Police Department in Mississippi to the New York State Police—the program is in danger of becoming a victim of its own excess. The problems have become so obvious to the CHP that the agency recently embarked on a major overhaul of its Pipeline program.

Two months before Curtis Rodriguez had his car tossed, a reporter had asked a veteran California Highway Patrol sergeant to explain the operating principle behind this campaign to remove contraband from highway travelers. The answer: volume, volume, volume.

"It's sheer numbers," he said. "Our guys make a lot of stops. You've got to kiss a lot of frogs before you find a prince." California Highway Patrol canine units kissed nearly thirty-four thousand frogs in 1997. Only 2 percent of them were carrying drugs. In other states, up to 95 percent of all Pipeline searches have been found to be dry holes.

An Ohio trooper testified in a drug-seizure case a few years ago that he'd personally conducted 786 searches in a single year, sometimes for no other reason than to keep in practice. The state judge, James Brogan, was outraged.

"If we multiply this among all agencies and officers who are currently using routine traffic stops to search the vehicles of citizens they suspect of no crime, the number of individual citizens being asked to relinquish their privacy rights . . . is staggering," Brogan wrote.

Within the past year, according to one DEA official, Attorney General Janet Reno and her top aides have begun asking questions about Pipeline, wondering why the program keeps spawning complaints from black and Hispanic motorists and lawsuits accusing the police of racism and selective enforcement.

Frankly, it's not much of a mystery. The answer can he found in the muddy median strip of I-95, a four-lane concrete corridor that cuts through the desolate coastal swamps of Florida. It's where Operation Pipeline arose and where it grew to become what it is today.

LIKE THE PHRENOLOGISTS of the nineteenth century, who believed that a person's personality could be divined from the shape of his skull, Robert L. Vogel Jr. believes he can spot drug traffickers from the general cut of their jib.

"Bob has a God-given sixth sense," Vogel's dark-haired wife, Jeannie, says earnestly. "A lot of people are jealous of that or can't understand it."

Vogel discovered his unusual talent in the mid-1980s, while working as a Florida state trooper, cruising I-95 outside Daytona Beach and Port

Orange, looking for traffic miscreants. Certain drivers, he noticed, just gave him a bad feeling inside. When he searched their cars, he would frequently find drugs or weapons.

A compact, soft-spoken Vietnam vet who bears a faint resemblance to Richard Gere, Bob Vogel is a deliberate, methodical man, serious about his job, so he began compiling his observations about the drivers who set off the alarm bells in his head. He discovered common traits among them and gathered these together into a list of "indicators," which he began mentally checking off whenever he pulled someone over.

He broke down the indicators into two types: physical and behavioral. The physical indicators were the ones he could see as he scanned the interior of his quarry's car. Such things as car phones and pagers, radar detectors and radio scanners, were obvious. But there were many others. Cops regard the indicators as something akin to a magician's secrets. Our Pipeline instructor warned against disclosing them in court lest "the bad guys" find out. But in truth, records of them can be found in a good public library. Among the most common:

- Air fresheners, especially the ones that look like leaves or little pine trees. Pipeline cops call them "the felony forest." They can be used to mask the odor of drugs. Having fabric softener, coffee grounds, or laundry detergent lying around is also a sign something could be amiss.

- Fast-food wrappers on the floor. Evidence of "hard travel"; suggests a desire not to leave the drug load, even to get a sit-down meal. Pillows and blankets in the car fall under this rubric as well.

- Maps with cities circled on them. A circled "drug source" or "drug destination"—which covers just about all major cities—is more evidence of a motorist's true nature.

- Tools on the floor, for easy access to those hidden compartments full of drugs and money. Tinted windows, new tires on an older car, or high mileage on a new car are also worrisome signs.

- A single key in the ignition. Most people, presumably, have lots of keys on their key chains. Solitary keys suggest someone just handed the driver a key.

■ Not enough luggage for a long trip or too much luggage for a short one. Rental cars are extremely suspicious, as is an auto-registration certificate in someone else's name.

Vogel acknowledges that each of these indicators can be found in the cars of innocent citizens and, by itself, is no indication of criminal activity. But when they are found in combination, he insists, it means you've got a potential drug mule on your hands. Spotting them is nothing more than good, basic police work, he says, and, as shown by the thousands of drug seizures Pipeline units make every year, obviously he is right.

But it's when you get to the next step—the behavioral indicators—that things get a bit trickier, that Vogel's sixth sense comes into play. It's also when good, basic police work can sometimes mutate into racism and stereotyping. In a deposition in 1997, Utah state trooper Paul Mangelson, one of the nation's best-known Operation Pipeline instructors and a frequent consultant to other police agencies, offered an insight into how the behavioral indicators work: "The secret of criminal interdiction is being able to read people. And there are things about people and things they do that are a definite tip-off," Mangelson explained. "I don't necessarily teach this, but on a freeway, prior to stopping somebody, I like to pull up in the inside lane, traffic permitting, and observe the individual."

"Now, when you pull up alongside of somebody and take a look at them," Mangelson was asked, "would this be any joe motorist or somebody that has already attracted your attention?"

"Somebody that I've already decided I'm going to stop. I want to see his reaction as I pull up alongside of him. For example, will he make eye contact with me? And I maintain that if a guy is doing something illegal, ninety-nine times out of a hundred he won't look at you. Number two, he knows good and well that you are there, and he is going to have a death grip on that steering wheel, and you can probably see that his knuckles are turning white. That's a very good indicator that guy is dirty. Something is illegal in that car."

Other indicators, he said, are adornments like "earrings, nose rings, eyelid rings. Those are things that are common denominators with people who are involved with crimes. Tattoos would go along with that," particularly tattoos of "marijuana leaves."

Bumper stickers also give him a feel for the soul of the driver.

"Deadhead stickers are things that almost—the people in those kinds of vehicles are almost always associated with drugs."

How about ACLU stickers? "Yeah, I look for them."

"What about, for instance, Hispanics in an out-of-state vehicle?"

"A lot of Hispanics are transporting narcotics," Mangelson said. "That's common knowledge. I don't think it matters whether they're in an out-of-state vehicle or not."

What if he saw pornography in the car? "I would certainly have a belief that drugs could be in the vehicle."

Not surprisingly, such unorthodox crime-fighting techniques were not immediately embraced by the courts. In Florida, Bob Vogel was viewed as something of an oddball at first. Judges, he learned, were simply unwilling to make allowances for a cop with clairvoyance.

When the federal eleventh-circuit court of appeals got a look at Vogel's police work, the judges denounced it as illegal, unconstitutional, and possibly un-American. You mean you pulled over someone because you thought he *looked* like a drug dealer? the judges gasped. What was your probable cause?

"That trooper Vogel's 'hunch' about the appellants proved correct is perhaps a tribute to his policeman's intuition, but it is not sufficient to justify, ex post facto, a seizure," the judges wrote in a 1986 opinion. To condone Vogel's methods, they wrote, would mean that every car on the road could be pulled over and searched, which "would run counter to our Constitution's promise against unreasonable searches and seizures."

Undeterred by the stinging judicial rebuke and the queasiness of some of his bosses, Vogel plowed ahead. "No one else was doing this but me, and there were some people who were nervous about it, but there always has to be someone to test the waters," Vogel says quietly. "I've never been a quitter."

He looked over the legal opinions and slightly changed his approach. Instead of pulling over a driver merely for looking suspicious, he would find other reasons to stop the shifty-looking ones. He found them by the hundreds in the thick volumes of the Florida vehicle code: rarely enforced laws against driving with burned-out license-plate lights, out-of-kilter headlights, obscured tags, and windshield cracks. State codes bulge with such niggling prohibitions, some dating from the days of the horseless carriage.

"The vehicle code gives me fifteen hundred reasons to pull you over," one CHP officer told me.

For Vogel, it was the perfect solution to his problem. Since it's nearly impossible for drivers to go ten feet without violating some obscure ordinance, Vogel would simply tag along and wait for it to happen. Then he would pounce. Nobody could complain about that; he was duly enforcing the traffic laws of the State of Florida. And with that one refinement, Operation Pipeline was up and running.

After Vogel pulled a car over, he would search it, and, sure enough, sometimes he would find drugs. Once in a while, he would find a lot of drugs. Newspaper reporters started writing stories about him, marveling at the way he was able to turn a routine traffic stop into a major drug bust.

Within a year of being publicly flayed by the highest federal appeals court in the Southeast, Bob Vogel was honored four times with law-enforcement awards. *60 Minutes* sent down a camera crew and produced a flattering profile depicting a dedicated, hardworking policeman trying his best to fight the drug war. Vogel became a local hero. In 1988, he was elected sheriff of Volusia County, and one of his first official acts was to set up a special antidrug unit in his image: the oddly named Selective Enforcement Team, handpicked deputies who had Vogel's training methods instilled by the master himself.

Vogel had his admirers in Washington as well. By 1987, the DEA had formally adopted his highway drug-interdiction system and begun funding a training program to preach Vogel's gospel around the country. (Though Vogel did not invent the notion of using profiles to spot potential drug couriers, he pioneered their adaptation to highway travelers, and my CHP instructors credited him as Pipeline's creator. Previous police use of drug-courier profiles had been largely confined to airports.)

With DEA financing, training courses were set up, and they began churning out thousands of Pipeline graduates a year, officers who would return home and train thousands more.

It spread like a virus.

IF YOU COME INTO CONTACT with one of the estimated twenty-seven thousand Operation Pipeline grads currently cruising the highways, chances are you'll never know it. The officer who pulls you over will look the same as any other traffic cop. Same hat. Same badge. Same car. He will not tell you he is a narcotics officer, and you will never suspect it, because, after all, who ever heard of drug agents passing out tickets for broken taillights?

The mechanics of a Pipeline stop are much like a minuet, except the trooper is the only one who hears the music or knows the steps—all of which lead inexorably to a thorough search of your car.

"I'm looking for anything that will get me in that car or get him out of the car," Utah trooper Mangelson explained in his 1997 deposition.

Because of various court rulings and constitutional impediments, things must be done delicately and in the proper order, so as not to overtly violate your rights.

It will begin like any traffic stop. You'll be asked for your license and registration, and while looking over your papers, the officer will ask you a series of questions about your travel plans. He'll be friendly and polite: Where are you heading? How long will you be there? He'll ask what you do for a living, or something equally innocuous.

"And when I'm doing this, you know, I'm not sitting there grilling you," Mangelson said. "I'm doing it in a way that you probably don't even realize what I'm doing."

What he's doing is called an interrogation, and your responses are being watched very closely. Did you have to think before answering? Did you repeat his questions? Are you being too helpful, too cooperative, or too talkative? Those are all bad signs, as bad as monosyllabic answers. If you have a passenger, the passenger will be taken off to the side and interrogated separately. The officer will check to see if your stories match.

"Criminals on the road are—how can I put it? I've always used this theory. If a guy can convince me of his legitimacy of being where he is or where he's going, then there's probably not much criminal activity going on," Mangelson said. "But by the same token, if he tells me he's going to Salt Lake, and I say, 'What takes you to Salt Lake?' and he goes, 'I'm going to see a friend.' If I say, 'What's your friend's name?' and he doesn't know the friend's name or he rattles some name off the wall, [I ask] 'What's his address?' He's now becoming extremely nervous, and he can't tell me the friend's address, doesn't know the phone number. 'How are you going to visit your friend if you don't know his address or phone number?' By now, he's trembling. The veins are poking out on the side of the neck and you can see his heart beating there and his hands are shaking and his mouth is so dry, he can't even talk to you. You know he's dirty. And he knows I'm on to him."

The indicators are tallied up. No indicators, no problem. Unless you've got a gun or a kilo of cocaine lying on the front seat, you'll be kicked loose.

You may not even get a ticket. Many Pipeline officers don't write them or write only enough of them to maintain the facade that they are traffic policemen.

If your indicators are on the high side, however, this is what will happen. You'll be given your papers back, and then the officer will hang around and strike up a conversation. What most drivers don't realize is that at this point, they have magically crossed into a whole new legal universe. At the moment your license and registration are returned, you are technically free to leave. In the eyes of the law, the traffic stop is over. Now you and Officer Friendly are just having a "consensual" chat. And your new friend is free to ask you anything.

From here, it's almost a script.

You'll be told that the local police have been having a problem with people ferrying guns and drugs along this part of the highway, but they're doing their best to stop it. Good, you may say. Glad to hear it. The officer will nod and say he's happy you see it that way. By the way, you wouldn't happen to have any guns or drugs in your car, would you?

Me? you will ask. Oh, no. Of course not.

Then the officer will look at you and say, Then you don't mind if I take a look-see, do you?

If you're like nine out of ten people who get asked this question, you'll gulp and say, No, no, officer, go right ahead.

You'll be asked to consent—orally or on paper—to a search, but don't think too hard or hesitate to comply, because those are more indicators of drug trafficking, as is refusing to allow the search. (And here's where things can get dangerous, where the psychopath who won't be taken might pull his gun. A 1992 Pipeline stop in South Carolina resulted in a shoot-out that killed the officer and wounded his suspect. And this past January, a veteran Pipeline officer in Georgia was murdered during a stop.)

"If they refuse, the stuff's in the trunk," our CHP instructor tells us matter-of-factly. A refusal justifies calling out the dogs and letting a drug-sniffing canine take a walk around your car. If Fido gets a whiff of something, the cop doesn't need your permission anymore.

Most drivers consent. This can authorize a complete search of everything, including your luggage and your person. It allows the officer literally to take your car apart with an air hammer, which has happened. One of the CHP's first Pipeline officers, Richard Himbarger, was legendary for carrying an electric screwdriver in his patrol car and removing heater ducts, fenders, trunk lids, and interior body panels, right by the side of the road.

"Once they've given consent," our CHP instructor tells us, "they've dug their own grave."

DEPUTY LOU GARCIA was assigned to Sheriff Vogel's selective enforcement Team in 1989. A canine-unit officer, Garcia would be summoned at all hours to walk his drug dog, Condor, near the cars the SET squad had pulled over on I-95. Lots of times, he'd be out on the highway at 3:00 A.M., splashing through swamps with Condor, chasing down panic-stricken motorists who'd bolted into the darkness. He didn't mind. Garcia was thrilled to have been chosen to work with Vogel's crew. The sheriff took good care of his boys: overtime, fancy Stetson hats, rapid promotions. By all accounts, Vogel was equally thrilled to have Lou Garcia on his team, and he commended the officer repeatedly.

"Thanks to you, our drug- and money-interdiction program is working," Vogel wrote in one enthusiastic letter.

The son of a New Mexico coal miner, Garcia had come to the Volusia County Sheriff's Office after fifteen years in the US Army as a paratrooper, a military policeman, and a drill instructor. He hired on at the sheriff's office in 1985 at $10.50 an hour and was in paradise. "When I finally got to be a deputy, I felt I had achieved my goal in life."

But his wife, Angie, began noticing that her husband was increasingly moody after his shift. "He'd get home sometimes after being out on that highway," she says, "and he'd just be shaking his head, and I'd ask him what was wrong, and he'd say, 'You won't believe what they're doing out there.'"

Garcia says he soon discovered the secret of Vogel's highly touted highway interdiction program: The cops concentrated on minority drivers, narrowing the universe of motorists to those they thought most likely to have drugs or guns, even though, in reality, drugs and guns turn up in searches of their vehicles with the same frequency as in those of white drivers. Garcia says he was present at a gathering of deputies on the median of I-95 when Vogel instructed them to focus their attention on black and Hispanic drivers. Vogel denies that happened, but another deputy, Frank Josenhans, corroborates Garcia's story.

Still, it wasn't as if Garcia needed to hear it from the sheriff's mouth.

"I knew who they were stopping. I saw the people. It was blacks, mostly, and they were all being pulled over for weaving. The black race was the only race I knew of that wasn't able to stay in a lane. Black people just couldn't seem to do it."

What Garcia was witnessing in Volusia County was not an aberration. As more and more police departments signed up for Operation Pipeline, it began happening in other places, too. Sometimes the police didn't even bother to hide it. Georgia state troopers told an Atlanta reporter in 1987 that they watched for rented cars from south Florida driven by blacks or Latinos.

Officer Richard Curtis of the Lexington, Kentucky, police department admitted under oath in a drug-interdiction case that race was one of the indicators looked at, as were out-of-state license plates. In another case, Alabama state trooper John Guthrie testified that his indicators included "Texas plates" and "Mexicans."

The "cocaine-courier profile" used by the New Mexico State Police along I-40 surfaced in court in the late 1980s. The very first indicator: "The vehicle occupants are usually resident aliens from Colombia." This profile, it turned out, had been sent to police departments nationwide by the DEA's El Paso Intelligence Center, the department that manages the Pipeline program and provides its annual funding of roughly $800,000.

Ironically, that's the same amount of money the taxpayers of Eagle County, Colorado—which encompasses the ski resort of Vail—forked over to settle a class-action suit filed on behalf of 402 black and Hispanic drivers who had been stopped and searched by the High County Drug Task Force, a Pipeline unit funded directly by the DEA. The task force "systematically violated the constitutionally protected rights of blacks and Hispanics to travel and be free from unreasonable seizures," US district judge James Carrigan wrote in a blistering criticism of the program in 1990. The evidence that race was used as an indicator, Carrigan ruled, was "undeniable," and such practice amounted to "a racist assumption."

Federal public defender Bryan Lessley obtained internal Oregon State Police records showing that the number of Hispanics being stopped on the highways near Grants Pass by a Pipeline unit was "grossly out of proportion" to the number of Hispanics on the road. He uncovered state-police training manuals that told Pipeline students a "high percentage" of narcotics traffickers were Hispanic.

In New Jersey, state-police Pipeline units assigned to the southern end of the New Jersey Turnpike were found by a superior-court judge to have had "at least a de facto policy . . . of targeting blacks for investigation and arrest," which resulted in the dismissal of six hundred cases. A former New Jersey state trooper, Kenneth Wilson, admitted in a sworn statement that he was trained to target blacks and Hispanics. A statistical analysis by John Lamberth of Temple University backed up Wilson's claims. Lamberth found that though blacks made up only 13 percent of the drivers on the turnpike, they accounted for nearly half the stops made by drug-seeking troopers.

The Maryland State Police made perhaps the biggest tactical blunder in the program's history in 1992, when a Pipeline unit pulled over a black family in a rental car outside Washington, D.C., ordered them out into the rain, and then ran a drug-sniffing dog in and out of their car, over their repeated objections. The driver turned out to be a Harvard Law graduate, Robert Wilkins, a public defender who was on his way home from a family funeral in Chicago. Wilkins slapped the Maryland State Police with a civil-rights suit and accepted a settlement that forced the cops to keep detailed records of their Pipeline stops for the next three years. The results were more proof of Pipeline's unique affinity for minorities: Of the 732 people who were detained and searched during 1995 and 1996, 75 percent were black and 5 percent Hispanic. The Maryland ACLU has filed another civil-rights suit based on those figures.

A GRANDMOTHERLY WOMAN in a slab sided Plymouth Fury III zips by. Not a chance, I think. Next is man in a suit, driving a gigantic white Lincoln Navigator, cell phone pressed to his ear. Mr. Business. With my luck, he'd turn out to be a lawyer. Pass. A teenage girl in her mom's station wagon. Ditto. Then comes the carload of Mexicans.

They look as though they're having one hell of a time, laughing, arms hanging out the window. Then they spot the CHP cruiser I'm sitting in, and the party is over. They look around furtively, sit up straight, won't meet my steely gaze. The driver begins practicing the ten-and-two hand position on the steering wheel that he probably hasn't used since driver's ed. Bingo. A whole bunch of indicators right there. These guys are mine.

That is the result of my first drill using the lessons I gained from Pipeline school. I am sitting in the front seat of the head instructor's patrol car, shaded by a giant oak. We are parked perpendicular to a bucolic two-lane highway in the hills beyond Susanville, California, checking out the sparse midmorning traffic. It is day two of my Pipeline training class, and I am putting my newly acquired observational skills to the test.

No one has instructed me to *look* for Mexicans; in fact, we were informed that racial profiling is illegal and frowned upon. But we were also taught that it is the Colombians and the Mexicans whose cartels are bringing most of the dope in and that a lot of drug mules are hired off the streets of Tijuana for $500 in cash. Not many gringos I've seen fit that description.

Plus, the Mexicans just look shifty to me. What are they doing, I wonder, driving around, yukking it up at 10:30 in the morning in the middle of the week? I am at work. Why aren't they? And if they are unemployed, where'd they get the money for that nice Mercury?

And then I realize the problem with Operation Pipeline.

If I were looking for unsafe drivers, as most patrolmen do, it wouldn't make any difference to me what the driver looked like or how he acted when he drove by or whether I thought he could afford his car. All I would care about would be how he was driving.

But that's not my job as a Pipeline officer. My job is to get drugs and guns off the highway, so I look for people who look like they might have them. And since I have only a limited time out on the highway each day, I'm not going to waste it pulling over people who look like upstanding citizens—people who look like me and my friends, for instance.

I remember what my instructors told me repeatedly. If something appears "abnormal," investigate. Always ask yourself whether this is something that you would do or say. If not, be suspicious. And suddenly, the baseline for determining who gets pulled over and searched is a forty-three-year-old white suburbanite's vision of normalcy. Most of the white people I have seen driving by, I have to admit, look pretty normal to me. But the Mexicans don't. Plus, there are all those indicators: their nervousness upon seeing a police car, the air freshener dangling from the mirror, their goddamn refusal to look at me.

It's no wonder, I realize, that 90 percent of the people arrested by the CHP's Pipeline units during the last two years have been minorities. They never stood a chance.

If I were empowered to do so, I could pull them over on some pretext to satisfy my curiosity. Maybe I would find something—drug-tainted money, a loaded gun, a kilo or two of cocaine or methamphetamine. Or maybe just a peaceable carload of people going from here to there, not owing me or anyone else an explanation. But if I do this long enough and use the indicators I've learned to pull over a volume of people, I will invariably find criminals. That was a big bag of dope in the Screamer's trunk, after all. But does that justify scaring the bejesus out of the thousands of other motorists—the honest ones whose taxes pay my salary and pave these roads—whom I will misjudge? Will they think being interrogated and searched was a fair trade?

And what of the enormous waste of police manpower that goes into stopping and searching thousands of cars in which nothing more incriminating than old gum wrappers is found? Even the cops admit that highway seizures don't make a dent in the quarter-trillion-dollar-a-year American narcotics industry. So, in the end, one is left to wonder: What is the point of all this harassment, this inefficiency, this futility? Is it really a way of finding contraband? Or is it, perhaps, a way of acclimating us to a future in which we will be routinely shadowed, stopped, and frisked by the police—a nation of suspects?

IN 1996, THE U.S. SUPREME COURT unanimously endorsed Bob Vogel's method of stopping people for minor traffic violations in order to search their cars for drugs. An officer's real reason for pulling over a car didn't matter a whit, the justices said, so long as some type of traffic offense—no matter how trivial—occurred first. It made no difference that the motor-vehicle codes gave the cops a license to "single out almost whomever they wish for a stop," Justice Antonin Scalia wrote. It was not the role of the Supreme Court to decide whether there were too many traffic laws or which ones should no longer be enforced.

Since that ruling, known as the Whren decision, state and local police participation in Operation Pipeline has soared. Enrollments in DEA training schools are way up. "After Whren," one of my CHP instructors told me, "the game was over. We won."

Last fall, another Supreme Court decision, rejecting the search of an Iowa motorist's car without probable cause, was widely hailed in the media as reinforcing the privacy rights of drivers. But since Pipeline officers are trained to legally justify a "reasonable suspicion," or, of course, get the driver's permission, before searching a car, this court decision may actually boost the popularity of Operation Pipeline.

That's why it's so ironic that Bob Vogel is no longer on the front lines of this particular war. Though his methods have received the stamp of unanimous approval from the highest court in the land, he's quit teaching and has mothballed his drug-interdiction program. After a while, he said, it just wasn't worth it.

In 1992, *The Orlando Sentinel* began printing stories that essentially accused Vogel's SET unit of being racist thugs who were stealing money from innocent travelers. The newspaper said it found nearly two hundred cases in which deputies had taken a driver's cash but made no arrests, and 90 percent of those cases involved minority drivers.

And then the tapes came out. It seemed Vogel's boys had been videotaping their stops for posterity, and 148 hours of them were turned over to the newspaper. Example: a May 16, 1990, stop of a white driver. SET sergeant Dale Anderson strolls up to the car and asks the man how he's doing.

"Not very good," the driver replies.

"Could be worse," Anderson reminds him. "Could be black."

The civil-rights suits flew fast and furious after that. The US Justice Department announced an investigation, and FBI agents started snooping around. A federal grand jury was empaneled.

The *Sentinel* won a Pulitzer prize for its exposé, a fact that grates on Vogel to this day. "Anybody who saw those stories would have thought I was some racist, tobacco-chewing, Billy Bob, redneck southern sheriff," he complains. He leans forward slightly and asks me, mistakenly, if I was aware that the editor who oversaw the *Sentinel's* coverage was an African-American.

"I'll bet they didn't tell you that part," he says.

Eventually, the hubbub subsided. The discrimination suits were dismissed after federal judges declared that they had not seen convincing evidence of racial injustice. And the Justice Department, while muttering darkly about Vogel's methods, declined to prosecute him on civil-rights charges, reportedly because it didn't think a jury would convict him.

Critics called the investigation a whitewash, but there was more involved than that. History, for one thing. For more than a decade, Bob Vogel's controversial system has been officially endorsed, financed, and espoused by the DEA—an arm of the Justice Department. Having Operation Pipeline's creator brought up on federal civil-rights charges would have put the Justice Department and every other police agency involved in a rather awkward spot, especially when so many civil-rights suits were pending.

Vogel sees this as total vindication. "I've been investigated by just about everyone—the FBI, the Justice Department, the NAACP, the ACLU—and they haven't been able to win a solitary case," he says. "This whole thing is something that drug lawyers grabbed ahold of to try to beat some arrests by dragging race into it."

If that's true, he is asked, then why has this program had such lopsided racial results in state after state? Why are the statistics so one-sided?

Vogel stiffens. "Let me have my assistant, Lenny Davis, come in and answer that question for you. He might have an explanation for it." A few minutes later Chief Deputy Davis, a large, friendly black man, sits down and solemnly assures me that the reason so many blacks and Hispanics are being pulled over is because so many of them are involved in the drug business.

Vogel sits next to his chief deputy, nodding. But he doesn't say a word.

Sex and the Internet

Gary Webb

Yahoo! Internet Life magazine (May 2001)

INTRODUCTION BY LARRY SMITH

Back in 2001, the tech community was working its way through what would be one of many cycles of glory and gloom, and I was working as an editor of *Yahoo! Internet Life*. We considered ourselves a sort of "people's *Wired*," a print magazine less obsessed with the latest business fads, hotshot start-ups, and faraway techno-futures, and more focused on how technology was changing the way regular folks lived, worked, and played. It was an exciting time to be helping to set the agenda for a publication read by millions of people who were excitedly, cautiously—and, in fact, often quite skeptically—trying to make sense of a world that was looking a lot different from the one into which they'd been born. The internet felt like the biggest story of our time. And at the swirling center of that story was sex.

So how would the largest-circulation magazine about Net culture approach *such a hot-button topic*? Carefully, for starters. That my boss, editor-in-chief Barry Golson, had been the legendary articles editor at *Playboy* during its heyday didn't help. We'd have to find the perfect angle, the perfect writer, and the perfect tone.

Meanwhile, a cover story in *Time* magazine on internet porn, as well as a column by respected *New York Times* health writer Jane E. Brody comparing it to crack cocaine, set off a wave of hysteria (as porn reports always have, no matter the medium). Which is to say: If and when we decided to discuss sex and the internet in our pages—and there was no way we weren't going to—we had to do it exactly right.

I had come from the alternative press, working at the independent news outlet *AlterNet*, and knew Gary Webb's work well. What we at *YLife* asked him to do was just what he does so well: crunch the numbers, read the reports, talk to the experts, and, as always, follow the money. (He reports that the online sex business, back then, was a $366 million to $1 billion industry with as many as

60 million unique visitors coming to 26,000 sites. Quaint numbers now, of course.)

In the wonderfully personal and insightful piece he delivered, "Sex and the Internet," he examines the topic with a 360-degree perspective—and, most importantly, with clear eyes. All of which was to be expected. What I didn't expect (in part because I knew Gary only through his work and had never met him personally) was how he was able to weave so much humanity into a topic that had been sorely missing a human element in most of the coverage. He posits that the story of sex and the internet is not just the story of smutmongers and puritans, of a burgeoning business and a growing world of worried parents, but a complicated coming-of-age story for us all.

□   □   □

I discovered pornography shortly after shooting and killing my first living thing, so maybe that's why the memory clings with such tenacity 30 years later.

It's likely I was already in a state of shock when I spotted the magazine lying there in the pine woods behind my parents' house in North Carolina. Moments earlier, I had watched dumbstruck as a bird I'd half-seriously fired a BB at fell from its perch like a bright red pinecone. Rushing up to inspect my prize I saw for the first time the effect of a speeding ball of metal has upon the head of a cardinal, and the sight horrified me. So it was with some relief that I noticed the faded old magazine poking out of the underbrush nearby. Anything to take my mind off the terrible flipping and flapping I'd just witnessed.

The magazine had been lying in the woods for a while. Many of its pages were missing. But what the elements and the insects had left behind was more than enough to inflame my 12-year-old mind. Naked men and naked women—doing odd, mystifying things that made me feel embarrassed and excited and afraid all at the same time. Under normal circumstances, I might have flung it down immediately. But not that day. That day I kept looking, my heart beating faster with every weather-beaten page I turned. I stole back the next day after school and looked some more. And the next day. And the day after that. By the time the magazine mysteriously disappeared a few weeks later, I was a different boy—older, vastly wiser. Now I knew what was hidden under the clothes of grown women.

Now I knew what sex organs were for, and where they went, and what you did with them, and I began wondering how soon I would get to use mine like those happy-looking people in the magazine. Some slumbering part of my brain had clicked on, a part that has never clicked off.

I've been thinking about that wintry day a lot lately, since discovering that my 16-year-old son was downloading pornography from the internet when he got home from high school in the afternoons. His previous experience with the family computer had been limited to playing games and doing homework. But according to the history file of my internet browser, he'd been hitting a lot of sites with the words *teens* and *nude* in the domain name.

I asked him about it. I wasn't mad, just curious. He told me he'd been surfing porn sites since he was 14, like a lot of his friends.

"I was in a chatroom on AOL, and someone had written something about getting free porn in your e-mail," he said. "I knew it was around, but I had never seen it, so I guess I was curious to see what it was." The next day, his e-mailbox was overflowing with hardcore JPEGs. "Some of it was funny, really odd-looking stuff. Peeing pictures. Foot fetishes. All this weird stuff. You can get anything." But some of the other images intrigued him— pinup pictures of nude young women particularly—and soon he was spending hours online, jumping from one teen site to another. Sometimes he and his friends held contests to see which one of them could snag the first naked picture of the latest Hollywood babe.

Not long after our talk, he got himself a girlfriend, and one thing ultimately led to another. The result was the same it had been for me. But what a difference 30 years had made upon the method of delivery. I found my first porn in the woods by some freakish accident, and it was many years before I saw anything like it again. My son had it delivered to him in the family room, where he was able to see it whenever he wanted, as often as he liked. And he could see things men of my generation had only heard about in the form of the vilest rumors—women and donkeys being a prime example—stories we dismissed as the product of fevered and possibly unbalanced minds. Yet here they are (along with eels, horses, dogs, and pigs), proclaiming their existence in flaming 32-bit color, on my computer screen.

At no time in American history has pornography been so widely available and so easily accessible to the general public. It is now possible for anyone from nine to 90 to watch full-color, full-motion pictures of every kind of sexual act imaginable. Instant porn, free of charge, delivered to your home 24 hours a day, 365 days a year. And millions of us, young and old, male and female, are consuming it.

Indeed, online porn is one of the most profitable areas of e-commerce. It may even be *the* most profitable. Estimates of annual sales for the industry overall range from $366 million to nearly $1 billion. (While there are no reliable statistics on how many adult sites are scattered throughout the Web, a widely accepted minimum number is 50,000.) And traffic volume is staggering. Sex Tracker, a Web service that keeps an eye on some 26,000 adult sites, reports that on an average day as many as 60 million unique visitors land upon those sites. Taken together, the top five sex sites—with names like Smut Server and Erosvillage—receive just under 4 million unique visitors every day. To put that in perspective: the world's top five news site, including such heavyweights as MSNBC.com and CNN.com, receive a total of only about 2.5 million unique visitors per day.

"If any one analyst started covering [the online porn industry], they would never be able to do anything else," internet analyst Eric Scheirer told *Adweek* magazine last year. "It's not only such a large percentage of e-commerce, it's just as large for the obvious reasons." Adds Andy Sernovitz, a former Washington lobbyist for the internet industry, "I think we should accept that porn in quantity is here to stay and we're never going to be able to block it."

By a quirk of technology, we have become history's guinea pigs—America's first postcensorship generation. In just five years, the Net has rendered 250 years' worth of antiobscenity laws as quaint as chastity belts. All the barricades that past generations erected to keep graphic depictions of sex at the outskirts of our society have fallen and, for the moment at least, everything under the sun is clambering over them. Nothing is hidden; it's advertised, boasted about in banner ads with moving pictures and money shots. Want pictures of midgets fornicating? Click this moving vagina here. Transsexuals with lesbians? Click here. Dads 'n' daughters? Right this way. No questions asked, at least not seriously.

"It's endless, it's free, it's unfettered, and you can really achieve a perfect goodness of fit between what you want to see on your monitor and what's going on in your head," says Bill Fisher, a Canadian psychology professor who is currently researching internet sex. "That would be the case to be made that this stuff is different. It's different than a copy of *Playboy*; it's different from anything that went on before it."

Thanks to the Net, we and our kids become a living laboratory that scientists will plumb for answers to long-elusive riddles: What does pornography do to people deep down inside? Is it addictive, as some researchers claim? Does it destroy marriages? Does a sexually repressed society suddenly immersed in smut retain its sexual values, or do people start edging towards darker extremes? Does it, as some researches fear, push unstable men toward rape or child molestation?

"I think the best example to use is child pornography," says Storm A. King, a Palo Alto, California, doctoral student in psychology who has been researching the internet's effects on behavior since 1993, "In order to know that you like child pornography, you have to be exposed to it somewhere along the line. Prior to the internet—maybe even five years ago—in order to acquire child pornography you had to really risk a lot, find it on some sort of black market. Things have changed dramatically in the last couple of years. People are routinely exposed to child pornography just in surfing these other porn sites, looking for what they want. The rate of the exposure now is way higher. So the big question is: Now that initial exposure has gone up, is that going to increase the number of people who find themselves attracted to this stuff? I would speculate that yes, this is true." (A recent investigation by *Newsweek* magazine likewise concluded that, after having been largely eradicated in the '80s, child porn has recently "exploded" because of the internet.)

On the other hand, King argues, perhaps the availability of child pornography on the Net will satiate pedophiles to the point of where they don't feel the need to actually molest a child. If child-molestation rates were to decline as a result, might we be more willing to tolerate the existence of child porn on the Net?

Which raises a host of other questions. What if we find that everything we've been told about pornography since the 18th century has been nothing but Puritan propaganda? What if it turns out that sexual material on the internet is harmless or even, as some researchers argue, good for you?

Will such arguments ever hold sway among the general population? Will we change our mind and go the way of Amsterdam and Denmark? More to the point: Will we even have a choice?

The young girl plops herself down at her mother's computer and quickly signs on to America Online. She's just turned 13, a seventh-grader, but she looks even younger. She has braces, likes Britney Spears, plays a mean game of soccer, wears sweatshirts with Angel and Princess written on them in sparkly cursive, and wants to be a singer. Her mother, a single parent in her early forties, is standing behind her, seeming a bit anxious. The modem screeches, and the girl announces she's online. "So," she asks, "now what do you want me to do?"

"You told me you knew how to find dirty pictures on the internet," I say. "Show me. I don't believe it." The girl rolls her eyes. "*Anybody* can do that." She turns back to the keyboard and starts writing. "Look. I'll just type in *porn.com.*"

Up flashes a screen filled with pictures of women performing oral sex on men, women licking each other's breasts, a flashing red sign that reads BOOBS! and various little pop-up boxes showing tiny animated pictures of fellatio. The girl spins and covers her eyes as if blinded by a light. "I don't want to see those pictures!" she shouts. "Get it off the screen!"

Her mother does so, and looks nonplussed. "I don't even know how to do that!" she tells her daughter. "How come you know?"

The girl looks at her mother quizzically. "It's easy, Mom. You just think of a word."

"But how did you know to go to that Web page?" her mother persists.

"I *didn't.* Don't you get it? You just type in a word. I could have thought of any word. Sometimes you get sex pages even when you're not thinking of anything dirty. I was in the computer lab at school, and I was looking for Britney Spears and I got a sex page. And we have filters on our computers. I got embarrassed and turned it off, and the boys behind me were, like, 'No! No! Leave it on! Leave it on!'"

When it comes to sex, American parents have always managed to keep at least one hand clamped firmly over their children's eyes. In many areas of the country, it was for a long time easier to get drugs and moonshine than it was to find pornography. For countless generations of American males, seeing any kind of porn—whether hard core or soft—was a formidable task. As difficult as it may be to remember, ticket sellers at movie houses actually refused to admit anyone under the age of 17 to an R-rated movie. During the '60s and '70s, magazines like *Playboy* and *Penthouse* were often kept behind the drugstore counter, safely out of sight or covered with black plastics. At home, most dads refused to acknowledge they even looked at such things (though millions of sock drawers were searched nonetheless by sons who fervently hoped otherwise). And until the '70s, the sexual fare was limited to women with their tops off. As for pubic hair, forget about it.

"I remember when I was in the fifth or sixth grade and Stevie Owens— who had been to reform school once already—brought in a pack of playing cards with pornographic images on them, and we thought it was the most amazing thing we'd ever seen," recalls Jennings Bryant, a professor at the University of Alabama and director of the school's Institute of Communications Research. "I couldn't believe that such things even existed."

For two decades, Bryant has been looking at pornography and studying its effects on the human mind. He and his colleagues at the institute have shown volunteers dirty movies for weeks on end and measured their psychophysiological responses (that is, their heart rate, blood pressure, etc.) and their subsequent attitudes toward the opposite sex. They've made their subjects watch violent porn film and the put them on mock juries to decide a rape case. They have gauged junior-high students' exposure to pornography and studied the impact that massive consumption of pornography has on behavior, marriages, and society. They have poked and probed and prodded pornography and sexuality from a dozen different angles. But in this field, little is ever settled.

In fact, for almost every university study suggesting that pornography is harmful, an equally convincing study can be found saying it's not. The same is largely true in the government arena. Take the case of the dueling presidential commissions. One, appointed by Richard Nixon in 1970, concluded after two years of study and $2 million in research that there was insufficient evidence to show that porn caused antisocial behavior. Fifteen years later, another presidential panel—this time appointed by Ronald Regan, with a far smaller budget and half the time to investigate—declared pornography to be a menace that led to rapes and sexual violence against women.

"Research on the consequences of exposure to pornography has been subjected to extreme scrutiny and devastating criticism," writes Professor Dolf Zillman, another sex expert who teaches at the University of Alabama. "The bottom line is that research on pornography effects cannot be definitive . . . [T]he research leaves us with considerable uncertainty about exposure consequences."

Since that's the state of current scientific research into traditional forms of pornography, it's little wonder that next to nothing is known about porn distributed over the internet. During the US Senate's first hearing into the issue in 1995, Sen. Herbert Kohl complained loudly that lawmakers were being stampeded into censoring the internet in the absence of even the most rudimentary information. "In the last few months, horror stories have dominated the news. Yet no one—absolutely *no one*—has conducted a systematic and balanced study of the extent of the obscenity, pornography, or indecency on the internet," Kohl declared. "Anyone who tells you otherwise is wrong."

Professor Bryant agrees. "We really are on the frontier in terms of doing research in this area," he says. "We are way behind the curve. I think we're a good two years away from having anything in terms of reliable research." Part of the problem, he explains, is that "there just are not any good, clean data out there. Exposure data, for example, is very limited. We can't tell who is looking at it, or for how long. There's been limited content analysis done. And all of that makes it hard to do effects studies."

In this scientific vacuum, strange things can happen. One of the most notorious centered on an article that appeared in 1995 in the *Georgetown Law Journal*. Written by Martin Rimm, an electrical-engineering student at Carnegie Mellon University, the article claimed that the internet was awash in filth, child porn, and bestiality, and that nearly everything being downloaded was pornographic. Rimm, at the time a 30-year-old undergraduate, cut a deal with *Time* to give his report exclusively in exchange for a cover story. The newsweekly agreed. Almost immediately, the story touched off an online-porn hysteria in the media and in Congress. Within months, Rimm's study was transformed into the Communications of Decency Act of 1995, which outlawed online porn, and the bill rocketed through Congress with barely a hearing, to be passed in 1996.

But even as the *Time* story was being memorialized in the *Congressional Record* as proof of the perverted nature of the Net, scientists and statisticians were tearing Rimm's conclusions apart, calling them wildly inaccurate, statistically unsound, and politically suspect. The CDA passed anyway. Though the law was later rejected by the Supreme Court as unconstitutional, the image of the internet as a dark, porn-drenched alley stuck. Ironically, Rimm may have been merely ahead of the times; his study was done before porn pages truly began to proliferate on the World Wide Web.

Many argue that scientific evidence isn't necessary, because common sense tells us that pornography—especially hard-core pornography—is bad for us, and even worse for our kids. "Our children are consuming it, and it will affect their hearts, their minds, and their lives for years to come," insisted Dee Jepsen at a 1995 Senate hearing on online porn. Jepsen, president emeritus of a group called Enough Is Enough, which lobbies Congress for restrictions on internet porn, continued: "If we do nothing to stem this flood of pornography available to children by computer, we will be changing the baseline on the availability of illegal material. It will be comparable to inviting children to have free access into adult X-rated bookstores and theaters."

At the same hearing, Sen. Charles Grassley, an Iowa Republican and co-sponsor of a bill similar to the CDA, said: "The home is supposed to be safe and is supposed to be a barrier between your children and the dark forces which seek to corrupt and destroy our youth. Suddenly, now not even the home is safe. Now the dark forces which were once stopped by the front door have found their way into the home through personal computers."

According to some, the dark forces are already far beyond that. They're actively messing with our mind.

Last spring, the august *New York Times* printed a lurid, lengthy piece by the widely respected health writer Jane E. Brody comparing internet porn to crack cocaine. Beyond the allegedly addictive qualities of page views full of pornographic images, the story announced "a brand-new psychological disorder—cybersex addiction—that appears to be spreading with astonishing rapidity and bringing turmoil to the lives of those affected." One sex therapist was quoted saying that "sex on the Net is like heroin. It grabs them and takes over their lives."

"Those most strongly hooked on internet sex," the *Times* found, "are likely to spend hours each day masturbating to pornographic images."

The story, which was picked up by dozens of newspapers and magazines across the country, was prompted by a survey published in March 2000 by Stanford University psychologist Alvin Cooper, who called the internet "the crack cocaine of sexual compulsivity."

But Cooper's survey, and the *Times* story that immortalized it, were hardly models of either scientific or journalistic inquiry. Virtually all sources quoted by the *Times* were sex therapists with businesses to promote. One oft-cited expert was Dr. Kimberly S. Young, who in addition to treating Net sex addiction also offers counseling sessions for eBay and day-trading "addicts." At her Center for On-Line Addiction, cyberaddicts can pay from $25 per consultation (for a single e-mail reply) up to $124 (for an hour-long office visit). And like porn-site charges themselves, these porn-addiction treatments can be "discreetly billed" to your credit card, Dr. Young assures. (Reached via email, Dr. Young insists that "cybersexual addiction, as it is often referred to, is a legitimate and credible mental disorder.")

But Cooper's survey itself was a self-administered online poll taken by visitors to MSNBC's website, and anyone who admitted to looking at internet porn for more than 11 hours per week (that is, 90 minutes per day) was deemed to be a "cybersex compulsive." Even with those generous boundaries, however, only about 1 percent of the 9,265 people who took the MSNBC poll admitted to indulging to such an extent. Applying those same standards to other online activities, one could argue that the Net is producing addicts by the legion: e-mail addicts, chatroom addicts, Napster addicts, role-playing game addicts—the list is endless.

Such Web-based surveys are "really bogus," says Storm King, the Palo Alto doctoral student, "because who is most likely to find that survey? People who are online all the time! My Aunt Martha, who sends two e-mails a week to her niece in Georgia, is never going to take that survey. So the numbers are highly inflated. There's a huge methodological issue here called sampling bias."

Cooper, for his part, declined to be interviewed, saying he was busy writing a book "and am only able to do really major interviews where our center and my work are featured."

It's perhaps unsurprising that not all academic studies about internet porn get the same sort of clanging publicity that has been afforded to the work of Rimm and Cooper. Bill Fisher, a professor in the psychology department of the University of Western Ontario, and Azy Barak, a psychology professor at the University of Haifa in Israel, have published three studies in the past two years that found internet porn had no effect on men's attitudes toward women, sexual harassment, and rape. So far, there have been no major news stories or magazine articles about their findings, though they are all available online—see construct.haifa.ac.il/~azy/azy/htm.

"I have to keep an open mind as a scientist," Fisher says, "that there may well be serious negative effects of internet sexuality. But I have to be guided by data, and I don't know of any such data. The data I do know about is that in earlier eras, when there was a legalization of all forms of sexual materials in Denmark and Sweden and Germany, there was no increase in the rate of sexual assault. If you seek to be guided by relevant data, you are not brought to a body of research that rings alarm bells. The effect of internet pornography on sexuality are open questions."

But doesn't the idea of impressionable children getting their first glimpse of sex from a hardcore porn site ring alarm bells? "I'll adopt the Talmudic approach and throw a question back at you," Fisher replies. "One hundred years ago a common, perhaps *the* most common, first experience with sexuality was a visit to a prostitute. That was certainly a much more comprehensive introduction to sexuality than internet sex is. Do we want to go back to that?"

Serena Beltran is, as usual, running late. Her job behind the Chanel counter at Macy's department store requires her to be the living embodiment of what her expensive line of cosmetics can do for a woman, and it takes time to put on her makeup, style her hair, and select the right outfit. Today it takes longer than normal, so she has little time to spare. If I want to talk to her, she tells me, I'll have to share her ride to Macy's.

An attractive and exotic-looking 18-year-old, Serena is seldom without a boyfriend. She goes to clubs and parties with her friends every weekend; she speaks unself-consciously of hoping to find a man who loves her enough to buy her breast implants. When she's not at work or with her friends, she's home watching the daytime TV shows, where every sort of atypical sexual behavior is discussed in raucous and often distressing detail. So it surprises me a bit that Serena professes scant interest in Net sex. She uses the internet only occasionally, she says.

"The only kind of things I've ever gotten from the internet is weird, funny sex stuff," she tells me as we head toward the mall. "Like Madonna having sex with a horse. That was probably the first thing I ever saw. It was fake, I think. But it looked realistic. I've seen other pictures of Madonna having sex that I know were real." Serena guesses she was about 16 when she first discovered what one could find on the internet. "I probably went to PicPost. That's where everybody goes."

"How did you find out about that site?"

"I don't know. It's like one of those things everybody just *knows*, you know? And even if you didn't, you could always go to a chatroom and ask, and someone will tell you."

While Net porn hasn't yet had an effect on Serena's life, it had quite an effect on one of her girlfriends, a tall, thin blonde who partied with Serena's friends. "She wasn't shy about her body at all," Serena tells me. "She decided to go to a studio here in town and find out about posing for pictures on the internet. And she didn't want to go in there by herself, so she asked me to go with her. We go in, and there's this big, fat, ugly black guy who ran the place, and he told her what she'd have to do. Like, take her clothes off in front of a camera, and she had to do what the guys wanted her to do, and she couldn't be shy or anything, you know, and they had her sign this contract. She was supposed to get, like, $50 for every picture of her they put up, and every time someone clicked on her, she'd get part of the money."

Serena's friend began doing live Web cam shows, stripping and masturbating in from of a small video camera in the studio, her gyrations beamed to dozens of people who could, in turn, communicate with her via keyboard, telling her how to pose, how to touch herself, and so forth. "She was underage," Serena informs me as we pull up outside Macy's. "She had a fake ID, and the guy at the studio knew she was underage, but he told her that it was like working in a liquor store. As long as you had an ID showing that you were over 18, he was covered . . . I don't know what happened to her. I think she moved to LA."

Even if there aren't any hard and fast scientific answers about the psychological effects this deluge of porn will have on us, there is little disagreement among experts that the societal effects will be significant—changing, perhaps permanently, the way we think about sex and pornography. In myriad ways, it's already happening.

In a special issue of *CyberPsychology & Behavior* published last August, researchers concurred that "the internet is affecting human sexuality and human sexual behavior in profound and complex ways." Dr. Marlene Maheu of the California School of Professional Psychology sees us repeating the sexual revolution of 40 years ago: "It's back to the experimentation of the '60s, because now people don't have to worry about venereal disease. They don't have to worry about their reputations. They could be standing in the grocery line next to the person they had cybersex with last night and not even know it," Maheu told a Canadian reporter.

My son, Ian, and his 17-year-old friend Matt both say they found internet porn helpful in shaping their ideas of what they found sexually alluring. "It kind of helped me out in terms of the different types of women out there," says Matt, a high-school junior. "You find out what kind of taste you have. I feel like I'm a little more educated about sex, and it's made me more relaxed about it."

My son echoes those sentiments. "How else can you find out about different types of positions and things like that?" he asks. It's a perfectly legitimate question, since I've never broached the subject with him—nor did my father ever broach it with me. I could have listened to my father talk about the pros and cons of sports careers all day, but I would have been mortified if he'd started lecturing me on, say, doggy style.

Ian's question also reminds me of the cold anxieties I felt as a young insecure lover: What if she knows more about sex than I do? She'll think I'm a clod. Despite our age difference, my son and I both got essentially the same sex-ed course in high school—the one that never answers the only question most teenage males have: What do I do when the impossible happens and I wind up in bed with someone?

In spite of its rudeness and lack of intimacy, pornography certainly educates one in the intricacies of sexual intercourse, even if only in a how-to sense. And now that's easily available, kids will learn how to have sex sooner. Does that mean they actually will? Some of them, almost certainly. Does it also mean that young gays and lesbians will awaken to their sexual preferences earlier and realize that, no matter how isolated and scared they might feel, they are certainly not alone? Probably.

At the University of Alabama, Professor Bryant isn't ready to announce a sexual revolution yet, and certainly not one on the scale of the 1960s, which he says was influenced less by pornography than by the sudden availability of birth-control devices. "We haven't seen the same kinds of shifts yet in sexual attitudes than we saw in the '60s. But I certainly think that what you have so far is a revolution in sexual voyeurism. I think the other area in which it is causing a revolution is in terms of exposure to young people. We have no gatekeepers any longer. Anything goes."

As Bryant and others see it, there are several potential pitfalls. For one thing, kids may think that what they see portrayed on the Net is real sex and not an idealized or fantasized depiction of it. Adolescent males may grow up with the impression that in order to be a satisfactory sex partner, an organ the size of porn star Lexington Steele's is required. Indeed, the vast majority of porn sites are awash in banner ads touting penis-enlargement techniques that promise to turn any normal guy into a Genoa salami who no longer needs a personality to attract women—and the free pictures on the porn sites only reinforce that idea. Young girls, notoriously sensitive about their bodies, may conclude that in order to be wanted and desired, enormous breast implants and anal sex are a must. Internet porn, Bryant says, has already become "a weird form of sex education"—and it's one that isn't countered by anything suggesting, for example, that not all women want sex with multiple partners, or enjoy ending a lovemaking session by having their sweetheart ejaculate in their face (a universal theme in hard-core Net porn).

A second concern is that the wealth and variety of internet porn may dull the sexual senses of viewers, leading them to seek out increasingly shocking fare, and spurring the porn industry to provide ever-edgier material, once again raising the titillation bar in a never-ending spiral. That effect has been demonstrated to some degree in lab studies conducted by Bryant and others, though the effect is a temporary one. "It takes more to get your batteries charged the second time around," Bryant says. Still, others caution that most people have a saturation point that, once reached, causes them to tire of porn and lose interest in it. And many others will never develop a liking for it at all.

A third potential problem is that, because it is depicted so infrequently in internet porn, safe sex will be given short shrift by teenagers who view it. "That is something that concerns me a great deal and something we really need to study," says Fisher, the Canadian psychology professor. In exploring porn sites for the past few months, I have noticed more photos of men wearing condoms, but unprotected sex is far more frequently depicted—including unprotected anal sex. While schools generally do a good job of telling kids of the dangers of AIDS, students may have to be taught it earlier owing to the growing reach of porn.

Lastly, because kids will be exposed to the facts of life at an earlier age, that much more of the innocence of childhood is being denied to them. And the facts that they are being exposed to are sometimes brutal and almost always shocking. "There's no poetry to it, no gentleness to it," says Dr. William Bronston, a California physician who runs a youth organization focused on teens and computers. "There is a complete loss of the sacredness of the spiritual context."

Dave Roberts shrugs when I ask him how he feels about his two teenagers seeing hard-core pornography in his home. "I've just sort of accepted it," he says. "What else can you do? It's out there, it's easy to find, and they're on the computer all the time. It's bound to happen."

Roberts, 50, is a cheerful ex-hippie who came of age in the Bay Area during the early '60s. It was, he remembers, "before the drugs came in. My friends and I used to go up to Golden Gate Park every weekend, and you know what that was like. Girls sunbathing without their tops, the whole scene. So that was the era in which I learned about sex. I'll tell you, it was a great time to be 17. Sometimes I feel sorry for the kids today." After attending college in Seattle, where he got arrested in some student demonstrations, Roberts married and raised a family; he now lives in an upscale neighborhood in Sacramento, California, where he owns a landscape-design and construction company. His wife, Linda, is a contract administrator. They have four internet-connected computers in the house.

"I think if my daughter saw something like that on the internet, she'd totally freak out and come screaming to me," Linda says of 15-year-old Elisa. "She freaks out if I even say the *s-e-x* word out loud."

Did Dave think his 17-year-old son, Mark, was looking at porn sites? "I don't know—I've never asked him," Roberts says, then pauses and smiles. "I think I'd probably be disappointed if he wasn't, I mean, I sure remember how I was at his age, in high school. There were three things that were important to me: cars, girls, and money. And it wasn't always in that order. So, yeah, I guess I'd be surprised if he hadn't. My only concern with the porn thing is that there's a big gap between reality and the computer. And when they're this age, you just have to hope that you've given your kids a good grip on reality."

"We've escalated everything we do in our lives," the father of two laments. "It's no longer just sports, you know? Now it's *extreme* sports. *Extreme* skiing. *Extreme* football. Everything's extreme. And so now we've got extreme sex. About all we can do as parents is hope that our kids can tell the difference between hype and real life."

Luckily, his kids seem to have a pretty good grasp on reality. Roberts shows me to a back bedroom, which he and his son are in the process of converting into a computer animation studio, complete with a blue screen painted on a wall. Mark is at the computer when we walk in, listening to trance music pumping from a big pair of speakers in the corner. A thin, brown haired boy, he nods and smiles shyly as his father introduces me. Cables, CDs, audio and video equipment are piled everywhere. A flat-screen television monitor runs color bars, which Mark is adjusting from his computer screen.

I asked him how much time he spends on his computer every day. "Right now, because of school, only four hours a day. If I had my choice, it'd be eight or 18. I hope to start my own computer animation company." He shows me some of his work, which features cartoon characters spinning in ever-widening circles, crisscrossing the screen, appearing and disappearing. "That took me forever to figure out how to do," he says. "Now I'm working on blending, and that's pretty easy."

When he's online, he chats with friends at school or surfs for cartoon animations. He doesn't look at porn sites: "I don't really care for it. It's not like I don't know what's out there. I just don't have any interest in it."

What *does* interest him is *anime*, a unique kind of Japanese cartoon that features sweepingly drawn images of attractive women and men with oversize eyes and brightly colored costumes. They appear in all of Mark's animations and cover the background of his computer screen. "All of these characters are from the same show," he explains. "It's one of my favorite series—*Tenchi Muyo*. I think that's the best *anime* ever done."

The hero of the cartoon is a shy high-school boy who suddenly finds himself living with a host of marooned space aliens. Fortunately, some of them are of the long-legged, large-breasted, beautiful teen female variety, and are bent upon possessing the hero in one form or another. On the Net, fan sites devoted to the alien babes abound, some featuring nude and semi-nude drawings. "We only get the censored versions of the show over here," Mark tells me. "The Japanese versions are uncensored. There's a lot more violence and, uh, other stuff in them."

Mark's mother says she's never seen the show but knows of her son's fascination with it. "Now he wants to learn Japanese," she says.

Mark's father sighs. "Sometimes," he says, "I wish he'd just go out and get a date."

The irony of the current debate over Net porn is that those we wish to protect from it—our children—may wind up being better equipped to deal with it than we adults are. What hard data exists at this point—as opposed to the long-standing range of prejudices we bring to the subject—suggests that most people will not suffer any long-term negative effects by looking at internet porn. Like many unanticipated consequences of technological innovation, we will eventually learn to live with it.

"The generation coming up behind us is going to grow up accustomed to the fact that they have access to pornography you cannot find in many adult bookstores in the county," says King, the Palo Alto doctoral candidate. "Our children will grow up in an environment where this is preexisting. They're going to know this stuff is out there from the beginning. So it's not going to be as striking to them, or as problematic to them, as it is to this current generation that's sort of hit with it all at once in midstride."

So far, statistics bear out the notion that Net sex is far more intriguing to middle-aged men than it is to sex-crazed teens. According to a demographic data from SexTracker, two-thirds of all sex surfers are over 30, and fully one-third of them are 41 and 55. A majority are married and solidly middle class, and they are predominantly white. In other words, average guys who grew up with nothing to look at but breast magazines and grainy 16mm stag films. How different will those demographics be in 25 years, when the first crop of postcensorship teens attain middle age? Will those men, after a lifetime of exposure to it, still find Net porn something worth spending time and hundreds of millions of dollars on?

I'm not sure my own life would have been any different if I had first discovered pornography on the Web with my parents' computer than in the woods. I've been exposed to a considerable amount of porn in my lifetime. In the '70s, when *Deep Throat* made adult films somewhat mainstream, I reviewed porn films for my college paper. Yet my sex life has been relatively conservative. I've never been to an orgy, never had group sex, never been with a prostitute, never subscribed to an adult magazine, and rarely frequent strip clubs, because they embarrass me. I've certainly never committed a sex crime.

I suspect that my eldest son, who knows far more about sex than I did at his age, will probably turn out much like me in this regard. And if viewing porn on the internet makes him more sexually adventurous person than I am, I'm not sure I see the harm in that.

What concerns me as a parent is not that my kids will find porn, or even that they will enjoy it, but what they will take away from the experience when they are confronted with it. On the whole, Net porn gives them a very cheap, vulgar, often unappealing, and sometimes frightening portrait of sex. It robs a beautiful and infinitely intimate act of its sensual dignity, which may be porn's worst sin, along with its attraction. But if my sons grow up coarse and vulgar and view women as useful orifices and nothing more, it won't be the fault of some pictures they saw on the internet. It'll be mine.

The Mighty Wurlitzer Plays On

Gary Webb

From *Into the Buzzsaw: Leading Journalists Expose the Myth of a Free Press,* edited by Kristina Borjesson (2004)

INTRODUCTION BY KRISTINA BORJESSON

"Why haven't the media risen in revolt against this story? . . . Where are the media knocking it down . . . ?" From a soapbox on his CNN program ironically titled *Reliable Sources,* Bernard Kalb was leading a vilification campaign against Gary Webb's most famous work. It was 1996 and Webb's series, "Dark Alliance," had lifted the veil on the Reagan-Bush administration's scheme to arm the rightwing paramilitary Contras in Nicaragua using profits from the sale of literally tons of crack cocaine. The drugs had been smuggled into the US with the help of the CIA and other government operatives. Kalb, a spokesman for the Reagan administration while the Contra operation was underway, had been reinvented now as a journalist and media critic. He was furiously calling upon other high-powered journalists to attack Webb's credibility—and they did.

Walter Pincus and Roberto Suro at the *Washington Post,* as well as others at *The New York Times* and the *Los Angeles Times,* hacked away at Webb's work. Howard Kurtz, the *Post*'s media critic, snarkily weighed in with the quip, "Oliver Stone, check your voicemail." Meanwhile, Kalb brought former Reagan Justice Department spokesman Terry Eastland on to *Reliable Sources* to discredit "Dark Alliance." What Kalb failed to tell his audience about Eastland was that in May 1986, Eastland's deputy, Patrick Korten, had informed *The New York Times* that there was no evidence of Contra gunrunning and drug-smuggling—a claim others in the Justice Department immediately contradicted. As Joel Millman writes in his 1986 article, "Narcoterrorism: A Tale of Two Stories," *The New York Times*

> gave the [C]ontras a clean bill of health. Under the headline, CON-
> TRAS CLEARED ON GUNRUNNING, the unbylined story quoted an
> unidentified "senior official" of the Justice Department as saying that
> charges that the [C]ontras were implicated in gunrunning and drug
> smuggling were without foundation. "There just ain't any evidence,"

the source said. As it turned out, the "senior official" was one Pat Korten, a deputy to Justice Department spokesman Terry Eastland. Although Korten's statements to the *Times* were quickly contradicted by others in the Justice Department and by investigators for the Senate Foreign Relations Committee (which was about to begin hearings on the gunrunning and drug-smuggling charges), the *Times* did not run a correction. "The confusion was Justice's," says Phil Shenon, the *Times* reporter who interviewed Korten. "Our story was accurate. The guy told us what he told us."

Robert Parry reports on this same story in his book, *Lost History: Contras, Cocaine, the Press & "Project Truth"*(1999), as do Peter Dale Scott and Jonathan Marshall in *Cocaine Politics: Drugs, Armies, and the CIA in Central America* (1991). In the end, Kalb et al. not only succeeded in marginalizing Webb, but in disconnecting him from his raison d'être. Webb lived to do deep investigative reporting and their relentless, unfounded attacks on his credibility eventually killed his career.

I met Gary in person for the first and last time on March 21, 2003. He had flown across the country to attend the New York Public Library's annual Books to Remember presentation. The library was honoring a book that I had edited and Gary had contributed to entitled *Into the Buzzsaw: Leading Journalists Expose the Myth of a Free Press*. An anthology of mostly first-person accounts written by journalists about their encounters with censorship, *Buzzsaw* had been chosen as one of twenty-five "exceptional fiction and non-fiction titles" of 2002. While liberally punctuated with his signature dry wit, Webb's essay in the anthology, "The Mighty Wurlitzer Plays On," was searing.

Walking into the library, I recognized Gary immediately. As I shook his hand, he flashed a megawatt smile. His warm, rakish charm was immediately apparent. His blond hair was slightly untamed, and he had the kind of mustache that you see on guys who wear leather jackets. Glancing down, I saw that he was sporting a tweed blazer with leather elbow patches. It looked worn and didn't match Gary's macho image as a warrior journalist. Then it struck me that perhaps he'd come all this way just to feel like a journalist again, to be validated, if only for an hour or so.

Gary committed suicide a little less than two years later, tired, apparently, of the disconnection between his life and his raison d'être. I had no idea he had been suffering so much. He kept up a good front during our phone conversations. From time to time, I am haunted by my failure to have discerned his distress.

Webb is gone, but thanks to his work and that of other journalists who have found platforms on the internet, the media system in which Kalb and his coterie once thrived is hemorrhaging audience. Wise to the systemic corruption and bad reporting of Kalb and other traditional media insiders, droves of Americans now look elsewhere for real news and the truth behind big issues. Meanwhile, Webb's vindication is complete. "Dark Alliance" was not only accurate, but is now acknowledged as an example of high-level investigative reporting to which many aspire, but of which few are capable. As you'll see below, Gary Webb paid an exorbitant price for his journalistic excellence.

□   □   □

If we had met five years ago, you wouldn't have found a more staunch defender of the newspaper industry than me. I'd been working at daily papers for seventeen years at that point, doing no-holds-barred investigative reporting for the bulk of that time. As far as I could tell, the beneficial powers the press theoretically exercised in our society weren't theoretical in the least. They worked.

I wrote stories that accused people and institutions of illegal and unethical activities. The papers I worked for printed them, often unflinchingly, and many times gleefully. After these stories appeared, matters would improve. Crooked politicians got voted from office or were forcibly removed. Corrupt firms were exposed and fined. Sweetheart deals were rescinded, grand juries were empanelled, indictments came down, grafters were bundled off to the big house. Taxpayers saved money. The public interest was served.

It all happened exactly as my journalism-school professors had promised. And my expectations were pretty high. I went to journalism school while Watergate was unfolding, a time when people as distantly connected to newspapering as college professors were puffing out their chests and singing hymns to investigative reporting.

Bottom line: If there was ever a true believer, I was one. My first editor mockingly called me "Woodstein," after the pair of *Washington Post* reporters who broke the Watergate story. More than once I was accused of neglecting my daily reporting duties because I was off "running around with your trench coat flapping in the breeze." But in the end, all the sub rosa trench coat–flapping paid off. The newspaper published a seventeen-part series on organized crime in the American coal industry and won its first national journalism award in half a century. From then on, my editors at that and subsequent newspapers allowed me to work almost exclusively as an investigative reporter.

I had a grand total of one story spiked during my entire reporting career. That's it. One. (And in retrospect it wasn't a very important story either.) Moreover, I had complete freedom to pick my own shots, a freedom my editors wholeheartedly encouraged since it relieved them of the burden of coming up with story ideas. I wrote my stories the way I wanted to write them, without anyone looking over my shoulder or steering me in a certain direction. After the lawyers and editors went over them and satisfied themselves that we had enough facts behind us to stay out of trouble, they printed them, usually on the front page of the Sunday edition, when we had our widest readership.

In seventeen years of doing this, nothing bad had happened to me. I was never fired or threatened with dismissal if I kept looking under rocks. I didn't get any death threats that worried me. I was winning awards, getting raises, lecturing college classes, appearing on TV shows, and judging journalism contests. So how could I possibly agree with people like Noam Chomsky and Ben Bagdikian, who were claiming the system didn't work, that it was steered by powerful special interests and corporations, and existed to protect the power elite? Hell, the system worked just fine, as far as I could tell. It *encouraged* enterprise. It *rewarded* muckraking.

And then I wrote some stories that made me realize how sadly misplaced my bliss had been. The reason I'd enjoyed such smooth sailing for so long hadn't been, as I'd assumed, because I was careful and diligent and good at my job. It turned out to have nothing to do with it. The truth was that, in all those years, I hadn't written anything important enough to suppress.

In 1996, I wrote a series of stories, entitled *Dark Alliance*, that began this way:

> For the better part of a decade, a Bay Area drug ring sold tons of cocaine to the Crips and Bloods street gangs of Los Angeles and funneled millions in drug profits to a Latin American guerrilla army run by the US Central Intelligence Agency, a *Mercury News* investigation has found.

This drug network opened the first pipeline between Colombia's cocaine cartels and the black neighborhoods of Los Angeles, a city now known as the "crack" capital of the world. The cocaine that flooded in helped spark a crack explosion in urban America—and provided the cash and connections needed for LA's gangs to buy automatic weapons.

It is one of the most bizarre alliances in modern history: the union of a US-backed army attempting to overthrow a revolutionary socialist government and the Uzi-toting "gangstas" of Compton and South Central Los Angeles.

The three-day series was, at its heart, a short historical account of the rise and fall of a drug ring and its impact on black Los Angeles. It attempted to explain how shadowy intelligence agencies, shady drugs and arms dealers, a political scandal, and a long-simmering Latin American civil war had crossed paths in South Central Los Angeles, leaving behind a legacy of crack use. Most important, it challenged the widely held belief that crack use began in African American neighborhoods not for any tangible reason, but mainly because of the kind of people who lived in them. Nobody was forcing them to smoke crack, the argument went, so they only have themselves to blame. They should just say *no*.

That argument never seemed to make much sense to me because drugs don't just appear magically on street corners in black neighborhoods. Even the most rabid hustler in the ghetto can't sell what he doesn't have. If anyone was responsible for the drug problems in a specific area, I thought, it was the people who were bringing the drugs in.

And so *Dark Alliance* was about them—the three cocaine traffickers who supplied the South Central market with literally tons of pure cocaine from the early 1980s to the early 1990s. What made the series so controversial is that two of the traffickers I named were intimately involved with a Nicaraguan paramilitary group known as the Contras, a collection of ex-military men, Cuban exiles, and mercenaries that the CIA was using to destabilize the socialist government of Nicaragua. The series documented direct contact between the drug traffickers who were bringing the cocaine into South Central and the two Nicaraguan CIA agents who were administering the Contra project in Central America. The evidence included sworn testimony from one of the traffickers—now a valued government informant—that one CIA agent specifically instructed them to raise money in California for the Contras. I found a photograph of one of the CIA agents huddled in the kitchen of a house in San Francisco with one of the traffickers and had interviewed the photographer, who confirmed its authenticity. Pretty convincing stuff, we thought.

Over the course of three days, *Dark Alliance* advanced five main arguments: First, that the CIA-created Contras *had* been selling cocaine to finance their activities. This was something the CIA and the major media had dismissed or denied since the mid-1980s, when a few reporters first began writing about Contra drug dealing. Second, that the Contras had sold cocaine in the ghettos of Los Angeles and that their main customer was LA's biggest crack dealer. Third, that elements of the US government knew about this drug ring's activities at the time and did little if anything to stop it. Fourth, that because of the time period and the areas in which it operated, this drug ring played a critical role in fueling and supplying the first mass crack cocaine market in the United States. And fifth, that the profits earned from this crack market allowed the Los Angeles-based Crips and Bloods to expand into other cities and spread crack use to other black urban areas, turning a bad local problem into a bad national problem. This led to panicky federal drug laws that were locking up thousands of small-time black crack dealers for years, but never denting the crack trade.

It wasn't so much a conspiracy that I had outlined as it was a chain reaction—bad ideas compounded by stupid political decisions and rotten historical timing.

Obviously this wasn't the kind of story that a reporter digs up in an afternoon. A Nicaraguan journalist and I had been working on it exclusively for more than a year before it was published. And despite the topic of the story, it had been tedious work. Spanish-language undercover tapes, court records, and newspaper articles were laboriously translated. Interviews had to be arranged in foreign prisons. Documents had to be pried from unwilling federal agencies, or specially declassified by the National Archives. Ex-drug dealers and ex-cops had to be tracked down and persuaded to talk on the record. Chronologies were pieced together from heavily censored government documents and old newspaper stories found scattered in archives from Managua to Miami.

In December 1995, I wrote a lengthy memo to my editors, advising them of what my Nicaraguan colleague and I had found, what I thought the stories would say, and what still needed to be done to wrap them up. It was also to help my editor explain our findings to her bosses, who had not yet signed off on the story, and most of whom had no idea I'd been working on it.

Two months ago, in an unheard-of response to a Congressional vote, black prison inmates across the country staged simultaneous revolts to protest Congress' refusal to make sentences for crack cocaine the same as for powder cocaine. Both before and after the prison riots, some black leaders were openly suggesting that crack was part of a broad government conspiracy that has imprisoned or killed an entire generation of young black men.

Imagine if they were right. What if the US government was, in fact, involved in dumping cocaine into California—selling it to black gangs in South Central Los Angeles, for instance—sparking the most destructive drug epidemic in American history?

That's what this series is about.

With the help of recently declassified documents, FBI reports, DEA undercover tapes, secret grand jury transcripts and archival records from both here and abroad, as well as interviews with some of the key participants, we will show how a CIA-linked drug and stolen car network—based in, of all places, the Peninsula— provided weapons and tons of high-grade, dirt cheap cocaine to the very person who spread crack through LA and from there into the hinterlands.

A bizarre—almost fatherly—bond between an elusive CIA operative and an illiterate but brilliant car thief from LA's ghettos touched off a social phenomenon—crack and gang-power—that changed our lives in ways that are still to be felt. The day these two men met was literally ground zero for California's crack explosion, and the myriad of calamities that have flowed from it (AIDS, homelessness, etc.)

This is also the story of how an ill-planned and oftentimes irrational foreign policy adventure—the CIA's "secret" war in Nicaragua from 1980 to 1986—boomeranged back to the streets of America, in the long run doing far more damage to us than to our supposed "enemies" in Central America.

For, as this series will show, the dumping of cocaine on LA's street gangs was the "back-end" of a covert effort to arm and equip the CIA's ragtag army of anti-Communist "Contra" guerrillas. While there has long been solid—if largely ignored—evidence of a CIA-Contra cocaine connection, no one has ever asked the question: "Where did all the cocaine go once it got here?"

Now we know.

Moreover, we have compelling evidence that the kingpins of this Bay Area cocaine ring—men closely connected to the assassinated Nicaraguan dictator Anastasio Somoza and his murderous National Guard—enjoyed a unique relationship with the US government that has continued to this day.

In a meeting to discuss the memo, I recounted for my editors the sorry history of how the Contra-cocaine story had been ridiculed and marginalized by the Washington press corps in the 1980s, and that we could expect similar reactions to this series. If they didn't want to pursue this, now was the time to pull back, before I flew down to Central America and started poking around finding drug dealers to interview. But if we did, we needed to go full-bore on it, and devote the time and space to tell it right. My editors agreed. My story memo made the rounds of the other editors' offices and, as far as I know, no one objected. I was sent to Nicaragua to do additional reporting, and the design team at Mercury Center—the newspaper's online edition—began mapping out a Web page.

At the end of my memo, I'd suggested to my editors that we use the internet to help us demonstrate the story's soundness and credibility which, based on past stories critical of the CIA, was sure to come under attack by both the government and the press.

I have proposed to Bob Ryan [director of Mercury Center] that we do a special Merc Center/World Wide Web version of this series. The technology is extant to allow readers to download the series' supporting documentation through links to the actual text. For example, when we are quoting grand jury testimony, a click of the mouse would allow the reader to see and/or download the actual grand jury transcript.

Since this whole subject has such a high unbelievability factor built into it, providing our backup documentation to our readers—and the rest of the world over the internet—would allow them to judge the evidence for themselves. It will also make it all the more difficult to dismiss our findings as the fantasies of a few drug dealers.

To my knowledge, this has never been attempted before. It would be a great way to showcase Merc Center and, at the same time, use computer technology to set new standards for investigative reporting.

The editors jumped at the idea. From our perch as the newspaper of Silicon Valley, we could see the future the World Wide Web offered. Newspapers were scrambling to figure out a way to make the transition to cyberspace. The *Mercury*'s editors were among the first to do it right, and were looking for new barriers to break. A special internet version of *Dark Alliance* was created as a high-profile way of advertising the *Mercury*'s Web presence and bringing visitors into the site. Plus, the newspaper could boast (and later did) that it had published the first interactive online exposé in the history of American journalism.

I remember being almost giddy as I sat with Merc Center's editors and graphics designers, picking through the pile of once-classified information we were going to unleash on the world. We had photos, undercover tape recordings, and federal grand jury testimony. In addition, we had interviews with guerrilla leaders, tape-recorded courtroom testimony, confidential FBI and DEA reports, Nicaraguan Supreme Court files, Congressional records, and long-secret documents unearthed during the Iran-Contra investigation. For the first time, any reader with a computer and a sound card could see what we'd found—could actually read it for themselves—and listen in while the story's participants plotted, schemed, and confessed. And they could do it from anywhere in the world, even if they had no idea where San José, California, was.

After four months of writing, rewriting, editing, and reediting, my editors pronounced themselves satisfied and signed off. The first installment of *Dark Alliance* appeared simultaneously on the streets and on the Web on August 18, 1996.

The initial public reaction was dead silence. No one jumped up to deny any of it. Nor did the news media rush to share our discoveries with others.

The stories just sat there, as if no one seemed to know what to make of them.

Admittedly, *Dark Alliance* was an unusual story to have appeared in a mainstream daily newspaper, not just for what it said, but for what it was. It wasn't a news story per se; nearly everything I wrote about had happened a dozen years earlier. Because my editors and I had sometimes vehemently disagreed about the scope and nature of the stories during the writing and editing process, the result was a series of compromises, an odd mixture of history lesson, news feature, analysis, and exposé. It was not an uplifting story; it was a sickening one. The bad guys had triumphed and fled the scene unscathed, as often happens in life. And there was very little anyone could do about it now, ten years after the fact.

So, I wasn't really surprised that my journalistic colleagues weren't pounding down the follow-up trail. Hell, I thought it was a strange story myself.

Had it been published even a year or two earlier, it likely would have vanished without a trace at that point. Customarily, if the rest of the nation's editors decide to ignore a particular story, it quickly withers and dies, like a light-starved plant. With the exception of newspapers in Seattle, some small cities in Northern California, and Albuquerque, *Dark Alliance* got the silent treatment big time. No one would touch it.

But no one had counted on the enormous popularity of the website. Almost from the moment the series appeared, the Web page was deluged with visitors from all over the world. Students in Denmark were standing in line at their college's computer waiting to read it.

E-mails came in from Croatia, Japan, Colombia, Harlem, and Kansas City, dozens of them, day after day. One day we had more than 1.3 million hits. (The site eventually won several awards from computer journalism magazines.)

Once *Dark Alliance* became the talk of the internet (in large part because of the technical wizardry and sharp graphics of the Web page), talk radio adopted the story and ran with it. For the next two months, I did more than one hundred radio interviews, in which I was asked to sum up what the three-day-long series said in its many thousands of words. Well, I would reply, it said a lot of things. Take your pick. Usually, the questions focused on the CIA's role, and whether I was suggesting a giant CIA conspiracy. We didn't know the CIA's exact role yet, I would say, but we have documents and court testimony showing CIA agents were meeting with these drug traffickers to discuss drug sales and weapons trafficking. And so, figure it out. Did the CIA know or not? The response would come back— So, you're saying that the CIA "targeted" black neighborhoods for crack sales? Where's your evidence of that? And it would go on and on.

There were other distractions as well. Film agents and book agents began calling. One afternoon Paramount Studios whisked me down to have lunch with two of the studio's biggest producers, the men who brought Tom Clancy's CIA novels to the screen, to talk about "film possibilities" for the still-unfolding story. This was about the time I realized the wind speed of the shit storm I had kicked up.

The rumbles the series was causing from black communities was unnerving a lot of people. College students were holding protest rallies in Washington, DC, to demand an official investigation. Residents of South Central marched on city hall and held candlelight vigils. The Los Angeles City Council soon joined the chorus, as did both of California's US senators, the Oakland city council, the mayor of Denver, the Congressional Black Caucus, Jesse Jackson, the NAACP, and at least a half dozen congressional members, mostly African American women whose districts included crack-ridden inner cities. Black civil rights activists were arrested outside the CIA after sealing off the agency's entrance with yellow crime scene tape. The story was developing a political momentum all of its own, and it was happening despite a virtual news blackout from the major media.

Some Washington journalists were alarmed. "Where is the rebuttal? Why hasn't the media risen in revolt against this story?" fretted former newsman and government flack Bernard Kalb, host of CNN's *Reliable Sources*. Kalb expressed frustration that the story was continuing to get out despite the best efforts of the press to ignore it. "It isn't a story that simply got lost," Kalb complained, during the show, "It, in fact, has resonated and echoed and the question is, 'Where is the media knocking it down?'"

It was an interesting comment because it foretold the way the mainstream press finally did respond to *Dark Alliance*. A revolt by the biggest newspapers in the country, something columnist Alexander Cockburn would later describe in his book *White Out* as "one of the most venomous and factually inane assaults . . . in living memory."

I remember arguing with a producer at a CNN news show shortly before I was to go on the air that I didn't want him asking me to explain "my allegations" because these stories *weren't* my allegations. I was a journalist reporting events that had actually occurred. You could document them, and we had.

"Well, you gotta understand my position," he mumbled. "The CIA isn't admitting it. So we're going to call it an allegation. You can understand that, right?"

"Are you telling me that until the day the CIA confesses to drug trafficking, CNN's position is that these events may not have happened?" I snapped. "What the fuck is that? When did we give the CIA the power to define reality?"

After nearly a month of silence, the CIA responded. It admitted nothing. It was confident that its agents weren't dealing drugs. But to dispel all the rumors and unkind suggestions my series had raised, the agency would have its inspector general take a look into the matter.

The black community greeted this pronouncement with unconcealed contempt. "You think you can come down here and tell us that you're going to investigate yourselves, and expect us to believe something is actually gonna happen?" one woman yelled at CIA director John Deutch, who appeared in Compton, California, in November 1996 to personally promise the city a thorough investigation. "How stupid do you think we are?"

The conservative press and right-wing political organizations were equally hostile to the idea of a CIA-crack investigation, but for different reasons. It meant the story was gaining legitimacy, and might lead to places that supporters of the Reagan and Bush administrations would rather not see it go. John Deutch was blasted on the front page of the *Washington Times* (which had also helped finance the Contras, hosting fundraisers and speaking engagements for Contra leaders while supporting their cause editorially) as a dangerous liberal who was undermining morale at the CIA by even suggesting there might be truth to the stories.

Ultimately, it was public pressure that forced the national newspapers into the fray. Protests were held outside the *Los Angeles Times* building by media watchdogs and citizens groups, who wondered how the *Times* could continue to ignore a story that had such an impact on the city's black neighborhoods. In Washington, black media outlets were ridiculing the *Post* for its silence, considering the importance the story held for most of Washington's citizens.

When the newspapers of record spoke, they spoke in unison. Between October and November, the *Washington Post*, the *New York Times*, and the *Los Angeles Times* published lengthy stories about the CIA drug issue, but spent precious little time exploring the CIA's activities. Instead, my reporting and I became the focus of their scrutiny. After looking into the issue for several weeks, the official conclusion reached by all three papers: Much ado about nothing. No story here. Nothing worth pursuing. The series was "flawed," they contended. How?

Well, there was no evidence the CIA knew anything about it, according to unnamed CIA officials the newspapers spoke to. The drug traffickers we identified as Contras didn't have "official" positions with the organization and didn't really give them all that much drug money. This was according to another CIA agent, Adolfo Calero, the former head of the Contras, and the man whose picture we had just published on the internet, huddled in a kitchen with one of the Contra drug traffickers. Calero's apparent involvement with the drug operation was never mentioned by any of the papers; his decades-long relationship with the CIA was never mentioned either.

Additionally, it was argued, this quasi-Contra drug ring was small potatoes. One of the Contra traffickers had only sold five tons of cocaine during his entire career, the *Washington Post* sniffed, badly misquoting a DEA report we'd posted on the website. According to the *Post*'s analysis, written by a former CIA informant, Walter Pincus, who was then covering the CIA for the *Post*, this drug ring couldn't have made a difference in the crack market because five tons wasn't nearly enough to go around. Eventually, those assertions would be refuted by internal records released by both the CIA and the Justice Department, but at the time they were classified.

"I'm disappointed in the 'what's the big deal' tone running through the *Post*'s critique," *Mercury News* editor Jerry Ceppos complained to the *Post* in a letter it refused to publish. "If the CIA knew about these illegal activities being conducted by its associates, federal law and basic morality required that it notify domestic authorities. It seems to me that this is exactly the kind of story that a newspaper should shine a light on." Ceppos posted a memo on the newsroom bulletin board, stating that the *Mercury News* would continue "to strongly support the conclusions the series drew and will until someone proves them wrong." It was remarkable, Ceppos wrote, that the four *Post* reporters assigned to debunk the series "could not find a single significant factual error."

Privately, though, my editors were getting nervous. Never before had the three biggest papers devoted such energy to kicking the hell out of a story by another newspaper. It simply wasn't done, and it worried them. They began a series of maneuvers designed to deflect or at least stem the criticism from the national media. Five thousand reprints of the series were burned because the CIA logo was used as an illustration. My follow-up stories were required to contain a boilerplate disclaimer that said we were not accusing the CIA of direct knowledge, even though the facts strongly suggested CIA complicity. But those stunts merely fueled the controversy, making it appear as if we were backing away from the story without admitting it.

Ironically, the evidence we were continuing to gather was making the story even stronger. Long-missing police records surfaced. Cops who had tried to investigate the Contra drug ring and were rebuffed came forward. We tracked down one of the Contras who personally delivered drug money to CIA agents, and he identified them by name, on the record. He also confirmed that the amounts he'd carried to Miami and Costa Rica were in the millions. More records were declassified from the Iran-Contra files, showing that contemporaneous knowledge of this drug operation reached the top levels of the CIA's covert operations division, as well as into the DEA and the FBI.

But the attacks from the other newspapers had taken the wind out of my editors' sails. Despite the advances we were making on the story, the criticism continued. We were being "irresponsible" by printing stories suggesting CIA complicity without any admissions or "a smoking gun." The series was now described frequently as "discredited," even though nothing had surfaced showing that any of the facts were incorrect. At my editor's request, I wrote another series following up on the first three parts: a package of four stories to run over two days. They never began to edit them.

Instead, I found myself involved in hours-long conversations with editors that bordered on the surreal.

"How do we know for sure that these drug dealers were the first big ring to start selling crack in South Central?" editor Jonathan Krim pressed me during one such confab. "Isn't it possible there might have been others before them?"

"There *might* have been a lot of things, Jon, but we're only supposed to deal in what we know," I replied. "The crack dealers I interviewed said they were the first. Cops in South Central said they were the first, and that they controlled the entire market. They wrote it in reports that we have. I haven't found anything saying otherwise, not one single name, and neither did the *New York Times*, the *Washington Post* or the *Los Angeles Times*. So what's the issue here?"

"But how can we say for *sure* they were the first?" Krim persisted. "Isn't it possible there might have been someone else and they never got caught and no one ever knew about them? In that case, your story would be wrong."

I had to take a deep breath to keep from shouting. "If you're asking me whether I accounted for people who might never have existed, the answer is no," I said. "I only considered people with names and faces. I didn't take phantom drug dealers into account."

A few months later, the *Mercury News* officially backed away from *Dark Alliance*, publishing a long column by Jerry Ceppos apologizing for "shortcomings" in the series. While insisting that the paper stood behind its "core findings," we didn't have proof that top CIA officials knew about this, and we didn't have proof that millions of dollars flowed from this drug ring, Ceppos declared, even though we did and weren't printing it. There were gray areas that should have been fleshed out more. Some of the language used could have led to misimpressions. And we "oversimplified" the outbreak of crack in South Central. The *New York Times* hailed Ceppos for setting a brave new standard for dealing with "egregious errors" and splashed his apology on their front page, the first time the series had ever been mentioned there.

I quit the *Mercury News* not too long after that.

When the CIA and Justice Department finished their internal investigations two years later, the classified documents that were released showed just how badly I had fucked up. The CIA's knowledge and involvement had been far greater than I'd ever imagined. The drug ring was even bigger than I had portrayed. The involvement between the CIA agents running the Contras and the drug traffickers was closer than I had written. And DEA agents and officials had protected the traffickers from arrest, something I'd not been allowed to print. The CIA also admitted having direct involvement with about four dozen other drug traffickers or their companies, and that this too had been known and effectively condoned by the CIA's top brass.

In fact, at the start of the Contra war, the CIA and Justice Department had worked out an unusual agreement that permitted the CIA not to have to report allegations of drug trafficking by its agents to the Justice Department. It was a curious loophole in the law, to say the least.

Despite those rather stunning admissions, the internal investigations were portrayed in the press as having uncovered no evidence of *formal* CIA involvement in drug trafficking and no evidence of a conspiracy to send crack to black neighborhoods, which was hardly surprising since I had never said there was. What I *had* written—that individual CIA agents working within the Contras were deeply involved with this drug ring—was either ignored or excised from the CIA's final reports. For instance, the agency's decade-long employment of two Contra commanders—Colonel Enrique Bermudez and Adolfo Calero—was never mentioned in the declassified CIA reports, leaving the false impression that they had no CIA connection. This was a critical omission, since Bermudez and Calero were identified in my series as the CIA agents who had been directly involved with the Contra drug pipeline. Even though their relationship with the agency was a matter of public record, none of the press reports I saw celebrating the CIA's self-absolution bothered to address this gaping hole in the official story. The CIA had investigated itself and cleared itself, and the press was happy to let things stay that way. No independent investigation was done.

The funny thing was, despite all the furor, the facts of the story never changed, except to become more damning. But the perception of them did, and in this case, that is really all that mattered. Once a story became "discredited," the rest of the media shied away from it. *Dark Alliance* was consigned to the dustbin of history, viewed as an internet conspiracy theory that had been thoroughly disproved by more responsible news organizations.

Why did it occur? Primarily because the series presented dangerous ideas. It suggested that crimes of state had been committed. If the story was true, it meant the federal government bore some responsibility, however indirect, for the flood of crack that coursed through black neighborhoods in the 1980s. And that is something no government can ever admit to, particularly one that is busily promoting a multibillion-dollar-a-year War on Drugs.

But what of the press? Why did our free and independent media participate in the government's disinformation campaign? It had probably as many reasons as the CIA. The Contra-drug story was something the top papers had dismissed as sheer fantasy only a few years earlier. They had not only been wrong, they had been terribly wrong, and their attitude had actively impeded efforts by citizens groups, journalists, and congressional investigators to bring the issue to national attention, at a time when its disclosure may have done some good. Many of the same reporters who declined to write about Contra drug trafficking in the 1980s—or wrote dismissively about it—were trotted out once again to do damage control.

Second, the *San Jose Mercury News* was not a member of the club that sets the national news agenda, the elite group of big newspapers that decides the important issues of the day, such as which stories get reported and which get ignored. Small regional newspapers aren't invited. But the *Merc* had broken the rules and used the internet to get in by the back door, leaving the big papers momentarily superfluous and embarrassed, and it forced them to readdress an issue they'd much rather have forgotten. By turning on the *Mercury News*, the big boys were reminding the rest of the flock who really runs the newspaper business, internet or no internet, and the extents to which they will go to protect that power, even if it meant rearranging reality to suit them.

Finally, as I discovered while researching the book I eventually wrote about this story, the national news organizations have had a long, disappointing history of playing footsie with the CIA, printing unsubstantiated agency leaks, giving agents journalistic cover, and downplaying or attacking stories and ideas damaging to the agency. I can only speculate as to why this occurs, but I am not naïve enough to believe it is mere coincidence.

The scary thing about this collusion between the press and the powerful is that it works so well. In this case, the government's denials and promises to pursue the truth didn't work. The public didn't accept them, for obvious reasons, and the clamor for an independent investigation continued to grow. But after the government's supposed watchdogs weighed in, public opinion became divided and confused, the movement to force congressional hearings lost steam and, once enough people came to believe the stories were false or exaggerated, the issue could safely be put back at the bottom of the dead-story pile, hopefully never to rise again.

Do we have a free press today? Sure we do. It's free to report all the sex scandals it wants, all the stock market news we can handle, every new health fad that comes down the pike, and every celebrity marriage or divorce that happens. But when it come to the real down and dirty stuff—stories like Tailwind, the October Surprise, the El Mozote massacre, corporate corruption, or CIA involvement in drug-trafficking—that's where we begin to see the limits of our "free" press. In today's media environment, sadly, such stories are not even open for discussion.

Back in 1938, when fascism was sweeping Europe, legendary investigative reporter George Seldes observed (in his book *The Lords of the Press*) that "it *is* possible to fool all the people all the time—when government and press cooperate." Unfortunately, we have reached that point.

The Arnold

Gary Webb

High Times magazine (May/June 2004)

INTRODUCTION BY ANNIE NOCENTI

Gary Webb was his own kind of all-American. He believed in this lumbering, yearning, slapdash nation that he, in the same breath, did not trust. It is not easy to believe in something you do not trust, but he did. It was his faith in the ideal of an unfettered, uncensored country that drove his scrupulous style of journalism. Gary had a modern cowboy swagger in both life and work: a quicksilver adventurousness rooted in profound principles.

When I hear people citing and trusting the "facts" in Wikipedia, I think of Gary Webb. I can imagine the manic fun Gary would have as he hit random pages and raged about all the misinformation. There are so many moments in this decade of emerging social media when I miss Gary: "transparency journalism"; Wikileaks; privacy issues; the fight for a decentralized, revenue-free, bottom-up, net neutrality. I long for a touchstone like Gary to reach for and ask: What do you think of this?

Gary Webb was old-school. Check and recheck and triple-source every single piece of information. Question and rethink. That's why they couldn't take him down after his explosive reporting at the *San Jose Mercury News.* They called him a conspiracy theorist but Gary was the most red, white, and blue of all. What a symbolic tale of journalistic decline: the small paper that believed in Gary, the small paper that folded under pressure, the lone journalist who persevered and exonerated himself. Gary simply went back to his mountainous research files and proved every single word. I think of Gary Webb every time I'm cleaning the "dead weight" out of my life and I almost toss a box of notes and old interview tapes that are the basis of my reporting in one story or another. It's not dead weight; it's fail-safe.

I met Gary Webb in Mexico when we were both visiting professors at the School of Authentic Journalism. As we taught and drank and traveled we became friends. When I think of Gary now, I think of the movie *The Wild*

Bunch . . . how men who knew how to live in an untamed frontier also heard the train coming and knew its whistle as a portent for them to get off the tracks . . . it was their death song and they knew how to die.

When I became editor of *High Times* in 2004, I thought of Gary. I was brought into *High Times* to bring it back to its 1970s-early 80s heyday when the magazine wasn't just potporn for potaholics. I wanted to publish not just stories about marijuana, but stories that somehow embodied the kind of questioning, radical thinking a heightened consciousness could inspire.

That year, the Governator had already caught miles of ink, but Gary thought that ink had focused too much on celebrity and pop culture, when in fact, something a bit more grassroots and subterranean was brewing in California . . .

□   □   □

On the day Arnold Schwarzenegger was to be sworn in as California's 38th governor, a grizzled legislative staffer—a democrat—spied what he assumed was one of the governor-to-be's aides hurrying down the hallway of the 19-century capitol building.

"I stopped him and asked him if he was one Arnold's advance men," the staffer recalled. He said the young man looked at him uncomprehendingly for a second, then shook his head.

"No. I'm in production."

In the midst of the most dire financial crisis in California's history, nearly five million voters decided to overthrow their government. It was a feat unprecedented in the state's political annals and nearly unprecedented in the nation's. Not since 1921, in North Dakota, had voters banded together to kick a sitting governor out of office.

But what makes California's case even more remarkable is that they replaced him with a man once described by a *Village Voice* film critic as a "hydrant-headed dummkopf." A Hollywood action hero. When he was sent to Sacramento to run the biggest state in the nation, Arnold Schwarzenegger's most noteworthy achievements had been winning muscle-man contests and starring in mediocre movies. Now his brawny hands are at the controls of a state that strongly resembles an impending train wreck. Yet, by and large, people seem delighted—inspired even.

On Inauguration Day, they drove to Sacramento from all over the state, lining up four and five deep behind fences hundreds of yards away, just to glimpse the man. They mob his every appearance and cheer him lustily. The state's television media swoons at the mention of his name, and so does much of the press. When he finished his State of the State address in January, the mood was such that, had decorum and strength allowed it, the solons would have hoisted him on their shoulders and carried him from the legislative chambers.

Rid yourself of the notion that California's voters were stupid, bamboozled by slick PR or starstruck by Arnold's celebrity. What they did may have been irrational, but they knew precisely what they were doing—turning the political establishment on its head. What California experienced with Schwarzenegger's election was nothing less than a populist revolution, an unexpected aftershock from a political earthquake that happened 93 years ago. In his latest role, Schwarzenegger isn't playing a visitor from the future. Rather, he's a ghost from the past.

I knew Governor Gray Davis was dead politically the day I went to Home Depot to buy some glue. Outside the main exit, on a warm Saturday last spring, an older fellow wearing a white undershirt had set up a little folding table and a camp chair. Then, like a carnival barker, he began shouting at passersby, urging them to stop and sign a petition.

In and of itself, that isn't an uncommon sight. California's constitution allows any issue to be put on the ballot as long as enough people can be hectored, tricked or persuaded to sign a petition for it. (A few years ago, a petition was going around to mandate publicly televised, commercially sponsored executions—with the victim's family choosing the means, and the sale of raffle tickets to select the executioner. Amazingly, it failed to get enough signatures.)

Because these paid signature-gatherings ask such personal questions—such as whether you're a registered voter and willing to take a stand on a political issue—shoppers tend to regard them with a mixture of apprehension and dread, as if they were fanatics instead of retirees and college students trying to make a little money on the side. Usually they walk by brusquely. But not that day.

"Want to get rid of the governor?" the man in the undershirt yelled. "Sign here! Want to throw out the governor? Sign right here!" Shoppers halted as if angels were trumpeting. An overweight man with an armload of shopping bags froze mid-step, galloped back toward the little table, set each bag down one by one and breathlessly asked, "Where do I sign?" The table was quickly surrounded by do-it-your-selfers, young and old, black and white, Hispanic and Asian, male and female, many of them leaving long lines at the cash register to stand happily in line once again. In two decades covering state government, I'd never seen that level of enthusiasm exhibited over anything having to do with politics, particularly gubernatorial politics. Voter turnout has been in a death spiral for years.

Yet here was supposedly somnolent middle class eagerly signing up for something as radical as deposing a governor they had just re-elected. And, at that point, their excitement had little to do with the former Mr. Universe. Arnold was still shooting *Terminator 3* and making plans for another movie. Nor was it due to any particular animus toward Davis, a dull man with a whiny voice and funny haircut. While it is true that Davis has been a cold fish his whole career and is regarded as a bloodless striver, a self-promoter and a shameless fund-raiser, that never stopped him from winning. He'd waltzed into a second term just as if his first hadn't been an unqualified disaster. "I've won every statewide election, every general election I've ever been in," Davis boasted in *Newsweek* last July. "And I intend to win this one."

But his last victory had been exceedingly hollow, and a syndicated columnist named Tom Elias was among the first to recognize it. People didn't vote for Davis because they *wanted* him as governor, Elias wrote in an internet column in late 2002. Most people stayed home because they couldn't stomach either candidate. The public was disillusioned and angry, and Davis was ripe to be brought down by a good dose of populism, he opined. In Sacramento, a political gadfly named Ted Costa read that and started circulation petitions for a recall, which ultimately led to the man in the T-shirt sitting outside Home Depot that day and then thousands of others like him, stationed outside supermarkets, 99-cent stores, swap meets and flea markets up and down the state.

The experts and most political columnists initially laughed off the idea of a recall. It had been tried 32 times since 1911, they chorused, and not once had it ever made the ballot. It was a pipe dream, they scoffed. Yet it qualified for the ballot easily, and the political establishment reacted with shock and alarm. Democrats showed their contempt by refusing to run any candidate *except* Davis—probably not the wisest prank to pull on an already angry electorate. Major political figures from Bill Clinton down denounced the recall as irresponsible, un-American, extremist and the work of radicals—echoing almost word-for-word the epithets used against the 1911 campaign that put the recall provision in the constitution in the first place.

In both cases, the establishment wasn't entirely wrong: It *was* the work of radicals. In 1911, it had been the firebrand Republican Hiram Johnson, a burly, trust-busting former D.A., who broke the stranglehold that the Southern Pacific Railroad then had on state politics. In 2003, it was the far-right wing of the California GOP. But while they were correct in sensing that people were again on the verge of revolt, and for generally the same reasons as their great-grandparents, the effort blew up in their faces; voters wanted nothing to do with right-wingers. The day Schwarzenegger announced his candidacy on *The Tonight Show*, Darrell Issa, the conservative multimillionaire congressman who'd bankrolled the recall, dropped out of the race in tears. The far right, in the end, merely served as doormen for Schwarzenegger, a man they view suspiciously as the best.

In late July, a Democratic state senator I knew asked if he should break ranks and run against Davis. I thought he should. "It's a mistake to look at this as a situation where people just don't like Gray Davis," I wrote him. "They don't like the whole fucking system. They're tired of getting stuck with lousy choices, they feel like politics doesn't include them anymore, and that's why this recall effort has worked so well: It tapped into this vast undercurrent of general discontent, and it's given them a chance to directly effect a change, not just to swap one boring machine politician for another. People feel like they really have a say in government right now—even if it's just to say, Hey, fuck all of you guys."

Ironically, it was an actress, Bo Derek, who probably best summed up the giddy, exhilarating feeling that swept California voters last summer. "I have to say I was uncomfortable with the idea of a recall. I did not sign the petition every time I went in and out of a supermarket," she told an interviewer in September. "But now that it's happening, I'm really excited and I feel empowered and I want to shake things up . . . This is our moment, our opportunity, to sort of buck the system a little bit."

The Schwarzenegger campaign fully exploited that feeling. Arnold transformed himself into the living embodiment of Hiram Johnson—only bigger, tougher and handier with a grenade launcher. His campaign let it be known that Johnson was one of Arnold's personal heroes, and Schwarzenegger paid homage to the old rabble-rouser during an early campaign stop at the State Railroad Museum, where he stood before an old locomotive engine and vowed to resume Johnson's ancient campaign against the corruption of special interests. "The people of this state do not trust their government," Arnold declared. "They feel it is corrupted by dirty money, closed doors and backroom dealings." In his only debate, the first words out of Arnold's mouth were these: "I thank God every day that we have Hiram Johnson that created this more than ninety years ago. His intention was to create this recall because of special interests controlling politicians, which is exactly what is the case today."

Despite all the snickering in the national media about those goofy Californians and their political circus, Schwarzenegger's message was serious enough: Politics sucks. The system's corrupt and doesn't work anymore. It's time for a revolution. The populist streak running though Arnold's campaign rhetoric was stunning, considering the fact that it was coming from a moderate Republican.

Schwarzenegger could have run as a Democrat and easily beaten Davis, so wide was his appeal. Plus, he had the wide-open nature of a recall election working in his favor. For the first time in their lives, voters could actually pick someone they actually *wanted* as governor, as opposed to a party hack. Which meant that if they wanted a Hollywood action hero, then goddamnit, they'd have him. Now they do. And now we will see just who it was they elected during this once-in-a-century explosion of direct democracy, and whether it remains Left Coast aberration or it spreads to other states whose laws allow recall elections.

A few years back, I covered a political corruption trail during which an influential corporate lobbyist was heard on tape bragging that a Republican state senator was "our main robot." That wisecrack came back to me the other night as I watched *The Terminator*, in which Schwarzenegger plays a hunter-killer robot from the future. The first generation of his kind, we are told, had been made of rubber and was easily spotted as a machine disguised as a human. But Arnold's generation was different. He was a cyborg, a robot with human skin, sweat glands and real hair, who could walk among the people undetected. This is the question California's voters now face. Is the man they put in the governor's office one of them, or is he a cyborg? Will he turn out to be the two-fisted populist he portrayed himself to be— the little man's Big Friend, as former Louisiana governor Huey Long once described himself? Or was his transformation into Hiram Johnson merely a skin to conceal the metal skeleton of a machine politician?

The Killing Game

Gary Webb

Sacramento News & Review (October 14, 2004)

INTRODUCTION BY MELINDA WELSH

It was October of 2004, two months after he'd joined the reporting staff at the *Sacramento News & Review*, when Gary Webb wrote what was to be his most definitive story for the *SN&R*. "The Killing Game" was testament to Webb's obsession at that time with the growing popularity of "first-person shooter" video games that featured a single player in a combat zone with a weapon and a mission to hunt down and kill other players in a torrent of explosions, blood, and guts. Why were games like Counter-Strike—ones that were especially fascinating to middle-class teenage males—suddenly so riveting to Webb? Because he'd discovered that the US Army had spent $10 million in taxpayer dollars to develop its own first-person shooter. In fact, the US military had figured out that violent video games were a great way to recruit (and even test the aptitude of) their target market for potential soldiers.

To write "The Killing Game," Webb hung out with loads of Sacramento-area players and logged endless hours himself on first-person shooters. He unearthed obscure military documents and interviewed dozens of people, among them computer and military psychologists, game designers, and Army research engineers. In other words, he did what good reporters do in pursuit of any important story—he brought all his smarts and skills. It was no surprise, when his reporting was done, to find that Gary Webb had nailed the story.

□   □   □

For young men, first-person shooters are the hottest computer games around. That's why the Army spent $10 million making one of its own. But there's a catch. Big Brother gets to watch you play.

It's Tuesday, practice night for the LANatomas *Counter-Strike* clan. Five young men wearing headphones are sitting side by side before a bank of computer monitors, fingers flickering over keyboards, mouses clicking, yelling out warnings to each other. The room, a narrow computer-gaming center in a suburban strip mall, is pleasantly dim, lit with black light and neon. Blue Oyster Cult thrums through the sound system, but not loudly.

On-screen, the clan creeps quietly down a dark hallway of an oil pumping station in Russia, assault rifles and flash-bang grenades in hand, looking to kill five terrorists who are attempting to dynamite the complex. They think their enemies are hiding somewhere in ambush, hoping to draw LANatomas into a trap, and they're right.

"They're in CT spawn!" one of the clan shouts suddenly. "Left side!"

"I see them!" his neighbor yells back. "They're stacked!"

"Don't peek," their clan leader warns. "I'll get them." Before he can move, he is riddled with terrorist bullets and slumps to the ground. The rest of the clan quickly meets the same bloody fate, and the message "terrorists win" flashes on the screen. The game resets, and they begin another round.

LANatomas is an hour into its twice-weekly practice, getting ready for its season opener Sunday night against res.ilience, a clan from the Seattle area. In preseason standings, the LANatomas is the top-ranked team in the Pacific Conference of the Cyberathlete Amateur League's Main Division, and the members hope to claw their way into Premier Division this season, one step from the big time. But at the moment, the Premier Division clan they're practicing against—Eminence, from Dallas—is mowing them down.

"Dude, we are getting raped," clan leader Jeff Muramoto mutters.

Looking over their shoulders is Craig Wentworth, a slight, pale blond man wearing narrow glasses and a red T-shirt. Wentworth, 20, is the clan's veteran and has been playing *Counter-Strike* fanatically for five years. A junior at California State University, Sacramento, he decided recently to step back, citing the time required to remain competitive in league play. Now he just drops by to watch and advise.

"We were playing seven days a week, hours and hours a day, and I just got burned out," he says. Playing under the name Las1K, Wentworth says he won about $2,000 in cash and another $2,000 in computer parts in *Counter-Strike* tournaments. "Not bad for a hobby. I was one of the most famous players around here. A lot of people knew me."

Muramoto, 21, looks up at Wentworth with a grin of affirmation. "Dude, you were *own*-ness."

But Las1K hasn't laid down his weapons for good and he knows it. "You always come back," he says quietly, watching his friends blast their way through a phalanx of terrorists. "You get pissed, take off for a few months, but you always come back to it."

For anyone who hasn't seen one of these games—known as first person shooters—here's the gist of them. You're placed in a combat zone, armed with a weapon of your choice, and sent out to find and kill other players. Knife them, club them, blow them apart with a shotgun, set them afire, vaporize them with a shoulder-launched missile, drill them through the head with a sniper rifle—the choice is yours. Depending on the game, blood will spray, mist, or spout. Sometimes your kills collapse in crumpled heaps, clutching their throats and twitching convincingly. Sometimes they cry in pain with human voices. Their bodies lay there for a while so you can feed off them if necessary, restoring your own health. Then you can grab their weapons and set off to find another victim, assuming you don't get killed first.

It may not be everyone's cup of tea, but among young males it's far and away the most popular genre of computer game. Some psychologists and parents worry that such games are desensitizing a large, impressionable segment of the population to violence and teaching them the wrong things. But that depends on your point of view. If, like the US Army, you need people who can become unflappable killers, there's no better way of finding them. It's why the Army has spent more than $10 million in tax-payer funds developing its very own first-person shooter, and why the Navy, the Air Force and the National Guard are following suit. For anyone who thinks kids aren't learning playing shooter games, read on.

First person shooters originally were designed as contests between man and machine, but, as with many things, the advent of high-speed internet connections changed that. Now, from the privacy of your home, you can take on players the world over. Best of all, it costs nothing to play other than the initial price of the game. (Playing from an internet café or gaming center, such as LANatomas, costs a few dollars an hour.) Bearing names like "JizMack's California Slaughterhouse," "Let the Corpses Fall" and "Newbie Cemetery," free game servers abound. It is endless war, day or night. On a recent Wednesday morning, more than 29,500 servers were hosting games of *Counter-Strike*, and more than 66,000 people were playing.

For gamers, the attraction of online play is obvious. In the cyberworld, you're not hunting down slow computer-generated Nazis. You're matching wits with real humans (sometimes real Germans), which somehow makes a kill all the more satisfying. Moreover, computer graphics and sound have evolved to the point that it is quite easy to think you're in a tangible world. Your immediate surroundings vanish. Crickets chirp, bushes rustle, bullets whiz by your head and shower you with chips of concrete. Shell casings clatter to the floor. Mortars crump in the distance, and grenades send up gouts of rock and dirt. It's a loud, bloody, violent and altogether alarming world. Yet it's oddly exhilarating.

"I have to laugh when someone says, 'Oh, the people playing these games know it's not real,'" said Dr. Peter Vorberer, a clinical psychologist and head of the University of Southern California's computer game research group. "Of course they think it's real! That's why people play them for hours and hours. They're designed to make you believe it is real. Games are probably the purest example yet of the internet melding with reality."

LANatomas clan member Rob McCarthy, 17, a senior at Sacramento High School, couldn't agree more.

"What's interesting to me is that you can become famous in the cyber-world, and that fame can carry over into the real world," McCarthy said. "In the cyberworld, you can earn respect, just like in real life. Most parents can't get their minds around that."

It may sound fanciful, but he's right. Top *Counter-Strike* teams and top players have developed cult followings, and with that has come fame and fortune. Management teams have sprung up to develop new talent, and cash tournaments are commonplace. Clans from 50 countries attended the World Cyber Games last weekend in San Francisco, competing for a $25,000 top prize and lucrative corporate sponsorships.

Team 3D, arguably the best clan in the United States, boasts sponsor-ships from Subway, Hewlett Packard, Nvidia (which makes graphics processors) and Sennheiser (which makes audio equipment). The world's No. 1 ranked clan, Schroet Kommando of Sweden is sponsored by Intel and has its own clothing line. Fatal1ty, a legendary *Counter-Strike* gamer, also has a clothing line and a Fatal1ty-brand computer motherboard coming out. In addition, top players make extra money by giving private lessons for anywhere from $50 to $120 an hour, schooling players on strategies, gunnery, weapons selections and squad tactics.

For thousands of *Counter-Strike* players, the game quite literally has *become* their life. "This is what I want to do," said Carson Loane, 18, a LANatomas clan member who has played *Counter-Strike* for 20 consecutive hours. "But if I'm going to do it competitively, I have to practice at least 10 hours a day. And I'm prepared to do that. But the catch is you've got to find four other people to do it with you. The only way to win this game is as a team."

Stanford University psychology professor B.J. Fogg isn't surprised to see such dedication to a computer game.

"Video games, better than anything else in our culture, deliver rewards to people, especially teenage boys," said Fogg, who studies the effects of computer games. "Teenage boys are wired to seek competency. To master our world and get better at stuff. Video games, in dishing out rewards, can convey to people that their competency is growing, you can get better at something second by second."

But what is it kids are better *at* when they play first-person shooters, hour after hour? Many would assume it's a complete waste of time. But the US government would disagree.

As the number of people playing *Counter-Strike* soared into the millions, the US Army could only watch wistfully. For years, Army recruiters had diligently pursued the very same demographic—middle-class teenage males—with dwindling success.

In late 1999, after missing their recruiting goals that year, Army officials got together with the civilian directors of a Navy think tank at the Naval Postgraduate School in Monterey to discuss ways of luring computer gamers into the military.

Combat games not only happened to target the right age for the Army's purposes but, more importantly, possessed exactly the kind of information-processing skills the Army needed: the ability to think quickly under fire.

"Our military information tends to arrive in a flood . . . and it'll arrive in a flood under stressful conditions, and there'll be a hell of a lot of noise," said Col. Casey Wardynski, a military economist who came up with the idea for an official Army computer game. "How do you filter that? What are your tools? What is your facility in doing that? What is your level of comfort? How much load can you bear? Kids who are comfortable with that are going to be real comfortable . . . with the Army of the future."

From an Army report: "Aptitudes related to information handling and information culture values are seen as vital to the effectiveness of the high-tech, network-centric Army of the future, and young American gamers are seen as especially proficient in these capabilities. More importantly, when young Americans enter the Army, they increasingly will find that key information will be conveyed via computer video displays akin to the graphical interfaces found in games."

With the vast funding of the US government behind them, the Army/Navy team began developing a game that hopefully would turn some of its players into real soldiers. "The overall mission statement . . . was to develop a game with appeal similar to the game *Counter-Strike*," wrote Michael Zyda, the director of the Navy think tank. "We took *Counter-Strike* as our model, but with heavy emphasis on realism and Army values and training."

An experimental psychologist from the Navy helped tweak the game's sound effects to produce heightened blood pressure, body temperature and heart rate. It was released in digital double surround sound, which few games are. In terms of game play, it was designed as a "tactical" shooter, slow-paced, more deliberate, but with *Counter-Strike*'s demanding squad tactics and communications—a "serious" game for kids who took their war gaming seriously.

After two years of development, *America's Army* was released to the public on the first Fourth of July after 9/11. The gaming world gasped and then cheered. Contrary to expectations, the government-made shooter was every bit as good as a $50 retail shooter and, in some ways, better. Plus, it was free—downloadable from the internet at www.americasarmy.com. That, too, was a calculation—one the Army hoped would weed out people who didn't know much about computers. The game and its distribution system were difficult by design, Zyda said.

"That was a very key thing. First, they would have to be smart enough to download the game off the internet. Then, they would have to become good at [the game], which isn't easy. To attract those kinds of people, that was the mission. That's what we were looking for."

The game does a good job separating the wheat from the chaff. Before you're allowed to join an online game, you must undergo weapons training and send your firing range scores to the Army. If you're a lousy shot, you can't play. Once inside the game, it gets no easier. The virtual battlefield is enormous, and your enemy is often hidden under a cover of darkness.

"Newbies" are quickly cut to pieces. Unlike *Counter-Strike*, *America's Army* players aren't allowed to be on the terrorists' side. Your team always looks like American soldiers, and the other team always looks like terrorists (or "OPFORs" in Army lingo, meaning "opposing forces").

In the wake of 9/11, the public and media reaction was, in the Army's words, "overwhelmingly positive." *Salon*'s Wagner James Au, for example, gushed that the game would help "create the wartime culture that is so desperately needed now" and excitedly anticipated the day when youngsters raised on *America's Army* would pick up real weapons and cleanse the globe of real terrorists. Most media accounts focused on the novelty of using a video game to help find recruits and carried jocular headlines like "Uncle Sim Wants You."

"We thought we'd have a lot more problems," Zyda said. "But the country is in the mood where anything the military does is great . . . 9/11 sort of assured the success of this game. I'm not sure what kind of reception it would have received otherwise."

There are now more than 4 million registered users, more than half of whom have completed weapons training and gone online to play, making it the fourth most-played online shooter. The Army says there are 500 fan sites on the Web, and recruiters have been busy setting up local tournaments and cultivating an *America's Army* "community" on the internet, hoping to replicate the *Counter-Strike* phenomenon.

"With respect to recruitment, actual results won't be known for four to five years, when the current raft of 13- and 14-year-olds will be old enough to join," Zyda wrote.

But not everyone saw the game as a good thing. A Miami attorney named Jack Thompson went on ABC News and threatened to seek an injunction, saying it wasn't the government's job to provide kill 'em games to youngsters. He was deluged with angry emails and allegedly received death threats.

"The Army and the Defense Department have a very long history of conducting unethical, illegal experiments upon soldiers and civilians," Thompson angrily reminded players in a posting to the official Army website. "This 'game' is yet another experiment upon the unsuspecting pawns who play it. You are the latest guinea pigs."

Thompson was more right than he knew. Recruiting computer gamers was only one of the goals behind the creation of *America's Army*.

The other purpose, aptitude testing of potential recruits, has gotten virtually no publicity.

In Germany, a group of *America's Army* fans created a sophisticated statistic-tracking system, AAO Tracker, which can tell how much time a player spends online (top players average four hours a day), how many kills he's made, which battlefields he's best at, how many kills he averages an hour, and similar minutiae.

But the creator of the popular AAO Tracker system, a 23-year-old German computer engineer, quit in disgust after learning that the Army was rolling out its own statistics tracker for the game.

"You can understand that I don't want to spend (much) time on our stats-tracking system when I know that all my work is useless and for the trash when the official stats tracking system goes online," the engineer complained on his website.

One of the Army's game developers, in an interview with a fan site, confirmed that "we have started some development on an integrated stats tracker. As far as what we can track, that is really up to what we want to track, as every single event in the game can be recorded and logged. From every shot fired to every objective taken. It simply becomes a matter of which events we want to parse out."

Why would the Army spend tax dollars tracking and collecting arcane statistics about the players of the game? Because the data can be used to scientifically predict what kind of soldier they'd be.

"Suppose you played extremely well, and you stayed in the game an extremely long time," Wardynski explained in an interview last year. "You might just get an e-mail seeing if you'd like any additional information on the Army."

America's Army isn't merely a game, recruiting device or a public-relations tool, though it certainly is all of those things. It's also a military aptitude tester. And it was designed that way from the start.

In a paper written while he was still developing the game, Navy computer expert Zyda said that "the research focus is to determine if games can be instrumented to be able to determine the aptitude, leadership abilities and psychological profile of the game player."

That work was done by a senior psychologist for the Army Research Institute of Behavioral Science in Alexandria, Va. Zyda said the goal was to "instrument the game" so that it would perform the functions of the Armed Services Vocational Aptitude Battery, a test new recruits take to help the Army figure out what kind of job to give them. Zyda was told the research was a success, but couldn't discover any details.

"It was odd. I had people tell me (the researcher) had done PowerPoint presentations and research papers on it, but I was never able to see any of that, and I asked to see it. I know at one point the Army's lawyers had some problems with the whole idea of using that data, and we certainly did, too, from a personal privacy angle. We didn't think it was a good idea. But I don't know the status of it," Zyda said.

Wardynski confirmed that the aptitude testing research had been successful. "That's as far as we've taken it. It's something we'll be moving ahead with in the coming year."

In a posting deep inside the official *America's Army* website, the Army reveals that "players who request information (about the Army) . . . may have their gaming records matched to their real-world identities for the purpose of facilitating career placement within the Army. Data collected within the game, such as which roles and missions players spent the most time playing could be used to highlight Army career fields that map into these interest areas . . ."

The Army has been collecting player information in a vast relational database system called "Andromeda" Wardynski said, which recruiters will be able to use to look up a player's statistics if one of them shows up in a recruiting office. A version of *America's Army* now in development will take that a step further, allowing players to create a "persistent" online alterego, one that steadily progresses through virtual ranks by taking additional training or specialized missions, generating valuable data along the way.

Recently, an updated version of the game called *Special Forces* was released, and there was a reason why that particular theme was chosen—one that had little to do with entertainment value. "Specifically, the Department of Defense wants to double the number of Special Forces soldiers, so essential did they prove in Afghanistan and northern Iraq; consequently, orders have tickled down the chain of command and found application in the current release of *America's Army*, which features Special Forces roles, missions, and equipment," a Navy-produced booklet states.

Paolo Banzon is a harried man. He looks around the Yobags internet Café in Hayward, where he works as technical engineer, taking in the sight of dozens of milling teenagers, most of them Asian, many of them wearing backpacks, shorts, chains and expensive tennis shoes. From all over Northern California, clans have flocked to this flat, sun-baked industrial park on a Saturday morning for a chance to win the $650 top prize in Yobags' *Counter-Strike* tournament. They're fussy customers. Banzon has been running from table to table, answering questions about unacceptable frame rates and lagging processor speeds, rebooting computers, loading and unloading drivers. It has been bedlam, but Banzon is excited. Yobags is the area's first internet gaming parlor owned and operated entirely by Filipinos, he says proudly, and "this tournament will put us on the map. It's the first one we've held since we opened, and *look* at this place!"

The LANatomas clan quietly sets up its computers and checks out the competition. Jon Loane, 16, strolls over to watch a clan named Ninjas practice and comes back shaking his head. "That's TAG," he says. "They shouldn't even be here." TAG had been a Premier Division clan last season when, during the playoffs, it was caught using a "ringer," an expert player not on its roster. As punishment, the Cyberathlete League banished it to the Intermediate division for a season. Ironically, the penalty made TAG technically eligible to play in the Yobags tournament, which is closed to Premier Division clans.

It was not good news. LANatomas members haven't been playing well, and they know it. After handily winning their season opener, they were steamrolled by the Schooled in Killing clan, a team the online experts predicted would lose. Overconfident, LANatomas barely practiced. In addition, clan leader Muramoto skipped the game to attend a concert "with a girl," which did not sit well.

Today, there was more than pride riding on their performance. There was also the matter of the $125 entry fee.

In competitive play, a game consists of 30 rounds, each clan playing 15 rounds as terrorists and 15 rounds as counter-terrorists. The first clan to win 16 rounds—either by killing its opponents or thwarting their mission—wins the game.

LANatomas' first match, against the clan Effortless from San Jose, is close. After falling behind 2-0, Effortless—a young team thrown together just for the tournament—overcomes its nervousness, and, by the end of the first half, the San Jose kids have jumped to a 10–5 lead. "Settle down, guys," Muramoto messages his troops. "Take a deep breathe and remember: It's just a game." The second half goes a little better. With their backs to the wall, the LANatomas players dig in and start winning. But they stumble in the last round, and Effortless ekes out a 16–14 victory. "We're OK," McCarthy insists. "We were doing better at the end." Besides, it's double-elimination. As long as they don't lose again, they're in the hunt.

Two hours later, they're out in the parking lot stowing their gear in their cars, having earned the unwelcome distinction of being the first clan ousted from the tournament. "This is what happens when we don't practice," Carson Loane says disgustedly. "If we're not going to practice, these tournaments are a waste of money." No one says anything. "So, we're going to practice tonight, right? Anyone got a concert to go to?"

Muramoto looks unhappy. "This is feeling like a job, dude. It's like a job."

Loane is persistent. "We're going to practice, right?"

Muramoto sighs. "OK. But just for a couple of hours."

That night at practice, Loane quit. "He said some of us weren't devoting enough time to practice," Muramoto said. "I'm working two jobs, seven days a week, and I'm already spending three or four nights a week on this. I can't do any more. I need a life outside this game." But that idea may be put on hold for a while. The next day Muramoto received an offer from a Peruvian *Counter-Strike* clan. If all goes well, Muramoto said, LANatomas could be winging its way down to Peru to train with a South American clan, all expenses paid. Contracts were on the way. "This could be pretty good," he said.

Last March, with the success of *America's Army* assured, the Army cut the Navy out of the picture. Though it had been the Navy's civilian team of programmers, psychologists and game designers who'd brought *America's Army* to life, it was still the Army's game, and the Army was taking it in-house. "Differences between [the Navy] and Army management saw the game's production take a different turn," Zyda wrote. "The Army chose to take control of development."

According to the Army, it "expanded the *America's Army* development team to two new locations." One of them is the Army's Armament Research, Development and Engineering Center (ARDEC), which bills itself as the Army's "Center of Lethality."

Located on 6,500 rolling acres in northern New Jersey, a safe distance from any town, ARDEC is the Army's main weapons research plant. Its mission: to turn technology into weapons. Over the years, its labs have sprung such devices as laser-guided "smart" missiles, the "Bunker Buster" bomb and chemical weapons, as well as crowd-control devices like knockout gas, riot batons and—one of its current projects—incapacitating sound rays.

What could such a lethal outfit want with a kid's computer game? Unbelievable as it sounds, they're using it to test new weapons. Bill Davis, the head of the *America's Army* weapons research group, said the game's "graphics were well beyond what the military was able to match" and provided a virtual testing ground so lifelike "we can, in essence, try out a new weapons system before any metal is cut." Currently being tested is a computer-controlled airburst grenade launcher, which Davis said will probably be featured in a future release of *America's Army*, completing a circular journey from virtual reality, to reality, and back to virtual reality.

One month after the Army took over production of the game, it announced that it had signed an exclusive long-term contract with the French software company Ubisoft to bring *America's Army* to a wider, younger audience. By next summer, it will be out in a "console" version, for use with Xbox and Sony game machines. Currently, it is playable only on high-end PCs, "which reaches a certain demographic for household income," Wardynski told an interviewer. "We'd like to reach a broader audience, and consoles get you there. For every PC gamer, there are four console gamers."

Also in the works, he said, are an *America's Army* clothing line, comic books and toy action figures.

In a neurological laboratory at the University of Tuebingen in Germany a few months ago, the first of a dozen young German men slid into the claustrophobic confines of an ultra-high-resolution MRI machine and prepared to play the computer game *Tactical Ops: Assault on Terror.*

A *Counter-Strike* clone, *Tactical Ops* is bloodier, more frenetic and less strategic. It's known as a "twitch" shooter: Since the bullets fly so fast, instantaneous reaction time is needed to avoid death.

The experiment, funded by USC's Annenberg School of Communications, was designed to discover whether playing violent computer games induced aggressive brain activity. In other words, does your brain react the same way as it would if you were killing someone in real life, or does it realize that it's just a game?

Earlier studies, notably those done by Iowa State University psychologist Craig Anderson, have shown links between high video-game violence and heightened aggression, and not just casual links. Anderson says the connection is greater than the link between cancer and second-hand cigarette smoke. But, according to the Entertainment Software Association, "there is no compelling evidence that establishes a link between playing games and aggressive behavior."

If there were, obviously, it could be bad for the $7-billion-a-year game business, since half of all Americans over 6 play computer and video games. Last year, 239 million games were bought, nearly two for every household in America.

The Iowa studies were based on word-association test and psychological models. The USC experiment would be based on medical evidence. The scientists conducting it, USC media psychologist Rene Weber and German neurologist Klaus Mathiak, had spent a year designing their tests, and, as they turned on a giant magnetic imager, they were nervous. Foremost among their worries was whether their subjects could stand being trapped inside an MRI for an entire hour. Most patients, they knew, began demanding release within 20 minutes. But 20 minutes wasn't enough. They needed an hour.

The MRI began its ungodly hammering, and the young man—who had a trackball mouse by one hand and a keypad by the other—started to play, watching an image beamed into his glasses. The minutes ticked by without complaint. He seemed, Weber recalled, oblivious to everything but the game.

As the man blasted his way through *Tactical Ops,* the MRI scanner mapped his brain activities with such precision that the researchers could determine what it was doing at any given point in the game, frame by frame. The scientists focused their attention on a sliver called the anterior cingulate cortex (ACC), a beehive of emotional and problem-solving activity. Feelings, such as fear, sadness, and aggression originate here and send out marching orders to other parts of the brain. One study, for example, revealed that when Vietnam veterans with post-traumatic stress disorder are show words like "bodybag" and "firefight," their ACC's react far more aggressively than normal.

The results are still being analyzed, but Weber said it appears clear that the gamers' brains had the same reaction to computerized violence as they would to real violence. Aggressive brain activity was "quite remarkable . . . the results were consistent in nine of the twelve subjects," he said.

The scientist made another discovery as well. None of their subjects complained of being inside the MRI for an hour. In fact, Weber said, several asked if they could play longer.

Red Light, Green Cash

Gary Webb

Sacramento News & Review (November 24, 2004)

INTRODUCTION BY MELINDA WELSH

A classic case of an overlooked injustice sparked what became Gary Webb's last news story for the *Sacramento News & Review*. In "Red Light, Green Cash," regular people found themselves victims of an unfair judicial system when red-light cameras were installed at seventeen busy Sacramento-area intersections. Motorists found "guilty" of running red lights were mailed traffic citations but those who disputed their tickets got little more than assembly-line justice since they typically weren't even able to avail themselves of evidence of their crime (the photo), and were by rote ignored, pronounced guilty, and charged with a considerable fine. To report the story, Webb spent days in traffic court to watch and interview defendants disputing their tickets. He unearthed traffic safety studies that, in some cases, challenged the effectiveness of red-light camera systems. He interviewed California Highway Patrol officers versed in red-light-camera technology, district attorneys, and both advocates and assailants of the systems. He discovered that Affiliated Computer Services, the company that sold Sacramento its red-light-camera system and whose employees examined the photos and determined who got cited, received kickbacks from both the city and county for each ticket given, creating an incentive to cite on even marginal grounds. In the end, as with many such stories, Webb peeled back the onion to reveal that Sacramento's change to a red-light camera system turned out to be less about what it was supposed to be about—traffic safety—and more about the money.

□   □   □

If you think the idea of a $351 ticket is harsh, try fighting one. Even when the law's on your side, you're bound to lose.

Nearly two years ago, Clarksburg real-estate consultant John Alvin Bohl walked into the Carol Miller Justice Center to fight a traffic ticket. Having never challenged the People of California in court before, Bohl, a short, rotund man with thick classes, was nervous. He also was in agony. He'd woken up that morning with an abscessed tooth, which was causing him "splitting, splitting pain," but efforts to reach his dentist had failed.

His jaw throbbing, Bohl suffered silently as traffic Commissioner Raoul Thorbourne worked his way through the crowded docket. One after another of Bohl's fellow motorists trooped before the judge and attempted to plead their cases.

"My father always said that the president could be corrupted, and the Legislature could be corrupted, but there was one place that John Q. Public always had a chance of getting fair deal, and that was the legal system," the 60-year-old Vietnam veteran recalled. "He used to say that over and over."

But what Bohl was witnessing hardly seemed fair to him; it looked like an assembly line. The judge barely listened to the motorists' arguments, pronounced them all guilty and quickly trundled them off to the fines room.

"All right," the judge announced. "Then I have the matter of John Bohl."

The trial began. California Highway Patrol (CHP) officer John McCurry was sworn in and launched into the testimony he'd given a hundred times before. This was a red-light-camera case. He'd been trained in red-light-camera technology by a company called Affiliated Computer Services (ACS), which had sold the city and county of Sacramento their red-light-camera systems. McCurry had taken a two-days course from ACS and passed a written test. He explained briefly how the camera system worked, showed Bohl three photos taken of him allegedly running a red light on Martin Luther King Boulevard and asked that they be introduced into evidence.

"All right," the judge said. "Any objection, Mr. Bohl, to the photographs being made part of the record here?"

"Actually, I do, your honor," Bohl replied. "This is hearsay evidence. I don't believe the officer who testified has any personal direct knowledge." The judge paused and said he'd rule on that later.

McCurry brought out two maintenance log sheets from ACS, showing the red-light camera was working properly when it filmed Bohl. He asked that they be admitted into evidence, and then he rested his case. Once again, Bohl objected. McCurry didn't witness the inspection, Bohl argued.

The officer didn't know what the ACS inspector had done, he hadn't seen the log sheets being filled out, and the inspector wasn't in court to answer questions or even authenticate his maintenance logs. Every bit of the state's evidence against him was hearsay and was inadmissible, Bohl claimed, and he asked the judge to dismiss the ticket.

"I'm going to find you guilty of the violation, all right?" the judge said finally. "You have a seat out in the audience. Someone's going to come and walk you over to the cashier's office."

Bohl went off with the clerk and forked over $281. He'd lost on every point, and his tooth was killing him, but he was not unhappy. Far from it. His plan was working perfectly.

There are currently 17 intersections in Sacramento outfitted with red-light cameras. Over the past year, they generated 12,388 traffic tickets. Since red-light fines have now increased to $351—the harshest in the country—those tickets are worth $4.3 million. Considering that the county pays ACS roughly $1 million a year to rent and maintain the system, the cameras seem to have been a profitable investment. The sheriff's department, which runs the county-wide system and receives a lion's share of the revenues, has plans to install more.

Sheriff Lou Blanas likes them so much, in fact, that he's teamed up with ACS to help sell red-light cameras to other cities and towns. But, for such an apparent success story, Blanas' office either doesn't have or isn't eager to share much information about the program. A Public Records Act request filed more than a month ago—seeking basic records like contract documents and monthly reports—remained unfilled at deadline.

In truth, the red-light cameras have been a legal headache for local officials since they were installed in 1999, and they remain so to this day; Bohl is merely their latest migraine. The first came the same year the cameras went in. District Attorney Jan Scully was forced to dismiss nearly 800 tickets after a traffic commissioner decided the city hadn't followed state law on notifying the public that cameras were being used. The following year, another controversy flared up, and this one was more serious.

Because there are no eyewitnesses, the photos in red-light-camera cases—which ACS takes, digitizes and uploads to the sheriff's office—must be like Caesar's wife: beyond reproach. They are the only evidence the crime has been committed. But in San Diego in 2001, a judge ruled that they were "untrustworthy and unreliable." ACS was discovered to have a contract with the city of San Diego that paid the company a kickback each time a motorist was convicted—50 percent of the fine. That, Judge Ronald Styn ruled, gave ACS a clear financial motive to issue as many tickets as possible. Because the company was operating virtually unsupervised, it tainted the photos to the degree that they were inadmissible as evidence, he decided, and he tossed out 300 tickets.

"The judge said the way the program operates in San Diego is illegal," the motorists' attorney, Arthur Tate, said at the time. "And it basically operates the same way everywhere across the country."

That was certainly true in Sacramento. Both the city and county had identical kickback arrangements with ACS. As in San Diego, ACS employees were running Sacramento's system with little or no supervision. The company was reviewing the photos, deciding which motorists to cite, inspecting its own cameras and pocketing $87 dollars each time a motorist was convicted.

The city of San Diego suspended its red-light program and was hit with a class-action suit, which it eventually settled for more than $400,000. The ruling sent tremors through law enforcement and the red-light-camera industry. But not in Sacramento. Both the city and Blanas, whose red-light program had just begun when San Diego suspended its own, kept their cameras on, grinding out thousands of tickets. And the traffic-court judges kept returning guilty verdicts.

Until Ed Jaszewksi took the bench.

Jaszewksi, 54, is a civil attorney who had been volunteering his time at the Carol Miller Justice Center, hearing small-claim cases a few times a month. Because the traffic docket had become clogged, he was asked to help out for a half day on Fridays, presiding as a judge pro tem over traffic-court trials. On his first day in court, in mid-October 2001, his calendar was full of red-light cases. "I didn't know very much about them," he said. But what he was to learn would cause him no small amount of torment.

The policeman present knew nothing about the cases other than what ACS had told him. "He didn't know very much about how the system worked. And no one from ACS was there to ask. The defendants really had no ability to defend themselves," Jaszewski said. "It didn't seem to me that they were getting a fair trial at all."

But because it was his first day on the job, he did what the other judges did. He found the motorists guilty. Finally, he had enough.

"There was one case that was really borderline, so I acquitted him. A few minutes later, a clerk came up to the bench and told me the traffic commissioner wanted to see me." Calling a recess, Jaszewski found Commissioner David Foos waiting for him outside the courtroom. "Apparently, word had gotten back to him that I'd actually acquitted someone. He asked me if there was something about the red-light system that I was uncomfortable with or didn't understand." Jaszewski explained his concerns and brought up the San Diego case, which seemed to him to be right on point. Foos, he said, told him a Los Angeles court had reached a different conclusion and suggested he familiarize himself with that case. "It was all very diplomatic, but the intimation was pretty clear. I took his comments to mean that we just don't acquit these people." Foos said he did not recall the conversations but said, "It would be improper for me to tell someone how to reach a decision in a case."

Jaszewski went back to the bench and heard the last five cases on the calendar. But instead of finding them guilty, he told the motorists he wanted to research the law and would issue a ruling later. When he got home that evening, he opened his mailbox to find an ironic and unwelcome surprise: a traffic ticket, accusing him of running a red light two weeks earlier.

CHP officer McCurry could barely conceal his boredom. He'd been in traffic court since 8:30 that morning, and now it was closing in on 4 o'clock. He'd testified in 15 red-light-camera cases that day, had been asked the same questions dozens of times and had given virtually the same answers each time. It was no different this Friday, October 30, than it had been on any other Friday for the past two-and-a-half years.

McCurry, a trim, muscular man with dark eyebrows and a shaven head, has testified in more than 700 red-light cases. His conviction rate would make any prosecutor envious. Out of those 700-plus prosecutions, he's suffered only two or three defeats. "I only lost those because some pro-tem judge really didn't understand the program," he said.

One of the reasons he volunteered for his admittedly less-than-thrilling job was because it offered normal working hours and a chance to spend more time with his family. But this case, his last of the day, had all the earmarks of an interminably long one.

The defendant, a short man with a strong Germanic accent, had come to court armed with a thick three-ring binder, all of it tabbed and notated. It was filled with articles he'd culled from internet sites, the Caltrans traffic manual, court opinions, charts and photographs. For nearly 45 minutes, he worked his way through the binder, arguing in numerous ways that his ticket was illegally issued. At one point, he produced photos of the red-light-camera warning signs near the intersection of Fair Oaks Boulevard and Howe Avenue, where he'd been ticketed, and noted that on one sign, half of the letter "C" was missing. McCurry fidgeted in his seat and, very obviously, turned to look at the clock above the courtroom door. So did the judge.

"It's getting rather late," the judge said wearily. "Is that your argument, that the sign was illegible? Doesn't anyone shoot at traffic signs where you're from?"

Like everyone else who'd gotten a red-light ticket that day, the motorist was found guilty and sent to the fines room. McCurry gathered up his binders and briefcase and headed into the sunshine. "I honestly don't have a problem with people defending themselves," he said, as he walked through the courthouse parking lot to his car. "They have a right to do it. That guy, though . . ." McCurry smiled and shook his head. "I've heard every single one of those arguments a hundred times. And they never work."

McCurry, like many traffic cops, believes the cameras reduce accidents caused by red-light runners, and it's difficult to argue that point. In study after study (most of them funded by the insurance industry), red-light accidents went down after cameras went up. But there are other studies that are cited less frequently.

In 2002, San Diego hired a traffic engineering firm and a university professor to look at accidents at the intersections where the city had installed its controversial cameras. Sure enough, the number of car wrecks attributed to red-light running dropped by 60 percent. Unfortunately, rear-end collisions skyrocketed by 140 percent, due in large part to drivers making last-minute panic stops to avoid a ticket. Studies in North Carolina and Australia found the same thing happening there.

"If rear-end crashes do not decline," the San Diego study said, "then the validity of the traffic safety justification should be questioned." A similar study of Sacramento's intersections has never been taken, according to county traffic officials, who say Sheriff Blanas has never asked for one. Given Blanas' position as a national advocate for red-light systems, that might seem like an odd oversight. But Blanas isn't a neutral observer.

He helps direct a self-described "advocacy group" called the National Campaign to Stop Red Light Running. That organization aggressively promotes the sale of red-light-camera systems, which might be expected since it was founded and financed by ACS—specifically, its State and Local solution branch, which sells red-light cameras to government agencies. The ACS executive in charge of that division is former CHP Commissioner Maurice Hannigan.

Chris Galm, an executive with a Washington D.C., public-relations firm that ACS pays to run the right-light campaign, said Blanas was asked to join the campaign's National Advisory Board "because he's such an advocate of red-light cameras." As a board member, Galm said, Blanas "basically provides us our direction for the campaign." Blanas did not respond to questions about his role with the group.

In 2002, with Blanas' name on the inside cover, the campaign issued a slick 44-page promotional brochure extolling the virtues and infallibility of red-light systems and offering hints on how to respond to citizen complaints about them.

Increased rear-end collisions? Nothing to worry about. "That isn't surprising," the brochure sniffed. "The more people stop on red, the more rear-end collisions there will be . . . this appeared to be a temporary effect."

Blanas' group touted red-light systems as "violator-funded" money-makers but warned that some might accuse the government of profiteering. The best way to "overcome the perception that the program is simply a revenue generator for the jurisdiction," the brochure advises, "is to dedicate all or a portion of income to traffic safety, rather than the general fund."

Traffic-court Commissioner Foos, who helps train judges to hear red-light cases, has shown a similar fondness for ACS' wares. In a training manual Foos wrote, he tells judges to give great deference to all the evidence the company (formally called Lockheed Martin) submits. "Lockheed Martin is a reliable and large scientific and business identity and is therefore trustworthy," Foos wrote. "The private entity would not jeopardize their contract by altering the photos or allowing their mishandling. One would have to posses sophisticated equipment to do so."

Jaszewski had an ethical decision to make. He still had five red-light cases to decide, and he'd just gotten a red-light ticket himself.

"I asked some of the other traffic commissioners if I should rule on those cases, and they all laughed about the irony of it," he said. But none said they saw a problem. Jaszewski felt torn. The evidence presented, he knew, required him to find the motorists guilty. But the system that had snared them—and him—was wrong, he believed.

In a written memorandum of decision he mailed to the motorists, Jaszewski essentially apologized for finding them guilty. Sacramento's red light system, he wrote, "fails to satisfy traditional notions of fair enforcement of the law" and its "questionable enforcement methods can only demean the public's trust in and its respect for the law." But "even though doubt exists as to the methods with which the evidence in this case was obtained, I am compelled to accept that evidence."

He then resigned as a traffic-court judge and became a traffic-court defendant. Knowing that the district attorney's office only sends prosecutors to court when a motorist hires an attorney, Jaszewski represented himself. "I didn't want them sending some wiseguy from the DA's office over. I wanted the officer to do it," he said.

His judge turned out to be one of the commissioners he'd gone to for advice. Jaszewski raised the issue of the San Diego decision, the absence of prosecution witnesses and the fact that all the evidence against him was hearsay. The judge found him guilty and sent him off to the fines room.

In his appeal, he raised the issue of the kickbacks to ACS and the fact that the officer's expert testimony came from a pre-printed script. He wasn't questioning the government's right to install red-light cameras, Jaszweski argued. What he was objecting to was the kangaroo-court nature of the trials, calling them "an insult . . . to individual citizens and the legal system itself. In the name of revenue generation and streamlining legal processes, the trial court is routinely allowing time-tested and valuable legal rights to fall forfeit to saving a few minutes of time."

On April 29, 2002, Jaszewski filed his appeal and gave a copy to the district attorney's office. The next day, District Attorney Scully made a surprise announcement. The district attorney's office was halting all prosecutions of red-light traffic tickets because of unspecified "discrepancies between the manual prepared by the system's provider and the actual functioning of the system." More than 1,000 red-light tickets were dismissed, and the cameras were shut down, even though the sheriff's office and ACS insisted they'd been working perfectly. For the city of Sacramento, it was the final straw. Its cameras were turned off. But Blanas stuck by ACS and resumed issuing tickets three months later. In mid-2003, he took over the city's dormant program, as well.

A month before his appeal was to be heard, Jaszewski got a call from the district attorney's office, offering to dismiss his ticket. Jaszewski was suspicious. "I believed they were trying to avoid a decision on the merits, and I'd heard of several other cases where the same thing had happened. People appealed and got their cases dismissed before an appeal hearing. This was the way the DA was dealing with it. So, I declined. I'd written a strong brief, and I wanted to get this looked at by a higher court," he said.

He never got a chance. When his hearing came up, the district attorney's office told the judge that "in the interests of justice," they wanted to drop the ticket, but Jaszweski was being obstinate. The judge, over Jaszewski's objections, dismissed the case, never addressing his legal arguments. The system has protected itself once again.

After Bohl got his ticket, he threw himself into a frenzy of legal research. His wife, Margaret, thought he'd been possessed. He was on the internet constantly. He walked around their house muttering about approach speeds and Caltrans manuals. He'd taken the family video camera out to the intersection and filmed the yellow light changing, returning triumphantly to announce that the light in question was a few milliseconds shorter than the law allowed. He was calling friends, lawyers and people he knew in the media. Surely, he thought, he couldn't be the only person who was outraged by this whole thing.

One day in November 2003, Bohl was doing another internet search, and his browser turned up a week-old newspaper story about Jaszewski's unsuccessful struggle to have his case heard. Bohl had found a kindred spirit. He went to the State Bar of California's website, looked up Jaszewski's law license and got his number from at the State Compensation Insurance Fund, where Jaszewski was now working.

Impressed by his caller's fervor, Jaszewski agreed to help Bohl fight his ticket, but only as an unofficial advisor. "He was a pretty resourceful guy. I didn't have to do much," Jaszewski recalled. "I told him not to tip off the DA's office by hiring a lawyer, object to every piece of evidence that was entered at his trial, and then I faxed him my appeal brief."

Bohl followed Jaszewski's advice to the letter. After losing in traffic court, Bohl took Jaszewski's brief, changed a few dates and names and submitted it as his own. He got what Jaszewski's had been unable to get: a hearing before the appellate division of the Sacramento Superior Court.

Two months ago—more than two years after he got his ticket—Bohl finally got his answer. ACS' camera-maintenance logs were hearsay, a three-judge appellate panel unanimously agreed. They never should have been admitted. All they showed, wrote Judge Maryanne Gilliard, is that someone at some point of time did four minutes of maintenance on some cameras.

"The system appears to involve technology that has not been established as reliable in any published cases," Gilliard wrote. "It is unreasonable, as a matter of law, to assume that logs showing four minutes of weekday maintenance would be all that is necessary to ensure that the system reliably worked." Because no one from ACS bothered to appear at Bohl's trial, she wrote, he'd been deprived the right to cross-examine his accusers. The conviction was reversed, and she ordered the ticket dismissed.

CHP officer McCurry said the decision is meaningless. "That happened two years ago, and we do everything differently now. The contract with ACS has been changed, so they no longer get paid per ticket. We lay a better foundation for the maintenance logs. And the officer who handled that case was a city policeman who really didn't know how to present the case." (According to the trial transcripts, however, McCurry was the prosecuting officer, and the testimony he gave then is no different from the testimony he gives now. Moreover, ACS' contract had no bearing on the court's ruling.)

Private attorneys say the decision means that the prosecutor's office should be bringing ACS field inspectors to court to authenticate the evidence in red-light cases. Doing that, obviously, would increase the costs of the red-light program, so perhaps that's why nothing has changed in the two months since the decision came down.

On a recent Friday in traffic court, for instance, a burly woman in nurse's scrubs asked where the ACS technician was so she could cross-examine him about the cameras. He wasn't available, the judge informed her, because she hadn't subpoenaed him.

"Why is it my job to subpoena their witness?" she asked angrily. "I assumed he'd be here. Since he's not, I want a continuance until he is."

"You had your chance," the judge said and sent her to the fines room.

"This is a racket," she said loudly, storming from the courtroom.

Traffic Commissioner Foos said the appeals-court decision isn't binding on traffic judges but acknowledged that "it would be foolish for a judge not to take a look at it." However, it hasn't changed the way he has decided cases involving the admissibility of the maintenance logs. "In those cases, I think there was additional evidence that overcame the hearsay objections." Foos couldn't recall what that evidence was.

The district attorney's office says it's not too concerned with the Bohl decision, because—like the vast majority of appellate-court decisions—it wasn't ordered published in law books. "Since it's unpublished, it means it can't be cited as a precedent," said Lana Wyant, a spokeswoman for the district attorney's office. Does that mean the attorney's office thinks the judges are wrong about the evidence problems? "I'll have to get back to you on that," Wyant said. She didn't.

Because the case is unpublished doesn't make it invalid. It makes it obscure and hard for defendants to learn about.

One judge who knew of the decision was asked how he could continue to find motorists guilty based on evidence that, according to the appeals court, shouldn't be admitted. "I can't rule on objections that aren't made," the judge said. "People don't object to them."

To cure that problem, attorney Robert Pacuinas was at the courthouse a few days after the Bohl decision came down, handing out copies of it to motorists awaiting trial. The ruling, according to him, was a breakthrough in the war against "the money machine they've set up at the Carol Miller Injustice Center . . . I thought people should know about it since nobody down there was going to tell them."

A deputy district attorney, Richard Clark, and a court administrator approached Pacuinas and told him to stop handing out the opinion or leave the building.

Pacuinas, a former CHP Trooper of the Year, laughed. "I asked them to tell me what law or court rule I was breaking by handing out court opinions at a courthouse," the stocky lawyer said. Unable to think of one, the pair walked off, warning him against "soliciting."

"That's typical of their attitude down there," Pacuinas said. "They don't want motorists knowing they have any rights. They want them to come in, pay the fine and get out." Clark did not return a phone call, and the district attorney's office refused to comment.

Pacuinas' battle against red-light cameras is entering its fourth year; like Bohl, he has become something of a zealot on the issue. Some traffic judges regard him as a pest who stretches out routine cases for hours, even days, backing up the dockets and tying up courtroom personnel. He recently concluded an eight-day red-light trial, lost and promptly filed a 48-page appeal listing 46 separate reasons for reversal.

But he's won more than 20 red-light cases and slowly has forced the courts and the sheriff's office to change the way they run the system. Because of his badgering, defendants no longer are shown a court-produced videotape suggesting red-lights are infallible. And after Pacuinas secretly filmed an ACS technician doing a slapdash job of inspecting and calibrating the camera, Blanas' office was forced to hire a retiree to go out with the techs occasionally and make sure they were doing what their log sheets claimed they had done.

"The thing that pisses me off is that they say it's all about traffic safety," Pacuinas snorted. "It isn't. It's about money. That's why our fines are so high. Fines on the East Coast are $50. Does that mean we care more about traffic safety than New York City? Or do we just care more about taking people's money away from them?"

Afterword

Robert Parry

I first spoke with Gary Webb in 1996 when he was working on his "Dark Alliance" series for the *San Jose Mercury News*. He called me at my home in Arlington, Virginia, because, in 1985, I and my Associated Press (AP) colleague Brian Barger had been the first journalists to reveal the scandal of Ronald Reagan's Nicaraguan Contras, who were funding themselves partly by collaborating with drug traffickers.

Webb explained that he had come across evidence that one Contras-connected drug conduit had funneled cocaine into Los Angeles, where it helped fuel the early crack epidemic. Unlike our AP stories a decade earlier—which focused on the Contras helping to ship cocaine from Central America into the United States—Webb said his series would examine what happened to the Contra cocaine *after* it reached LA.

Besides asking about my recollections of the Contras and their cocaine smuggling, Webb wanted to know why the scandal never gained any real traction in the US national news media. I explained that the ugly facts of the drug trafficking ran up against a determined US government campaign to protect the Contras' image. In the face of that resistance, the major publications—the likes of the *New York Times* and the *Washington Post*—had chosen to attack the revelations and those behind them rather than to dig out more evidence.

Webb sounded confused by my account, as if I were telling him something that was foreign to his personal experience, something that just didn't compute. I had a sense of his unstated questions: Why would the prestige newspapers of American journalism behave that way? Why wouldn't they jump all over a story that important and that sexy, about the CIA working with drug traffickers? I got the impression that he might be judging me to be either a timid journalist who had gotten scared off of a tough story or maybe a conspiracy buff who shared the belief that top news executives collude to control what Americans get to see and read.

I took a deep breath, sensing that he had no idea of the personal danger he was about to confront. Well, he would have to learn that for himself. And it surely wasn't my place to warn a journalist away from a significant story just because it carried risks. So, I simply asked Webb if he had the strong support of his editors. He assured me that he did. I said their backing would be crucial once his story was out. He sounded perplexed, again, as if he didn't know what to make of my cautionary tone. I wished him the best of luck, thinking that he would need it.

When I hung up, I wasn't sure that the *Mercury News* would really press ahead with the story, considering how the big national news outlets had dismissed and ridiculed the notion that President Reagan's beloved Contras had included a large number of drug traffickers. It never seemed to matter how much evidence there was. It was much easier—and safer, career-wise—for Washington journalists to reject testimony from drug traffickers, disgruntled Contras, and even US law-enforcement officials who could be dismissed as overzealous or congressional investigators who could be painted as partisan.

In 1985, as we were preparing our first story on this topic, Barger and I knew that the evidence of Contras cocaine involvement was overwhelming. We had a broad range of sources both inside the Contras movement and within the US government, people with no apparent ax to grind who had described the cocaine-smuggling problem. One source was a field agent for the Drug Enforcement Administration (DEA); another was a senior official on Reagan's National Security Council (NSC) who told me that he had read a Central Intelligence Agency (CIA) report about how a Contras unit based in Costa Rica had used cocaine profits to buy a helicopter.

However, after our AP story was published in December 1985, we came under attack from the right-wing *Washington Times*. That was followed by dismissive stories in the *New York Times* and the *Washington Post*. The notion that the Contras, whom President Reagan had likened to freedom fighters on par with the Founding Fathers, could be implicated in the drug trade was simply unthinkable. It was always odd to me that many of the same newspapers had no problem accepting the fact that the CIA-backed Afghan mujahideen were involved in the heroin trade, but bristled at the thought that the CIA-backed Nicaraguan Contras might be cut from the same cloth.

A key difference, which I learned both from personal experience and from documents that surfaced during the Iran-Contra scandal, was that Reagan had assigned a young group of ambitious intellectuals such as Elliott Abrams and Robert Kagan to oversee the Contras war, who became known as the neo-conservatives. They worked with old-line anticommunists from the Cuban-American community, such as Otto Reich, and CIA propagandists, such as Walter Raymond Jr., to aggressively protect the Contras' image. And, unlike the Afghan rebels who had strong congressional support, the Nicaraguan Contras were always on the edge between getting congressional funding or having it cut off, with many Democrats opposed to the Contras war and many Republicans fighting furiously to secure additional money.

That combination—the propaganda skills of Reagan's Contras support team and the fragile consensus for continuing Reagan's pet Contras war—meant that any negative publicity about the Contras would be met with a fierce counterattack. The neoconservatives were also proving adept at ingratiating themselves with senior editors at major news outlets. They were bright, well-schooled, and facile in their manipulation of language and information, a process they called "perception management."

By the mid-1980s, these patterns had become entrenched in Washington. If a journalist dug up a story that put the Contras in a negative light, he or she could expect the Reagan administration's propaganda team to make contact with a senior editor or bureau chief and lodge a complaint, apply some pressure, and often offer up some dirt about the offending journalist. Also, many news executives in that time frame were sympathetic toward Reagan's hard-line foreign policy, especially after the humiliations of the Vietnam War and the Iranian revolution. Supporting US initiatives abroad—or at least not allowing your reporters to undercut those policies—was seen as patriotic.

At AP, general manager Keith Fuller was known to be a strong Reagan supporter. At the *New York Times*, executive editor Abe Rosenthal was one of the news media's most influential neoconservatives. At the *Washington Post* and *Newsweek* (where I went to work in 1987), there was also a strong sense that Reagan-era scandals should not reach the president. The operative phrase was "we don't want another Watergate," that is, another scandal where investigative journalism might take down another Republican president and thus create even more antimedia anger on the Right. It was considered "good for the country"—a phrase favored by *Newsweek*'s executive editor Maynard Parker—for editors to exercise discretion in handling "scandal" stories that had impeachment potential.

In other words, on the issue of Contras drug trafficking, there was a confluence of interests between the Reagan administration, which was determined to protect the Contras' public image at all costs, and senior news executives, who wanted to adopt a "patriotic" posture after convincing themselves that the country shouldn't endure another wrenching battle over wrongdoing by a Republican president. The popular image of courageous editors standing up for their reporters in the face of government pressure was not the reality, at least not where the Contras were concerned.

So, instead of a process that outsiders might imagine—where journalists who dig out tough stories get rewarded—the actual system worked in the opposite way. There was a steady weeding out of journalists who wouldn't toe the line. The clever careerists in the news business quickly grasped that the smart play when it came to the Contras was either to be a booster or at least to pooh-pooh evidence of the Contras' wanton brutality in the field and especially their moonlighting as drug traffickers.

The same rules applied to congressional investigators. Anyone who pried into the dark corners of the Nicaraguan Contras war faced ridicule, as happened to Democratic Senator John Kerry of Massachusetts when he followed up the AP stories with a courageous investigation that discovered more ties between cocaine traffickers and the Contras. When his report was released in 1989, its findings were greeted with yawns and smirks. News articles were buried deep inside the major newspapers and the stories focused more on alleged flaws in his investigation than on his discoveries about Contras cocaine trafficking.

For his hard work, *Newsweek* summed up the prevailing "conventional wisdom" on Senator Kerry by calling him a "randy conspiracy buff."[1] Being associated with breaking the Contras-cocaine story was also regarded as a major black mark on my own career.

To function in this upside-down world, where reality and perception clashed, the big news outlets developed a kind of cognitive dissonance that accepted two contradictory positions. On one level, the news outlets did accept the undeniable reality that some of the Contras and their backers, including the likes of Panamanian General Manuel Noriega, were implicated in the drug trade, but then simultaneously treated this reality as a conspiracy theory. Only occasionally did a major news outlet seek to square this circle, such as during Noriega's drug-trafficking trial in 1991 when US prosecutors called as a witness Colombian Medellín cartel kingpin Carlos

Lehder, who—along with implicating Noriega—testified that the cartel had given $10 million to the Contras, an allegation first unearthed by Senator Kerry.

"The Kerry hearings didn't get the attention they deserved at the time," a *Washington Post* editorial on November 27, 1991, acknowledged. "The Noriega trial brings this sordid aspect of the Nicaraguan engagement to fresh public attention."[2] However, the *Post* offered its readers no explanation for why Kerry's hearings had been largely ignored, with the *Post* itself a leading culprit in this journalistic misfeasance. Nor did the *Post* and the other leading newspapers use the opening created by the Noriega trial to do anything to rectify their past neglect. And, everything quickly returned to the status quo in which the desired perception of the noble Contras trumped the clear reality of their criminal activities.

So, from 1991 until 1996, the Contras-cocaine scandal remained a disturbing story not just about the skewed moral compass of the Reagan administration but also about how the US news media had lost its way. The scandal was a dirty secret that was best kept out of public view and away from a thorough discussion. After all, the journalistic careerists who had played along with the US government's Contras defenders had advanced inside their media corporations. As good team players, they had moved up to be bureau chiefs and other news executives. They had no interest in revisiting one of the big stories that they had downplayed as a prerequisite for their success.

Meanwhile, those journalists who had exposed these national security crimes mostly saw their careers sink or at best slide sideways. We were regarded as "pariahs" in our profession. We were "conspiracy theorists," even though our journalism had proven to be correct again and again. The *Post*'s admission that the Contras-cocaine scandal "didn't get the attention it deserved" didn't lead to any soul-searching inside the US news media, nor did it result in any rehabilitation of the careers of the reporters who had tried to put a spotlight on this especially vile secret.

As for me, after losing battle after battle with my *Newsweek* editors (who despised the Iran-Contra scandal that I had worked so hard to expose), I departed the magazine in June 1990 to write a book (called *Fooling America*) about the decline of the Washington press corps and the parallel rise of the new generation of government propagandists. I was also hired by PBS *Frontline* to investigate whether there had been a prequel to the

Iran-Contra scandal—whether those arms-for-hostage deals in the mid-1980s had been preceded by contacts between Reagan's 1980 campaign staff and Iran, which was then holding fifty-two Americans hostage and essentially destroying Jimmy Carter's reelection hopes.[3]

In 1995, frustrated by the pervasive triviality that had come to define American journalism—and acting on the advice and with the assistance of my oldest son Sam—I turned to a new medium and launched the internet's first investigative news magazine, known as *Consortium-News.com*. The website became a way for me to put out well-reported stories that my former mainstream colleagues seemed determined to ignore or mock.

So, when Gary Webb called me that day in 1996, I knew that he was charging into some dangerous journalistic terrain, though he thought he was simply pursuing a great story. After his call, it struck me that perhaps the only way for the Contras-cocaine story to ever get the attention that it deserved was for someone outside the Washington media culture to do the work.

When Webb's "Dark Alliance" series finally appeared in late August 1996, it initially drew little attention. The major national news outlets applied their usual studied indifference to a topic that they had already judged unworthy of serious attention. It was also clear that the media careerists who had climbed up their corporate ladders by accepting the conventional wisdom that the Contras-cocaine story was a conspiracy theory weren't about to look back down and admit that they had contributed to a major journalistic failure to inform and protect the American public.

But Webb's story proved hard to ignore. First, unlike the work that Barger and I did for AP back in the mid-1980s, Webb's series wasn't just a story about drug traffickers in Central America and their protectors in Washington. It was about the on-the-ground consequences, inside the United States, of that drug trafficking, how the lives of Americans were blighted and destroyed as the collateral damage of a US foreign policy initiative. In other words, there were real-life American victims, and they were concentrated in African-American communities. That meant the ever-sensitive issue of race had been injected into the controversy. Anger from black communities spread quickly to the Congressional Black Caucus, which started demanding answers.

Secondly, the *San Jose Mercury News*, which was the local newspaper for

Silicon Valley, had posted documents and audio on its state-of-the-art internet site. That way, readers could examine much of the documentary support for the series. It also meant that the traditional "gatekeeper" role of the major newspapers—the *New York Times*, the *Washington Post*, and the *Los Angeles Times*—was under assault. If a regional paper like the *Mercury News* could finance a major journalistic investigation like this one, and circumvent the judgments of the editorial boards at the Big Three, then there might be a tectonic shift in the power relations of the US news media. There was something revolutionary about this breakdown of the established order.

This combination of factors led to the next phase of the Contras-cocaine battle, the counterattack. However, the first major shot against Webb and his "Dark Alliance" series did not come from the Big Three but from the rapidly expanding right-wing news media, which was in no mood to accept the notion that some of President Reagan's beloved Contras were drug traffickers. That recognition also would have cast a shadow over the Reagan Legacy, which the Right was busy elevating into mythic status.

It fell to Reverend Sun Myung Moon's right-wing *Washington Times* to begin the vendetta. Moon, a South Korean theocrat who fancied himself the new Messiah, had founded his newspaper in 1982 partly to protect Ronald Reagan's political flanks and partly to ensure that he had powerful friends in high places. In the so-called "Koreagate" scandal of the late 1970s, Moon's religious cult had been exposed as a money-laundering front for South Korean intelligence and other corrupt right-wing political forces in Asia (including some elements of organized crime).

As a result, Moon had been convicted of tax evasion and spent time in federal prison. He was determined to prevent a recurrence of those investigations and thus began pouring what came to total several billion dollars of his mysterious money into the *Washington Times*, creating a propaganda bulwark for the Republican Party and guaranteeing himself a phalanx of powerful defenders. In the mid-1980s, the *Washington Times* even raised money to assist Reagan's Contras "freedom fighters."

To refute Webb's three-part series, the *Washington Times* turned to some ex-CIA officials, who had participated in the Contras war, and quoted them denying the story. Soon, the *Washington Post*, the *New York Times*, and the *Los Angeles Times* were lining up behind the *Washington Times* to trash Webb and his story. On October 4, 1996, the *Washington Post* published a front-page article knocking down Webb's series, although acknowledging that some Contras operatives did help the cocaine cartels.

The *Post*'s approach was twofold, fitting with the national media's cognitive dissonance on the topic of Contras cocaine: first, the *Post* presented the Contras-cocaine allegations as old news—"even CIA personnel testified to Congress they knew that those covert operations involved drug traffickers," the *Post* sniffed—and second, the *Post* minimized the importance of the one Contras smuggling channel that Webb had highlighted in his series, saying that it had not "played a major role in the emergence of crack." A *Post* sidebar story also dismissed African-Americans as prone to "conspiracy fears."

Next, the *New York Times* and the *Los Angeles Times* weighed in with lengthy articles castigating Webb and "Dark Alliance." The big newspapers made much of the CIA's internal reviews in 1987 and 1988—almost a decade earlier—that supposedly had cleared the spy agency of any role in Contras-cocaine smuggling. But the CIA's cover-up began to weaken on October 24, 1996, when CIA Inspector General Frederick Hitz conceded before the Senate Intelligence Committee that the first CIA probe had lasted only twelve days, and the second only three days. He promised a more thorough review.

Webb, however, had already crossed over from being a serious journalist to a target of ridicule. Influential *Post* media critic Howard Kurtz mocked Webb for saying in a book proposal that he would explore the possibility that the Contras war was primarily a business to its participants. "Oliver Stone, check your voice mail," Kurtz chortled.[4]

However, Webb's suspicion was no conspiracy theory. Indeed, White House aide Oliver North's chief Contras emissary, Robert Owen, had made the same point in a March 17, 1986, message about the Contras leadership. "Few of the so-called leaders of the movement . . . really care about the boys in the field," Owen wrote. "THIS WAR HAS BECOME A BUSINESS TO MANY OF THEM."[5]

In other words, Webb was right and Kurtz was wrong. But accuracy had ceased to be relevant in the media's hazing of Gary Webb. While Webb was held to the strictest standards of journalism, it was entirely all right for Kurtz—the supposed arbiter of journalistic integrity who was also featured on CNN's *Reliable Sources*—to make judgments based on ignorance. Kurtz would face no repercussions for mocking a fellow journalist who was factually correct.

The Big Three's assault—combined with their disparaging tone—had a predictable effect on the executives of the *Mercury News*. Clearly, Webb's confidence in his editors had been misplaced. By early 1997, executive editor Jerry Ceppos, who had his own corporate career to worry about, was in retreat. On May 11, 1997, Ceppos published a front-page column saying the series "fell short of my standards." He criticized the stories because they "strongly implied CIA knowledge" of Contras connections to US drug dealers who were manufacturing crack cocaine. "We did not have enough proof that top CIA officials knew of the relationship," Ceppos wrote.[6]

Ceppos was wrong about the proof, of course. At AP, before we published our first Contras-cocaine article in 1985, Barger and I had known that the CIA and Reagan's White House were aware of the Contras-cocaine problem. However, Ceppos was right in a more cynical fashion. He was recognizing that he and his newspaper were facing a credibility crisis brought on by the harsh consensus delivered by the Big Three, a judgment that had quickly solidified into conventional wisdom throughout the major news media and inside Knight-Ridder, Inc., which owned the *Mercury News*. The only career-saving move, career-saving for Ceppos even if career-destroying for Webb, was to jettison Webb and his journalism.

The big newspapers and the Contras defenders celebrated Ceppos's retreat as vindication of their own dismissal of the Contras-cocaine stories. Ceppos next pulled the plug on the *Mercury News*' continuing Contras-cocaine investigation and reassigned Webb to a small office in Cupertino, California, far from his family. Webb resigned from the paper in disgrace. For undercutting Webb and other *Mercury News* reporters working on the Contras investigation, Ceppos was lauded by the *American Journalism Review* and was given the 1997 national Ethics in Journalism Award by the Society of Professional Journalists.

While Ceppos won raves, Webb watched his career collapse and his marriage break up. Still, Gary Webb had set in motion internal government investigations that would bring to the surface long-hidden facts about how the Reagan administration had conducted the Contras war.

The CIA published the first part of Inspector General Hitz's findings on January 29, 1998. Though the CIA's press release for the report criticized Webb and defended the CIA, Hitz's *Volume One* admitted that not only were many of Webb's allegations true but that he actually understated the seriousness of the Contras-drug crimes and the CIA's knowledge of them. Hitz acknowledged that cocaine smugglers played a significant early role in the Contras movement and that the CIA intervened to block an image-threatening 1984 federal investigation into a San Francisco–based drug ring with suspected ties to the Contras, the so-called "Frogman Case."

After Volume One was released, I called Webb (whom I had met personally since his series was published). I chided him for indeed getting the story "wrong." He had understated how serious the problem of Contras-cocaine trafficking had been. It was a form of gallows humor for the two of us, since nothing had changed in the way the major newspapers treated the Contras-cocaine issue. They focused only on the press release that continued to attack Webb, while ignoring the incriminating information that could be found in the body of the report. All I could do was highlight those admissions at *ConsortiumNews.com*, which sadly had a much, much smaller readership than the Big Three.

The major US news media also looked the other way on other startling disclosures. On May 7, 1998, for instance, Representative Maxine Waters, a California Democrat, introduced into the Congressional Record a February 11, 1982, letter of understanding between the CIA and the Justice Department. The letter, which had been requested by CIA Director William Casey, freed the CIA from legal requirements that it must report drug smuggling by CIA assets, a provision that covered both the Nicaraguan Contras and the Afghan mujahideen. In other words, early in those two covert wars, the CIA leadership wanted to make sure that its geopolitical objectives would not be complicated by a legal requirement to turn in its client forces for drug trafficking.

The next break in the long-running Contras-cocaine cover-up was a report by the Justice Department's Inspector General Michael Bromwich. Given the hostile climate surrounding Webb's series, Bromwich's report also opened with criticism of Webb. But, like the CIA's *Volume One*, the contents revealed new details about government wrongdoing. According to evidence cited by Bromwich, the Reagan administration knew almost from the outset of the Contras war that cocaine traffickers permeated the paramilitary operation. The administration also did next to nothing to expose or stop the crimes.

Bromwich's report revealed example after example of leads not followed, corroborated witnesses disparaged, official law-enforcement investigations sabotaged, and even the CIA facilitating the work of drug traffickers. The report showed that the Contras and their supporters ran several parallel drug-smuggling operations, not just the one at the center of Webb's series. The report also found that the CIA shared little of its information about Contras drugs with law-enforcement agencies and on three occasions disrupted cocaine-trafficking investigations that threatened the Contras.

As well as depicting a more widespread Contras-drug operation than Webb had understood, the Justice Department report provided some important corroboration about a Nicaraguan drug smuggler, Norwin Meneses, who was a key figure in Webb's series. Bromwich cited US government informants who supplied detailed information about Meneses's drug operation and his financial assistance to the Contras. For instance, Renato Pena, a money-and-drug courier for Meneses, said that in the early 1980s the CIA allowed the Contras to fly drugs into the United States, sell them, and keep the proceeds. Pena, who was the northern California representative for the CIA-backed Nicaraguan Democratic Force (FDN) Contras army, said the drug trafficking was forced on the Contras by the inadequate levels of US government assistance.

The Justice Department report also disclosed repeated examples of the CIA and US embassies in Central America discouraging DEA investigations, including one into Contras-cocaine shipments moving through the international airport in El Salvador. Inspector General Bromwich said secrecy trumped all. "We have no doubt that the CIA and the US Embassy were not anxious for the DEA to pursue its investigation at the airport," he wrote. Despite these new disclosures, the big newspapers still showed no inclination to read beyond the criticism of Webb in the press release and the executive summary.

By fall 1998, Washington was obsessed with President Bill Clinton's Monica Lewinsky sex scandal, which made it easier to ignore even more stunning Contras-cocaine disclosures in the CIA's *Volume Two*. In *Volume Two*, published on October 8, 1998, CIA Inspector General Hitz identified more than fifty Contras and Contras-related entities implicated in the drug trade. He also detailed how the Reagan administration had protected these drug operations and frustrated federal investigations throughout the 1980s.

According to *Volume Two*, the CIA knew the criminal nature of its Contras clients from the start of the war against Nicaragua's leftist Sandinista government. The earliest Contras force, called the Nicaraguan Revolutionary Democratic Alliance (ADREN) or the 15th of September Legion, had chosen "to stoop to criminal activities in order to feed and clothe their cadre," according to a June 1981 draft of a CIA field report. According to a September 1981 cable to CIA headquarters, two ADREN members made the first delivery of drugs to Miami in July 1981. ADREN's leaders included Enrique Bermúdez and other early Contras who would later direct the major Contras army, the CIA-organized FDN, which was based in Honduras, along Nicaragua's northern border. Throughout the war, Bermúdez remained the top Contras military commander. The CIA later corroborated the allegations about ADREN's cocaine trafficking, but insisted that Bermúdez had opposed the drug shipments to the United States that went ahead nonetheless.

The truth about Bermúdez's supposed objections to drug trafficking, however, was less clear. According to Hitz's *Volume One*, Bermúdez enlisted Norwin Meneses, a large-scale Nicaraguan cocaine smuggler and a key figure in Webb's series, to raise money and buy supplies for the Contras. *Volume One* had quoted a Meneses associate, another Nicaraguan trafficker named Danilo Blandón, who told Hitz's investigators that he and Meneses flew to Honduras to meet with Bermúdez in 1982.

At the time, Meneses's criminal activities were well-known in the Nicaraguan exile community. But Bermúdez told the cocaine smugglers that "the ends justify the means" in raising money for the Contras. After the Bermúdez meeting, Contras soldiers helped Meneses and Blandón get past Honduran police who briefly arrested them on drug-trafficking suspicions. After their release, Blandón and Meneses traveled on to Bolivia to complete a cocaine transaction.

There were other indications of Bermúdez's drug-smuggling tolerance. In February 1988, another Nicaraguan exile linked to the drug trade accused Bermúdez of participation in narcotics trafficking, according to Hitz's report. After the Contras war ended, Bermúdez returned to Managua, Nicaragua, where he was shot to death on February 16, 1991. The murder has never been solved.

Along the Southern Front, the Contras' military operations in Costa Rica, on Nicaragua's southern border, the CIA's drug evidence centered on the forces of Edén Pastora, another top Contras commander. But Hitz discovered that the US government may have made the drug situation worse, not better. Hitz revealed that the CIA put an admitted drug operative—known by his CIA pseudonym "Ivan Gomez"—in a supervisory position over Pastora. Hitz reported that the CIA discovered Gomez's drug history in 1987 when Gomez failed a security review on drug-trafficking questions.

In internal CIA interviews, Gomez admitted that in March or April 1982, he helped family members who were engaged in drug trafficking and money laundering. In one case, Gomez said he assisted his brother and brother-in-law in transporting cash from New York City to Miami. He admitted that he "knew this act was illegal."[7] Later, Gomez expanded on his admission, describing how his family members had fallen $2 million into debt and had gone to Miami to run a money-laundering center for drug traffickers. Gomez said "his brother had many visitors whom [Gomez] assumed to be in the drug trafficking business."[8]

Gomez's brother was arrested on drug charges in June 1982. Three months later, in September 1982, Gomez started his CIA assignment in Costa Rica. Years later, convicted drug trafficker Carlos Cabezas alleged that in the early 1980s, Ivan Gomez was the CIA agent in Costa Rica who was overseeing drug-money donations to the Contras. Gomez "was to make sure the money was given to the right people [the Contras] and nobody was taking . . . profit they weren't supposed to," Cabezas stated publicly.[9]

But the CIA sought to discredit Cabezas at the time because he had trouble identifying Gomez's picture and put Gomez at one meeting in early 1982 before Gomez started his CIA assignment. While the CIA was able to fend off Cabezas's allegations by pointing to these discrepancies, Hitz's report revealed that the CIA was nevertheless aware of Gomez's direct role in drug-money laundering, a fact the agency hid from Senator Kerry in his 1987 investigation.

There was also more to know about Gomez. In November 1985, the FBI learned from an informant that Gomez's two brothers had been large-scale cocaine importers, with one brother arranging shipments from Bolivia's infamous drug kingpin Roberto Suarez. Suarez already was known as a financier of right-wing causes. In 1980, with the support of Argentina's hard-line anticommunist military regime, Suarez bankrolled a coup in Bolivia that ousted the elected left-of-center government. The violent putsch became known as the Cocaine Coup because it made Bolivia the region's first narco-state. Bolivia's government-protected cocaine shipments helped transform Colombia's Medellín cartel from a struggling local operation into a giant corporate-style business for delivering cocaine to the US market.

Flush with cash in the early 1980s, Suarez invested more than $30 million in various right-wing paramilitary operations, including the Contras forces in Central America, according to US Senate testimony by an Argentine intelligence officer, Leonardo Sanchez-Reisse. In 1987, Sanchez-Reisse said the Suarez drug money was laundered through front companies in Miami before going to Central America. There, other Argentine intelligence officers—veterans of the Bolivian coup—trained the Contras in the early 1980s, even before the CIA arrived to first assist with the training and later take over the Contras operation from the Argentines.

Inspector General Hitz added another piece to the mystery of the Bolivian-Contras connection. One Contras fund-raiser, Jose Orlando Bolanos, boasted that the Argentine government was supporting his Contras activities, according to a May 1982 cable to CIA headquarters. Bolanos made the statement during a meeting with undercover DEA agents in Florida. He even offered to introduce them to his Bolivian cocaine supplier.

Despite all this suspicious drug activity centered around Ivan Gomez and the Contras, the CIA insisted that it did not unmask Gomez until 1987, when he failed a security check and confessed his role in his family's drug business. The CIA official who interviewed Gomez concluded that "Gomez directly participated in illegal drug transactions, concealed participation in illegal drug transactions, and concealed information about involvement in illegal drug activity," Hitz wrote.[10]

But senior CIA officials still protected Gomez. They refused to refer the Gomez case to the Justice Department, citing the 1982 agreement that spared the CIA from a legal obligation to report narcotics crimes by people collaborating with the CIA who were not formal agency employees— Gomez was an independent contractor who worked for the CIA but was not officially on staff. The CIA eased Gomez out of the agency in February 1988, without alerting law enforcement or the congressional oversight committees.

When questioned about the case nearly a decade later, one senior CIA official who had supported the gentle treatment of Gomez had second thoughts. "It is a striking commentary on me and everyone that this guy's involvement in narcotics didn't weigh more heavily on me or the system," the official acknowledged to Hitz's investigators.[11]

A Medellín drug connection arose in another section of Hitz's report, when he revealed evidence suggesting that some Contras trafficking may have been sanctioned by Reagan's NSC. The protagonist for this part of the Contras-cocaine mystery was Moises Nunez, a Cuban-American who worked for Oliver North's NSC Contras support operation and for two drug-connected seafood importers, Ocean Hunter in Miami and Frigorificos De Puntarenas in Costa Rica. Frigorificos De Puntarenas was created in the early 1980s as a cover for drug-money laundering, according to sworn testimony by two of the firm's principals—Carlos Soto and Medellín cartel accountant Ramon Milian Rodriguez.

Drug allegations were swirling around Moises Nunez by the mid-1980s. Indeed, his operation was one of the targets of my and Barger's AP investigation in 1985. Finally reacting to these suspicions, the CIA questioned Nunez about his alleged cocaine trafficking on March 25, 1987. He responded by pointing the finger at his NSC superiors.

"Nunez revealed that since 1985, he had engaged in a clandestine relationship with the National Security Council," Hitz reported, adding: "Nunez refused to elaborate on the nature of these actions, but indicated it was difficult to answer questions relating to his involvement in narcotics trafficking because of the specific tasks he had performed at the direction of the NSC. Nunez refused to identify the NSC officials with whom he had been involved."[12] After this first round of questioning, CIA headquarters authorized an additional session, but then senior CIA officials reversed the decision. There would be no further efforts at "debriefing Nunez."

Hitz noted that "the cable [from headquarters] offered no explanation for the decision"[13] to stop the Nunez interrogation. But the CIA's Central American Task Force chief Alan Fiers Jr. said the Nunez-NSC drug lead was not pursued "because of the NSC connection and the possibility that this could be somehow connected to the Private Benefactor program [the Contras money handled by North] a decision was made not to pursue this matter."[14]

Joseph Fernandez, who had been the CIA's station chief in Costa Rica, confirmed to congressional Iran-Contra investigators that Nunez "was involved in a very sensitive operation" for North's "Enterprise."[15] The exact nature of that NSC-authorized activity has never been divulged. At the time of the Nunez-NSC drug admissions and his truncated interrogation, the CIA's acting director was Robert Gates, who nearly two decades later became President George W. Bush's second secretary of defense, a position he has retained under President Barack Obama.

The CIA also worked directly with other drug-connected Cuban-Americans on the Contras project, Hitz found. One of Nunez's Cuban-American associates, Felipe Vidal, had a criminal record as a narcotics trafficker in the 1970s. But the CIA still hired him to serve as a logistics coordinator for the Contras, Hitz reported. The CIA also learned that Vidal's drug connections were not only in the past. A December 1984 cable to CIA headquarters revealed Vidal's ties to Rene Corvo, another Cuban-American suspected of drug trafficking. Corvo was working with Cuban anticommunist Frank Castro, who was viewed as a Medellín cartel representative within the Contras movement.

There were other narcotics links to Vidal. In January 1986, the DEA in Miami seized 414 pounds of cocaine concealed in a shipment of yucca that was going from a Contras operative in Costa Rica to Ocean Hunter, the company where Vidal (and Moises Nunez) worked. Despite the evidence, Vidal remained a CIA employee as he collaborated with Frank Castro's assistant, Rene Corvo, in raising money for the Contras, according to a CIA memo in June 1986.

By fall 1986, Senator Kerry had heard enough rumors about Vidal to demand information about him as part of his congressional inquiry into Contras drugs. But the CIA withheld the derogatory information. On October 15, 1986, Kerry received a briefing from the CIA's Alan Fiers Jr., who didn't mention Vidal's drug arrests and conviction in the 1970s.

But Vidal was not yet in the clear. In 1987, the US Attorney's Office in Miami began investigating Vidal, Ocean Hunter, and other Contras-connected entities. This prosecutorial attention worried the CIA. The CIA's Latin American division felt it was time for a security review of Vidal. But on August 5, 1987, the CIA's security office blocked the review for fear that the Vidal drug information "could be exposed during any future litigation."

As expected, the US Attorney's Office did request documents about "Contra-related activities" by Vidal, Ocean Hunter, and sixteen other entities. The CIA advised the prosecutor that "no information had been found regarding Ocean Hunter,"[16] a statement that was clearly false. The CIA continued Vidal's employment as an adviser to the Contras movement until 1990, virtually the end of the Contras war.

Hitz also revealed that drugs tainted the highest levels of the Honduran-based FDN, the largest Contras army. Hitz found that Juan Rivas, a Contras commander who rose to be chief of staff, admitted that he had been a cocaine trafficker in Colombia before the war. The CIA asked Rivas, known as El Quiche, about his background after the DEA began suspecting that Rivas might be an escaped convict from a Colombian prison. In interviews with CIA officers, Rivas acknowledged that he had been arrested and convicted of packaging and transporting cocaine for the drug trade in Barranquilla, Colombia. After several months in prison, Rivas said, he escaped and moved to Central America, where he joined the Contras.

Defending Rivas, CIA officials insisted that there was no evidence that Rivas engaged in trafficking while with the Contras. But one CIA cable noted that he lived an expensive lifestyle, even keeping a $100,000 Thoroughbred horse at the Contras camp. Contras military commander Bermúdez later attributed Rivas's wealth to his ex-girlfriend's rich family. But a CIA cable in March 1989 added that "some in the FDN may have suspected at the time that the father-in-law was engaged in drug trafficking."[17]

Still, the CIA moved quickly to protect Rivas from exposure and possible extradition to Colombia. In February 1989, CIA headquarters asked that the DEA take no action "in view of the serious political damage to the US Government that could occur should the information about Rivas become public."[18] Rivas was eased out of the Contras leadership with an explanation of poor health. With US government help, he was allowed to resettle in Miami. Colombia was not informed about his fugitive status.

Another senior FDN official implicated in the drug trade was its chief spokesman in Honduras, Arnoldo Jose "Frank" Arana. The drug allegations against Arana dated back to 1983 when a federal narcotics task force put him under criminal investigation because of plans "to smuggle 100 kilograms of cocaine into the United States from South America."[19] On January 23, 1986, the FBI reported that Arana and his brothers were involved in a drug-smuggling enterprise, although Arana was not charged.

Arana sought to clear up another set of drug suspicions in 1989 by visiting the DEA in Honduras with a business associate, Jose Perez. Arana's association with Perez, however, only raised new alarms. If "Arana is mixed up with the Perez brothers, he is probably dirty," the DEA said. Through their ownership of an air services company called SETCO, the Perez brothers were associated with Juan Matta-Ballesteros, a major cocaine kingpin connected to the murder of a DEA agent, according to reports by the DEA and US Customs and Border Protection. Hitz reported that someone at the CIA scribbled a note on a DEA cable about Arana stating: "Arnold Arana . . . still active and working, we [CIA] may have a problem."[20]

Despite its drug ties to Matta-Ballesteros, SETCO emerged as the principal company for ferrying supplies to the Contras in Honduras. During congressional Iran-Contra hearings, FDN political leader Adolfo Calero testified that SETCO was paid from bank accounts controlled by Oliver North. SETCO also received $185,924 from the State Department for ferrying supplies to the Contras in 1986. Furthermore, Hitz found that other air transport companies used by the Contras were implicated in the cocaine trade as well.

Even FDN leaders suspected that they were shipping supplies to Central America aboard planes that might be returning with drugs. Mario Calero, the chief of Contras logistics, grew so uneasy about one air freight company that he notified US law enforcement that the FDN only chartered the planes for the flights south, not the return flights north.

Hitz found that some drug pilots simply rotated from one sector of the Contras operation to another. Donaldo Frixone, who had a drug record in the Dominican Republic, was hired by the CIA to fly Contras missions from 1983 to 1985. In September 1986, however, Frixone was implicated in smuggling 19,000 pounds of marijuana into the United States. In late 1986 or early 1987, he went to work for Vortex, another US-paid Contras supply company linked to the drug trade.

By the time that Hitz's *Volume Two* was published in fall 1998, the CIA's defense against Webb's series had shrunk to a fig leaf: that the CIA did not *conspire* with the Contras to raise money through cocaine trafficking. But Hitz made clear that the Contras war took precedence over law enforcement and that the CIA withheld evidence of Contras crimes from the Justice Department, Congress, and even the CIA's own analytical division.

Besides tracing the evidence of Contras drug trafficking through the decade-long Contras war, the inspector general interviewed senior CIA officers who acknowledged that they were aware of the Contras-drug problem but didn't want its exposure to undermine the struggle to overthrow Nicaragua's leftist Sandinista government.

According to Hitz, the CIA had "one overriding priority: to oust the Sandinista government. . . . [CIA officers] were determined that the various difficulties they encountered not be allowed to prevent effective implementation of the Contra program."[21] One CIA field officer explained, "The focus was to get the job done, get the support and win the war."[22]

Hitz also recounted complaints from CIA analysts that CIA operations officers handling the Contras hid evidence of Contras drug trafficking even from the CIA's analysts. Because of the withheld evidence, the CIA analysts incorrectly concluded in the mid-1980s that "only a handful of Contras might have been involved in drug trafficking."[23] That false assessment was passed on to Congress and the major news organizations—serving as an important basis for denouncing Gary Webb and his "Dark Alliance" series in 1996.[24]

Although Hitz's report was an extraordinary admission of institutional guilt by the CIA, it went almost unnoticed by the big American newspapers. On October 10, 1998, two days after Hitz's *Volume Two* was posted on the CIA's website, the *New York Times* published a brief article that continued to deride Webb but acknowledged the Contras-drug problem may have been worse than earlier understood. Several weeks later, the *Washington Post* weighed in with a similarly superficial article. The *Los Angeles Times* never published a story on the release of Hitz's Volume Two.

In 2000, the House Intelligence Committee grudgingly acknowledged that the stories about Reagan's CIA protecting Contras drug traffickers were true. The committee released a report citing classified testimony from CIA Inspector General Britt Snider (Hitz's successor) admitting that the spy agency had turned a blind eye to evidence of Contras drug smuggling and generally treated drug smuggling through Central America as a low priority. "In the end the objective of unseating the Sandinistas appears to have taken precedence over dealing properly with potentially serious allegations against those with whom the agency was working," Snider said, adding that the CIA did not treat the drug allegations in "a consistent, reasoned or justifiable manner."[25]

The House committee—then controlled by Republicans—still downplayed the significance of the Contras-cocaine scandal, but the panel acknowledged, deep inside its report, that in some cases, "CIA employees did nothing to verify or disprove drug trafficking information, even when they had the opportunity to do so. In some of these, receipt of a drug allegation appeared to provoke no specific response, and business went on as usual." Like the release of Hitz's report in 1998, the admissions by Snider and the House committee drew virtually no media attention in 2000—except for a few articles on the internet, including one at *ConsortiumNews.com.*

Because of this misuse of power by the Big Three newspapers—choosing to conceal their own journalistic failings regarding the Contras-cocaine scandal and to protect the Reagan administration's image—Webb's reputation was never rehabilitated.

After his original "Dark Alliance" series was published in 1996, Webb had been inundated with attractive book offers from major publishing houses, but once the vilification began, the interest evaporated. Webb's agent contacted an independent publishing house, Seven Stories Press, which had a reputation for publishing books that had been censored, and it took on the project. After *Dark Alliance: The CIA, the Contras, and the Crack Cocaine Explosion* was published in 1998, I joined Webb in a few speaking appearances on the West Coast, including one packed book talk at the Midnight Special bookstore in Santa Monica, California. For a time, Webb was treated as a celebrity on the American Left, but that gradually faded.

In our interactions during these joint appearances, I found Webb to be a regular guy who seemed to be holding up fairly well under the terrible pressure. He had landed an investigative job with a California state legislative committee. He also felt some measure of vindication when CIA Inspector General Hitz's reports came out.[26] However, Webb never could overcome the pain caused by his betrayal at the hands of his journalistic colleagues, his peers.

In the years that followed, Webb was unable to find decent-paying work in his profession—the conventional wisdom remained that he had somehow been exposed as a journalistic fraud. His state job ended; his marriage fell apart; he struggled to pay bills; and he was faced with a move out of a modest rental house near Sacramento, California.

On December 9, 2004, the forty-nine-year-old Webb typed out suicide notes to his ex-wife and his three children; laid out a certificate for his cremation; and taped a note on the door telling movers—who were coming the next morning—to instead call 911. Webb then took out his father's pistol and shot himself in the head. The first shot was not lethal, so he fired once more.

Even with Webb's death, the big newspapers that had played key roles in his destruction couldn't bring themselves to show Webb any mercy. After

Webb's body was found, I received a call from a reporter for the *Los Angeles Times* who knew that I was one of Webb's few journalistic colleagues who had defended him and his work.

I told the reporter that American history owed a great debt to Gary Webb because he had forced out important facts about Reagan-era crimes. But I added that the *Los Angeles Times* would be hard-pressed to write an honest obituary because the newspaper had not published a single word on the contents of Hitz's final report, which had largely vindicated Webb. To my disappointment but not my surprise, I was correct. The *Los Angeles Times* ran a mean-spirited obituary that made no mention of either my defense of Webb, nor the CIA's admissions in 1998. The obituary was republished in other newspapers, including the *Washington Post*.

In effect, Webb's suicide enabled senior editors at the Big Three newspapers to breathe a little easier—one of the few people who understood the ugly story of the Reagan administration's cover-up of the Contras-cocaine scandal and the US media's complicity was now silenced.

To this day, none of the journalists or media critics who participated in the destruction of Gary Webb has paid a price for their actions. On the contrary, many were rewarded with professional advancement. None of them have faced the sort of humiliation that Webb had to endure. None have had to experience that special pain of standing up for what is best in the profession of journalism—taking on a difficult story that seeks to hold powerful people accountable for serious crimes—and then being vilified by your own colleagues, the people that you expected to understand and appreciate what you had done.

Instead of any justice, the tragic saga of Gary Webb has remained one of the US news media's dirty little secrets.

NOTES

1. As quoted in Robert Parry, "Contra-Crack Story Assailed," *ConsortiumNews.com*, October 28, 1996, http://www.consortiumnews.com/archive/crack2.html (accessed November 1, 2010).
2. Editorial, "The Contras and the Cartel," *Washington Post*, November 27, 1991, http://pqasb.pqarchiver.com/washingtonpost/access/74754368.html?FMT=ABS&FMTS=ABS:FT&date=Nov+27%2C+1991&author=&pub=The+Washington+Post+%28pre-1997+Fulltext%29&edition=&startpage=a.16&desc=The+Contras+and+the+Cartel (accessed November 1, 2010).
3. For more on this topic, see Robert Parry, *Secrecy & Privilege: Rise of the Bush Dynasty from Watergate to Iraq* (Arlington, VA: The Media Consortium, 2004).

4. Howard Kurtz, "Time Lets Writer Run Interference," *Washington Post*, October 28, 1996, http://pqasb.pqarchiver.com/washingtonpost/access/21930757.html?FMT=ABS&FMTS=ABS:FT&date=Oct+28%2C+1996&author=Howard+Kurtz&pub=The+Washington+Post+%28pre-1997+Fulltext%29&edition=&startpage=D.01&desc=Time+Lets+Writer+Run+Interference (accessed November 1, 2010).

5. Memo from Robert Owen to Oliver North, as quoted by Stephen Engelberg, "In Public, Praise for Contras; In Private, a Darker U. S. View," *New York Times*, May 21, 1987, http://www.nytimes.com/1987/05/21/world/in-public-praise-for-contras-in-private-a-darker-us-view.html; and Douglas Foster, "Ollie And His Friends," *Mother Jones* (August/September 1987) 8, http://books.google.com/books?id=ROcDAAAAMBAJ&lpg=PP10&ots=3kg3fvZejb&dq=robert%20owen%20%22this%20war%20has%20become%20a%20business%20to%20many%20of%20them%22&pg=PP10#v=onepage&q=robert%20owen%20%22this%20war%20has%20become%20a%20business%20to%20many%20of%20them%22&f=false (accessed November 1, 2010). Emphasis in the original.

6. Todd S. Purdum, "Expose on Crack Was Flawed," *New York Times*, May 13, 1997, http://www.nytimes.com/books/98/09/27/specials/cia-flawed.html (accessed November 1, 2010). Summary available at Central Intelligence Agency, Reports, "Introduction: the California Story," https://www.cia.gov/library/reports/general-reports-1/cocaine/report/intro.html (accessed November 1, 2010).

7. Central Intelligence Agency, *Allegations of Connections Between CIA and the Contras in Cocaine Trafficking to the United States. 96-0143-IG. Volume II: The Contra Story* (issued as a classified report on April 27, 1998; declassified October 8, 1998) paragraph 673, http://www.namebase.org/hitz.html (accessed November 1, 2010).

8. Ibid., para. 674.

9. Ibid., para. 678.

10. Ibid., para. 675.

11. Ibid., para. 711.

12. Ibid., para. 490.

13. Ibid., para. 491.

14. Ibid., para. 494.

15. As reported in Robert Parry, "Why Journalist Gary Webb Died," *ConsortiumNews.com*, December 9, 2009, http://www.consortiumnews.com/2009/120909.html (accessed November 1, 2010).

16. Central Intelligence Agency, *Allegations of Connections Between CIA and the Contras in Cocaine Trafficking to the United States. 96-0143-IG. Volume II: The Contra Story* (issued as a classified report on April 27, 1998; declassified October 8, 1998) para. 528, http://www.namebase.org/hitz.html (accessed November 1, 2010).

17. Ibid., para. 567.

18. Ibid., para. 569.

19. Ibidi., para. 610.

20. Ibid., para. 615.

21. Ibid., para. 121.

22. Ibid., para. 147.

23. Ibid., para. 1091.

24. For more details on Hitz's report, see Robert Parry, *Lost History: Contras, Cocaine, the Press & 'Project Truth,'* (Arlington, VA: The Media Consortium, 1999).

25. As reported in Robert Parry, "CIA Admits Tolerating Contra-Cocaine Trafficking in 1980s," *ConsortiumNews.com*, June 8, 2000, http://www.consortiumnews.com/2000/060800a.html (accessed November 1, 2010).

26. Hitz's investigation was eventually included in the paperback edition of *Dark Alliance*.

Acknowledgments

"The Coal Connection" (1980) series was reprinted by permission of the *Kentucky Post*. "I Create Life" (1983) and "Doctoring the Truth" (1985) were likewise reprinted by permission of the *Cleveland Plain Dealer*. "Caltrans Ignored Elevated Freeway Safety" (1989) and "Good Cop Bad Cop: The Thin Blue Line" (1990) were reprinted by permission of the *San Jose Mercury News*, and "Driving While Black" (1999) was reprinted by permission of *Esquire* magazine.

"The Mighty Wurlitzer Plays On" from Kristina Borjesson, *Into the Buzzsaw: Leading Journalists Expose the Myth of a Free Press*, revised edition (Amherst, NY: Prometheus Books, 2004). Copyright © 2004 by Kristina Borjesson. All rights reserved. Reprinted by permission of the publisher.

"The Arnold" (2004) was reprinted by permission of *High Times* magazine, and "The Killing Game" (2004) and "Red Light, Green Cash" (2004) were reprinted by permission of the *Sacramento News & Review*.

Seven Stories Press wishes to thank all the contributors for dedicating their time and words, on short notice, to making Gary's book sing with his unique and irreplaceable voice.

ABOUT THE AUTHOR AND EDITOR

An award-winning investigative reporter, GARY WEBB is best known for the "Dark Alliance" series that linked a Northern California drug ring with elements within the US government and the advent of crack cocaine. It first appeared in August 1996 in the *San Jose Mercury News* and became the first explosive internet news story, the newly minted *Mercury News* website receiving up to 1.3 million hits daily, spreading the story far and wide. The book of the same name appeared in 1998, and a revised and updated paperback edition came in 1999.

Before "Dark Alliance," Webb was a star reporter at various major metropolitan daily newspapers, including the *Kentucky Post* (where, in 1980, he won an Investigative Reporters and Editors Award for co-authoring, with Tom Scheffey, a seventeen-part series on organized crime in the American coal industry), the *Cleveland Plain Dealer*, and the *San Jose Mercury News* (which he joined in 1988 and where in 1990 he was one of a team of reporters who received a Pulitzer Prize for reporting on the San Francisco earthquake that year).

Webb wrote the kinds of stories that made newspapers proud, that exposed corruption and put fear into the hearts of the rich and powerful, stories to remind us why investigative reporting is a cornerstone of democracy, and why any open society needs freedom of the press.

Gary Webb was born on August 31, 1955, in Corona, California, to a military family. At the age of fifteen, while growing up in Indianapolis, Indiana, he began writing for his suburban high school newspaper, creating his first controversy when he criticized the use of a female drill team to rally students in favor of the Vietnam War. He attended journalism school at Northern Kentucky University where—until he dropped out—he wrote for the student newspaper, the *Northerner*, receiving several awards from the Kentucky Intercollegiate Press Association.

The "Dark Alliance" series appeared in the *San Jose Mercury News* on three consecutive days beginning on August 18, 1996. Southern Californians began to hear about how the crack cocaine phenomenon that had begun in LA had been the direct result of US government collusion to support drug dealers—who in turn were funneling money to the Contras, whose funding had been cut off by the US Congress. This clear case of our government harming and betraying its own citizens in its pursuit of foreign adventures inflamed LA residents. Local politicians like US Congresswoman Maxine Waters held public meetings. At one, in November 1996, CIA Director John Deutch came to Compton, California to promise a thorough investigation and was shouted down by community residents.

But by then the reaction had already begun. It started at the rightwing *Washington Times*, was picked up by rightwing media beat television journalists like Bernard Kalb, and quickly spread to newspapers of record. On October 4, 1996, the *Washington Post* published a front-page article by Walter Pincus attacking Webb's reporting, followed by similarly prominent coverage in the *New York Times* and the *Los Angeles Times*.

None investigated Webb's breaking news story itself. Nor were any of the allegations of inaccuracies in Webb's reporting ever substantiated. On the contrary, the US Senate and CIA investigations would later confirm and elaborate on the network of mutual support between drug dealers and our government that Webb had exposed. But none of the parties that had brought Webb down would later take any actions to undo the harm they had done. On December 10, 2004, only eight years after the publication of the "Dark Alliance" series, Gary Webb died by gunshot wound, and his death was subsequently ruled to have been a suicide.

ERIC WEBB is Gary Webb's youngest son. Surrounded by journalism all his life, he is now a journalism student in Northern California.

ABOUT THE CONTRIBUTORS

KRISTINA BORJESSON has produced for major American and European television networks and published two groundbreaking books on the problems of the US press: *Into the Buzzsaw: Leading Journalists Expose the Myth of a Free Press* and *Feet to the Fire: the Media After 9/11, Top Journalists Speak Out.* Her awards include an Emmy and Murrow Award in TV, and the National Press Club's Arthur Rowse Award for Press Criticism and two Independent Publisher Awards for her books.

PETE CAREY is a long-time reporter for the *San Jose Mercury News* who is now covering the economy.

GARY CLARK spent thirty years as a reporter and editor at four newspapers, including *The Plain Dealer* in Cleveland, Ohio, where he worked a variety of reporting and editing assignments, including ten years as managing editor. He was also city editor at *The Columbus Dispatch* and, for six years, managing editor of *The Denver Post.*

JEFFREY KLEIN spent a decade editing *West*, the *San Jose Mercury News'* Sunday magazine. One of the founding editors of *Mother Jones* magazine, he subsequently served as its editor-in-chief.

TOM LOFTUS has been a newspaper reporter for thirty-four years. He lives in Frankfort, Kentucky, where for the past twenty-three years he has been the state capital bureau chief for the (Louisville) *Courier-Journal*. In 2008, Loftus's coverage of state government won him the James Madison Award for Service to the First Amendment from the Scripps Howard First Amendment Center at the University of Kentucky.

ANNIE NOCENTI's journalism has appeared in *Details, Utne, HEEB, Stop Smiling, PRINT, Filmmaker, Scenario,* and more. Her story about Baluchistan, "The Most Expensive Road Trip in the World," was chosen for Best Travel Writing 2008. Her series about teaching film in Haiti, *Goudou Goudou,* can be found at http://hilobrow.com/tag/goudou-goudou, and her website is www.annienocenti.com.

ROBERT PARRY is a Washington-based investigative reporter who broke many of the early stories about President Ronald Reagan's secret operations in support of the Nicaraguan Contra rebels in the 1980s. Parry's stories, including the first article identifying White House aide Oliver North as a key figure in the operation, fed into what later became known as the Iran-Contra Affair. Parry worked for the Associated Press from 1974 to 1987, was national correspondent for *Newsweek* from 1987 to 1990, and was a reporter/correspondent for the PBS *Frontline* documentary series until 1994. In 1995, Parry founded the internet's first investigative magazine, *ConsortiumNews.com,* where he still serves as editor. Parry also worked for Bloomberg News as an editor handling securities regulation coverage from 2000 to 2004. Among Parry's journalistic awards are the Polk Award for National Reporting and the AP Managing Editors Association Award for Top Reportorial Performance. He was a Pulitzer Prize finalist in 1985. Parry lives in Arlington, Virginia.

THOMAS B. SCHEFFEY worked at the *Kentucky Post* from 1974 to 1980. He is currently the senior writer at *The Connecticut Law Tribune.* For the past twenty years, he has covered the legal scene in Connecticut, with a focus on issues of professionalism and government accountability. Notably, he discovered Connecticut's "Super-secret" court file system in 2003 that had permitted some cases to be filed without any public knowledge, lacking names or docket numbers. The system was abolished by the Judicial Branch, which has overhauled its open government practices. Before joining the *Law Tribune,* Scheffey practiced law in Philadelphia and Princeton, NJ.

Seven Stories founder and publisher DAN SIMON is co-author of *Run Run Run: The Lives of Abbie Hoffman* (Putnam/Tarcher, 1994) and translator of *Van Gogh: Self-Portraits* by Pascal Bonafoux (Alpine, 1989). His articles have appeared in the *Nation,* the *Progressive,* and the *Monthly Review.* He is a contributor to the four-volume *History of the Book in America* and the *Oxford Companion to the Book.* In 1996, Simon was named a *Chevalier des Arts et Lettres* by order of the French Ministry of Culture. He lives in New York City with his partner and two children, Asha and Miles.

LARRY SMITH was executive editor at *Yahoo! Internet Life* magazine from 2000 to 20002, and is the founder and editor of the online community *SMITH Magazine* (smithmag.net), home of the Six-Word Memoir project and bestselling book series.

MARK WARREN is executive editor of *Esquire*, where he has worked since 1988, directing much of the magazine's feature writing.

MELINDA WELSH is editor of the *Sacramento News & Review*, an award-winning alternative weekly newspaper she helped found in 1989. On leave from this post on a few occasions, she has also written dozens of long-form journalism pieces and served as an adjunct journalism professor at Sacramento City College.

ABOUT SEVEN STORIES PRESS

SEVEN STORIES PRESS is an independent book publisher based in New York City, with distribution throughout the United States, Canada, England, and Australia. We publish works of the imagination by such writers as Nelson Algren, Russell Banks, Octavia E. Butler, Ani DiFranco, Assia Djebar, Ariel Dorfman, Coco Fusco, Barry Gifford, Hwang Sok-yong, Lee Stringer, and Kurt Vonnegut, to name a few, together with political titles by voices of conscience, including the Boston Women's Health Collective, Noam Chomsky, Angela Y. Davis, Human Rights Watch, Derrick Jensen, Ralph Nader, Loretta Napoleoni, Gary Null, Project Censored, Barbara Seaman, Alice Walker, Gary Webb, and Howard Zinn, among many others. Seven Stories Press believes publishers have a special responsibility to defend free speech and human rights, and to celebrate the gifts of the human imagination, wherever we can. For additional information, visit www.sevenstories.com.